P9-DWH-833

LA JOLLA MUSEUM OF CONTEMPORARY ART
700 Prospect Street
La Jolla, California 92037

Copyright of the first edition is assigned to
LA JOLLA MUSEUM OF CONTEMPORARY ART. All rights reserved.

Library of Congress Catalog Card Number: 82-82515
ISBN 0-934418-14-4

© PIERO SARTOGO. 1982.
Stampato in Italia da Nava Milano s.p.a.

ITALIAN RE EVOLUTION

DESIGN IN ITALIAN SOCIETY IN THE EIGHTIES

Conceived by/*ideata da* PIERO SARTOGO
Organized by/*organizzata da* LA JOLLA MUSEUM OF CONTEMPORARY ART

The exhibition "ITALIAN RE EVOLUTION"
design in Italian Society in the eighties
is presented under the patronage
of the Italian Ministry for Cultural Affairs

La Mostra "ITALIAN RE EVOLUTION"
design nella società italiana degli anni ottanta
è posta sotto il patrocinio
del Ministero dei Beni Culturali

NK
1452
A1
I82
1982

Exhibition directed and installed by
Ordinamento della mostra e progetto dell'allestimento
PIERO SARTOGO

Exhibition Coordinator
Coordinatore della mostra
GIANNI RATTO

Advisory committee
Comitato scientifico
GIAMPAOLO FABRIS
FABIO MAURI
ALESSANDRO MENDINI
BRUNO ZEVI

LA JOLLA MUSEUM OF CONTEMPORARY ART

BOARD OF TRUSTEES
Mr. Donald K. Ballman, President
Mrs. Lynn G. Fayman, Executive Vice President
Mr. John McKenna Case, Vice President
Mrs. Jack M. Farris, Vice president
Mrs. Charles Edwards, Secretary
Mr. Edgar Marston, Jr., Treasurer
Mrs. Charles Arledge
Mrs. Rea A. Axline
Mr. Christopher Calkins
Mr. Everitt Carter
Mrs. Alfred W. Chandler, Jr.
Charles G. Cochrane, MD
Mr. James Colachis
Mr. Murray Galinson
Mr. Murray Gribin
Mr. Joseph Hibben
Mr. Gerald P. Hirshberg
Mrs. Nancy Hoover
Mrs. Frank Kockritz
Mr. Barry McComic
Mrs. George E. Osborn
Mrs. Roland Sahm
Mr. Robert Shapiro
Mrs. Forrest Shumway
Mrs. Mark Yorston

STAFF
Sebastian J. Adler, Director
Robin Bright, Preparator
Janet Ciaffone, Administrative Assistant
Bolton Colburn, Registrar
Lynda Forsha, Curator
Michael Golino, Building Manager
Prudence Hutshing, Public Information Officer
Greg Kahn, Curator of Film
Racthel Lindgren, Finance Officer
Verna Loy, Museum Bookstore Manager
Robert McDonald, Chief Curator
Gail Richardson, Librarian

CONTRIBUTORS TO THE EXHIBITION
HANNO CONTRIBUITO ALLA MOSTRA

CONTRIBUTORS TO THE CATALOGUE
HANNO CONTRIBUITO AL CATALOGO

Mr. and Mrs. Mark Yorston

BULGARI

J. DAVID & COMPANY

Mr. and Mrs. Roland Sahm
Buitoni
Piaggio

Borsalino
Cassina Design Ltd.
Cinelli
Olivetti
Sirp - Italdesign

Artemide
Brionvega
Brunati
Busnelli Gruppo Industriale
Driade
Heron Parigi
Kartell
Molteni
Nuova Faema
Nazareno Gabrielli
Poltrona Frau
Skipper
Uniform
Ermenegildo Zegna
Alfatec
Alfeo
Casanova
Castelli
Jadi Luisa
Missoni
Stilnovo
Vortice Elettrosociali
Zanotta
Alessi
Arteluce
Bieffeplast
Bialetti
Bloom
Caber Italiana
Carpigiani Bruto
Cimbali
Danese
Elam
Gianfranco Ferré
Ferragamo
Flos
Giovannetti
Icaro Olivieri
Lorenz
Krizia
Nordica
Rossi di Albizzate
Sames
Saporiti
Seim - Moto Guzzi
Tecno
Venini

EXHIBITION
MOSTRA

Curator of the Exhibition
Ordinamento della Mostra
Piero Sartogo
Nathalie Grenon

Exhibition Coordinator and staff
Coordinamento
Gianni Ratto
Adalberto Marchetti
Rita Persich
Françoise Rousseaux

Installation Design
Progetto dell'allestimento
Sartogo Architetti Associati
Piero Sartogo
Nathalie Grenon

Collaborators
Collaboratori
Sergio Micheli
David Griffin
Massimo Magistri
Carlo Evangelista

Statistics research consultants
Consulenti per la ricerca statistica
Demoskopea

Industrial products Consultant
Consulente per i prodotti industriali
Aurelio Picco

Fashion Consultants
Consulenti per la Moda
Research / *Ricerca*
Cristina Morozzi
Image / *Immagine*
Studio Alchimia

Movie's Program Coordinator
Coordinamento per la rassegna del Cinema
Patrizia Pistagnesi

External relations
Relazioni esterne
Pierluigi Vaccario
Paolo Ceratto

Secretary
Segreteria
Rosetta Lapponi

EXHIBITION CATALOGUE
CATALOGO DELLA MOSTRA

Edited by
A cura di
Piero Sartogo
Nathalie Grenon

Collaborators
Collaboratori
Industry / *Industria*
Aurelio Picco
Movies / *Films*
Michele Mancini
Food Drawings / *Disegni del cibo*
Gian Piero Bodino

Research
Ricerca
Emanuela Bompiani
Umberto Silva
Stefano Casciani
Benedetta Torrani

Translations
Traduzioni
James Pallas
Ronald Strom
Robert Kleyn
Kate Singleton
Richard Dury

Graphic layout
Progetto grafico
Ettore Vitale

Printed in Italy by
Stampato da
Nava Milano spa, 1982

ACKNOWLEDGEMENTS
SI RINGRAZIA

Beverly Pepper
Folco Quilici
Umberto Tirelli
Milton Gendell
Ralph Caplan
Niels Diffrient
Luciano Damiani
Pierre Richès
Simonetta Scalfari
Renato Pedio
Maddalena Capotondi - Ministero degli Affari Esteri
Graziella Lonardi
Italo Lupi

Carlo Maria Badini - Sovraintendente del Teatro alla Scala
Gabriele De Vecchi - Segretario Nazionale del W.C.C. World Craft
Council
Monsignor Pietro Van Lierde - Vicario Vaticano
Le case editrici: Bompiani - Einaudi - Mondadori - Feltrinelli - Vallecchi
- Garzanti - Adelphi
Domus - rivista di Architettura, Design, Arte
L'Architettura - cronache e storia
Demoskopea - Istituto per le ricerche sociali e di mercato
A.D.I. - Associazione Disegno Industriale
Laboratorio Cinematografico della Facoltà di Lettere e
Filosofia, Università di Palermo
Centro Marca - Centro di Studi e Coordinamento tra Industrie di Beni
di Consumo
R.A.I. Radio Televisione Italiana
Cineteca nazionale Roma
Antonio Casolini
Foto Pierluigi
Teatro Comunale di Firenze
Associazione Filarmonica Romana
Lega Nazionale Calcio
Assoarredo
Federazione Scarpe
Camera Nazionale Moda

CONTENTS

INDICE

FOREWORD

Italian Re evolution" is a multi-media, multi-dimensional slice of Italian life. In addition to the objects displayed, it includes, notably, films and the exhibition catalogue, a unique document that encapsulates the exhibition visually and adds literary content to it. The varieties of objects, covering all aspects of Italian life, from common, daily activities to special, religious events, are too numerous to list here. They range from espresso machines to papal vestments.

Our focus as a museum is on contemporary aesthetics. The exhibition is, moreover, multi-disciplinary may be considered from the perspectives of history, sociology, anthropology, economics, politics, literature, engineering and these categorizations do not exhaust its contents. It is cultural history in its broadest sense.

The exhibition has been actively in the making for four years. It was in the late 1970's that I perceived a need for it and started to seek means to realize it. On the other hand, the germ of the idea was planted many years ago when I personally first became interested in design as one of the expressions of fine art and in designers as artists. Evidence of this long-term interest is the Design Collection which I initiated at the La Jolla Museum of Contemporary Art.

Since World War II Italian design has been preeminent among connoisseurs, although Scandinavian design also enjoyed a period of favor, and more recently Japanese design has begun to emerge as significant internationally. It is surely not by accident that Italy, which has the oldest continuous history of civilized societies in the western world, should produce design which is the standard for other societies to acquire and copy. Great Italian artists in all fields for over two millenia are too numerous to mention. Suffice it to say that Italians, even the least advantaged, are aware of their rich cultural heritage, live with its evidence daily in their environment, appreciate the achievements of Italian artists, and take pride in them. It is this shared experience of the present with the past and the anticipation of the future which has created, I feel, the Italian look, which uniquely expresses utility in imaginative and elegant forms.

To make the exhibition a reality I have appointed the internationally renowned architect, Piero Sartogo, of Sartogo Architects and Associates, Rome, as Guest Curator. He conceptualized and organized the exhibition and its catalogue as visitors see and experience them. I wish to express my thanks to him and to architect Nathalie Grenon for her collaboration to the project. We are all grateful to Gianni Ratto of Milan, who, as Exhibition Coordinator, was responsible for the complex arrangements involved in bringing the exhibition materials together and getting them transported to the United States.

I wish also to acknowledge the assistance of an advisory committee of distinguished Italians: Bruno Zevi, Giampaolo Fabris, Fabio Mauri and Alessandro Mendini. The instructive essays and perceptive comments by numerous cultural figures included in the catalogue are integral to it and much appreciated.

Even with all this talent, the exhibition and catalogue could not have been realized without the very substantial financial assistance of Bulgari and of J. David and Company. We are grateful to them. For introducing Piero Sartogo to me, I wish to express my thanks to sculptor, Beverly Pepper.

I wish also to acknowledge the support of the Museum's Trustees, and among them especially Donald Ballman, President, and Edgar Marston, Treasurer, for their support in this project.

All the Museum's staff have worked with me over a long period of time to make this exhibition a reality. Those most closely associated with it are Administrative Assistant Janet Ciaffone, Financial Officer Rae Lindgren, Public Relations Officer Prudence Hutshing, Registrar Bolton Colburn, Building Superintendent Michael Golino, Preparator Robin Bright, Curator Lynda Forsha, and Chief Curator Robert McDonald.

Sebastian J. Adler
Director
La Jolla Museum of Contemporary Art

Negli ultimi due decenni, l'Italia è il paese che maggiormente ha influenzato il design a livello internazionale. "Italian Re evolution" rappresenta i molteplici aspetti del modello di vita italiana. Oltre agli oggetti esposti, alla rassegna di films la mostra si completa e integra con questo catalogo. Documento che visualizza il percorso della mostra, e ne esemplifica i contenuti con il supporto della letteratura e del cinema. La varietà dei prodotti rappresenta i diversi aspetti della vita italiana, sia quelli che scandiscono il quotidiano che quelli che connotano momenti particolari dei riti di massa, dalle macchine da caffè agli abiti del Papa. Pertanto la mostra ha un carattere interdisciplinare; le varie dimensioni storica, sociologica, antropologica, economica, politica, letteraria, tecnologica, si integrano con la visione estetica, fondamento delle attività del Museo.

È dalla fine degli anni settanta che ho perseguito l'obiettivo di realizzare questa mostra. Il mio interesse al design come espressione artistica risale a molto prima. Non a caso in questi anni ho dotato il Museo di Arte Contemporanea di La Jolla della collezione permanente di design. È dal dopoguerra che il design italiano, a detta dei connaisseurs, è il più importante anche se negli anni cinquanta fiorì il design scandinavo, e se oggi si fa sentire la presenza del design giapponese. L'Italia, che è stata la culla della civiltà occidentale, produce oggi design che è modello per altre società. Non sarebbe possibile enumerare qui tutti i grandi artisti italiani che nell'arco di duemila anni di storia si sono distinti nei diversi settori.

Questo patrimonio culturale si riflette nel paesaggio, nell'ambiente, nello spazio e qualifica i momenti, i luoghi, le cadenze della vita quotidiana. L'Italian look si sviluppa sulla base di questa dialettica tra passato e presente, e di proiezione nel futuro.

Questa mostra e questo catalogo sono oggi una realtà, grazie all'Architetto Piero Sartogo che l'ha ideata ed organizzata. Voglio esprimere i miei ringraziamenti all'Architetto Nathalie Grenon, per la sua collaborazione al progetto e a Gianni Ratto, che ha coordinato la partecipazione delle industrie italiane. Voglio anche ringraziare il Comitato Scientifico composto da Bruno Zevi, Giampaolo Fabris, Fabio e Alessandro Mendini e gli autori dei saggi contenuti nel catalogo. Questo catalogo è stato realizzato con il contributo di Bulgari e J. David & Company ai quali va la mia gratitudine.

Un particolare ringraziamento all'artista Beverly Pepper che mi ha fatto conoscere Piero Sartogo.

Tengo anche a ringraziare i Trustees del Museo, e in particolare il Presidente Donald Ballman, e il Tesoriere Edgar Marston, per il loro apporto a questo progetto.

L'intera equipe del Museo ha lavorato a lungo con me per realizzare la mostra. Tra quanti hanno partecipato desidero citare Janet Ciaffone Administrative Assistant, Rae Lindgren Financial Officer, Prudence Hutshing Public Relations Officer, Bolton Colburn Registrar, Michael Golino Building Superintendent, Robin Bright Preparator, Lynda Forsha curator, e Robert McDonald Chief Curator.

Sebastian J. Adler
Direttore
La Jolla Museum of Contemporary Art

INTRODUCTION

PIERO SARTOGO

INTRODUZIONE

PIERO SARTOGO

The look of the object is often inviting, provocative, aggressive, seductive, depending on the ways and procedures attending its predicted encounter with the user. An event, this, which is repeated innumerable times in the course of the day, at different moments and in various places, in accordance with the customary time divisions of activities.

The intermediary between the person and the object is the fact of its use, which infuses life into products and illuminates them: more than for any single person, it speaks for the social group.

The aim of this exhibition is to exemplify this phenomenon, to testify to its continual evolution and its structural changes in respect to models of living and of production. This is not an exhibition of the Italian way of life nor of objects, but an exhibition of the object-user relationship. We all know these objects; there are a great number of them, but they are of no significance whatsoever without knowing *who* is going to use them, *how, when,* and *why.* The sociological analysis and the statistical survey add up to a revelation of preferences and inclinations with regard to products and the where and when of their consumption; and they offer some important reasons why. If we examine the Italian way of life closely, we realize that the activities that make up a day are carried on with specific rhythms, peculiarities and cadences in the relationship between the place where the Italian works, his home, the street and the places for socializing and leisure time.

The cultural significance of this exhibition lies in its demonstration that the analysis of design is rooted in the complex conditions of life and context.

We know that the objective of design is generally to delineate strongly standardized processes and outcomes. Among industrial countries this usually takes place widely, but not in Italy where production and its diversification seem to respond to the slogan: personalized design for one and all. One need only reflect on the fact that in one of the most highly industrialized sectors, automobiles, there are now 132 models of cars produced by only eight industries. This cultural rejection of imported models has over the years guaranteed the safeguarding of a recognizable identity and a physiognomy that continues the relationship with the past. This is why such phenomena, sprung of mass-civilization elsewhere have, in terms of planning and programming, had quite a different impact here.

If the ritual of drinking coffee is as important as the statistics tell us, it comes as no surprise that there are myriads of coffee-makers produced, diversified as to cost, design and method of manufacturing.

If the street is not simply a thoroughfare but also a place where socializing takes place, it is no surprise that its paving (cobblestones, bricks, flagstones, etc.) is hardly meant for cars. For as soon as the car leaves the scene, the streets and squares are immediately reappropriated by people. This can be seen, for example, in the seasonal expansion and contraction of restaurants and coffee bars, which in winter relinquish and then in summer reacquire space for their café tables and hedges by invading the "parking space" of cars on the pavement outside.

If food is an institution, leaving to innumerable goings and comings to and from the home, its preparation explains the knowledgeable amassing of small quantities bought by the ounce. Pasta is the most important food in this institution: there are more than sixty kinds and they tend to multiply in the cooking process.

If clothing is to be understood as a means of participation, there is nothing surprising about the quick adoption of the latest model of uniform for all, which turns out to be different for everyone. One needs only think for a moment of the range of colors (from pastel to fluorescent) for the jogging-suits issued recently in Italy on the standard American model, which for years has been limited to grey, blue, red and green.

In a study carried out only a few years ago, George Nelson, photographed a good 1500 different types of signs off the autostrada del Sole, on roads running from Venice to Palermo. In a similar way the spatial layout of the Italian peninsula with its capillary differentations mortifies standards, simple repetitions and the linear development typical of industrialized models which, in Italy, have to be substantially

Lo sguardo dell'oggetto è spesso ammiccante, provocatorio, aggressivo, seducente, in funzione delle modalità e procedure del prevedibile incontro con l'utente. È questo un evento che si ripete innumerevoli volte nell'arco di una giornata, in momenti e luoghi diversi, secondo le scansioni temporali delle attività.

Intermediario tra la persona e la cosa è l'uso che decreta la vita dei prodotti, che li illumina: più che per le persone singole esso parla per il gruppo sociale.

La mostra si propone di esemplificare questo fenomeno evidenziandone la continua evoluzione, i mutamenti strutturali sia sul fronte del modello di vita che dei prodotti. Non è una mostra sugli italiani, né una mostra sugli oggetti: è una mostra sul rapporto oggetto-utente. Gli oggetti li conosciamo, sono tanti e diversi, restano insignificanti senza chi, come, quando e perché *li* usa. L'analisi sociologica e l'indagine statistica rivelano preferenze, inclinazioni, luoghi, tempi di consumazione dei prodotti ed anche alcuni importanti perché. Focalizzando l'osservazione sul modello di vita italiano, notiamo che le attività che compongono la giornata si svolgono con ritmi specifici, peculiarità e cadenze nel rapporto tra il luogo del lavoro, la casa, la strada etc.

La proposta culturale di questa mostra sta proprio nel radicare l'analisi del design in tali complesse condizioni di vita e contesto.

Sappiamo che l'obiettivo del design è, in genere, quello di delineare processi ed esiti fortemente standardizzabili, e ciò si verifica ampiamente nei paesi più industrializzati tranne che in Italia dove, vista la scala di industrializzazione e di iterazione la "diversificazione" dei prodotti sembra rispondere allo slogan: ad ogni cittadino il suo design personalizzato. Basti la constatazione che, in uno dei settori maggiormente industrializzati, quello dell'automobile, ci sono oggi sul mercato centotrentadue modelli di auto prodotti da solo otto industrie. Tale cultura del "rigetto" ai modelli d'importazione ha garantito, nel tempo, il mantenimento di una identità riconoscibile e di una fisionomia in continuità con il passato: per questo i fenomeni indotti dalla civiltà di massa altrove, in termini di pianificazione e programmazione, hanno avuto ed hanno qui, un impatto ben diverso.

Se il rituale del caffè è così importante come rivelano le statistiche, non sorprende scoprire sul mercato una infinità di modelli diversificati per costo, design e modi di fabbricazione.

Se la strada non è soltanto luogo di percorrenza ma anche spazio di socializzazione, non sorprende la sua pavimentazione anti-auto (sanpietrini, mattoni, pietra, ciottoli, ecc.). Non appena l'automobile si ritira, strade e piazze sono luogo di appropriazione del sociale che si manifesta anche nel dilatarsi e contrarsi, accompagnando le stagioni, di trattorie e bar che cedono e riconquistano con tavolini e siepi in vaso lo "spazio ai parcheggi".

Se il cibo è una istituzione, che induce gli innumerevoli spostamenti da e verso la casa, giustifica la preparazione di un singolo pasto come sapiente assemblaggio di quantità acquistate all'etto. Nell'ambito di questa istituzione la pasta è protagonista, i più di sessanta tipi si moltiplicano combinandosi in cucina.

Se l'abbigliamento è inteso come strumento di partecipazione, non sorprende la rapida adozione dell'ultimo modello uniforme per tutti, diverso per ciascuno. Basti pensare alle gamme di colore (dal pastello al fluorescente) delle tute per "jogging" nate, di recente, sul prototipo standard americano che per anni si è limitato al grigio, blu, bordeaux e verde.

In uno studio fatto pochi anni fa, George Nelson aveva fotografato ben 1500 campioni di segnaletica nel percorso, al di fuori dell'autostrada del Sole, tra Venezia e Palermo. Per analogia possiamo affermare che la strutturale complessità dell'assetto territoriale con le sue capillari differenziazioni, nega lo standard. l'iterazione semplice, lo sviluppo lineare, tipici dei modelli di industrializzazione.

Sulla base di queste considerazioni la ricerca si è orientata seguendo l'indicatore statistico inteso come strumento per penetrare, analizzare ed eventualmente interpretare, senza pregiudizi, la natura, i tempi comportamentali, le ritualità e i tabù della società italiana. Una società complessa e differenziata e che purtuttavia l'analisi sociologica riconduce ad alcuni modelli tipologici dei quali il dato statistico percentualizza preferenze, inclinazioni, riti e miti.

Anche la ricerca artistica con le sue intuizioni-anticipazioni, affidata

modified to be acceptable.

This being so, the methodological approach of this exhibition has tended to utilize statistical data mainly as a means of penetrating, analyzing, and possibly interpreting without preconceptions, the nature and times of behavioral patterns and the ritual aspects and taboos of Italian society. This is a complex and differentiated society, however, one which sociological analysis reduces to a few typological models, whose tendencies and prospects it endeavors to single out. Statistical data calculate in percentages preferences, inclinations, rites, and myths.

Artistic study, too, with its intuitive foreshadowings has entrusted the cinema and literature with the task of appraising products by taking the form of a quite "different" point of reference with respect to industrial products today, which entail modifications introduced in order to bring productive systems up-to-date and to cope with great quantities. Technicians, specialists, producers, designers and planners here represent the kind of conceptual, manual, mechanized, individual and group work which is inherent of the process of fabrication.

All together these points of observation (sociology, statistics, art, films, literature, etc.) make up the framework within which the object-user relationship is analized.

The result, is a system of cataloguing which puts on the same critical plane objects of quite different extraction: these differences enhance the quality and trace lines of tendency, affinity, and distance. Signed products, anonymous products, single piece, mass-production objects reveal on the physiognomy of the daily encounter-clash with the user and contribute to the definition of the Italian way of life.

This picture reflects *Italian Re Evolution*, a model of development which utilizes its own great leaps forward, situations and moments of great transformation (which are never radical or definitive) but considers them objectives not worth achieving. What really counts is the impulse towards transformation which the prospect generates simultaneously in our daily lives in all sectors. Much the same thing occurs in design: the multiplicity of products and their appearance are more significant and decisive than any specialization on one field, which would of necessity be limited to only a few industrial sectors. This apparent non-specialization is its specialization.

There was evidence of this quite recently: the Italian team that won the Mundial '82 world soccer series has no "system", but with its "non system" time after time it turned out to be the most versatile and adaptable one in beating much better-trained teams which based their game on a rigidly applied "system".

cinematografia e alla letteratura, marca i prodotti configurandosi come referente "altro" alle modifiche e agli aggiornamenti verificatesi nei sistemi produttivi, per il grande numero, che i prodotti industriali di oggi connotano. I tecnici, gli specialisti, i produttori ed i progettisti danno voce al lavoro concettuale, manuale, meccanizzato, individuale o di gruppo, che è interno ai processi di fabbricazione.

Questo insieme di punti di osservazione compongono il quadro entro il quale è analizzato il rapporto oggetto-utente.

Il risultato, includendo criteri non solamente estetici, è una catalogazione tale da mettere sullo stesso piano critico oggetti di estrazione stilistica diversi: le disomogeneità esaltano la qualità delineando linee di tendenza, affinità e lontananze. Prodotti d'autore, prodotti anonimi, pezzi unici o di grande serie, rivelano la fisionomia dell'incontro-scontro quotidiano con l'utente contribuendo a definire il modello di vita degli italiani.

Questo fenomeno riflette l'Italian Re Evolution: un modello di sviluppo che si avvale di salti in avanti, di situazioni e momenti di grande trasformazione (mai radicali e definitori) come obiettivo da non raggiungere. Quello che conta è l'impulso di trasformazione che tale prospettiva genera sul presente-quotidiano simultaneamente in tutti i settori. Altrettanto si verifica per il design: è più significativa e determinante la molteplicità dei prodotti e delle loro fisionomie che la specializzazione di punta, la quale non può che essere limitata ad alcuni settori.

Questa apparente non specializzazione è la sua specialità.

È successo anche di recente: la squadra che ha vinto il Mundial 82 non ha un suo "gioco" ma con il "non gioco" è risultata la più versatile ed adattabile, di volta in volta, a superare squadre ben più dotate ma impostate su di un rigido modello di "gioco".

ITALIAN DESIGN

GIULIO CARLO ARGAN

IL DESIGN DEGLI ITALIANI

GIULIO CARLO ARGAN

Everything that industry turns out is designed with several things in mind, economics, technology, and esthetics. All products, however, have another value that does not depend on the value of the raw material or the amount of work but on the way they were designed. Not infrequently products that are considered examples of good industrial design cost less or are things that were created without any attempt at making them beautiful forms. Something is well designed not when practical and esthetic features have been combined or superimposed but when they form a whole because they were designed together. The objects shown on the present occasion were not chosen because of their particular beauty. The aim has been to illustrate the role that industrial design has played in the development of Italian society and in Italy's efforts to rebuild its culture and revive its economy after the Second World War.

Even before the war, there was a tendency in Italian industry to aim for quality. Although it was not exactly obstructed by the Fascist regime, it was subtly contrary to Fascist nationalism, rhetoric, and the demand for cultural as well as economic autarky. It expressed the italian entrepreneur class's wish to stay in touch with European bourgeois democracies, where technological advancement went hand in hand with social progress. Adriano Olivetti was a great promoter of Italian industrial design. An intelligent and well-educated manager, he was politically on the side of labor. His typewriter company in Ivrea was a model of advanced technology and of the social organizing of labor at the same time. Olivetti may have been the first to understand that a country like Italy, which had to rely heavily on manufacturing because of its dearth of raw materials, would have to wager everything on product quality, and this meant rigorous design, the latest in technology, and highly efficient companies. The chief requirement from industrialists was an ability to set themselves social and cultural goals beyond the immediate profits. And since then industrial production has earned its right to be considered an important factor in Italian culture and not just a factor in the Italian economy.

The government made little effort to conceal its mistrust and preferred the showy, illogical monumentality of the official architects of the Fascist regime; but for almost twenty years the *Triennale* shows in Milan made Italy a world meeting place and reference point in architecture and in high quality standardized industrial production. Heavy industry was already engaged in the armaments race, readying for war, while architects and designers, taking up the call of Le Corbusier and Gropius, were still asking that the extraordinary new possibilities of technology be applied to the creation of homes and household objects instead of cannons. Those triennial meetings were held in Italy, where industry may have been younger than elsewhere but it was livelier too, for Italy still kept alive the tradition of a culture in which art and craftsmanship had been leading actors. The triennial show displayed highly sophisticated products of modern technology alongside the latest creation in Fine Venetian glass and the ceramics of Faenza. Together with full-fledged industrial designers, there were artists with a free, precise, and dazzling inventiveness like Lucio Fontana and Fausto Melotti, and the combination seemed to prove that the free creativity of artists and the methodic research of designers were part and parcel of the same avant-garde.

This was the premise for what, in an altogether different cultural situation, was later to be the second phase of Italian industrial design. Italy came out of the Second World War undone but keen to end its long cultural isolation and eager to catch up with the more industrially advanced nations. The country seemed to want to preserve in its industrial work the same taste and the quality of inventiveness that had marked its artists and craftsmen in the past. A host of small and medium-sized industries were scattered throughout the Italian peninsula. They were out of touch with each other, and yet they worked along fairly similar lines. They tried to maintain the iconic aspect of objects while freely reinventing them. They paid great attention to the pleasure in the look and feel of things, so that objects could simultaneously stand out and yet blend, or almost disappear, in a setting. These products of Italian industry received a warm welcome throughout Europe and America.

People began to speak of the Italian look, and indeed almost everything Italian aimed at immediately pleasing visual effects. But

Tutte le cose che l'industria produce sono progettate da più punti di vista: economico, tecnico, estetico. Per ogni tipo di prodotto, tuttavia, si danno differenze di valore che non dipendono dal pregio del materiale o dal tempo di lavorazione, ma dal metodo della progettazione. Non di rado i prodotti che si considerano rappresentativi di un buon disegno industriale sono i meno costosi o quelli in cui non è stata cercata un'appariscente bellezza formale: un progetto è ben disegnato quando i fattori pratici e gli estetici non si sommano o sovrappongono, ma si integrano perché sono stati progettati insieme. Il disegno industriale italiano non è qui rappresentato attraverso una serie di oggetti particolarmente belli: ciò che si vuole dimostrare è il ruolo che ha avuto il disegno industriale nell'evoluzione della società italiana e nel suo sforzo di ricostruzione culturale e di ripresa economica dopo la seconda guerra mondiale.

Già nel periodo precedente la guerra si era delineata nell'industria italiana una tendenza alla ricerca di valori di qualità. Non era stata propriamente ostacolata dal regime fascista, ma era sottilmente in contrasto con il nazionalismo, la retorica, la pretesa di un'autarchia culturale non meno che economica del fascismo. Fu l'espressione del proposito della classe imprenditoriale italiana di tenersi in rapporto con le democrazie borghesi europee, dove l'avanzamento tecnologico era connesso col progresso sociale. Grande promotore del disegno industriale in Italia fu infatti Adriano Olivetti, manager intelligente e preparato, politicamente di tendenza laborista, titolare di quella fabbrica di macchine per scrivere a Ivrea che fu, nello stesso tempo, un modello di tecnologia avanzata e di organizzazione sociale del lavoro. Olivetti fu forse il primo a capire che in un paese come l'Italia, costretto ad una industria di trasformazione dalla povertà di materie prime, si doveva puntare tutto sulla qualità del prodotto, e questa esigeva progettazione rigorosa, tecniche aggiornate, operatori qualificati. Esigeva soprattutto, da parte degli industriali, la capacità di proporsi finalità sociali e culturali al di là dell'immediato profitto. È da allora, infatti, che la produzione industriale è diventata di pieno diritto un fattore importante della situazione non soltanto economica ma culturale italiana.

Nonostante la malcelata diffidenza del governo, che preferiva la vistosa e sgrammaticata monumentalità degli architetti di regime, con le mostre della Triennale di Milano, l'Italia è rimasta, per circa vent'anni, il punto di incontro e di riferimento dei ricercatori di tutto il mondo nel campo dell'architettura e della qualificazione dei prodotti industriali di serie.

Quando la grande industria aveva già cominciato la corsa agli armamenti e alla guerra, architetti e designers, facendo eco agli appelli di Le Corbusier e a Gropius, chiedevano ancora che si impiegassero le nuove, straordinarie possibilità della tecnica a fabbricare case e suppellettili invece che cannoni. In Italia, dove aveva luogo quell'incontro triennale, l'industria era forse più giovane che altrove ma più viva rimaneva la tradizione di una cultura di cui l'arte e l'artigianato erano i grandi protagonisti: alla Triennale Milanese accanto ai più sofisticati prodotti della tecnologia moderna, si potevano vedere gli ultimi saggi della raffinata vetreria veneziana o della ceramica faentina, e c'erano anche, accanto ai designers ormai integrati nelle industrie, artisti dall'invenzione libera, esatta e folgorante come Lucio Fontana e Fausto Melotti, quasi a dimostrare che la libera creatività degli artisti e la metodica ricerca dei designers facevano parte, in definitiva, di una stessa avanguardia.

Era la premessa di quella che sarebbe stata, in tutt'altra condizione di cultura, la seconda fase del disegno industriale italiano. Uscita dalla guerra disfatta ma impaziente di spezzare un lungo isolamento culturale e di allinearsi ai paesi industrialmente più avanzati, l'Italia sembra aver voluto conservare nella produzione industriale il gusto e il valore dell'invenzione che in passato era stato dei suoi artisti e artigiani. Molte medie e piccole imprese, disseminate nella penisola e prive di qualsiasi coordinamento tra loro, hanno avuto tuttavia orientamenti abbastanza concordi: ricercando da un lato l'evidenza iconica degli oggetti e dall'altra reinventandoli spregiudicatamente, ma sempre curando il piacere della vista e del tatto, la capacità degli oggetti così di spiccare come di dissimularsi e quasi sparire nell'ambiente lo sforzo dell'industria italiana è stato guardato con simpatia in tutta l'Europa e in America.

unlike Scandinavian production, there was never any indulgence in naturalistic, folk, or populist effects. The real innovation was that things were designed for a real society rather than projected forward into a hypothetical and utopian realm.

Before the war De Stijl and Bauhaus had offered architects and designers a model of beauty that was logical and moral, but after the unbridled violence of the war years, it would have been too much to expect that an orderly town plan, clean-lined geometric buildings, and soberly functional everyday objects would suffice to bring man back to reason. Who could still cherish illusions about a future world where everything would be measured in mathematical modules, a world that would never again destroy but only build? And perhaps it had been a mistake, a sin of pride, to think that a method of production could also become a political ideology, and that everything consisted in constant planning, to such a point that the design of a chair or a cup could, in essence, be the model of a new society.

The aims and intentions of Italian design after 1945 have something in common with what liberal French historians called the morality of the conquered-abstract nationalism had given way to good sense and reason. And, after all, why must planning always and only concern the future, as if it were up to us to preordain the environment and way of file of future generations?

Couldn't there be a way of designing at short terms, answering to the needs of the moment, and not only expressing a wish for future social reform? Certainly, the reformist and didactic viewpoint typical of constructivist design was to be abandoned, and short-term design would take the form of extemporaneous invention rather than planning. For this very reason it was to be nearer to the inventiveness of the artist, which also implied a planning phase; but rather than proclaim a plan, it went beyond and all but consumed planning in the work itself. Perhaps the striking iconic character that marks Italian design is nothing else than an ultimate form of art: in the very act of surrendering itself immediately and fully to the eyes, the work all but cancels out the last trace of its long evolution.

But this plastic and visual iconic substantiality could not harmonize with the immateriality of the constructivist object, which maintained the linear form of its original design and could be repeated in an infinite series in a limitless space. A basic premise of all Italian design is the limited series involving the coexistence of different types: not geometric and abstract space but a context of things including the users of the objects and their manufacturers, everything moving with endless possibilities of encounter and combination.

In this context, as in space, nothing can have a fixed and immutable meaning. Every object takes on value because of the meaning that is ascribed to it by the person who needs it or wishes to own it. The relationship is no longer normative, as if the object were equipped with a set of instructions on how to use it. The relationship becomes one of empathy and sympathy. The object must serve its purpose but allow the user total freedom of interpretation, and this capacity for interpretation betrays a residual link the work of art, which allows and evokes different interpretations on the part of different observers. Since objects no longer had a normative sense, they communicated only information. And together they created an environment that was itself an information and communication system. Since information is not a precept but a stimulus, it does not demand obedience from the user, simply attention and response. And a well-designed object is one that provides clear information and signals.

But more than the fearful anguished years of the Second World War, what it was that deprived history of its authority and banished confident expectations of the future was the sudden ending of the war in the pointles destruction of two Japanese cities. The world changed at that moment, because the atomic bomb existed. And a philosophy of the bomb immediately came to birth with Jaspers, Sartre, and Günter Anders: the irrevocable end of the world of discourse, history, politics, imagination, and freedom and the passive submission of nations and individuals to the blackmail of the bomb. There could be no further hope in the rationale of progress; the only thing certain was that progress would take the form of constant growth in the murderous potential of the bomb, and that sooner or later, for no good reason, the bomb would certainly go off. The perspective of history as

Si parlò di italian look, ed infatti quasi tutta la produzione italiana ha cercato effetti visivi immediati e piacevoli; ma a differenza della produzione scandinava non si è mai concessa indulgenze naturalistiche e vernacole, popolaresche o populiste. Tutta la sua novità sta nell'essersi rivolta a una società reale invece di proiettarsi in una società ipotetica e d'utopia.

Prima della guerra De Stijl e il Bauhaus avevano proposto ad architetti e designers il modello di una bellezza ch'era anche logica e morale: ma dopo cinque anni di scatenata violenza non si poteva certamente più supporre che l'ordine di un tracciato urbano, la nitida geometria degli edifici e la sobria funzionalità degli oggetti d'uso quotidiano bastassero a riportare gli uomini alla ragione. Chi poteva ancora illudersi nell'avvento di un mondo dove tutto potesse misurarsi in moduli matematici e non si sapesse più distruggere, ma soltanto costruire? E non era stato un errore, forse un peccato d'orgoglio, pensare che una metodologia della produzione fosse anche un'ideologia politica, e tutto fosse un progettare continuo, al punto che un progetto di sedia o di tazza fosse già, in nuce, il progetto di una società nuova?

C'è qualcosa che riporta l'intento e la finalità del design italiano dopo il 45' a quella che gli storici liberali francesi chiamavano la morale dei vinti. All'astratto razionalismo è succeduto il buon senso, la ragionevolezza. E, del resto, perché mai il progettare debba riguardare sempre e soltanto il futuro, come se spettasse a noi preordinare l'ambiente e il modo di vita delle generazioni future?

Non può eserci un modo di progettare per tempi ravvicinati, che risponda anche a bisogni del momento, e non solo al desiderio di lontane riforme sociali?

Indubbiamente si rinuncerebbe all'ottica riformistica e pedagogica ch'era propria del design costruttivista e la progettazione a tempi brevi sarebbe, più che progettazione, estemporanea invenzione; ma proprio perciò sarebbe più vicina a quell'inventare degli artisti, che implicava anch'essa una fase progettuale ma, invece di enunciarla, la sormontava e quasi bruciava nell'opera. Forse quel carattere marcatamente iconico che distingue il design italiano altro non è che un ultimo configurarsi dell'opera artistica che, nel suo darsi immediatamente e pienamente alla vista, quasi cancellava la traccia del suo lento formarsi.

Questa consistenza plastica e visiva, iconica, non si conciliava con l'immaterialità dell'oggetto costruttista che, conservando la linearità del progetto, poteva ripetersi in serie infinita in uno spazio illimitato. Premessa di tutto il design italiano è la serialità limitata, che comporta la coesistenza di tipi diversi: non lo spazio geometrico e astratto, ma un contesto di cose di cui fanno parte gli utenti delle cose e gli stessi operatori e nel quale tutto si muove, vi sono illimitate possibilità d'incontri e di combinazioni.

Nel contesto nulla può avere un significato fisso e immutabile come nello spazio.

Ciascun oggetto vale per il significato che gli viene attribuito da chi ne ha bisogno e lo desidera ed il rapporto non è più normativo, come se l'oggetto portasse in se l'istruzione per l'uso, ma di empatia e simpatia. L'oggetto dunque deve servire lasciando all'utente tutta la sua libertà d'interpretazione, ed anche questa interpretazione tradisce un residuo legame con l'opera d'arte, che consentiva e sollecitava interpretazioni diverse da parte dei diversi soggetti.

Non avendo più un senso normativo, gli oggetti comunicano soltanto informazioni; nel loro assieme formano un ambiente, che a sua volta è un sistema dell'informazione e della comunicazione. E poiché l'informazione non è precetto ma stimolo, non richiede all'utente obbedienza, ma soltanto attenzione e risposta. E l'oggetto ben disegnato è quello che fornisce informazioni e segnali ben chiari.

Più ancora che i cinque anni di paura e d'angoscia della guerra, a toglier via l'autorità della storia e la fiduciosa aspettazione del futuro è stata la repentina fine della guerra con l'inutile distruzione di due città giapponesi. Da quel momento tutto nel mondo è cambiato perché c'è la bomba atomica. È subito nata con Jaspers, Sartre, Günter Anders la filosofia della bomba: fine irrevocabile dell'universo del discorso, della storia, della politica, dell'immaginazione, della libertà; sottomissione passiva dei popoli e degli individui al ricatto della bomba. Non più speranze nella razionalità del progresso: soltanto si può essere certi

1. Shop-window, *Vetrina* / des. A. Persico e M. Nizzoli / 1934.
2. Fluorescent lighting, *Illuminazione fluorescente* / des. Lucio Fontana / IX Triennale di Milano / 1951.
3. Espresso coffee-machine, *Macchina per caffè espresso* / mod. 53 / des. Giò Ponti, Fornaroli, Rosselli / prod. Pavoni / 1953.
4. Armchair, *Poltrona* / mod. Joe / des. J. de Pas, D. d'Urbino, P. Lomazzi / prod. Poltronova / 1970.
5. Toy, *Giocattolo* / des. E. Mari / prod. Danese.
6. Folding chair, *Sedia pieghevole* / mod. Plia / des. G.C. Piretti / prod. Castelli / 1969.
7. Typewriter, *macchina da scrivere* / mod. Lettera 22 / des. M. Nizzoli / prod. Olivetti / 1950.

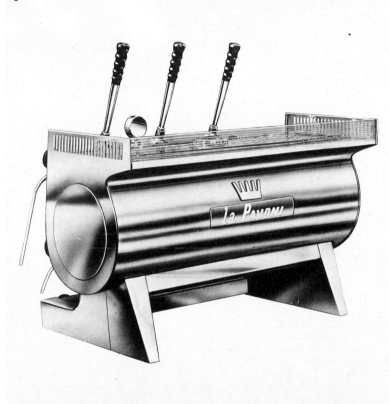

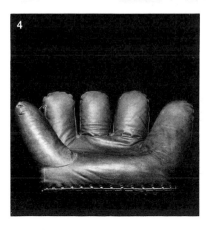

master had been destroyed, and the prospect of the future was a closed one rather than an inviting one. Then Bergson's idea that the present was nothing more than the ungraspable demarcation line between future and past became the only practicable dimension of existence, and this dimension acquired extension and weight, even though it was a restricted dimension where everything tended to swell up in order to be seen, heard, and touched. It was an easy equation: Bomb = destruction = consumption. After all, consumer society is the society of the bomb. Closing off the future is tantamount to denying the possibility of progress and ideology, but unless one is willing passively to submit to the intrusive physical presence of objects, they must be designed. It is no longer necessary that objects transparently display how they were designed, as in constructivist design, because what matters is not the gestation or formation of the objects buts its birth and coming into being, its surprising entry into the world.

Since design no longer had a moralistic intent, there was no shame in trying to beat the competition and conquer the marketplace. Thus design had an immediate practical end, it was not passed off as a model for behavior, it was a technical process that involved only production technicians. It was not aimed at an ideal society in the future, i.e., a designed society, but at a *de facto* community, and not an elite society at that, but the middle classes, blue-collar factory workers, women who combined office work with housework, young people, and adolescents. Objects were no longer models of perfection, using their visible forms to proclaim the rationality of their design. Designing was the techical task of designers, it did not concern users, and its only aim was to bring into the world things that made life easier and were pleasant to look at. The development of a design was no longer of interest. What was interesting was the sudden appearance of the object, its having been produced, nay, just produced and just put into the environmental context. It must look new, like a flower that has just bloomed, and at the same time like something familiar. All the efforts of post-war Italian design lay in combining these two contradictory conditions. Certainly there was no way one could pretend not to know that the technology that turned out the motor scooter and the electric razor was the same technology that was working, on a totally different scale, at the secret manufacture of the nuclear bomb. Technology had a dark and menacing face, but it had a bright and promising one as well. If one could not live without the threat of the bomb, one could at least enjoy the advantages that technology offered in daily life. And why be Manichaean when the technology that made the bomb was the same used for making rockets and space ships to the moon? The fall-out from ultra-sophisticated technology showered everyday life with the gadgetry that began to fill middle-class homes. People did not think of technology as either good or bad in itself; it all depended on the uses to which it was put. True, the presence of the bomb made any predictions for the future terrifying, but that was just one more reason not to make forecasts and to live the present as intensely and fully as possible.

Once design ceased to be considered a normative activity, the logical consequence was that it would part company with architecture. Italian postwar design is essentially nomenclature, an inventory of the things that form the real environment of existance. Perhaps the closest thing was the apparel sector, which in those very years was ridding itself of prescriptive norms, whether those of fashion or those of life's ceremonial rituals. What design had in common with apparel was that their objects were weak in meanings of their own and hence could easily take on attributed meanings. As with clothing so with everyday objects, the distinction between the new and the used collapsed. Casual clothes were tantamount to pre-used apparel, while construction became prefabricate and baby food was pre-digested. Things no longer *wore* out; objects were used until something broke down, and then they were discarded. Or an object was kept in service until another object was invented to take its place. New materials that could be used to press out objects nullified any interest in how an object might be formed or constructed. Obsolescence was no longer a process by which something wore out psychologically; it was simply an exit from the scene. Of course all objects are part of a context, but no object has an interest or value beyond the service it provides. Its striking appearance is no longer an evocation, it is merely an

che il progresso sarebbe stato l'aumento continuo della potenza micidiale della bomba e che presto o tardi la bomba sarebbe sicuramente esplosa senza alcun motivo razionale. Distrutta la prospettiva della storia, non più maestra, chiusa la prospettiva del futuro, non più invitante, quel presente che per Bergson non era che un'inafferrabile linea di demarcazione tra futuro e passato diventa la sola praticabile dimensione dell'esistenza: acquista un'estensione e un peso, anche se la sua è indubbiamente una dimensione ristretta dove ogni cosa tende a dilatarsi per farsi vedere, sentire, toccare. Era facile l'equazione: bomba = distruzione = consumo; la società del consumo è, in definitiva, la società della bomba. Chiudendo il futuro si nega il progresso e l'ideologia, ma se non si vuole subire passivamente l'invadente presenza fisica degli oggetti, bisogna progettarli, ma non occorre più che gli oggetti mostrino per trasparenza l'iter della progettazione, come nel design costruttivista, poiché ciò che importa non è la gestazione, la formazione dell'oggetto ma il suo nascere o prodursi, il suo sorprendente comparire nel mondo.

Non avendo più un intento moralistico, il design non si vergogna di progettare per battere la concorrenza e conquistare i mercati; la progettazione ha un fine pratico immediato, non si propone come modello di comportamento, è un procedimento tecnico che interessa soltanto i tecnici della produzione. Non si rivolge ad una società ideale e di là da venire, dunque ancora a un progetto di società, ma alla società di fatto, e neppure ad una élite, ma ai ceti medi, ai colletti bianchi delle fabbriche, alle donne che conciliano l'impiego in ufficio e le cure della casa, ai giovani, ai ragazzi. I prodotti non debbono più essere modelli di perfezione che dichiarino con le loro forme visibili la razionalità della progettazione: progettare è compito tecnico dei progettisti, non interessa gli utenti, non ha altro scopo che collocare nel mondo cose che aiutano a vivere e piacciono.

Se non interessa più l'iter progettuale, interessa tuttavia la subita apparizione dell'oggetto, il suo essere prodotto, anzi appena prodotto, appena entrato nel contesto dell'ambiente. Deve apparire nuovo come un fiore appena sbocciato e tuttavia già ambientato, familiare. Tutto lo sforzo del design italiano del dopoguerra è appunto nel combinare queste due condizioni contraddittorie. Certo non si poteva far finta di ignorare che la tecnologia che sfornava il ciclomotore o il rasoio elettrico era in definitva la stessa che, a tutt'altra scala, fabbricava all'oscuro la bomba nucleare; ma se quella tecnologia aveva una faccia scura e minacciava, ne aveva anche una chiara e propizia. Se non si poteva fare a meno di convivere con la minaccia della bomba, bisognava almeno godere i vantaggi che quella tecnologia offriva per l'esistenza quotidiana. E poi, perché fare del manicheismo quando la tecnica che faceva la bomba era la stessa con cui si facevano i razzi e i missili per andare nella Luna? Quelle tecnologie ultra-sofisticate avevano una ricaduta a pioggia sulla vita di ogni giorno, creavano quei gadgets che cominciavano a popolare le case borghesi. Si cominciava a pensare che la tecnologia non fosse in sé né cattiva né buona, e tutto dipendesse dall'uso che se ne faceva. È vero che la presenza della bomba rendeva terrificante qualsiasi previsione del futuro, ma era una ragione di più per non prevederlo e vivere nel modo più intenso, esauriente il presente.

Era logico che la rinuncia alla progettazione come attività paradigmatica avesse come conseguenza il distacco del design dall'architettura: il design italiano del dopoguerra è essenzialmente nomenclatura, elenco di cose costitutive dell'ambiente reale dell'esistenza. Il settore più affine è forse quello del vestiario, che negli stessi anni andava liberandosi da tutte le prescrizioni, sia inerenti alla moda sia inerenti alla ritualità cerimoniale. Col vestiario il design aveva in comune la debole significanza degli oggetti in sé e la conseguente prontezza a caricarsi di significati attribuiti. Come nel vestiario, così negli oggetti d'uso corrente è caduta la distinzione tra nuovo ed usato: negli abiti casual si è arrivati al pre-usato come nella costruzione al pre-fabbricato e nelle diete per bambini al pre-digerito. Non esiste più logorio, l'oggetto serve finché si rompe e si butta. O finché è stato inventato un altro oggetto che lo scosta e prende il suo posto. I nuovi materiali che permettono di stampare l'oggetto vanificano ogni interesse per la sua formazione o costruzione: lo stesso processo di obsolescenza non è più un processo di usura psicologica, ma semplicemente di uscita dal campo. Naturalmente tutti gli oggetti

indication of availability. There is no way of grasping an object's message or its signal without considering that the architecture of prefabricated houses (which often have some of the furnishings built in) has lost much of the communicativeness it once had. The prefabricated dwelling is a colorless and uniform setting, and the tenant knows that his apartment is exactly like the others next door, upstairs, and downstairs. It is up to the single tenant to give the apartment some character or accent, and a little picture is not sufficient to do the trick, because everyone is more or less aware of its mediocrity and shuns it. Yet, the very rooms that were once without any esthetic interest — the kitchen and the bathroom — have become the *loci* of the greatest concentration of object information. Those are the rooms that contain all the gadgets that producer industry has managed through publicity to invest with so much interest that they have become tokens of social success. Objects can diversify and personalize a characterless room the way a scarf or a necktie personalizes a mass-produced suit or dress. Another factor has all but replaced design and made a substantial contribution to creating the visual and fairly striking forms of Italian design, and that factor is advertising. The advertising image repeats the object with an emphasis and accent on beauty that reverberate back onto the product; consumers want the object the way the ads promised it, displayed it, and offered it. It is not an exiciting, deforming process like styling but a progressive process arising out of the interplay of an object and its image, image and object always trying to outdistance each other. This mechanism involves memory, perception, and imagination, and operates to combat the paralysis of the imagination induced by the overwhelming barrage of images to which so many of the mass media instruments subject the imagination. An analysis of that mechanism shows that it is ultimately still a design process, but what is designed is a use rather than a product, and this implies an involuntary and almost unconscious, yet direct, participation of the consumer. Of course, objects are no longer treated like something to be handed down from one generation to another, nor is durability considered a coefficient of worth. On the contrary, in the vast production of what might be called "poor" design, the ephemeral, the short-lived, or the no-lived becomes a coefficient of value. Nylon, plastic, resins, and acrylic have caught up our contemporaries in a joyous multicolored vortex of things that are picked up, used, and thrown away without a second thought. They have brightened our ordinary gray lifescape like a flight of birds or butterflies, and they have also altered a host of notions and ideas that were considered certain and final. They have changed the color and shape of objects. What was gray, colorless, dull, drab, and insignificant has become colorful, agile, and flexible. And all those extremely lightweight materials have changed our conventional concept of the relationship between weight and size. Everything floats, as if in defiance of the law of gravity we were living in the stratosphere. Polystyrene has made astronauts of us all. Our experience has changed where transparency, luminosity, reflection, and adhesiveness are concerned, and an infinity of actions that once seemed impossible are now available to everyone. The experience of a world where everything had weight, substance, duration, and value, i.e., a world in which things gave richness to life, now seems infinitely poorer than our experience of the world today, where nothing has value, nothing lasts, and where well-being, if it exists, is not something to be planned for but to be enjoyed. It is a world in which everyone is invited to throw things away with the prodigality of millionaires.

And the mass media system, rightly execrated for a whole host of reasons, has also played a part in accustoming us to live by images. The television image, above all, has altered that sense we once had of an image as something closely connected to an object, an image that was somehow an idealization or a sublimation of a thing. The television image is substantial, spaceless, instantaneous, and fragmentary. And it is stranger still, because we cosume this image in the solitude of the home, while at the same moment that image is being consumed by millions of other consenting persons. It is the enfranchisement of the image as created by the mass media that has radically changed what used to be the mythology of objects. The craftsmen of yesterday mythicized things, and that mythology in turn

fanno parte del contesto ambientale, ma nessuno conserva un interesse, un valore al di là del servizio che rende. La sua apparenza vistosa non è un richiamo, ma soltanto un avviso di disponibilità. Ma non si afferrano i valori del messaggio o del segnale degli oggetti se non si considera che l'architettura della casa pre-fabbricata, spesso con taluni mobili integrati, ha perduto molto della comunicativa di una volta: il suo è un ambiente scolorito e uniforme, chi vi abita sa che è uguale negli appartamenti adiacenti, sottostanti, soprastanti al suo. Compete ormai a ciascun inquilino dargli un qualche carattere o accento, e non soddisfa più il quadretto perché tutti più o meno riconoscono la mediocrità e ne rifuggono. D'altra parte proprio gli ambienti che una volta erano privi di qualsiasi interesse estetico, come la cucina e il bagno, sono diventati luoghi di massima concentrazione d'informazioni oggettuali, contengono tutti quei gadgets a cui l'industria che li produce è riuscita con la pubblicità ad annettere il massimo interesse, fino a farne dei segni di qualificazione sociale. Gli oggetti variano e personalizzano l'ambiente amorfo della casa, come una sciarpa o una cravatta, personalizzano l'abito in serie. Un altro fattore che, quasi sostituendosi allo studio progettuale, ha contribuito fortemente a determinare le forme visibili e moderatamente vistose del design italiano è la pubblicità: l'immagine pubblicitaria ripete l'oggetto con un'enfasi e un'accentuazione di bellezza che si ripercuote sulla produzione perché i consumatori vogliono l'oggetto così come la pubblicità l'ha promesso, presentato ed offerto. Non si tratta di un processo di deformazione eccitante com'è lo styling, ma di processo progressivo fondato sulla gara di sorpasso che sempre si stabilisce tra l'oggetto e la sua immagine.

È una meccanica che coinvolge memoria, percezione e immaginazione e che, col suo movimento, combatte gli effetti paralizzanti dell'immaginazione come il sistema della continua travolgente emissione di immagini da parte dei molti apparati di comunicazione di massa. L'analisi di quel meccanismo dimostra ch'esso in ultima analisi è ancora un processo di progettazione, che però è piuttosto progettazione dell'utenza che della produzione e quindi implica una partecipazione involontaria e pressoché inconscia ma diretta dei consumatori. Naturalmente non si può più parlare dell'oggetto come valore patrimoniale né della durata come coefficiente del suo valore: anzi in tutta la vastissima produzione di quello che potrebbe chiamarsi "design povero" l'effimero, cioè la durata nulla o minima, diventa un coefficiente di valore. Nylon, plastiche, resine, acrilici hanno coinvolto i nostri contemporanei in un turbinio coloratissimo e allegro di cose che si prendono, si usano e si buttano senza pensarci; e non soltanto hanno animato i nostri grigi paesaggi abituali come un volo d'uccelli o di farfalle, ma hanno mutato una quantità di idee e di nozioni, che credevamo certe e definitve. Hanno mutato i colori degli oggetti, le loro forme: ciò che era grigio, stinto, monotono, sciatto, trascurabile è diventato colorato, agile, flessibile, Hanno mutato, con tutte quelle materie leggerissime, la relazione, che ci era abituale, tra volume e peso: tutto levita come se ci trovassimo nella stratosfera, fuori legge di gravità. Il polistirolo ha trasformato tutti in astronauti. Sono mutate le nostre esperienze in fatto di trasparenza, di luminosità, di riflesso, di adesività: infinite azioni che credevamo impossibili sono ormai alla portata di tutti. L'esperienza che si aveva del mondo quando ogni cosa aveva un peso, una consistenza, una durata, una valore e, insomma, le cose formavano ricchezza, ci appare oggi infinitamente più povera di quella che abbiamo del mondo odierno dove nulla ha valore, nulla ha durata e il benessere, se c'è, non si progetta, si gode. E dove ciascuno è invitato a gettar via i valori della vita con una prodigalità da milionario. Anche ci ha abituati a questo vivere d'immagini il sistema, per tanti altri aspetti giustamente esecrato, dei mass media. L'immagine televisiva, soprattutto, ha mutato il senso che aveva una volta l'immagine: rigidamente connessa ad un oggetto di cui in qualche modo era un'idealizzazione o una sublimazione delle cose. L'immagine televisiva è inconsistente, aspaziale, frammetaria, tanto più strana in quanto la consumiamo nell'isolamento della nostra casa e tuttavia nel medesimo istante è consumata da milioni di persone consenzienti. È appunto lo statuto d'immagine creato dai mass media che ha radicalmente mutato quella che, nel passato, era la mitologia degli oggetti. Il vecchio artigianato mitizzava le cose e quella mitologia determinava le regole, la ritualità del loro impiego. Il design costruttivista mitizzava i progetti e

established the rules and the rituals governing the use of those things. Constructivist design mythicized the act of designing, and the ritual of use was a repetition of the orders embodies in the design. The contemporary world is forced into a precarious position by the constant appeal to consume joyously today and to destroy ferociously tomorrow. Thus the world has lost that old religious sense in which it was myth that conditioned rite. Now ritualism institutes myths, and it is no longer the object that is mythicized; the myth itself becomes material. Quite appropriately, it seems to me, the creators of the present Italian design show (and Mediterranean Italy is still strongly bound to the pagan cult of myths) have taken the rites of everyday life as the main strand of the exhibit: the unwritten law of mass society, where the repetition of the same gestures leads to encounters with the same objects. These objects act as signals of availability and then immediately leave our field of interest and remain inert. When the user passes by again, the objects turn on again. The encounter with habitual objects is never the same, for each of us arrives at the appointment in a state of mind conditioned by the experiences we have been through in the course of the day. And yet the objects will remain fixed luminous points, a myth created by ritual.

Structurally speaking, a culture in which myth is created by rite is a primitive, tribal type of culture, highly refined and advanced through its technology may be. Applying Levy-Strauss's distinction, it might be said that the first constructivist and rationalist stage of design was typical of an engineering culture, while the second stage, in which rite creates myth, is a culture of hunters, gatherers, nomads, and primitives. Modern man's religion is animist, though the reality with which he identifies is not nature but the world of things that he franticaly produces in order to consume them just as franticaly. There is no doubt that the industrial production that flourished in Italy after the Second World War was marked by a will to endow things with an overwhelming visual and tactile attractiveness. That is what makes it possible for people to make contact and enjoy an industrially-produced object, in order to discharge the inevitable frustration arising from the repetition of situations and gestures throughout a normal day's work, work inside the industrial system. In a world where the image is dominant, there is no stance possible except *bricolage*: after all, industrial design projects needs and the satisfaction of those needs, it is a do-it-yourself tool in a thoroughly artifical environment, almost a second and artificially created nature, where persons and things move to rhythms that are identical with the apparently senseless and convulsive rhythms of the modern industrial city. A society like ours, far removed as it is from the harmonious nature of old, is part and parcel of the city. But the city is no longer thought of as stable and historic monumental structure; it is a set of main arteries and capillary branches along which life runs like a river.

The dimensional categories of modern design are the apartment, the city, and the surrounding territory. We all move in this space, and the animated functional objects with which industry has filled it have a twofold valence in connection with our private life and life in public. We can enjoy the ownership and use of an object that belongs to us as well as to many other people, and an invisible solidarity is established between these owners. This double valence seems to have been in the minds of the creators of new types and forms of objects that are produced industrially. Things must be like garments, creating uniformity and personalizing at the same time.

What kind of city is this, for which industry has created this constantly changing wardrobe of things? The industrial city of constructivist town planning was like a chess board with people following set patterns of movement at a pre-calculated pace, a city structured like a Mondrian painting. Mondrian himself, in his final American period, realized that this was utopian. It is no accident that the ritual dynamism underlying the infinite little mythologies of the modern world, the urban image that corresponds to our experience, is that of Jackson Pollock's pictorial space. It is a dense network of strokes and lines that perhaps mark out habitual routes with no point of arrival, itineraries for thousands or millions of people incessantly on the go, crossing each other' s path and often ending up back where they started. That myriad of itineraries and trajectories, which vary from person to person, is studded with an infinity of intensely colored points: they

la ritualità d'impiego era la ripetizione dell'ordine progettuale. Il mondo contemporaneo, costretto alla precarietà dalla continua sollecitazione a un consumo ora allegramente e domani ferocemente distruttivo, ha perduto l'antica religiosità per cui era il mito a condizionare il rito: oggi la ritualità è istitutiva dei miti e non è più l'oggetto che si mitizza, ma il mito che si materializza. Opportunamente, mi pare, gli ideatori di questa mostra del design italiano (e l'Italia mediterranea è ancora fortemente legata al culto pagano dei miti) hanno preso come filo conduttore del discorso espositivo la ritualità quotidiana: la legge non scritta, per cui in una società di massa si ripetono i medesimi gesti che portano all'incontro con i medesimi oggetti, i quali perciò agiscono come segnali di disponibilità e, subito dopo, escono dal campo d'interesse e rimangono inerti fino al momento in cui l'utente dovrà ripassare nel loro raggio e si riaccenderanno. L'incontro con gli oggetti abituali non sarà mai uguale, ciascuno giungerà all'appuntamento in uno stato d'animo che l'esperienza vissuta nella giornata avrà condizionato: e quell'oggetto sarà comunque un punto fermo e luminoso, un mito creato dal rito.

Una cultura in cui il mito è creato dal rito è strutturalmente una cultura di tipo primitivo, tribale, anche se la sua tecnologia sia delle più raffinate e avanzate. Richiamando la famosa distinzione di Levy Strauss si può dire che la prima fase, costruttivista e razionalista, del design era tipica di una cultura di ingegneri, la seconda, in cui il rito crea il mito, è una cultura di raccoglitori, di cacciatori, di nomadi, di primitivi. La religione dell'uomo moderno è animistica, solo che la realtà con cui l'uomo si identifica non è la natura, ma l'universo delle cose che l'uomo produce freneticamente per poterle freneticamente consumare. Indubbiamente c'è, nella produzione industriale fiorita in Italia dopo la seconda guerra, una volontà di caricare i prodotti di una prepotente attrattiva visiva e tattile: è quella che permette alle persone di scaricare nel contatto e nel godimento di un oggetto fatto dall'industria, l'inevitabile frustrazione della ripetizione di situazioni e di gesti nel corso di una giornata di normale lavoro. Lavoro all'interno del sistema industriale. In un mondo in cui la dominante è l'immagine, non v'è altro atteggiamento possibile che quello del bricolage: il disegno industriale, che in definitiva, progetta il disegno e la sua soddisfazione, è uno strumento di bricolage in un ambiente tutto artificiale, quasi una seconda e artefatta natura in cui persone e cose si muovono con ritmi che sono quelli, apparentemente insensati e convulsi, della moderna città industriale. Una società come l'attuale, ormai lontanissima dall'antica ed armonica natura, è tutt'uno con la città, che però non è più pensata come una stabile, storica struttura monumentale, ma come un insieme di canali maggiori e capillari in cui la vita scorre come un fiume. Le categorie dimensionali del design moderno sono l'abitazione, la città vera e propria e il territorio: tutti ci muoviamo in questo spazio e gli oggetti animati e funzionali di cui l'industria l'ha riempito hanno una doppia valenza in rapporto all'esistenza privata e alla pubblica. Si gode il possesso e l'impiego di un oggetto che è nostro, ma anche di molte altre persone tra cui si stabilisce una invisibile solidarietà. Proprio questa doppia valenza sembrano essersi proposta i creatori di nuove tipologie e morfologie oggettuali della produzione industriale: l'oggetto dev'essere come un capo di vestiario, che uniforma e personalizza. Per quale città è pensato il guardaroba di oggetti, che l'industria continuamente rinnova? La città industriale dell'urbanistica costruttivista era come una scacchiera in cui la gente si muoveva secondo percorsi obbligati e tempi pre-calcolati: una città la cui struttura era come un quadro di Mondrian. Ma lo stesso Mondrian, nel suo ultimo periodo americano, si rese conto che era utopistica. Non certo per caso, ma il dinamismo rituale che sottende le piccole e infinite mitologie del mondo moderno, l'immagine urbana che corrisponde alla nostra esperienza è quella dello spazio pittorico di Pollock: fitto reticolo di segni, di linee traccianti, forse gli itinerari abituali e senza un punto d'arrivo di migliaia o milioni di persone che si muovono incessantemente, incrociandosi e spesso ritornando al punto di partenza. Quella miriade di itinerari e traiettorie, diverse per ciascun individuo, è costellata da un'infinità di punti intensamente colorati: stanno per le infinite cose o magari persone che nel vorticoso spazio cittadino trattengono per un istante lo sguardo. Tutto il design italiano, che pure non ha alcuna costante stilistica, si direbbe ispirato dalla diversità di ritmi o soltanto frequenze di moto a cui sono destinati gli

stand for countless things or perhaps countless persons who catch the eye for an instant in the swirling space of the city. Although there is no stylistic constant in Italian design, all of it could be said to take its inspiration from the diversity of rhythms, or merely the frequencies of motion, at which the objects are aimed: the bathroom, the kitchen, the living room, the street, the square, the highway.

What might paradoxically be called the artificial nature of the modern world is obviously based on our ideas of space and time. And these ideas are connected with our constant experience of cinema space and time. The space and time to which movies and television have accustomed us are fragmentary and involve several dimensions and several scales of magnitude. There is a rapid transition from the utmost distance to the maximum proximity, from a panoramic view to the detailed close-up. What matters most is the function or role that each object or each detail of an object is called upon to play. In a word, every object is on stage, because sooner or later the moment will come when that object enters into the action. It is in a waiting state until it performs its action, and then it returns to motionless silence. The fact that objects are set in a space that is never unitary and that they are presented in a fragment of space and time gives these prop objects an additional presence — the image is so highly charged that it takes on a substance that is in no way inferior to the substance of the real object. This may be why the objects that industry produces to equip our everyday city life are both honestly utilitarian and slightly emphatic and theatrical at the same time. They have to be artificially natural or naturally artificial, like the urban landscape they compose and enliven. Since the manufactured object is basically an image made concrete, it has to be capable of entering the mass communication channels and of being assimilated by the image that are in constant circulation. The image of the mass media is not a plan but an indirect model of industrial design. It is not just a matter of iconic derivation: it is that the structure of things made with techniques that manufacture objects is the same as the structure of the images manufactured by image-making techniques, and this shows that the two techniques are in fact one and the same. That is why the present exhibit of object is coordinated with an exhibition of contemporary motion pictures and television programs.

Industrial production is the leading factor in the cityscape, and its maximum symbolic charge is concentrated in vehicles, especially those designed for city traffic. This is the case with compact cars, certainly one of the product categories in which Italian industry has enjoyed its greatest successes on domestic and foreign markets alike. Many Italian cities have old structures of such historic value that they cannot be altered, and here the compact car clearly offers a practical and civil way of moving about. Small cars are certainly preferable to big ones, not only because they take up less room but because they constitute a less strident contrast to the older buildings that were designed to human dimensions. The motor scooter (the Vespa was the prototype) has had a more extensive and deeper influence on the life of Italian society. On its first appearance it was noisy and intrusive yet basically friendly, and it was clear at once that the motor scooter was closer kin to household gadgets than to roaring automobiles. It was not designed with social and didactic aims in mind, but one of its beneficial effects on Italian life, and this is something worth remembering: it brought people who lived in crowded outlying districts into contact with the life of the city center, and it tore down quite a few class distinctions and eliminated several taboos, especially among young people. The motor scooter might have been merely a new and practical means of transport, but it became a way of reinterpreting the city. This seems even more evident today, when industry is technologically more advanced but more exclusively concerned with profit. To a large degree, the domestic motor scooter has been supplented by powerful and dangerous motorcycles, which resemble more to machine guns than to gadgets and are totally unassimilable in a cityscape.

Italian design never had metaphysical ambitions, but it has certainly offered a multiform and lively phenomenology of custom and usage. It has not been a levelling factor but a factor of social aggregation. It establishes a kind of solidarity among people who use the same types of auxiliary objects. It follows the general rituals of daily life, but its own

oggetti: il bagno, la cucina, il soggiorno, la via e la piazza, l'autostrada. Quella che potremmo paradossalmente chiamare la natura artificiale del mondo moderno è ovviamente fondata sulle nostre nozioni di spazio e di tempo, che a loro volta sono connesse con l'esperienza che tutti hanno fatto e fanno continuamente della spazialità e temporalità cinematografica. Lo spazio ed il tempo a cui cinematografo e televisione ci hanno abituati sono frammentari, a molte dimensioni e a molte scale di grandezze; passano rapidamente dalla massima distanza alla massima vicinanza, dalla panoramica al particolare vicinissimo; di ogni oggetto o di particolare d'oggetto conta soprattutto la funzione o il ruolo a cui sarà chiamato ad adempiere. Ogni cosa, insomma, è presente in scena perché verrà prima o poi il momento in cui dovrà entrare in azione; la sua condizione è una condizione di attesa a cui succederà, conclusa l'azione, il rientro nell'immobilità e nel silenzio. Il fatto di inserirsi, poi, in uno spazio che non è mai unitario, e cioè di darsi in un frammento di spazio come di tempo, conferisce agli oggetti di scena un più-di-presenza: si carica l'immagine affinché assuma un peso non inferiore a quello dell'oggetto reale. È questo forse il motivo per cui gli oggetti che l'industria produce per attrezzarci a vivere la nostra giornata cittadina sono ad un tempo onestamente utilitari e leggermente enfatici, teatrali: debbono essere artificialmente naturali o naturalmente artificiali come il paesaggio urbano che compongono ed animano. Essendo in fondo un'immagine materializzata, l'oggetto fabbricato deve potere entrare nel canale della comunicazione di massa, assimilarsi alle immagini che vengono continuamente messe in circolo. L'immagine dei mass media, infine, non è certamente un progetto, ma un modello indiretto del design industriale. Non si tratta soltanto di derivazione iconica: è che la struttura delle cose prodotte dalle tecniche che fabbricano cose è la stessa delle immagini prodotte dalle tecniche che fabbricano immagini, ciò che prova come le due tecniche siano di fatto una sola. Perciò in questa mostra la rassegna degli oggetti è accompagnata dalla rassegna del cinema e della televisione dello stesso tempo.

Essendo il maggior fattore del paesaggio urbano, la produzione industriale ha concentrato il massimo di carica simbolica nei veicoli e specialmente in quelli destinati al traffico cittadino. È il caso delle automobili di piccola cilindrata, che sono indubbiamente una delle categorie di prodotti in cui l'industria italiana ha ottenuto i migliori successi, anche sui mercati stranieri. In città come le italiane, che spesso hanno strutture antiche e per il loro valore storico non modificabili, sono evidentemente un pratico e civile modo di muoversi: preferibile, comunque, alle grandi vetture non soltanto perché occupano meno spazio, ma perché meno urtante è la contraddizione con la scala a misura d'uomo degli edifici antichi. Ancora più estesa e profonda è stata l'influenza che sulla vita sociale italiana ha avuto il ciclomotore, di cui prototipo la famosa Vespa. Quando apparve, rumorosa e invadente ma in fondo simpatica, si vide subito ch'era parente piuttosto dei gadgets domestici che delle rombanti automobili. Non era progettata con un'intenzionalità sociale e didattica, ma tra i suoi effetti positivi sulla vita italiana non va dimenticato che contribuì a far partecipi della vita del centro gli abitanti delle decentrate, gremite periferie, che abbatté non poche distinzioni di classi e cancellò non pochi tabù, specialmente nei giovani. Poteva essere soltanto un nuovo, pratico mezzo di trasporto: fu un modo per reinterpretare la città. Lo si capisce meglio oggi, quando un'industria tecnologicamente più avanzata ma più esclusivamente volta al profitto ha in larga misura sostituito ai domestici ciclomotori motociclette potenti e pericolose, molto più vicine al mitra che al gadget e assolutamente non ambientabili in un paesaggio urbano.

Dopo l'euforia e le illusioni di una grande ripresa economica il design italiano non ha mai preteso di essere una metafisica, ma certo è una multiforme e animata fenomenologia del costume. Non è un fattore di livellamento, ma di aggregazione sociale: crea una solidarietà tra chi pratica le medesime tipologie di oggetti ausiliari. Aderisce alla generale ritualità della vita quotidiana ma il suo spazio vitale, il paesaggio in cui naturalmente si inserisce e per cui è fatto, prima ancora che la casa o l'ufficio o la strada, è il grande magazzino. È questo il vero foro della città contemporanea. È un paesaggio senza orizzonti, interamente fatto di cose concrete che l'industria ha prodotto e avvolte in involucri brillanti o colorate di tinte vivaci e finalmente ammassate in serie

1. Motor scooter, *Ciclomotore* / mod. Vespa / des. C. d'Ascanio / prod. Piaggio / 1946.
2. Automobile, *Macchina* / mod. Fiat 500 / des. D. Giacosa / prod. Fiat / 1957.
3. Department store, *Grande magazzino* / des. F. Albini / La Rinascente, Roma / 1958-62.
4. Reconstruction of the dinosaur, *Ricostruzione del dinosauro* / Pino Pascali / 1966-67.
5. Motorcycle, *Motocicletta* / mod. Guzzi 850 Le Mans III / prod. Guzzi / 1982.

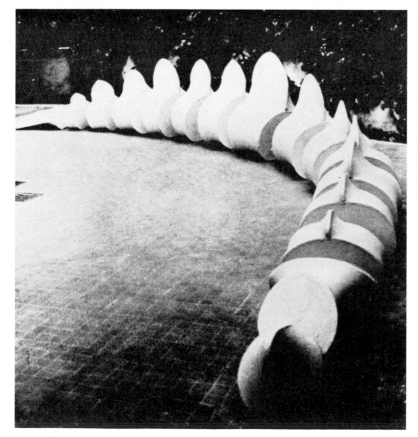

living space, the landscape in which it naturally has its being, is primarily the department store much more than the household or the office or the street. The department store is the real forum of contemporary cities. It is a horizonless landscape, totally made up of the tangible objects that industry produces and packages in brilliant containers or decorates with bright colors and stacks up in rows (small series) on overflowing shelves lined up in crowded, garishly lighted rooms. Every object emits its own visual call, often set off by a vaguely intoxicating sound background, like organ music during church services. It is the consumer's hand that answers the visual call of objects, a hand held out to take the object off the shelf the way you pluck ripe fruit from a tree. The rites of consumption are too important a social fact to be disturbed by economic concerns: the price is fixed, take it or leave it, and thus even dialogue disappears from the marketplace, that human intervention of the seller mediating between producer and consumer. In the department store, merchandise is transferred from producer to consumer in assembly-line fashion. The whole life of a modern city is a series of ritual acts, obviously served by their corresponding ritual instruments, but the department store is a veritable cathedral, where the solemnest and most highly practiced rite is performed from dawn till dusk, the rite of shopping. It would be no exaggeration to say that design is less concerned with the objective needs of the marketplace than it is with the sport of shopping. Once a product has been purchased it has fulfilled its function, it has been consumed.

Italy has a Catholic tradition, and in that church rites are revelatory, so they must be conspicuous and the appurtenances of the rites must also be eye-catching. Modern Italian mentality took shape during the Baroque period, when pomp and splendor were the very substance of ritual. And it was in function of that sacred splendor that craftsmanship enjoyed its last, exhuberant, and stunning blossoming, in antithesis to the aniconic and austere formality of Protestantism. It was an incredible technology of vision. Everything was manufactured for the religious service, which took the form of spectacle and theatrical performance. Streets, squares, churches, and homes were set designs and choreography. It made no difference whether an object was made of *papier maché* instead of precious stone, stucco instead of marble, or if flowers were made of cloth. (Nowadays flowers are made of plastic, and the realistic flora that industry turns out is the *kitsch* end-point of the artificial naturalism of the Baroque.) What was important then, and it still is, was technological pride in manufacturing a sense of nature. The department store is a veritable fair of the artificial, the *locus* of desire that is artificially aroused and satisfied and hence the *locus* of the collective imagination, the heart of the city in our time.

But that is not all: the rite of shopping is the typical occupation of people's free time, a way of making up for repetitiveness and frustration. And that is why objects need a substantial degree of attractiveness and visual efficiency, has to provide gratification the way a hand-crafted object used to gratify the craftsman, but the difference is that it is no longer the producer who derives the satisfaction; the consumer is far more important. It is this, I think, that provides the link, albeit at a remove, between the phenomenon of the industrial product and the Baroque in one sense, and in another sense between the industrial product and the carnival of objects turned out by American Pop Art and Italian *Arte Povera*. It is no surprise that it was in Italy that a brilliant young artist like Pino Pascali, who unfortunately died very young in 1968, was both the landscape artist of that artificial landscape and the statue-maker of the artificial figures in that landscape. He stressed the playful aspects, exaggerated the bad taste, and interpreted the rituality in a veritably tribal sense. In short, he understood that design was certainly not a form of austerity; it was rather an aid in overcoming the inhibition that persited in many strata of Italian society vis-à-vis objects as something to be preserved, as inheritable assets. That kind of design gave the Italian family economy a sense of security, a freedom from prejudice, and a new courage. It marked a period in which a country that felt too old recaptured its youth. It was a sign and an act of faith, Italian society's faith in the most advanced countries of Europe and America.

(piccole serie) in scaffali stipati e in ambienti gremiti e violentemente illuminati. Ciascun oggetto emette il proprio richiamo visivo, spesso armonizzato da un sottofondo sonoro e vagamente inebbriante, come la musica d'organo che accompagna le funzioni religiose. Al richiamo visivo degli oggetti risponde la mano protesa dell'utente, che prende l'oggetto dallo scaffale come coglierebbe un frutto maturo dall'albero. La ritualità del consumo è un fatto sociale troppo importante per essere turbato da preoccupazioni economiche: il prezzo è fisso, si prende o si lascia, e così scompare dal mercato anche il dialogo, la mediazione umana del venditore tra chi produce e chi consuma: nel grande magazzino la merce passa dalla produzione al consumo attraverso una catena di montaggio. Se tutta la vita di una città moderna è una successione di atti rituali a cui corrispondono ovviamente gli strumenti del culto, il grande magazzino è veramente la cattedrale in cui dalla mattina alla sera si celebra il rito più solenne e più praticato, lo shopping. Può dirsi addirittura che il design, più ancora che l'obiettiva necessità del mercato, ha di mira lo sport dello shopping. Una volta acquistato, il prodotto ha adempiuto alla sua funzione, è consumato.

Si sa che l'Italia è un paese di tradizione cattolica, dove il rito, essendo rivelatorio, deve essere vistoso così come appariscenti debbono essere i suoi attributi. L'epoca in cui si è formata la mentalità dell'italiano moderno è il periodo barocco, quando la fastosità era la sostanza stessa dei riti. È in funzione di quella vistosità sacrale che si è avuta, in antitesi all'aniconismo e all'austerità formale protestante, l'ultima, esuberante, sbalorditiva fioritura dell'artigianato: un'incredibile tecnologia della visione. Tutto si fabbricava per il rito, ch'era spettacolo, teatro: la via, la piazza, la chiesa, la casa erano scenografia e coreografia. Non importava che l'oggetto fosse fatto di cartapesta invece che di pietra rara, di stucco invece che di rame, e i fiori fossero di stoffa (oggi di plastica: la realistica flora di produzione industriale è la terminazione Kitsch del naturalismo artificiale barocco): l'importante era ed è l'orgoglio tecnologico di fabbricare il sentimento della natura. Fiera dell'artificiale, il grande magazzino è il luogo del desiderio artificialmente acceso e artificialmente soddisfatto, dunque il luogo dell'immaginazione collettiva, il cuore della città del nostro tempo.

C'è di più: il rito dello shopping è il tipico impiego del tempo libero dal lavoro, quello che ne compensa la ripetitività e la frustrazione. È perciò che l'oggetto deve avere un notevole grado di attrazione e di efficienza visiva: deve cioè essere gratificante così come l'oggetto fabbricato artigianalmente era gratificante per l'artigiano, ma con la differenza che non si gratifica più la produzione bensì, come di gran lunga più importante, il consumo. È questo, credo, che lega alla lontana la fenomenologia del prodotto industriale con il barocco da un lato e, dall'altro, con il carnevale degli oggetti del pop art americano o dell'"arte povera" italiana. E non sorprende che proprio in Italia un artista giovane e geniale come Pino Pascali, purtroppo morto giovanissimo nel '68, sia stato ad un tempo il paesaggista di quel paesaggio artificiale e lo statuario di quelle artificiali figure, e ne abbia sottolineato gli aspetti ludici, esagerato il cattivo gusto, interpretato la ritualità in senso addirittura tribale. Capì insomma che il design non era certamente una forma di austerità, ma piuttosto un aiuto a vincere l'inibizione che in molti strati della società italiana persisteva nei confronti dell'oggetto come cosa da conservare, bene patrimoniale. Quel design, infine, introdusse nell'economia familiare italiana un senso di sicurezza, di spregiudicatezza, di coraggio; caratterizzò un periodo di giovinezza recuperata da parte di un paese che si credeva troppo vecchio; fu un segno e un atto di fiducia della società italiana verso paesi europei e americani di più avanzato progresso.

DESIGN AND/OR DISEGNO IN ITALIAN ARCHITECTURE

BRUNO ZEVI

DESIGN E/O "DISEGNO" NELL'ARCHITETTURA ITALIANA

BRUNO ZEVI

The purpose of the following pages is not to offer an overall picture of Italian architecture since the end of World War II. The selection of buildings relates to the nature of this exhibit. It shows that the specific sensitivity to design or, rather, to shaping and *disegno* in the more restricted sense of the Italian term, has a strong impact even on the macro-objects of the urban scene.

Needless to say, architecture cannot be reduced to a design "object". It is involved in a vast complex of challenges: the human contents and functions, the different ways of representing and expressing them, the elaboration of volumes so as to overcome the static three-dimensionality of the Renaissance and to incorporate movement, the use of new structures. Above all, architecture deals with the creation of dynamic spaces in which people can freely behave. And it must cope with its context — be it natural, urban, historical, or contemporary — in order to establish a dialogue with it, often achieved through contrast or by deliberate discontinuity.

Italian designers touch to a greater or lesser degree upon all these aspects of the architectural process. To give a few examples, the matter of contents and functions is tackled courageously in the Passarelli building in Rome, where the commercial, office, and residential zones are kept polemically independent (fig. 1). There is asymmetry and dissonance in the Gorio house (fig. 2) and in the kinetic conception of Capobianco's University building in Salerno (fig. 3-4). There are original cavities, some compressed and some dilated, in the Pellegrin villa (fig. 5) and the Genoa museum by Albini, with its dialectic interchange between formal circular areas and formless intervals (fig. 6). Clear examples of relationship to context include the Monument of the Ardeatine Caves, on the outskirts of Rome, with its intelligently conceived passageways between the suspended prism and the natural grottoes (fig. 8), Petrignani's building in the historical core of Bari (fig. 10), and the Taormina Hotel by Gatti (fig. 11). Many other buildings illustrated here have similar features and do not need critical comment.

This, however, only a small part, almost a fragment of the Italian architectural panorama. As a rule, we have "boxes" and not articulated volumes, static voids instead of flexible spaces, symmetry, repetition, and anachronistic functional schemata. Hence there is recourse to visual and tactile expedients, those elements of refinement that manage to make even a substantially banal building attractive and personalized. In this sense design may be considered as something cosmetic, a kind of styling, a remedy and compensation for what is missing, namely a concept of space. But in many cases the intervention of design means something more than that. When it is not merely formalist and superficial, it aims to give an identity and a message on external volumes and interior spaces through a creative and sagacious choice of material, color, and light.

Surely, from a strictly architectural viewpoint, it would be preferable to have less *disegno* in the façade and more inventiveness in space and plastic values. But when you consider the works shown here as whole, and think that they could easily be multiplied, you perceive that the design factor is, under present conditions, stimulating and positive. It permeates architecture at all scales, at the highest professional level and in a remarkable number of average-quality works. And within its limits it makes Italy distinct from many other countries.

A brief analysis of some personalities and trends may emphasize the question. Let us concentrate on Carlo Scarpa, three engineers, and Giovanni Michelucci.

A splendid artist like Scarpa could be described as either a designer or an architect; he was somewhere between the two. Able to model a wonderful Murano glass, he could also set a statue diagonally on top of a wall of the Castelvecchio in Verona, thereby imposing on an old monument a new and modern physionomy (fig. 19). He did the same with the Palermo museum, several ancient building in Venice, stores and tombs (fig. 16-17-18). Even when he was involved in temporary exhibitions at the Venice *Biennale* and the Doge's Palace, his infallible instinct for how to display painting and sculpture was supreme. From a neutral or vulgar box he would extract an exciting and lyric architectural image. The same gifts, with differences in accent, are shared by Mollino (fig. 21-22), Gabetti (fig. 23), and others, all

Le pagine seguenti non intendono offrire un panorama esaustivo dell'architettura italiana dopo la seconda guerra mondiale. La selezione degli edifici è connessa al carattere di questa mostra: vuole indicare che la specifica sensibilità per il design industriale e artigianale o, meglio, per il "disegno" e la modanatura, esercita una forte influenza anche sui macroggetti dello scenario urbano.

Certo, l'architettura non può essere ridotta ad un "oggetto". È coinvolta in un vasto complesso di impegni e di sfide: i contenuti e le funzioni umane, il modo differenziato di rappresentarli e comunicarli, l'elaborazione di volumi che superino la statica tridimensionalità rinascimentale ed incorporino il movimento, l'uso di nuove strutture abitabili. Soprattutto, l'architettura riguarda l'invenzione di spazi dinamici dove la gente possa assumere liberi comportamenti; e deve stabilire un dialogo con l'ambiente, naturale o cittadino, storico o contemporaneo, magari basato su contrasti, su una calcolata discontinuità.

I progettisti italiani investono, più o meno, tutti questi aspetti del processo architettonico. Per dare alcuni esempi, i contenuti e le funzioni sono coraggiosamente aggrediti nell'edificio dei Passarelli a Roma, dove le porzioni commerciale, direzionale e residenziale mantengono la loro polemica autonomia (fig. 1). Asimmetrie e dissonanze sono presenti nella casa di Gorio (fig. 2) e nei percorsi della scuola di Capobianco a Salerno (fig. 3-4). Cavità originali, compresse o dilatate, sono evidenti nella villa di Pellegrin (fig. 5) e nel museo di Albini a Genova, in cui vibra una dialettica tra aree circolari formali e pause prive di forma (fig. 6). Quanto al rapporto con il contesto, è facile citare il Monumento alle Fosse Ardeatine per i suoi sapienti passaggi tra il prisma sospeso e le grotte (fig. 8), l'inserto di Petrignani nel centro antico di Bari (fig. 10), l'albergo dei Gatti a Taormina (fig. 11). Analoghi connotati sono reperibili in molte altre opere qui illustrate, e non richiedono commenti critici.

Questa, però, è solo una minima parte del quadro architettonico italiano. Di regola, abbiamo "scatole" e non volumi articolati, vuoti inerti e non spazi flessibili, simmetrie e reiterazioni, anacronistici schemi funzionali. Allora si ricorre ad espedienti visuali e tattili, a quei particolari raffinati che riescono a rendere attraente e personalizzato anche un edificio sostanzialmente banale. Il design, in questo senso, può essere considerato cosmesi, styling, rimedio e compenso per ciò che manca, la concezione spaziale. Ma il suo intervento significa spesso qualcosa di più. Quando non è meramente formalistico e superficiale, conferisce un'identità e un messaggio agli involucri e agli interni mediante la scelta intelligente e sagace di materiali, colori e luci.

Indubbiamente, da un rigoroso osservatorio architettonico preferiamo avere meno "disegno" nelle facciate e più fantasia nei valori spaziali e plastici. Tuttavia, esaminando l'insieme delle opere qui riprodotte, e pensando che potrebbero essere facilmente decuplicate, si è spinti a riconoscere che il fattore design, nelle condizioni attuali, appare stimolante e positivo. Permea l'architettura in ogni sua scala, al livello professionale più alto e in un largo settore di quello medio. Entro i suoi confini, distingue l'Italia da molti altri paesi.

Una breve analisi di alcuni protagonisti e di alcune tendenze può servire a chiarire meglio il fenomeno. Concentriamoci su Carlo Scarpa, tre ingegneri e Giovanni Michelucci.

Uno splendido artista come Scarpa può essere definito sia un designer che un architetto: è in bilico tra i due ruoli. Sapeva modellare un meraviglioso vetro di Murano, ma anche ubicare una statua diagonalmente in cima ad un muro del Castelvecchio di Verona, imprimendo una nuova, moderna fisionomia a un vecchio monumento (fig. 19); lo stesso nel museo di Palermo, in molti edifici di Venezia, in negozi e tombe (fig. 16-17-18). Anche quando si occupava di esposizioni temporanee alla Biennale o al Palazzo Ducale, il suo istinto nel situare dipinti e sculture era infallibile, supremo: da una scatola inerte e volgare sapeva estrarre emozionanti gesti lirici. Con accenti diversi, una vocazione simile si rintraccia in Mollino (fig. 21-22), in Gabetti (fig. 23) ed altri, tutti simultaneamente architetti e designers. Veniamo agli ingegneri. Nervi era legato ad impianti classici, cupole tipo Pantheon e sequenze di campate; ciò malgrado, è impossibile citare una sua opera in cui non ci sia un pilastro, una trave o un soffitto di straordinaria efficacia (fig. 26-27-28). Morandi, al contrario, non teme l'insicurezza: il suo salone sotterraneo a Torino sembra dover

architects and designers at the same time.
Engineering versus design. Nervi was bound to classical set-ups, Pantheon-like domes and a rather traditional repetition of bays. Despite this, there is not a single building by Nervi that does not have a pillar, a truss, or a ceiling of extraordinary significance (fig. 26-27-28). Morandi, however, is not intimidated by apparent insecurity. His underground Hall in Turin looks as if it might collapse at any moment, but the design of slanting supports and ribbed vault translates insecurity into an act of poetry (fig. 29-30). There was a unique timbre in Musmeci's kind of engineer. He shaped the structure of his bridge in Potenza in such a way that it would meet the ground and become a kind of vertebra of the landscape; you can play and stroll inside the bridge. He used mathematics to develop an expressionist theme and achieve an organic configuration (fig. 25).
Michelucci's itinerary is symptomatic. After the fundamental achievement of the 1936 railway station in Florence, he tried several paths: a simplified neoclassicism, which he rejected at once; then "poor" architecture, inspired by Tuscan peasant houses; later on an interweave of building and city with the aim of turning even a bank into an urban event, almost a street (fig. 31). Finally he took the plunge into Expressionism, which he describes as "a style that is not a style, but an anti-style", and modeled several churches, from the one on the highway near Florence to the one in Longarone (fig. 32-33). Expressionism yes, but with a particularly Italian flavor, without violence or protest, where the subtleties of moulding are an essential ingredient. These churches are conceived or "dreamt" of to be experienced from every angle, with automobiles running over their roofs. Crude and violently anticlassical skeleton structures blend with lacerated anti-geometric voids. However, suffice it to compare these churches with Le Corbusier's Ronchamp Chapel to show that all their elements are filtered and controlled by design, thus attenuating the drama of spaces, volumes and light.
Almost all other Italian architects share to some degree these trends. Ricci started out with a group of houses inspired by Wright, and he is still the most explicitly and courageously expressionist (fig. 34). In the Marchiondi Institute (fig. 37) and in the Arteluce store (fig. 38), Viganò offered provocative versions of British "New Brutalism". Savioli had two souls, one brutal and the other High-tech, both of them aristocratic. His bridge over the Arno River in Florence is a meeting point of the two (fig. 40). Many people have been trying to overcome the impasse of "disegno", including De Carlo in his work in Urbino (fig. 42), Loris Rossi in Naples (fig. 43), and Zacchiroli in Bologna (fig. 44). Are Piano's High-tech trend (fig. 47), the industrialized buildings by Zanuso (fig. 46), Valle (fig. 48), Morassutti and others, Pellegrin's prefabricated schools (fig. 50), Cappai and Mainardis' (fig. 51) "macro-machine" for Olivetti exceptions that postulate a sharp dividing line between design and industrial design in architecture? Only on the surface Technology and mass production are the preliminary motives, but the results always offer something more, elegant and formal signs and impulses that are often genuinely inventive.
Two other questions deserve consideration, the impact of tradition and anonymous architecture.
The problem of fitting new building into an old historical setting has dogged the Italians at least since the 1960s, both positively and negatively. A positive response consists in relating a new building to its surroundings by way of dissonance, as in the Termini railway station in Rome (fig. 55) and in the work of Samonà (fig. 56), Sartogo (fig. 53), and Pagliara (fig. 54). An acceptable alternative is to identify "modern stimuli" in the heritage of the past, but this calls for outstanding architects with a clear idiom of their own that can be reflected in the past, as B.B.P.R. did in the Torre Velasca in Milan (fig. 59) and Albini in the Rinascente department store in Rome (fig. 7). But to turn to tradition without a truly contemporary aesthetic awareness can only lead to passive attitude, to pseudo-classical and pseudo-baroque, neo-Islamic and neo-enlightenment abortions.
What about "architecture without architects", ordinary buildings, pop, and kitsch? Italian design has had no effect on this area of architecture. Attempts to revive vernacular styles have failed here just as elsewhere. Ordinary buildings are never simply anonymous; there is always something pretentious that makes them irritating. There is

crollare da un minuto all'altro, ma i profili dei supporti inclinati e della volta innervata traducono l'incertezza in atto poetico (fig. 29-30). Musmeci era un ingegnere di timbro singolare: nel ponte di Potenza, ha modulato una struttura che scende a terra vertebrando il paesaggio, sotto la quale si può giocare e passeggiare; con l'arma della matematica, ha realizzato un tema espressionista, una visione organica (fig. 25).
L'itinerario di Michelucci è sintomatico. Dopo la fondamentale Stazione di Firenze del 1936, ha sondato molteplici vie: una semplificazione neoclassica, subito rifiutata; poi, un'architettura "povera", ispirata alla casa contadina toscana; più tardi, un intreccio tra edificio e città, con l'obiettivo di tramutare persino una banca in un episodio urbano, quasi in una strada (fig. 31). Infine, si è tuffato nell'espressionismo, "uno stile che non è uno stile, ma un anti-stile", come dice, e ha plasmato una serie di chiese, da quella dell'Autostrada presso Firenze a quella di Longarone (fig. 32-33). Espressionismo, sì, e però di un sapore italiano, non violento e protestatario, in cui le sottigliezze delle modanature sono un ingrediente essenziale. Queste chiese sono concepite o sognate per essere percorse in ogni verso, con automobili che salgono sopra i tetti, con strutture a scheletro crude ed irruenti, con cavità lacerate, antigeometriche, che si fondono l'una nell'altra. Tuttavia, confrontandole con la cappella di Le Corbusier a Ronchamp, si scopre immediatamente che il design ne filtra e controlla elementi, attenuando il dramma degli spazi, dei volumi e delle luci.
A questi indirizzi, con varia enfasi, possono essere ricondotti quasi tutti gli architetti italiani. Ricci ha debuttato con un gruppo di case la cui matrice rievoca Frank Lloyd Wright, ed è tuttora il più esplicito e coraggioso espressionista (fig. 34). Viganò, nell'Istituto Marchiondi e nel negozio Arteluce (fig. 37-38), ha fornito provocanti versioni del "Nuovo Brutalismo" inglese. Savioli aveva due anime: una tecnologica, l'altra materica, ma entrambe aristocratiche, che si compongono nel ponte fiorentino aperto sull'Arno (fig. 40). Sforzi per liberarsi dai vincoli del "disegno" sono perseguiti da molti, fra cui De Carlo nell'attività ad Urbino (fig. 42), Loris Rossi a Napoli (fig. 43), Zacchiroli a Bologna (fig. 44).
La corrente High-Tech di Piano (fig. 47), gli edifici industrializzati di Zanuso (fig. 46), Valle (fig. 48), Morassutti ed altri, le scuole prefabbricate di Pellegrin (fig. 50), la "macchina" per la Olivetti di Cappai e Mainardis (fig. 51) sono eccezioni che postulano una netta linea divisoria tra design e industrial design in architettura? Solo apparentemente. La tecnologia e la produzione di massa sono i motivi di partenza, ma nei risultati c'è sempre qualcosa di più: segni e impulsi formali eleganti, spesso genuinamente inventivi.
Restano due questioni cui occorre accennare: 1) il peso della tradizione e 2) l'edilizia anonima.
Il problema dell'ambientamento nei contesti storici ha perseguitato gli italiani almeno dagli anni sessanta. In senso positivo e negativo. Una risposta positiva consiste nel relazionare il nuovo edificio al suo intorno per dissonanza, come nella Stazione di Roma (fig. 55) e nei lavori di Samonà (fig. 56), Sartogo (fig. 53), Pagliara (fig. 54). Un'alternativa accettabile mira a identificare "stimoli moderni" nel patrimonio antico, ma questa operazione richiede artisti di primissimo piano, che abbiano un loro preciso linguaggio e sappiano rispecchiarlo nel passato, come i BBPR hanno fatto nella Torre Velasca a Milano (fig. 59) e Albini nella "Rinascente" a Roma (fig. 7). Ispirarsi alla tradizione senza possedere una vera coscienza contemporanea sfocia invece in atteggiamenti passivi, in aborti pseudo-classici e pseudo-barocchi, neo islamici e neo-illuministi.
Quanto alla cosiddetta "architettura senza architetti", all'edilizia ordinaria, al pop e al Kitsch, il design italiano non ha inciso in questa area. Qualsiasi tentativo di risuscitare i vernacoli e i dialetti è fallito qui, come altrove. Gli edifici ordinari non sono mai semplicemente anonimi: hanno sempre qualche velleità che li rende irritanti. Un'architettura neutrale non esiste né nelle città né nei villaggi, dove anche gli artigiani imitano ciò che vedono in televisione. La pop-art e il Kitsch, quali incentivi per un arricchimento della scena urbana, sono esaltati in teoria e in numerosi progetti utopici, ma senza conseguenze concrete. L'architettura "firmata" domina quella "non firmata". Molti professionisti, specie nei quartieri popolari, cercano di cancellare le loro firme, per attingere effetti "spontanei", impersonali. I risultati sono

no such thing as neutral architecture in town or country, because even local craftsmen have taken to imitating what they see on television. Pop art and kitsch have been backed up by theory and in a host of utopian projects as means of enhancing the cityscape, but little or nothing has been done concretely. "Signed" architecture towers over "unsigned" architecture. Many architects, especially in low-income housing projects, have tried to erase their signatures in an attempt to achieve a kind of "spontaneous" and impersonal effect. The results are decent, simple, and correct, but they are always "signed". And this brings us to the last point. When you think that the glory of Italy consists in its squares, its streets, and the fabric of its cities and that modern architecture has not produced a single worthy *piazza* or street or city fabric, there is reason to wonder. There is much work yet to be done and essential goals to reach. It may be that the traditional notions of squares and streets have become obsolete in our day and that the modern city will have to acquire a look that is altogether different from that of the past. However the contrast between past and present is such a burning issue in Italy that it is a constant subject of discussion.

A small group with a loud voice recommends a self-destructive, nihilistic, and suicidal course. Their line is that modern architecture is doomed and that we must turn back to the academic and the eclectic to achieve a square or a street, even as frivolous as the Post-modern one at the 1980 *Biennale*. Fortunately there is an alternative to this abdication, and it is subscribed to by most Italian architects. Instead of throwing the baby out with the bath water, it would have him grow and develop a language of his own, one that is cultivated and popular at the same time, an idiom that could be used by major and minor architects and by non-architects as well. That way the brilliant fragments, of which the present exhibit offers a sampling could come out of their isolation and become part of a "continuum", of an enhanced and varied human environment.

In Italy too, the so-called "International Style" has been rejected, not because it denied the academic tradition but, on the contrary, because it quickly became academic itself and forgot modern principles. It did not express content and function, it proliferated "boxes", it was often a slave to the dogmas of symmetry, regularity, and proportion, it sought out *a priori* or *a posteriori* synthesis, it was formalist and symbolic, and hence it was essentially classical albeit stripped of decoration. What we have to do now is to reconquer and develop what was lost or dissipated in the postwar decades and forge a free, democratic, modern architecture, capable of interacting with the past, the authentic past an not a past polluted by the Beaux-Arts misinterpretations.

appropriati, semplici e corretti, ma sempre "firmati".
Arriviamo così alla conclusione. Quando si osserva che la gloria italiana è composta di piazze, strade, tessuti urbani, e che l'architettura moderna non ha prodotto né piazze, né strade, né tessuti validi, c'è motivo di restare perplessi: abbiamo ancora una lunga ricerca da svolgere ed essenziali traguardi da raggiungere. Forse le nozioni tradizionali della piazza e della strada sono anacronistiche nella nostra epoca, e la città moderna deve acquisire un volto totalmente differente da quello storico. Tuttavia il confronto tra passato e presente è così bruciante in Italia, che non si può evitare di discuterne continuamente. Una terapia autodistruttiva, nichilista e suicida propugnata da un piccolo, benché rumoroso, gruppo: afferma che l'architettura moderna è condannata e dobbiamo retrocedere all'accademia e all'eclettismo per ottenere una piazza o una strada, magari frivola come quella "post-modern" della Biennale 1980. Contro questa tesi abdicatoria c'è fortunatamente l'atteggiamento della maggioranza dei professionisti italiani: consiste nel non buttar via il bambino con l'acqua sporca del bagnetto, nel farlo crescere e nell'indurlo a maturare un linguaggio colto e insieme popolare, attraverso il quale architetti grandi e minori, ed anche non-architetti, possano comunicare. I brillanti, geniali "frammenti" documentati in queste pagine potrebbero allora rompere il loro isolamento e costituire un "continuum" vario, soddisfacente, umano.
L'"International Style", anche in Italia, è rifiutato non perché abbia negato la tradizione accademica ma, al contrario, perché ben presto si è accademizzato dimenticando i principi moderni. Non esprime i contenuti e le funzioni, moltiplica le "scatole", è spesso schiavo dei dogmi della simmetria, della regolarità e della proporzione, cerca una sintesi a priori o a posteriori, è formalistico e simbolico, cioè sostanzialmente classico, sebbene denudato dalle decorazioni. Dobbiamo riconquistare i valori perduti o dissipati in queste decadi del dopoguerra, e forgiare un'architettura moderna, libera e democratica, capace di dialogare con il passato, ma con il passato autentico, non con quello inquinato dall'ottica Beaux-Arts.

STUDIO PASSARELLI
1. Building on via Campania in Rome - 1963/65 / *Edificio in via Campania a Roma - 1963/65.*

FEDERICO GORIO
2. Maresciallo House in Rome - 1957/58 / *Casa del Maresciallo a Roma - 1957/58.*

MICHELE CAPOBIANCO
3.4. The School of Engineering - The University of Salerno - 1979 / *Facoltà di Ingegneria - Università di Salerno - 1979.*

LUIGI PELLEGRIN
5. Two-family house, Rome - 1964 / *Casa bifamiliare sull'Aurelia a Roma - 1964.*

FRANCO ALBINI
6. The San Lorenzo Museum in Genoa - 1956 / *Tesoro S. Lorenzo a Genova - 1956.*
7. The Rinascente Department Store, Rome - 1962 / *La Rinascente a Roma - 1962.*

NATALE APRILE - CINO CALCARINA - ALDO CARDELLI - MARIO
FIORENTINO - GIUSEPPE PERUGINI
8. Monument to the Martyrs of the Ardeatine Caves in Rome - 1945/48 /
Monumento ai Martiri delle Fosse Ardeatine a Roma - 1945/48.

LUIGI COSENZA
9. Olivetti Factory in Pozzuoli - 1954 / *Fabbrica Olivetti a Pozzuoli - 1954.*

MARCELLO PETRIGNANI
10. Apartment Building in Bari - 1978 / *Casa a Bari - 1978.*

ALBERTO E AMBRETTA GATTI
11. Hotel in Taormina - 1973 / *Albergo a Taormina - 1973.*

IGNAZIO GARDELLA
12. Apartment Buildings in Alessandria - 1951 / *Case per impiegati ad
Alessandria - 1951.*

ADALBERTO LIBERA
13. Malaparte House in Capri - 1940 / *Casa Malaparte a Capri - 1940.*

CARLO SCARPA
14. Olivetti Showroom in Venice - 1958 / *Olivetti a Venezia - 1958.*
15. Bridge to Querini Stampalia Gallery, Venice - 1963 / *Querini Stampalia a Venezia - 1963.*
16. Brion Family Tomb at San Vito (Treviso) - 1970/72 / *Tomba Brion a San Vito (Treviso) - 1970/72.*
17.18. Gavina Showroom in Bologna - 1962 / *Negozio Gavina a Bologna - 1962.*
19. Castelvecchio Museum in Verona - 1964 / *Museo Castelvecchio a Verona - 1964.*

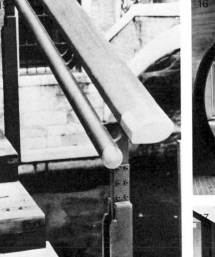

MARIO RIDOLFI
20. Apartment Buildings on Viale Etiopia in Rome - 1957 / *Edifici di abitazione in viale Etiopia a Roma - 1957.*

CARLO MOLLINO
21. House at Agra - 1953 / *Casa ad Agra - 1953.*
22. Lagonero Skiing Station at Sauze d'Ouix - 1946 / *Stazione della Slittovia di lagonero - Sauze d'Ouix - 1946.*

ROBERTO GABETTI - AIMARO D'ISOLA
23. Bottega d'Erasmo Building, Turin - 1956 / *Bottega d'Erasmo a Torino - 1956.*

GUIDO CANELLA - MICHELE ACHILLI - DANIELE BRIGIDINI - LAURA LAZZARI
24. Town Hall at Segrate (Milan) - 1962/63 / *Municipio di Segrate (Milano) - 1962/63.*

SERGIO MUSMECI
25. Bridge over Basento River - 1974 / *Ponte sul Basento - 1974.*

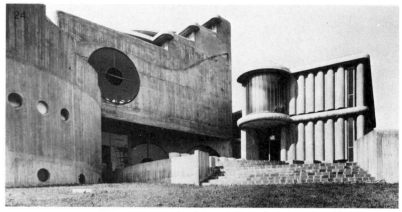

PIER LUIGI NERVI
26. Sports Palace in Rome - 1960 / *Palazzo dello Sport a Roma - 1960.*
27. Exhibition hall in Turin - 1948/49 / *Padiglione d'esposizione a Torino - 1948/49.*
28. Burgo Paper Factory in Mantua - 1962 / *Cartiera Burgo a Mantova - 1962.*

RICCARDO MORANDI
29. Underground exhibition salon in Turin - 1959 / *Padiglione sotterraneo dell'automobile a Torino - 1959.*
30. Viaduct over Polcevera River, Genoa - 1961/63 / *Viadotto del Polcevera a Genova - 1961/63.*

GIOVANNI MICHELUCCI
31. Savings Bank in Florence - 1953 / *Cassa di Risparmio a Firenze - 1953.*
32. The San Giovanni Battista Church near Florence - 1964 / *Chiesa S. Giovanni Battista detta dell'"Autostrada" presso Firenze - 1964.*
33. Church at Longarone - 1980 / *Chiesa a Longarone - 1980.*

LEONARDO RICCI
34. Sorgane Public Housing Complex in Florence - 1966 / *Quartiere Sorgane a Firenze - 1966.*

MARCELLO D'OLIVO
35. Children's Center in Trieste - 1955 / *Villaggio del Fanciullo a Trieste - 1955.*

LUIGI CARLO DANERI
36. Forte-Quezzi Public Housing Complex, Genoa - 1957 / *Quartiere Forte-Quezzi a Genova - 1957.*

VITTORIANO VIGANÒ
37. Marchiondi Medical Center in Milan - 1953/57 / *Istituto Marchiondi a Milano - 1953/57.*
38. Arte Luce Showroom in Milan - 1963 / *Negozio Arte Luce a Milano - 1963.*

LEONARDO SAVIOLI
39. Flower Market at Pescia - 1981 / *Mercato dei Fiori a Pescia - 1981.*
40. Bridge over Arno River in Florence - 1966/68 / *Ponte sull'Arno a Firenze - 1966/68.*
41. Apartment Building in Florence - 1966 / *Appartamenti a Firenze - 1966.*

GIANCARLO DE CARLO
42. University College at Urbino - 1966 / *Collegio Universitario ad Urbino - 1966.*

ALDO LORIS ROSSI
43. Port Authority Building in Naples - 1981 / *Edificio portuale a Napoli - 1981.*

ENZO ZACCHIROLI
44. Towers in Bologna - 1980 / *Torri a Bologna - 1980.*

MARCO ZANUSO
45. Apartment Houses in Milan - 1965 / *Edifici di abitazione a Milano - 1965.*

SERGIO LENCI
46. Rescoop Building in Lugo di Romagna - 1978 / *Sede Rescoop a Lugo di Romagna - 1978.*

42

44

43

46
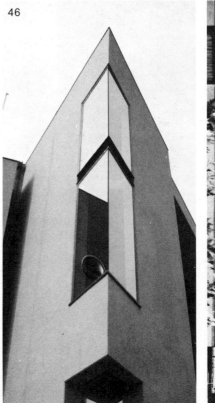

45

RENZO PIANO - RICHARD ROGERS
47. Beaubourg Center in Paris - 1972/77 / *Centro Beaubourg a Parigi - 1972/77.*

GINO VALLE
48. Zanussi Factory at Pordenone - 1960 / *Stabilimento Zanussi a Pordenone - 1960.*

VITTORIO GREGOTTI Associati - GINO POLLINI
49. School of Science - The University of Palermo - 1982 / *Dipartimento di Scienze - Università di Palermo - 1982.*

LUIGI PELLEGRIN
50. Vocational School at Rifredi, Florence - 1981 / *Scuola professionale a Rifredi a Firenze - 1981.*

IGINO CAPPAI - PIETRO MAINARDIS
51. Olivetti Residential and Social Service Center at Ivrea - 1969/74 / *Centro dei servizi sociali e residenziali Olivetti a Ivrea - 1969/74.*

CARLO AYMONINO - MAURIZIO AYMONINO - ALESSANDRO DE ROSSI - SACHIM MESSARÉ
52. Gallaratese Public Housing Complex in Milan - 1967/74 / *Quartiere Gallaratese a Milano - 1967/74.*

PIERO SARTOGO
53. Medical Center in Rome - 1972 / *Sede dell'Ordine dei Medici a Roma - 1972.*

NICOLA PAGLIARA
54. SIP Telephone Building at Benevento - 1959 / *Centrale SIP a Benevento - 1959.*

LEO CALINI - MASSIMO CASTELLAZZI - VASCO FADIGATI - EUGENIO MONTUORI - ACHILLE PINTONELLO
55. Termini Railroad Station in Rome - 1949/51 / *Stazione Termini a Roma - 1949/51.*

GIUSEPPE SAMONÀ
56. Theater at Sciacca - 1981 / *Teatro di Sciacca - 1981.*

BRUNO BARINCI - MASSIMO BATTAGLINI - CORRADO CAMELI - MARIO CAMPANELLA - CARLO COCCHIA - GIULIA DE LUCA - MARINO LOMBARDI - PIER LUIGI NERVI - LUIGI PICCINATO - GIUSEPPE VACCARO - UGO VIALE - BRUNO ZEVI
57. Central Railroad Station, Naples - 1955/60 / *Stazione di Napoli - 1955/60.*

LUDOVICO BELGIOIOSO - ENRICO PERESSUTTI - ERNESTO N. ROGERS
58. Museum of Castello Sforzesco, Milan - 1963 / *Castello Sforzesco a Milano - 1963.*
59. Velasca Tower, Milan - 1954/58 / *Torre Velasca a Milano - 1954/58.*

PAOLO MAURIZIO SACRIPANTI
60. School at Sant'Arcangelo di Romagna (Forlì) - 1979 / *Scuola a Sant'Arcangelo di Romagna (Forlì) - 1979.*

LUCIANO CELLI - DARIO TOGNON
61. Computer Center in Trieste - 1975 / *Centro di calcolo a Trieste - 1975.*

DESIGN AND INDUSTRY

SERGIO PININFARINA

It makes sense for an industrialist to write about an industrial design exhibit if he is fully aware of the importance of design as a vehicle of culture, when the objects that are designed convey the inventive resources that give them their proper meaning in direct relationship to the purpose they are meant to serve.

Among the things and objects that make up the present exhibit, those that were conceived for mass production invite us to linger a moment, for here the designer's creative freedom is subjected to a host of general conditioning factors. (During the current period of crisis one such factor is the demand for austerity of form, so that the object not conflict with the everyday reality of the consumer.) These constraints may limit a designer's creativity, but also enhance his capacity to adjust his view of the given object to fit a world of wide consumption and to bring an object into the life of consumers without any distinction between one class of society and another.

In no way does it diminish the designer to know that what he has designed will go through all the stages of an industrial product, the result of strategic theories that control the decision-making process to begin with, then the industrial phases, and finally the marketing.

All of this is nothing more than a demonstration of the fact that the life of the community and productive work are interlinked. A factory could not function properly under a bell jar, nor, since it is an aggregation of people, could it be uprooted from the reality that involves man, his passions, and his ideas.

Within certain limits at least, this interchange of experience brings with it cultural and human enrichment, and this is all to the good, for it makes growth possible.

The fact remains, however, that the host of variables inherent in the complex work of an industrialist are matched by a host of variables from outside the industrial system. I have earned the right to say so through direct experience. I am responsible for a research and development center that employs 150 people as well as for a company that turns out 25,000 car bodies a year and employs 2,000 people. I am not saying that an entrepreneur has to be an expert in political science; what I am saying is that he will not be doing his job fully unless he approaches with sensitivity and intelligence the problems of human, union, and indeed political relations.

What makes the case of Italy so exceptional is the enormous relevance of difficulties and uneconomic procedures that pour into the sphere of economics from the social sphere and, at the same time, the ability to respond, the flexibility and vitality that Italian civic society has shown even in periods of world crisis like the present.

But what are the chief peculiarities of the Italian situation and particularly the ones that have the most direct repercussions on the production system?

To begin with there is a cultural dualism. Italy has deep roots in the Catholic faith, but the recent success of a public referendum on abortion, which involves a very serious question of principle for Catholics, shows that a lay conscience is developing, and a clear distinction between religious faith and political behavior is making headway in a manner that has even surprised the Church.

There is a geographic duality. The north is very advanced industrially, while the south is so backward that per capita production is only two-thirds of the national average.

Labor is profondly split too. The Italian system provides more extensive job security than most other countries in the world, but unemployment and underemployment are widespread.

The employed and the unemployed are rigidly counterpoised. An employee is so protected that his job may be guaranteed even in the extreme case that the company may go out of business. This makes the labor market that much more rigid and inevitably increases the problems of those who set out to look for a job without special advantages.

There is another dualism that needs to be mentioned, one that affects the very structure of the industrial system.

There are businesses in Italy on a par with the most modern, advanced, and technologically equipped in the world, while there are others, those that are run by the state or owned mainly by the state, that are so weighted down because of a misguided sense of social responsibility that they can hardly fulfill their basic production

DESIGN E INDUSTRIA

SERGIO PININFARINA

Un industriale può presentare una mostra sul design italiano se ha la piena consapevolezza dell'importanza del design come veicolo di cultura presso gli utilizzatori quando nell'oggetto sono trasmesse le risorse inventive che gli danno il giusto significato in diretto rapporto con la sua qualificazione.

Tra i prodotti che fanno parte di questa rassegna ci si sofferma su quelli in particolare concepiti per la grande serie; per questi prodotti la libertà creativa del designer subisce un complesso di condizionamenti di carattere generale (in questo momento di crisi anche il condizionamento per la necessità di un'austerità formale così che l'oggetto non si ponga in contrasto con la realtà quotidianamente vissuta dall'utilizzatore). La serie di vincoli, se da una parte può limitare la creatività del designer, dall'altra però ne esalta la capacità di inserire la sua visione dell'oggetto in un mondo di largo consumo, portandolo nella vita degli utilizzatori senza distinzione tra una categoria sociale e l'altra.

Non è riduttivo per il designer sapere che esso passa attraverso tutti i processi di un prodotto industriale, frutto delle strategie teorizzate che guidano prima il processo decisionale, poi quello della industrializzazione ed infine della commercializzazione del bene.

Tutto ciò non è che la manifestazione dell'intreccio tra società e vita produttiva: infatti la fabbrica non può operare bene sotto una campana di vetro, e anch'essa — in quanto aggregazione di uomini — non può essere sradicata dalla realtà che riguarda l'uomo, le sue passioni, le sue idee.

Almeno entro certi limiti, dunque, viene un arricchimento culturale e umano da questo scambio di esperienze, e il fatto è positivo: consente ad un sistema di crescere.

Resta però il fatto che alle infinite variabili, già di per sé esistenti nel complesso lavoro dell'industriale, si aggiungono le non meno numerose variabili provenienti dall'esterno del sistema industriale. Ve lo posso dire perché ne ho una esperienza diretta; perché ho la responsabilità non solo di un Centro Studi e Ricerche che impiega 150 persone, ma anche quella di un'azienda che produce 25.000 carrozzerie di automobili all'anno e che impiega quasi altre 2.000 persone.

Non dico che l'imprenditore debba diventare un esperto di scienze politiche, dico che non può fare completamente bene il proprio mestiere senza accostarsi con sensibilità e intelligenza ai problemi delle relazioni umane, sindacali, e appunto politiche.

L'eccezionalità del caso Italia sta proprio nell'enorme rilevanza delle difficoltà e delle diseconomie che si riversano dal sociale sull'economico, e — nonostante questo — nella capacità di reazione, nella flessibilità e nella vitalità che la società civile italiana dimostra anche in un momento di crisi mondiale come questo.

Ma quali sono le principali anomalie del caso Italia, e in particolare quelle che si ripercuotono più direttamente sul sistema produttivo?

C'è innanzitutto una duplicità culturale che rende ogni cosa più difficile in un Paese di profonde radici cattoliche, ma che segnala ad esempio — con il recente esito di un referendum popolare su un problema di principio molto importante per i cattolici — che la coscienza laica, e una più lucida distinzione tra fede e comportamento politico, stanno avanzando in modo, per molti e per la stessa Chiesa, imprevedibile.

C'è poi la ben nota duplicità territoriale e geografica: con le regioni del Nord industrialmente molto avanzate, e quelle del Sud arretrate al punto che il prodotto per abitante del Mezzogiorno è circa due terzi di quello medio nazionale.

C'è inoltre una profonda divisione che percorre verticalmente il mondo del lavoro. Abbiamo in Italia un sistema di garanzie per il lavoratore occupato che è tra i più estesi e sicuri del mondo, ma al contempo riscontriamo una vasta area di disoccupazione e sottoccupazione.

L'uno è contrapposto all'altro in modo rigido: l'occupato viene difeso fino al punto di garantirgli il posto di lavoro anche nel caso estremo in cui l'azienda d'appartenenza non esista più, e questo rafforza la rigidità del mercato del lavoro e accresce fatalmente le difficoltà di coloro che cercano occupazioni partendo da posizioni sfavorevoli.

Vi è infine una quarta duplicità da segnalare, ed è quella che riguarda appunto la struttura stessa del sistema industriale nel suo insieme.

Vi convivono infatti imprese tra le più moderne, avanzate e tecnologicamente dotate del mondo, con altre, quelle a gestione dello

functions.

But to turn to my conception of design. What does the name Pininfarina mean? The Italian automotive body, Cisitalia, Lancias, Ferraris, rally racing.

Let me say at once that Pininfarina means something else as well. If we can keep the values of our past vital and alive and if we can look to expansion in the future, this is due not only to fifty years' experience in design and production but also to the fact that we are an integral part of the Italian cultural heritage.

What is it that links the industrial designing of an automobile with the phenomenon of Italian design?

I do not think our experience is much different from that of quality Italian design generally. We are all on the razor's edge between eclecticism and genius, improvisation and science, daring and intuition. Vittorio Gregotti once described this mysterious terrain as the "solution of the problem of the relationship between art and industry". What this means for the designer is a creative moment it is almost impossible to talk about without falling into contradiction, except by letting the products speak for themselves through their way of existing and lasting.

I think things are different in Japan, in other European countries, and in the United States.

In those countries roles are better divided professionally, and I think the designer is called upon more frequently as the product advances, but perhaps at a more superficial level. We are all aware of the importance of the first impact the look of something has on the consumer. The United States has led the world in developing one of the most complex design phenomena, styling and its application in industry.

I am reminded of a conversation between my father and Sir Alec Issigonis, who created the Mini, the vehicle that revolutionized Europe's idea of the automobile after the war. The Pininfarina company was called in to design new models for what was then the British Motor Corporation. At one point, my father asked Issigonis if he considered himself "a stylist or an engineer". Issigonis replied with mock indignation, "Sir, I could find your question offensive. I am an engineer, not a stylist".

The collaborative efforts that ensued between BMC and Pininfarina, I believe, convinced Sir Alec, that we were on his side. The results of that collaboration included some of the great advances in automobile design. The philosophy of the Berlina Break, for example, which resulted in the 1956 Austin A40 and the 1963 Morris 1100, is taken by many observers to be the fountainhead of all the two-cylinder cars that European manufacturers have brought out.

This collaboration was so important that Issigonis referred to us on the fiftieth anniversary of Pininfarina as "design engineers and not stylists".

If styling is understood as a purely formal attraction to the consumer of industrial products, then we must take our stand against that kind of persuasion. From the very beginning Pininfarina has been a deeply innovative force in automobile functions and in the formal response to the development of those functions.

This creative independence is certainly rooted in Italy's artistic culture. The centuries have made Italy a unique concentrate of works of art, but it would be pure rhetoric to cite the great names of the Renaissance as others have done in the past. What is important is that my father's work was not insensitive to the new artistic and design trends that emerged in this century, from futurism and its "machine esthetics" to rationalist composition and "integral planning". Speaking of such matters reminds me of something almost Dada or surrealist that happened to my father and me in Paris. It was 1947, and for reasons that I prefer not to think of, Italy was not allowed to take part in the Paris Salon. The Pininfarina company had two new cars ready, an Alfa and a Lancia. My father decided to go to Paris anyhow, and he took me, a schoolboy then, with him.

The Salon was held at the Grant Palais, and when we got there, my father put his plan into action. He parked the two automobiles right in front of the main staircase. Visitors to the Salon all stopped to look; this went on for the whole duration of the Salon, and thousands of people had a chance to see the new Pininfarinas. The day after the

Stato o a prevalente partecipazione statale, che ragioni di malintesa socialità appesantiscono a tal punto di oneri impropri che finiscono per non poter più svolgere la loro più elementare funzione produttiva.

Parliamo della mia concezione del design, di Pininfarina, di che cosa significa questo nome: la carrozzeria italiana, la Cisitalia, le grandi Lancia, le Ferrari, le competizioni nei rallies.

Ma vorrei subito dire che la Pininfarina significa non solo questo, e che se possiamo mantenere vivi ed attivi i valori del nostro passato ed espandere la nostra attività nel futuro, lo dobbiamo sì alla nostra esperienza di cinquant'anni di disegno e di produzione, ma anche al fatto di essere parte integrante del patrimonio culturale italiano.

Cosa lega allora il fenomeno della progettazione industriale dell'automobile con quel particolare altro fenomeno che è il design italiano?

Credo che la nostra esperienza non sia molto differente da quella della totalità del design italiano di qualità; siamo tutti sul sottile filo del rasoio che divide l'eclettismo dalla genialità, l'improvvisazione dalla scientificità: insomma quel territorio ancora misterioso che una volta Vittorio Gregotti ha definito "risoluzione del rapporto arte-industria", e che si traduce per il designer in un momento creativo di cui non è quasi possibile parlare, se non con definizioni anche contraddittorie, se non facendo parlare da soli i prodotti del proprio lavoro, il loro modo di essere e di durare nel tempo.

Io credo che in Giappone, ma anche negli altri Paesi europei, come del resto negli Stati Uniti, la situazione sia diversa.

I ruoli — in questi Paesi — sono professionalmente meglio individuati ed il designer ritengo venga chiamato ad intervenire sul prodotto più frequentemente, ma forse a livello più superficiale. Conosciamo tutti l'importanza del primo impatto formale del prodotto con l'utente; di questo il Paese che ci ospita è stato tanto maestro da dare vita e definizione a uno dei fenomeni progettuali più complessi del mondo contemporaneo: lo styling e la sua industrializzazione.

Mi viene in mente uno scambio di battute tra mio padre e Sir Alec Issigonis, Il creatore della Mini, il primo veicolo che dopo la guerra ha rivoluzionato il concetto europeo di automobile; al nostro primo incontro, nel periodo in cui la Pininfarina era stata chiamata per pianificare i nuovi modelli dell'allora British Motor Corporation, mio padre chiese ad un certo punto ad Issigonis se si sentisse "a stylist or an engineer"; Issigonis si finse un po' arrabbiato e rispose "Sir, I could find your question offensive. I am an engineer, not a stylist".

L'esperienza di collaborazione tra la BMC e la Pininfarina che seguì a quel primo incontro credo abbia convinto Sir Alec che noi eravamo dalla sua parte; le soluzioni che sono nate da quella collaborazione sono infatti tra le più avanzate nel campo delle automobili di grande serie: la filosofia nuova delle Berlina-Break, ad esempio, con l'Austin A40 del '56, o la Morris 1100 del '63, che a giudizio di molti critici si può considerare esteticamente e concettualmente la capostipite di tante due volumi prodotte successivamente dalle case europee.

Una collaborazione quindi tanto importante che Issigonis si è trovato recentemente ad affermare, in occasione dei cinquanta anni della Pininfarina, che di noi si dovesse parlare come di "design engineers and not stylists".

Se dunque intendiamo lo styling come puro incentivo formale al consumo dei prodotti industriali, dobbiamo dire che siamo avversi ad un simile mezzo di persuasione: e che, al contrario, l'opera della Pininfarina è stata fin dalla fondazione un'attività profondamente innovatrice delle funzioni dell'automobile e delle risposte formali all'evoluzione di tali funzioni.

Questa autonomia creativa ha certamente radici nella cultura artistica italiana, che nei secoli ha fatto del nostro Paese un concentrato unico di opere d'arte. Più importante è però chiarire che l'opera di mio padre non è stata insensibile alle nascenti tendenze artistiche e progettuali moderne: dal futurismo e la sua "estetica della macchina", al metodo compositivo del razionalismo: la "progettazione integrale".

E già che ci siamo con le illustri analogie di carattere artistico, vi divertirà sapere che subito dopo la guerra mio padre ed io fummo protagonisti, proprio a Parigi, di un'azione di genere quasi "dada" o surrealista: era il 1947 e, per una discriminazione i cui motivi non amo ricordare, l'Italia era stata esclusa dal salone di Parigi. Ma la Pininfarina aveva pronte due nuove vetture: un'Alfa ed una Lancia. E mio padre

inauguration the newspapers printed stories and pictures with the caption, "L'antisalon du carrossier turinois Pininfarina". My father remembered the word "antisalon" with pleasure and satisfaction all his life. It summed up his genius, as well as the authority and "weight" that the Carrozzeria Pininfarina already enjoyed.

Someone remarked that the Pininfarina style had a special meaning in the history of industry, the ability to translate the concept of the automobile immediately into an object, the concept and meaning of the automobile as speed. And the concept of aerodynamics was the most appropriate instrument of this design endeavor. This was how the slanted windshield of the 1932 Alfa Romeo 2300 coupe came into being, not to mention the streamlined 1936 Lancia Aprilia, and the formal perfection of the 1947 Cisitalia, the Pininfarina automobile that Arthur Drexler put on display in 1951 at New York's Museum of Modern Art as an example of "sculpture in motion", and it is still on display there.

From the very beginning Pininfarina decided to produce small numbers of cars itself and to have other companies produce its models in large quantity. An industrial stance was forced to take account of its context, and the Italian context was certainly not yet industrial. So at the outset it was creative intuition that generated forms that were later to influence industrial production, a kind of dialectical relationship and constant feedback between design and product.

Of course a prophetic gift would not have been enough to turn Pininfarina into an industrial reality. Yet such was the company's influence that what was then the Nash Motor Corporation (now American Motors Corp.) asked Pininfarina in 1950 to design its Ambassador, and it was so successful that when the car was introduced in 1952 thousands of posters were printed with my father's photograph.

Success in America reverberated in Europe, and the geographic and industrial distance between the two continents enhanced the prestige.

That was the period in which two developments of great importance for our image got started. The company restructured for large-scale production, and collaborative efforts with Ferrari got under way. And it was this that brought us into automobile racing with its brutally urgent and incessant demands for progress. But this has also made it possible for us to create the most beautiful sports cars, the Italian sports cars *par excellence*.

It was also in the 1950s that Pininfarina formalized its collaboration with the great companies in the automobile field, with all the Italian producers, several European companies, and several across the oceans. To mention the most important and longest-lasting, Peugeot. Our relationship with Peugeot has grown closer and closer since 1951, and all its basic models have started out from Pininfarina design. More than twenty million automobiles have been built to Pininfarina design, and this fact best expresses the importance of the company in automotive industrial design.

In terms of quality we have tried to express our ideas and concepts in vehicles that could offer a positive response to all the new demands made on the automobile; we have tried to give new concepts in technology material form in prototypes.

I should like to mention three examples. The first is the safety idea embodied in the 1963 Sigma. We submitted 14 basic concepts, and 8 of them subsequently became legally mandatory. One of these concepts was for a centrally reinforced body that was less rigid at the ends. Although this is not mandatory, it is fundamental in the technological thinking behind all cars today.

The second example is Formula 1 racing safety. In 1969, with the help of an international team of experts, we designed a safety Formula 1 car, the Sigma Grand Prix. The idea was to reduce risks for racing drivers and to apply racing experience to everyday cars. Thus we have made more than a technical and sporting contribution. Several of the basic ideas of this prototype were later to be incorporated in international regulations.

The third example involves aerodynamics. Through a combination of intuition and dangerous road testing, we have developed a host of aerodynamic vehicles since 1936, including the streamlined Aprilia,

decise di partire lo stesso, con me, allora ancora studente, per Parigi. Arrivati al Grand Palais, dove si teneva il salone, mio padre mise in atto il suo piano. E cioè posteggiò le due automobili proprio davanti al grande scalone di ingresso, così che i visitatori che affluivano, si avvicinavano incuriositi e interessati; e così andò avanti per tutta la durata del salone, finché tutte le migliaia di visitatori ebbero modo di vedere le nuove Pininfarina. I giornali pubblicarono la notizia, con il titolo "L'antisalon du carrossier turinois Pininfarina". La parola "antisalon" mio padre la ricordò sempre con piacere e convinzione.

È stato detto che lo stile Pininfarina ha significato, nella storia delle formule industriali, la capacità di tradurre immediatamente in oggetto, il concetto stesso dell'automobile. E il concetto di aerodinamicità è stato lo strumento più appropriato di quest'operazione progettuale. Così sono nati il parabrezza inclinato del coupé Alfa Romeo 2300 del 1932, le intuizioni aerodinamiche, pure di una Lancia Aprilia del 1936, la perfezione formale della Cisitalia del 1947, l'automobile Pininfarina che Arthur Drexler volle presentare nel 1951 al Museum of Modern Art di New York, come esempio di "scultura in movimento"; una scultura che ancora oggi è esposta in quel museo.

Ma fin dall'inizio della sua attività la Pininfarina si propose di riprodurre in piccola serie i propri prodotti o di farli riprodurre da altri in quantitativi molto più grandi. Un atteggiamento di tipo industriale doveva forzatamente fare i conti con un contesto, come quello italiano, che industriale non era ancora certamente; fu quindi inizialmente la capacità di intuizione creativa a generare forme che poi avrebbero influenzato la successiva produzione industriale; una specie di rapporto dialettico, un feedback continuo tra progetto e prodotto.

Certo, la sola capacità profetica non sarebbe stata sufficiente alla Pininfarina per diventare una realtà industriale; tuttavia era tale la sua influenza che la allora Nash Motor Corporation americana (ora la American Motors Corp.) volle nel 1950 affidare a noi la progettazione del suo modello Ambassador e l'entusiasmo fu tale che vollero presentare negli Stati Uniti — nel 1952 — il nuovo modello con migliaia di manifesti riproducenti il volto di mio padre.

Il successo americano rimbalzò in Europa, ingigantito proprio dalla lontananza geografica ed industriale dei nostri continenti.

Ed è proprio in quell'epoca che si avviano contemporaneamente due processi decisivi per la nostra immagine; da una parte la creazione di una struttura produttiva per la serie, dall'altra la collaborazione con la Ferrari. Essa ci avrebbe avvicinato per anni — e lo fa anche oggi — al mondo delle corse automobilistiche, alle sue necessità di progresso brutalmente urgenti e senza mai sosta. Allo stesso tempo ci permise — per anni ed ancora oggi — di dare vita alle più belle auto sportive che sono diventate le sportive italiane per eccellenza.

Gli anni cinquanta segnarono anche l'inizio delle collaborazioni con i grandi dell'automobile: tutte le case italiane, molte europee, alcune al di là degli oceani. Ne cito fra tutte una: quella più importante e duratura: quella con la Peugeot. Dal 1951 ad oggi, il nostro rapporto di collaborazione continua sempre più stretto, tutti i modelli base della casa di Parigi sono nati da allora con design Pininfarina.

Dal punto di vista qualitativo abbiamo cercato di esprimere le nostre idee, i nostri concetti in veicoli che rispondessero positivamente a quanto di nuovo si richiedeva all'automobile; abbiamo cercato di materializzare i nuovi concetti tecnici in prototipi di studio.

A titolo di esempio ne citerò tre. Il primo: l'idea sicurezza, espressa nella Sigma (1963). Proponevamo 14 concetti base, 8 divenuti in seguito norma di legge: uno, quello della cellula centrale rigida e delle estremità deformabili, senza essere prescrizione legale è tuttavia alla base della concezione tecnica di tutti gli autoveicoli di oggi.

Secondo esempio: la sicurezza nelle corse di formula 1. Costruimmo nel 1969, con l'aiuto di un team internazionale di esperti, una formula 1 di sicurezza, la Sigma Grand Prix. L'idea era di diminuire i pericoli per i piloti in corsa ma anche di usare l'esperienza delle corse per le macchine di tutti i giorni, quelle che tutti noi usiamo. Aggiungere alle corse un altro scopo oltre a quello tecnico e sportivo.

Molte idee base di questo prototipo, divennero in seguito parte integrante dei regolamenti internazionali.

Terzo esempio: l'aerodinamica. Basandoci sull'intuizione e sul supporto tecnico di pericolose prove su strada, concepimmo, fin dal 1936, numerosi studi di veicoli aerodinamici come l'Aprilia

which increased speed by 15 per cent.

Then in 1967 and 1968 came the two streamlined BMC sedan prototypes. These two automobile concepts were behind a host of models that created the image of the European sedan, including the Citroen GS, Alfa Sud, Lancia Gamma and the Rover 3500.

It was also clear that there would have to be changes in the hardware as well if progress were to continue. We were the first in Italy, between 1965 and 1972, to build a natural size wind tunnel. And it is here that we carry out sophisticated testing, including aerodynamic tests, the effect of side winds on the regularity of a vehicle's course, and air flow noise measurement inside and outside the car.

The interesting thing is that we built the wind tunnel mainly to improve performance, that is to say, to make cars faster, road hugging, and manageable.

Then came the oil crisis to upset the world economy, and our wind tunnel served a new and even more important purpose in developing energy-saving vehicles.

It was thanks to the wind tunnel that we were able to develop the "ideal aerodynamic form", the result of research promoted by Italy's National Research Center as part of a project to develop a "body for a medium-size European car to achieve a substantial reduction in energy consumption". 1971 was the year we set up our automated calculation and design center, which is equipped to gather data, develop management programs, and, starting out from master models (models taken from life), make all the necessary changes in dimension. The object under examination can be turned around in space, shown in perspective and three-dimensional section, reduced in scale, turned over, and many other things as well.

In recent years there have been changes in industrial design and in production at Pininfarina, including designs for industrial vehicles, interior and exterior design for pleasure craft, aircraft interiors, cable cars, and more recently farm tractors and earth-moving equipment. Thus we have achieved an industrial dimension and further extended our research and development (a larger and more modern research center is being built), and our design and engineering work is being supplemented by large-scale production of our own vehicles.

The current exhibit offers a broad view of Italian design. It shows how it entered industry and from there into the life and culture of a whole people without diminishing the classical working of objects intended for an elite clientele. Thus something that traditionally was part of the nation's heritage of artisanry and closed to the mass of citizens has become available to all.

The exhibit offers a view of design in mass rites during twenty-fours in the life of an Italian city, and this section of the show illustrates the role industry has played in the transformation of society, since the 1950s, from a predominantly agricultural society into one of the world's most industrialized countries.

Industry can proudly claim to be the irreplaceable instrument that has conveyed the beauty and culture inherent in design into all our everyday lives. The present exhibit bears witness to this. And this ample view of the history of Italian design offers a host of stimuli for those in the field, since it is consideration of what has already been done that provides the basis for future development. Italian design has made a name for itself throughout the world, and there is every reason to believe that vital elements continue to ferment and that it will continue to be one of the finest testimonies of Italian endeavor and imagination.

aerodinamica con la quale ottenemmo un incremento di velocità, a pari potenza, del 15%.

In seguito realizzammo nel 1967 e nel 1968 i due prototipi di berline aerodinamiche BMC. Queste macchine-idea furono le capostipiti di una numerosa serie di modelli che costituiscono oggi l'immagine della berlina europea: dalla Citroën GS all'Alfa Sud, dalla Lancia Gamma alla Rover 3500.

Ma ci parve evidente che per avere ulteriori consistenti progressi avremmo dovuto intervenire anche sull'hardware. Siamo stati i primi in Italia, a costruire — dal 1965 al 1972 — una galleria del vento, scala 1:1. Qui effettuiamo prove tra le più complesse: dal determinare l'azione aerodinamica attraverso la misura delle forze e dei momenti che agiscono sull'oggetto in prova, allo studio di veicoli che non alterino la loro traiettoria, se soggetti a vento laterale, alle misurazioni delle rumorosità aerodinamiche all'esterno ed all'interno dei veicoli.

Ed il bello è che la nostra galleria del vento nacque principalmente per migliorare le prestazioni a parità di potenza: più velocità, più aderenza al suolo, più stabilità direzionale.

È grazie anche alla galleria del vento che siamo giunti alla definizione della "forma aerodinamica ideale"; cioè il risultato di una ricerca tecnico-sperimentale promossa dal Centro Nazionale delle Ricerche, nell'ambito del Progetto Finalizzato Energetica, "per definire una forma di carrozzeria per autovettura europea di media cilindrata in grado di realizzare una sensibile riduzione".

Abbiamo cercato sempre di anticipare i tempi, introducendo nel progetto nuovi strumenti di ricerca e di supporto. Nel '71 abbiamo dato vita al Centro di Calcolo e Disegno automatico; con le attrezzature di cui disponiamo possiamo acquisire dati, elaborare programmi per gestire lavori di controllo numerico, e partendo da master models cioè da modelli dal vero, possiamo realizzare tutte le trasformazioni metriche necessarie: cioè, dato l'oggetto di studio ruotarlo nello spazio, renderlo in prospettiva, isometria, ridurlo alle varie scale, ribaltarlo e molte altre cose.

Negli ultimi anni è iniziato alla Pininfarina un processo di diversificazione non solo nel campo dell'industrial design, ma anche in quello produttivo: dagli iniziali progetti di veicoli industriali, di interni ed esterni di imbarcazioni da diporto ed interni di aeromobili, fino alle vetture per cabinovie.

Abbiamo così potuto raggiungere una dimensione industriale, estendere la nostra attività di ricerca, ed affiancare all'attività di progetto e di ingegnerizzazione, la produzione in serie dei nostri modelli.

Questa mostra dà una larga visione del design italiano, su come esso sia entrato nell'industria e da essa nella civiltà e nella cultura di un popolo senza niente togliere al classico lavoro degli oggetti destinati ad una clientela di élite che appartengono come riferimento storico-culturale, alle tradizioni del grande artigianato del paese, ma che proprio per la loro natura di élite rimangono estranei alla massa dei cittadini.

D'altra parte già la mostra stessa, inserendo nel suo piano schematico il "design dei riti di massa in 24 ore di una città italiana", esalta il ruolo dell'industria nel settore visto attraverso la trasformazione del Paese che dagli anni '50 ad oggi, è passato da una struttura eminentemente agricola a quella di uno dei paesi più industrializzati del mondo.

In fondo, l'industria può avere l'orgoglio di rappresentare il veicolo insostituibile attraverso il quale gli elementi di bellezza e di cultura che appartengono al design possono trasferirsi nella vita di tutti i giorni e di tutti. Questa mostra ne è la chiara testimonianza e permette a chi opera nel design italiano, attraverso un'ampia visione della sua storia, di ricavare gli stimoli per il futuro che sempre discendono da una riflessione su ciò che è stato fatto.

THE SIX ITALIES

GIAMPAOLO FABRIS

LE SEI ITALIE

GIAMPAOLO FABRIS

The instruments of interpretation and analysis usually employed with reference to a society whose characteristics of complexity are now being increasingly often brought out by social scientists are exceptionally simplified in the great majority of cases: to such a degree, indeed, as to become simplistic and risk giving a distorted picture of the social reality. This attempt to reduce complexity by recourse to ideology or universalistic categories or conceptual instruments (which may have had their appropriateness in different historical periods but are now definitely irrelevant) is clearly of little use in trying to understand what is happening around us. Take, for instance, the clichés about the *mass society* which used to be so widely debated in the social sciences (and not only by these disciplines: just look at some of the most thought-provoking of Pasolini's articles in the "Corriere della Sera") during the sixties and seventies, all of them derived in some way from a best-seller by David Riesman. Mass-society was founded on/produced mass individuals, mass workers, mass consumers and so forth: other-directed individuals, characterized by preferences, expectations, needs and behaviour patterns which were all markedly standardized and homogeneous.

It looked as if what was happening was a process of cultural homologation of world-wide dimensions, at least on the level of industrial societies, involving standardized life styles and value systems, all of which amounted to so-called mass culture. The extraordinary range and variety of cultures, ethnic differences, and local traditions seemed destined shortly to disappear, after having shrunk around a basic common denominator. The success of the Frankfurt school, within the social sciences, helped in the same years to reinforce the stereotype of a society which had become "massified" around a set of extremely homogeneous values, which the ruling classes, through the massa media and the main agencies of socialization (education, the culture industry etc.) succeeded in enforcing with great effectiveness and lucid awareness.

On the contrary, there is a continuous flow of evidence that, instead of a progressive homogenization of behaviour and attitudes, societies are becoming further differentiated internally. Italian society, for instance (as we shall see in a minute) has never before been so highly differentiated, fragmented, diversified as at present; never has there been such a marked co-existence of sub-cultures so diverse and remote from one another, such accentuated cultural pluralism.

2. The research permits a substantial qualitative breakthrough in the instruments of analysis of Italian society, passing from population *aggregates* (those just considered, substantially heterogeneous) to homogeneous *segments* (or types, groups), those which manifest internally a notable homogeneity in terms of behaviour and attitudes. The typology which we are proposing – drawn from the Monitor 3SC survey (1) of social change, which Demoskopea is conducting continuously within the ambit of an international project coordinated by the RISC (Research Institute on Social Change) – seems capable of identifying the underlying features of Italian society, even in its increasing complexity. The six types (or population segments, groups) which the calculator has constructed (2) – on the basis of the location of every individual component of the representative sample of the Italian population – on each of the thirty socio-cultural currents (3) taken into consideration – delineate six sub-cultures sufficiently differentiated from one another. *Six Italies* displaying different and absolutely specific values, attitudes, behaviour patterns and life-styles.

The six Italies form a continuum in the process of modernization of the country and enable us to perceive patterns of consumption and purchasing, choice and preferences for products and brands, which are peculiar to each segment.

3. We can try to describe, though in very summary form, each of these six Italies (each one of which has been described elsewhere, in a detailed monograph which gives analytical consideration to the most significant values, life-styles and behaviour patterns, as well as the socio-demographic features defining each segment), starting with the most backward types along the plane of modernization. The denominations given to the types are, obviously, to some extent arbitrary and perhaps not always very felicitous.

Gli strumenti di interpretazione e di analisi solitamente impiegati per riferirsi ad una società le cui caratteristiche di complessità sono ormai sempre più spesso richiamate dagli scienziati sociali risultano, nella grande maggioranza dei casi, eccezionalmente semplificati. Tanto da divenire semplicistici e rischiare di fornire una visione deformata della realtà sociale.

E questo tentativo di riduzione della complessità, mediante il ricorso all'ideologia o a categorie universalistiche o a strumentazioni concettuali appropriate forse a diversi periodi storici ma oggi decisamente inattuali, non aiuta certo a comprendere ciò che sta accadendo intorno a noi. Pensiamo, ad esempio, ai luoghi comuni della società di massa che avevano massicciamente alimentato il dibattito delle scienze sociali (ma non solo di queste: si pensi ad esempio ad alcuni fra i più suggestivi articoli di Pasolini scritti per il "Corriere della Sera") negli anni sessanta/settanta e che, in qualche modo, traevano tutti ispirazione da un fortunato best-seller di David Riesman. La società di massa si fondava/produceva individui massa, lavoratori di massa, consumatori di massa e via dicendo: individui eterodiretti, caratterizzati da preferenze, aspettative, bisogni, comportamenti fortemente standardizzati e omogenei. Sembrava cioè fosse in atto un processo di omologazione culturale di dimensioni planetarie, almeno a livello delle società industriali, intorno a stili di vita e sistemi di valori unificati, quelli appunto della cosiddetta cultura di massa. Lo straordinario variegarsi di culture, etnie, tradizioni locali sembrava destinato a tempi brevi a scomparire, rattrappito intorno ad un massimo di comun denominatore. La fortuna, nell'ambito delle scienze sociali, della scuola di Francoforte contribuisce in quegli anni a rafforzare lo stereotipo di una società massificata intorno a un set di valori estremamente omogeneo che le classi dominanti con i mezzi di comunicazione di massa e tramite le principali agenzie di socializzazione (scuola, famiglia, industria culturale, ecc.) riescono ad imporre con grande efficacia e lucidità.

Vi sono, all'opposto, continue evidenze che, in luogo di una progressiva omogeneizzazione dei comportamenti e degli atteggiamenti, le società vadano, al loro interno, ulteriormente differenziandosi. Mai ad esempio la società italiana — come vedremo fra breve — è apparsa tanto differenziata, frammentata, diversificata come nel momento attuale: mai come adesso si è verificata una tanto marcata coesistenza di sub-culture così diverse e distanti fra loro, un tanto accentuato pluralismo culturale.

La ricerca consente un sostanziale salto di qualità negli strumenti di analisi della società italiana passando dagli aggregati di popolazione (quelli appena considerati: cioè sostanzialmente eterogenei) a segmenti (o tipi, gruppi) omogenei che manifestano cioè al loro interno una notevole omogeneità in termini di comportamenti ed atteggiamenti. La tipologia che proponiamo — ricavata dalla ricerca Monitor 3SC (1) sul cambiamento sociale che Demoskopea conduce continuativamente nell'ambito di un progetto internazionale coordinato dal RISC (Research Institute on Social Change) — appare adeguata a cogliere, anche nella sua crescente complessità, i lineamenti di fondo della società italiana. I sei tipi (o segmenti, gruppi di popolazione) che l'elaboratore ha costruito (2) — sulla base del posizionamento di ogni individuo componente il campione rappresentativo della popolazione italiana — su ciascuna delle trenta correnti socio-culturali (3) prese in considerazione — delineano sei sub-culture sufficientemente differenziate l'una dall'altra. Sei Italie che manifestano valori, atteggiamenti, comportamenti, stili di vita diversi e assolutamente specifici.

Le sei Italie si dispongono lungo un continuum. nel processo di modernizzazione del Paese, e consentono di cogliere modelli di consumo, patterns di acquisto, scelte e preferenze per prodotti e marche peculiari a ciascun segmento.

Cerchiamo di descrivere, sia pure con il massimo della sintesi, ciascuna di queste sei Italie — ognuna delle quali è stata descritta in altra sede in una circostanziata monografia in cui sono analiticamente considerati valori, stili di vita, comportamenti più espressivi insieme alle caratteristiche socio-demografiche che definiscono ciascun segmento — iniziando con i tipi più arretrati lungo l'asse della modernizzazione. Le denominazioni attribuite ai tipi sono, ovviamente, in qualche modo arbitrarie e forse non sempre felici.

ARCHAICS. This is the first of the Italies we have to consider, the most numerous quantitatively (28% of the population) but also the first we encounter along the continuum of modernization: on the socio-cultural map it appears oriented towards the Old pole. That is to say, it is found in correspondence to that cluster of social trends that we have defined as the Umbelical Cord, to stress precisely this continuity and also closeness with the most traditional values present in Italian society, the leading ones, shared by a large majority of the population down to the immediate postwar years. If we postulate a three-stage evolution of Italian culture — diachronically: traditional (or peasant), industrial, post-industrial — the Archaics are unquestionably anchored to the first stage. The Archaics seem at times not to be aware of the wave of innovation which, over the last thirty years, has pervaded Italy, or else, though aware of it, try to repel it. This is a segment left behind by the process of modernization through cultural isolation, personality type, social and economic pressures: a group (surprisingly large, to tell the truth) living in the Italian past. The Archaics appear as characterized by strict social and religious traditionalism; by acceptance of a structure of inequality and social hierarchization; by a conception of life governed by transcendence and "the will of God"; by the restriction of social space to a sphere consisting of the family, relatives and the neighbourhood; by a sacrificial ethic and rejection of hedonism; by rigid differentiation of the sexes, and so forth. The life of Archaics tends to be centred around two poles: on the one hand religion, on the other the family understood in a sense very close to the traditional extended family. In the world of work they do not seek any special fulfilment; work is, in Weber's terms, nearly always a value in itself, whatever its content. As consumers, the Archaics appear still strongly linked to an ethic of saving: the Archaic is unquestionably a saver, not a consumer, apart from the satisfaction of his elementary needs.

Cultural consumption in this segment is almost non-existent and there is little exposure to the mass media, with the outstanding exception of Famiglia Cristiana (the most widely read weekly in Italy), of which the Archaics are the most assiduous readers. Appreciation of the TV newscasts by the RAI (Italian government TV network) is also high. The Archaic is little interested in politics: he tends to vote for the Christian Democrat party, but mainly out of inertia.

CONSERVATIVES. This second Italy occupied a marked position in the private-old area of the socio-cultural map: i.e. the socio-cultural currents which appear in that area of the map characterize this segment. The Conservatives (16.1% of the Italian population) seem to have cut their ties with that area of the Umbelical cord that still runs all the way back to the traditional past and to have taken rather more than the first step towards modernization, understood as acceptance of industrial society. However, the Conservatives — very close to the sort of petit-bourgeois Weltanschauung wholly centred on propriety, respectability, decorousness — have been left behind by the "movements" of the last decade and seem to have developed an authentic form of rejection and aversion towards stimuli of the post-industrial type which those movements transmitted. In all probability, they see them as a potential danger to the status and relative affluence they have recently acquired and on which they appear to vaunt themselves. The simultaneous rejection both of the lines of conduct suggested by the traditional type of ethic and also of a modern lay morality seems, however, to give rise to a certain vulnerability and loss of bearings in this second Italy.

At work, the Conservatives require above all to be well-paid so as to permit privileged access to the consumption they desire so intensely. Scope for "getting on" in terms of their career also sees the Conservatives at the top of the table in terms of expectations from their work. From the point of view of consumption, the Conservatives are eager and easily influenced consumers. For Conservatives, consumption is the yardstick to measure the degree of affluence achieved, and possessions are considered a significant attribute of social identity. It is the segment where mechanisms connected with emulation/display in consumption, consumption as a status symbol, and so on, are most active and important.

Cultural consumption is limited while exposure to the mass media is

GLI ARCAICI. E la prima Italia che consideriamo, la più numerosa quantitativamente (pari al 28% della popolazione) ma anche la prima che incontriamo lungo il continuum del processo di modernizzazione: sulla Mappa socio-culturale si colloca infatti tutta orientata verso il polo Vecchio. In corrispondenza cioè di quel cluster di correnti socio-culturali che abbiamo definito del Cordone Ombelicale per sottolineare appunto la continuità, e la vicinanza insieme, ai valori più tradizionali presenti nella società italiana, quelli egemoni e condivisi da una larga maggioranza della popolazione sino all'immediato dopoguerra. Postulando una evoluzione a tre stadi della cultura italiana — diacronicamente: tradizionale (o contadina), industriale, post-industriale — gli Arcaici sono senza dubbio ancorati al primo stadio. Gli Arcaici appaiono a volte non rendersi conto dell'ondata di novità che, nell'ultimo trentennio, ha pervaso il nostro Paese oppure, pur rendendosene conto, appaiono respingerla. Si tratta di un segmento lasciato indietro dal processo di modernizzazione per isolamento culturale, per tipo di personalità, per pressioni sociali ed economiche: di gruppo (sorprendentemente vasto a dire il vero) che vive nel nostro passato. Gli Arcaici appaiono caratterizzati da un severo tradizionalismo sociale e religioso; dall'accettazione di una struttura di diseguaglianza e gerarchia della società; da una concezione della vita ispirata alla trascendenza e "alla volontà di Dio"; alla restrizione dello spazio sociale ad un ambito composto dalla famiglia, dalla parentela e dal vicinato; da un'etica sacrificale e rifiuto dell'edonismo; da una rigida differenziazione dei sessi e via dicendo. La vita degli Arcaici tende a ruotare intorno a due poli: da un lato la religione, dall'altro la famiglia intesa in senso ancora molto vicino alla famiglia estesa tradizionale. Nel mondo del lavoro non cercano particolari soddisfazioni, il lavoro è, weberianamente, quasi sempre un valore di per sé, qualsiasi ne siano i contenuti. Come consumatori gli Arcaici appaiono ancora fortemente legati ad un'etica del risparmio: l'arcaico senza alcun dubbio è un risparmiatore, non un consumatore, al di là della soddisfazione dei bisogni elementari.

Quasi inesistenti i consumi culturali e scarsa l'esposizione ai mezzi di comunicazione di massa, con la vistosa eccezione del periodico Famiglia Cristiana (il settimanale più diffuso in Italia) di cui gli Arcaici sono i più assidui lettori. Elevato anche l'apprezzamento per il Telegiornale della RAI. L'arcaico è assai poco interessato alla politica; vota prevalentemente, ma più per inerzia che per altro, per la Democrazia Cristiana.

I CONSERVATORI. Questa seconda Italia si colloca con estrema evidenza nel quadrante privato-vecchio della Mappa socio-culturale: sono cioè le correnti socio-culturali che si situano in tale parte della Mappa a caratterizzare il segmento. I Conservatori (16,1% della popolazione italiana) sembrano aver tagliato i ponti con quell'area del Cordone Ombelicale che collega ancora con il passato tradizionale ed aver compiuto qualcosa di più del primo passo verso una modernizzazione intesa nel senso di accettazione del tipo di società industriale. Tuttavia i Conservatori — che ricalcano molto da vicino quel tipo di weltanshauung piccolo borghese tutta incentrata sul decoro, il perbenismo, la rispettabilità — sono rimasti tagliati fuori dai "movimenti" del decennio passato e sembrano aver sviluppato, nei confronti degli stimoli di tipo post-industriale da questi trasmessi, una vera e propria forma di rigetto e di avversione. Vedendoli, con ogni probabilità, come un potenziale pericolo per quello status di relativo benessere da poco conseguito e di cui appaiono così orgogliosi. Il rifiuto contemporaneo sia delle direttive di condotta dettate dall'etica di tipo tradizionale che della morale laica moderna sembrano comunque generare una certa vulnerabilità e disorientamento in questa seconda Italia.

Al lavoro i Conservatori richiedono soprattutto di essere ben pagato così da consentire un accesso privilegiato ai consumi a cui intensamente aspirano. Anche la possibilità di "fare carriera" vede i Conservatori al primissimo posto in termini di aspettative verso il lavoro. Da un punto di vista dei consumi i Conservatori sono dei consumatori avidi e fortemente influenzabili. Il consumo per i Conservatori è il metro per misurare il benessere raggiunto e ciò che si possiede è considerato un attributo rilevante per l'identità sociale: è il segmento per cui sono più attivi ed operanti meccanismi legati

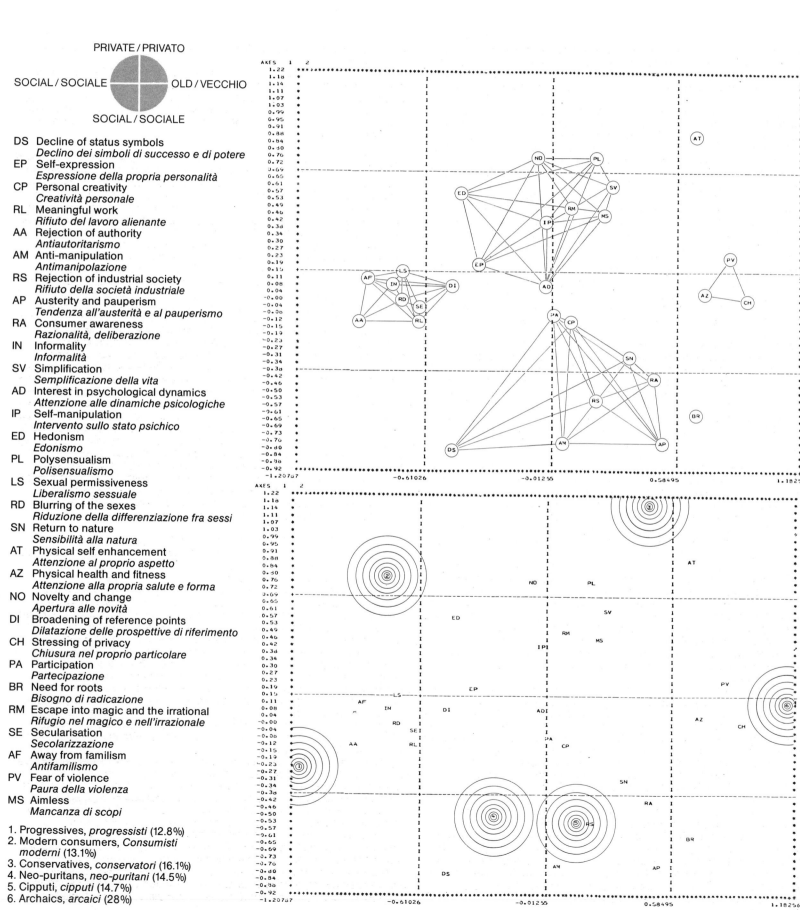

PRIVATE / PRIVATO

SOCIAL / SOCIALE — OLD / VECCHIO

SOCIAL / SOCIALE

DS Decline of status symbols
    Declino dei simboli di successo e di potere
EP Self-expression
    Espressione della propria personalità
CP Personal creativity
    Creatività personale
RL Meaningful work
    Rifiuto del lavoro alienante
AA Rejection of authority
    Antiautoritarismo
AM Anti-manipulation
    Antimanipolazione
RS Rejection of industrial society
    Rifiuto della società industriale
AP Austerity and pauperism
    Tendenza all'austerità e al pauperismo
RA Consumer awareness
    Razionalità, deliberazione
IN Informality
    Informalità
SV Simplification
    Semplificazione della vita
AD Interest in psychological dynamics
    Attenzione alle dinamiche psicologiche
IP Self-manipulation
    Intervento sullo stato psichico
ED Hedonism
    Edonismo
PL Polysensualism
    Polisensualismo
LS Sexual permissiveness
    Liberalismo sessuale
RD Blurring of the sexes
    Riduzione della differenziazione fra sessi
SN Return to nature
    Sensibilità alla natura
AT Physical self enhancement
    Attenzione al proprio aspetto
AZ Physical health and fitness
    Attenzione alla propria salute e forma
NO Novelty and change
    Apertura alle novità
DI Broadening of reference points
    Dilatazione delle prospettive di riferimento
CH Stressing of privacy
    Chiusura nel proprio particolare
PA Participation
    Partecipazione
BR Need for roots
    Bisogno di radicazione
RM Escape into magic and the irrational
    Rifugio nel magico e nell'irrazionale
SE Secularisation
    Secolarizzazione
AF Away from familism
    Antifamilismo
PV Fear of violence
    Paura della violenza
MS Aimless
    Mancanza di scopi

1. Progressives, *progressisti* (12.8%)
2. Modern consumers, *Consumisti moderni* (13.1%)
3. Conservatives, *conservatori* (16.1%)
4. Neo-puritans, *neo-puritani* (14.5%)
5. Cipputi, *cipputi* (14.7%)
6. Archaics, *arcaici* (28%)

high: private TV stations in particular (the Conservatives are assiduous viewers) and some magazines (Gente, Oggi, women's magazines etc.). Politically the Conservatives are found in the centre-right area and their preferences go to the Liberals, Christian Democrats and MSI.

CIPPUTI. This is the name coined by Altan for one of his cartoon characters: a sort of ideal type representing the traditional working class. We have borrowed the term to designate this Italy — comprising 14.7% of the population — shown by the calculator, because the group seems in many ways a sort of speaking portrait of the members of the "old-fashioned" working class (among other things, it is the population segment containing the greatest number of workers). This is the working class which traditionally represents the backbone of the historical left in Italy. The cultural map shows this third Italy in an ambiguous position in relation to the Old/New pole (about half-way along: i.e. there is a certain underlying schizophrenia between old and new which characterizes the segment) but very clearly placed on the vertical axis: a marked tendency towards the social pole. There is a definite rejection of the currents belonging to the Private area and at the same time a social grouping that feels somehow betrayed, disappointed in its expectations, dissatisfied with the present state of society but at the same time ready to struggle, if necessary, to change it: these are the group's characteristics. Strongly secularized — to the extreme limit of anticlericalism — the Cipputi seem to ask of their work — which, on the whole, they like and want to carry out competently — above all stability, security and a fair wage. As consumers, they are cautious and wary, very suspicious and critical of consumism even if in reality their choices are of the consumist type. The cultural horizon of this third Italy is generally restricted, but readership of daily papers is high, almost exclusively local ones. Fairly highly politicized, the Cipputi vote for the traditional left-wing political parties (especially the Italian Communist Party and Socialist Party, but also the Social-Democrats), while they are little attracted by the new left.

NEO-PURITANS. These make up 14.5% of the Italian population and represent the first (along the continuum we have been following) of the three types oriented towards the New pole of the horizontal old-new axis (the previous three Italies tended towards the Old pole). The Neo-Puritans display some similarities with the Cipputi in that, like them, they appear on the socio-cultural map as wholly tending towards the Social pole. But as we have said, they constitute a more modern type than the Cipputi. Adherence to many of the socio-cultural currents fo the strongly innovatory area of the New Frontier and simultaneous rejection of some of the most emblematic currents of the area of the Private justify the designation of this type as Neo-Puritans. Extremely religious, the group shares in many aspects of the process of modernization but is characterized by repudiation of the more escapist, frivolous and sensorial aspects of everyday experience. The Neo-Puritans appear also to be characterized by a strong social commitment aiming to effect a profound transformation in society in the direction of both egalitariansim and anti-authoritarianism.

Life-styles fo the Neo-Puritans appear to differ widely from those of the three Italies we have just considered. As a pastime, reading emerges strongly to take the place of television for the first time, while on Sundays meeting with friends takes the place of family gatherings. With regard to work, the Neo-Puritans ascribe particular importance to the possibility of sharing in decision-making: it is the segment of the population which gives greatest importance to interpersonal relationships and human contacts at work. As consumers, their attitude is on the whole cautious, reflective, to a great extent suspicious.

The Neo-Puritans dislike self-indulgence and its ostentation, they weigh up the "costs and benefits" of all expenditure with great care, they read labels attentively, distrust advertising which emphasises the image of a product rather than its intrinsic qualities: they are, in short, the most consumerist of consumers. Interest in politics is markedly above the national average. The area of their ideological sympathies ranges from the Christian Democrats, towards which the majority tends, to the centre of the lay and socialist area.

all'emulazione/ostentazione nei consumi, al consumo come status symbol e via dicendo.
Scarsi i consumi culturali mentre assai forte è l'esposizione ai mass media: in particolare le televisioni private (di cui i Conservatori sono degli assidui spettatori) e alcune pubblicazioni periodiche (Gente, Oggi, i settimanali femminili, ecc.). Politicamente i Conservatori si collocano in un'area di centro-destra e distribuiscono le loro preferenze tra Pli, Dc e Msi.

I CIPPUTI. *E questo il termine con cui Altan chiama uno dei protagonisti dei suoi cartoons: una sorta di idealtipico rappresentante della classe operaia tradizionale. Abbiamo preso a prestito il termine per designare questa terza Italia — che comprende il 14,7% della popolazione — che l'elaboratore ha evidenziato perché questo gruppo sembra, per molti versi, una sorta di ritratto parlante degli esponenti della classe operaia di "vecchio stampo" (tra l'altro è il segmento di popolazione a cui partecipa un maggior numero di operai). Quella classe operaia che costituisce, per tradizione, la spina dorsale della sinistra storica nel nostro Paese. Il posizionamento sulla Mappa socio-culturale colloca questa terza Italia in una posizione ambigua rispetto al polo vecchio/ nuovo (pressappoco a metà strada: ciò è alla base di una certa schizofrenia fra nuovo e vecchio che connota il segmento) e molto chiara invece rispetto all'asse verticale: tutta spostata appunto verso il polo sociale. Un marcato rifiuto delle correnti che appartengono all'area del Privato e insieme l'impressione di un raggruppamento sociale che si senta in qualche modo tradito, deluso nelle proprie aspettative, insoddisfatto dello stato attuale della società ma al tempo stesso disposto a battersi, se necessario, per cambiarlo caratterizzano il tipo. Fortemente secolarizzati — sino al limite dell'anticlericalismo — i Cipputi sembrano richiedere al lavoro — che tutto sommato amano e desiderano svolgere con competenza — soprattutto stabilità, sicurezza ed una equa retribuzione. Come consumatori sono consumatori cauti e sospettosi, fortemente diffidenti e critici verso il consumismo anche se spesso, di fatto, le scelte di consumo dei Cipputi sono di stretto stampo consumistico. L'orizzonte culturale di questa terza Italia è complessivamente limitato: buona invece la lettura dei quotidiani quasi esclusivamente locali. Assai politicizzati i Cipputi votano per i partiti della sinistra storica (soprattutto Pci e Psi, ma anche Psdi), mentre manifestano scarsissimi consensi per la nuova sinistra.*

I NEO PURITANI. *Costituiscono il 14,5% della popolazione italiana e rappresentano il primo, nel senso del continuum che stiamo seguendo, dei tre tipi orientati verso la polarità nuova dell'asse orizzontale vecchio-nuovo (le tre Italie precedenti gravitano invece prevalentemente verso il polo vecchio). I Neo Puritani manifestano alcune similarità con i Cipputi in quanto come questi risultano, sulla Mappa socio-culturale, tutti spostati verso la polarità sociale. Ma, come abbiamo detto, costituiscono un tipo più moderno dei Cipputi. L'adesione a molte delle correnti socio-culturali dell'area fortemente innovativa della Nuova Frontiera e il contemporaneo rifiuto di alcune delle più emblematiche correnti dell'area del Privato legittimano il nome di Neo Puritani con cui abbiamo denominato il tipo. Estremamente religiosi, condividono molti aspetti del processo di modernizzazione, ma si caratterizzano per un ripudio degli aspetti più evasivi, frivoli e sensoriali dell'esperienza quotidiana. I Neo Puritani appaiono altresì caratterizzati da un forte impegno sociale mirante ad ottenere una trasformazione profonda della società sia in senso egalitario che antiautoritario.
Gli stili di vita dei Neo Puritani appaiono assai diversi da quelli delle tre Italie che abbiamo appena considerato: come modo di passare il tempo in casa emerge prepotente la lettura che soppianta per la prima volta la televisione, mentre alla domenica il trovarsi con gli amici prende il posto della riunione familiare. Nei confronti del lavoro i Neo Puritani attribuiscono particolare importanza alla possibilità di partecipare alle decisioni, codeterminandole, relative al lavoro: è il segmento di popolazione che più attribuisce importanza alle relazioni interpersonali, ai rapporti umani nell'ambiente di lavoro. Per ciò che riguarda il consumo ci troviamo di fronte ad un atteggiamento nel complesso cauto, meditato, in gran parte sospettoso. I Neo Puritani odiano il lusso e la sua ostentazione, soppesano "costi e benefici" di*

MODERN CONSUMERS. This is our term for the fifth Italy identified by the computer, as before on the basis of a homogeneous grouping of replies to about a hundred questions contained in the survey questionnaire, which here emphasize a marked inclination towards consumption, on the one hand — levels of consumption are in fact high — but also an instrumental and modern attitude towards consumption. The Modern Consumers, making up 13.1% of the population, occupy the area defined by the New/Private polarity of the socio-cultural map. Unlike the Conservatives — the other segment with a high tendency to consunmption occupying the Private area but oriented towards the Old pole — who see possesssion of an item as, at bottom, more important than its enjoyment, and consumption as above all else a status symbol, the Modern Consumers see consumption in purposeful relation to other existential experiences. Consumption is high because this segment is extremely sensitive to anything that can make life richer and more intense and consumption is seen in this perspective: but is instrumental, subordinated to individual goals such as personal maturation, the quest for new experiences, experimenting with sensory gratification rather than seeking status or a social identity. Extremely sensitive to everything related to the Private Area, the Modern Consumers express a desire for change in relation to existing society, but this does not concern political aspects or the macro-social structure — except incidentally and to a secondary degree — so much as the individual's place in society and the norms affecting his behaviour. In other words, the "New society" desiderated may well be stratified and contain inequalities but it should permit everyone to act as he chooses, or rather in the way that gives him most pleasure. Strongly narcissistic, deeply involved in the themes of the body, personal growth, the limits of the expansion of awareness, the Modern Consumers display a high degree of cosmopolitanism, a strong inclination towards material pleasures, the enjoyment of life in the short term: an antipuritanism but all told of a modern kind. In their attitude to work there is a strong demand for fulfilment, for a job that is interesting in itself over and above the question of a good salary. Work has to give scope for personal self-determination, opportunity for initiative and creativity. Cultural horizons are broad: the cinema occupies a central position, but attendance at theatres, concerts, lectures/debates and art exhibitions is well above average. Level of interest in political development is not very high, but the area of political sympathies is definitely on the left.

PROGRESSIVES. The sixth Italy to emerge from analysis of the data covers 12.8% of the Italian population. This is a type centred on the New pole and in a position that is practically central and balanced in relation to the Private/Social axis. Generally speaking this is the type whose ideal of society comes nearest to what has been theorized as the post-industrial society. In this segment we find the aspiration to a society both egalitarian and non-authoririan; a marked tendency towards inner-directedness, with a definite rejection of fashions and induced consumption; complete secularization, involving rejection of the Church as both a source of conventional morality and centre of power in society (the Progressives constitute the least religious and most secularized group within the six Italies identified). They also display a desire to supersede national boundaries to adopt the models supplied by contemporary cosmopolitan culture as their guidelines, together with a tendency to reject discrimination of sexual roles in society, along with aspiration towards a new type of family in which the roles would be more equal and consensual. Overall, the pattern of needs for Progressives is not very different from the Modern Consumer: the most prominent element of difference is that while the latter see individual fulfilment as paramount, the Progressives consider there can be no fulfilment without a broader and more comprehensive design for the emancipation of society as a whole. Strongly politicized, the sympathies of the Progressives are wholly directed towards far left-wing radical movements. Leisure time of Progressives appears distributed between reading and music, which acquires notable importance: activity outside the home tends to centre on the friendship group and cultural activities, to which the Progressives devote themselves to a far greater degree than any other

ogni spesa con grande accuratezza, leggono attentamente le etichette, diffidano della pubblicità che insiste non sulle caratteristiche intrinseche dei beni, ma sulla loro immagine: sono insomma i più consumeristi fra i consumatori. L'interesse per la politica è nettamente più elevato della media nazionale. L'area delle affinità ideologiche si estende dalla Dc, su cui si concentra il maggior numero di scelte, all'area laica e socialista di centro.

I CONSUMISTI MODERNI. Abbiamo così denominato la quinta Italia che il calcolatore ha individuato, sempre sulla base di una omogeneità di risposte ad oltre un centinaio di domande contenute nel questionario della ricerca per sottolineare da un lato l'elevata propensione al consumo — e di fatto gli elevati livelli di consumo — ma anche un atteggiamento strumentale e moderno nei confronti dei consumi. I Consumisti Moderni, che costituiscono il 13,1% della popolazione, si collocano nel quadrante definito dalle polarità Nuovo/Privato della Mappa socio-culturale. A differenza dei Conservatori — l'altro segmento di elevata propensione al consumo che si colloca nell'area del Privato ma orientato verso il polo Vecchio — per cui il possesso del bene appare, al limite, più importante della sua fruizione e il consumo è considerato soprattutto come status symbol per i Consumisti Moderni il consumo è finalizzato ad altre esperienze esistenziali. Il consumo è elevato perché questo è un segmento estremamente sensibile a tutto ciò che può rendere più intensa e ricca la vita e il consumo è appunto visto in questa ottica: ma il suo ruolo è strumentale, subordinato ad obiettivi individuali, di maturazione personale, di ricerca di nuove esperienze, di sperimentazione di gratificazione sensoriale più che di attribuzione di status o di identità sociale. Estremamente sensibili a tutto ciò che concerne l'area del Privato, i Consumisti Moderni esprimono un'esigenza di mutamento rispetto alla società esistente che non riguarda tuttavia, se non in maniera secondaria e derivata, gli aspetti politici e di struttura macrosociale, quanto piuttosto la collocazione dell'individuo nella società e le norme che riguardano il suo comportamento. In altre parole la "nuova società" desiderata potrà essere stratificata e sperequata ma dovrà consentire ad ognuno di comportarsi come ritiene più opportuno o, meglio, come ritiene più gratificante. Fortemente narcisisti, estremamente coinvolti nelle problematiche che concernono il corpo, la crescita personale, al limite la dilatazione della coscienza i Consumisti Moderni manifestano, insieme ad un elevato grado di cosmopolitismo, un'ampia propensione ai piaceri materiali, al godersi la vita nell'immediato: un antipuritanesimo sia pure di stampo moderno insomma. Nei confronti del lavoro troviamo una forte richiesta di realizzazione nel lavoro, di lavoro interessante in sé oltre, e più, che ben pagato: il lavoro deve concedere ampi spazi di autodeterminazione personale, occasioni di imprenditività e creatività. Gli orizzonti culturali sono ampi: in posizione centrale appare il cinema, ma nettamente più frequente rispetto alla media nazionale risulta la frequentazione al teatro, ai concerti, alle conferenze/dibattiti, alle mostre d'arte. Il livello di interesse prestato alle ricerche politiche non è molto elevato: tuttavia l'area di affinità politica è decisamente spostata a sinistra.

I PROGRESSISTI. La sesta Italia, che emerge dall'analisi dei dati, include il 12,8% della popolazione italiana: si tratta di un tipo incentrato sul polo nuovo ed in posizione praticamente centrale ed equilibrata rispetto all'asse Privato/Sociale. In linea di massima è il tipo il cui ideale di società più si avvicina a quello che è stato teorizzato come società post-industriale. Troviamo in questo segmento l'aspirazione ad una società contemporaneamente egualitaria e non autoritaria; una spiccata tendenza all'autodirezione, con un netto rifiuto delle mode e dei consumi indotti; una completa secolarizzazione che comporta anche il rifiuto della Chiesa come fonte di morale convenzionale e centro di potere nella società (i Progressisti costituiscono il gruppo meno religioso e più secolarizzato delle sei Italie individuate). Si registra anche un'aspirazione al superamento delle frontiere nazionali per assumere come modelli di riferimento quelli forniti dalla cultura cosmopolita contemporanea, la tendenza a rifiutare la discriminazione dei ruoli sessuali nella società e l'aspirazione ad una famiglia di nuovo tipo i cui ruoli siano più paritari e consensuali. Complessivamente il

segment. Sport also has a certain importance, especially in its cheaper and/or non-competitive forms: athletics, jogging, cross-country skiing, are commoner than amongst other segments of the population. The degree of job-satisfaction, among those who work, is lower than in any other segment considered: the causes are probably to be sought in the incompatibility between the world of work as it is at present and expectations in relation to work in post-industrial culture. Those who share in this culture want a job, not necessarily a regular one, but one that will provide fulfilment for the individual's personality, intrinsically interesting, self-determined and socially significant: all qualities that, objectively, are found only to a minimal degree in public or private employment nowadays. The attitude towards consumption is one of deliberate and open indifference: it often displays an — unperceived — contradiction between markedly anti-consumist attitudes, often involving disapproval or ideological condemnation of high levels of consumer expenditure, frequently directed towards good-quality and highly priced goods.

sistema di bisogni dei Progressisti non è molto dissimile di quello dei Consumisti Moderni: l'elemento più rilevante di differenziazione è che, mentre per questi ultimi la via maestra è quella della realizzazione individuale, per i Progressisti non può esservi realizzazione al di fuori di un progetto più ampio e globale di emancipazione della società tutta. Fortemente politicizzati, le simpatie dei Progressisti sono tutte rivolte ai movimenti radicali e di estrema sinistra. Il tempo non lavorativo dei Progressisti appare distribuito tra la lettura e la musica che assume una notevole importanza: l'attività rivolta al di fuori della casa si incentra intorno al gruppo amicale ed alle attività culturali a cui i Progressisti si dedicano con incidenza di gran lunga superiore a qualsiasi altro segmento. Discretamente importante anche il ruolo dello sport, specie di quelli più poveri e/o non competitivi: atletica leggera, jogging, sci da fondo risultano praticati assai più che non dagli altri segmenti di popolazione. Il tasso di soddisfazione del lavoro, per coloro che lavorano, è più basso che non per tutti gli altri segmenti considerati: le cause sono probabilmente da ricercarsi nell'incompatibilità tra il mondo del lavoro quale esso è oggi e le aspettative relative al lavoro proprie della cultura post-industriale. Coloro che partecipano di questa cultura chiedono un lavoro, al limite anche precario, ma che permetta la realizzazione della personalità di ciascuno, intrinsecamente interessante, autodeterminato e socialmente rilevante: tutte caratteristiche queste che, oggettivamente, non si riscontrano che in misura minima nelle imprese pubbliche o private di oggi. L'atteggiamento nei confronti dei consumi è di studiata ed ostentata indifferenza: di fatto registra una, sia pure non percepita, contraddizione tra atteggiamenti marcatamente anticonsumistici, spesso di biasimo o di condanna ideologica nei confronti dei consumi a livelli di spesa elevati, sovente rivolti a beni di buona qualità e di prezzo elevato.

(1) The Monitor 3SC is based on a phase of ethnoanthropological analysis conducted continuously on Italian society by a team of researchers and on a survey repeated every 18 months on a representative sample of the Italian population made up of 2500 subjects.

(2) The criterion on which the computer proceeds to this grouping is that of statistical analysis of the variance finalized to aggregate the data so as minimize *intragroup* variance or maximize *intergroup* variance. Among all the possible solutions, that one is therefore chosen which makes the population groups as far as possible *internally homogeneous* and, at the same time, as far as possible *different from one another*.

(3) The social trend which can be briefly described as a vector of change/of measurement of the social structure is a synthetic indicator of the subjective type, made up of about ten questions inserted in the questionnaire. The social trends are individuated, described, and related to a theoretical model in the ethnoanthropological phase of the study: subsequently, during the survey, their measurement and quantification is completed. The social trends are then arranged by the computer by compression and distortion on a two-dimensional space (the socio-cultural map). The two dimensions are respectively defined as follows: horizontal dimension (absciss) by the New/Old polarity; the vertical dimension (ordinate) by the Private/Social polarity. The social trends have been grouped in their turn by a *cluster analysis* on the map in four areas: the New Frontier (coinciding with the New pole), the Private (Private pole), the Umbelical cord (Old pole), Social Sensitivity (Social pole).

(1) Il Monitor 3SC si basa su una fase di analisi etnoantropologica che viene svolta senza soluzioni di continuità sulla società italiana da un team di ricercatori e su un survey che viene ripetuto ogni 18 mesi su un campione rappresentativo della popolazione italiana composto da 2500 soggetti.

(2) Il criterio con cui il calcolatore procede a questo rappruppamento è quello dell'analisi statistica della varianza finalizzata ad aggregare i dati in modo da minimizzare la varianza intragruppo o massimizzare la varianza intergruppo. Tra tutte le possibili soluzioni viene pertanto scelta quella che rende i gruppi di popolazione il più possibile omogenei al loro interno e, contemporaneamente, il più possibile diversi fra loro.

(3) La corrente socio-culturale (social trend) che può essere sinteticamente descritta come un vettore di cambiamento/di misurazione della struttura sociale è un indicatore sintetico di tipo soggettivo, formato da una decina circa di domande inserite nel questionario. Le correnti socio-culturali sono individuate, descritte e ricollegate ad un modello teorico nella fase etnoantropologica della ricerca: successivamente mediante il survey si procede ad una loro misurazione e quantificazione. Le correnti socioculturali vengono poi, per compressione e torsione, disposte dall'elaboratore su uno spazio a due dimensioni (la Mappa socio-culturale). Le due dimensioni sono rispettivamente definite da: quella orizzontale (ascissa) dalle polarità Nuovo/Vecchio; quella verticale (ordinata) dalle polarità Privato/Sociale. Le correnti socio-cultrali sono state a loro volta raggruppate da una cluster analysis sulla Mappa in quattro aree: la Nuova Frontiera (in coincidenza con il polo Nuovo), il Privato (polo Privato), il Cordone Ombelicale (polo Vecchio), la Sensibilità Sociale (polo Sociale).

WAKING UP
FACING THE OBJECTS OF THE DAY

THE ALARM CLOCK.
COFFEE AS RITUAL.
CONFRONTING THE MIRROR.
BAREFOOT.
GETTING DRESSED, OR THE PHENOMENOLOGY OF DISGUISE.
WHEN ARE YOU COMING BACK?
THE TRAUMA OF LEAVING THE HOUSE.

RISVEGLIO
GLI OGGETTI QUOTIDIANI

LA SVEGLIA.
RITUALE DEL CAFFÈ.
L'IMMAGINE ALLO SPECCHIO.
IL PIEDE NUDO.
TRAVESTIMENTO EPOCALE.
NOTIZIE DAL MONDO.
QUANDO TORNI? IL TRAUMA DELL'USCITA.

Italo Calvino
Invisible Cities

The city of Leonia refashions itself every day: every morning the people wake between fresh sheets, wash with just-unwrapped cakes of soap, wear brand-new clothing, take from the latest model refrigerator still unopened tins, listening to the last-minute jingles from the most up-to-date radio.
On the sidewalks, encased in spotless plastic bags, the remains of yesterday's Leonia await the garbage truck. Not only squeezed tunes of toothpaste, blown-out light bulbs, newspapers, containers, wrappings, but also boilers, encyclopedias, pianos, porcelain dinner services. It is not so much by the things that each day are manufactured, sold, bought that you can measure Leonia's opulence, but rather by the things that each day are thrown out to make room for the new. So you begin to wonder if Leonia's true passion is really, as they say, the enjoyment of new and different things, and not, instead the joy of expelling, discarding, cleansing itself of a recurrent impurity. The fact is that street cleaners are welcomed like angels, and their task of removing the residue of yesterday's existence is surrounded by a respectful silence, like a ritual that

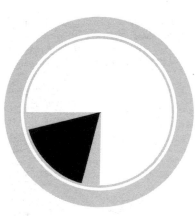

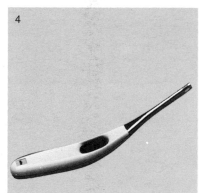

Only 12% have a real breakfast.
56% (66% in the South and the Islands) drink coffee but eat nothing else.
Italians drink of 3-4 coffees a day.
Coffee is prepared in various ways:
– in the South, using the "Napoletana" filter pot;
– in the more modern urban areas, with the Moka Express;
– instant coffee has a negligible share of the market.

Solo il 12% fa una vera colazione.
Il 56% (il 66% al Sud e nelle Isole) beve solo caffè.
In media l'Italiano beve da 3 a 4 caffè al giorno.
Il caffè viene preparato con modalità diverse da regione a regione:
– con la napoletana al Sud;
– con la Moka nei centri più moderni;
– il caffè istantaneo, solubile in acqua calda, ha una quota di mercato ridotta.

How Italians take their coffee:

strong	14%	*ristretto*	*14%*
normal	79%	*normale*	*79%*
weak	7%	*lungo*	*7%*
with sugar	82%	*con zucchero*	*82%*
without sugar	13	*senza zucchero*	*13%*
with sweeteners	5%	*con dolcificante*	*5%*
with some milk	23%	*con un po' di latte*	*23%*
with grappa/whisky, etc.	4%	*corretto con grappa/whisky, ecc.*	*4%*
black	73%	*senza nessuna aggiunta*	*73%*
primarily at home	65%	*più spesso in casa*	*65%*
primarily out	33%	*più spesso fuori casa*	*33%*
– at a coffee-bar	20%	*– al bar*	*20%*
– at the home of friends	5%	*– in casa di amici*	*5%*
– at work	2%	*– sul posto di lavoro*	*2%*
alone	20%	*da solo*	*20%*
with family	57%	*in compagnia di familiari, parenti*	*57%*
with guests	2%	*in compagnia di ospiti*	*2%*
with friends	23%	*in compagnia di amici*	*23%*
with colleagues	8%	*in compagnia di colleghi di lavoro*	*8%*

1. Shutter, *Persiana* / mod. Genovese.
2. Alarm clock, *Sveglia* / mod. Static / des. R. Sapper / prod. Lorenz / 1960.
3. Coffee Grinder, *Macinatore caffè* / mod. JO-JO / des. Ufficio Tecnico / prod. Bialetti.
4. Gas Cricket, *Accendigas* / des. A. Vanonck / prod. Flash / 1974.

L'APE REGINA

1963

MARCO FERRERI

Ugo Tognazzi
Marina Vlady

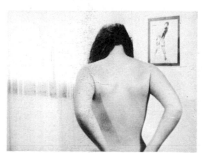

inspires devotion, perhaps only because once things have been cast off nobody wants to have to think about them further.

Nobody wonders where, each day, they carry their load of refuse, outside the city, surely; but each year the city expands, and the street cleaners have to fall farther back. The bulk of the outflow increases and the piles rise higher, become stratified, extend over a wider perimeter. besides, the more Leonia's talent for making new materials excels, the more the rubbish improves in quality, resists time, the elements, fermentations, combustions. A fortress of indestructible leftovers surrounds Leonia, dominating it on every side, like a chain of mountains. This is the result: the more Leonia expels goods, the more it accumulates them; the scales of its past are soldered into a cuirass that cannot be removed. As the city is renewed each day, it preserves all of itself in its only definitive form: yesterday's sweepings piled up on the sweepings of the day before yesterday and of all its days and years and decades.

Leonia's rubbish little by little would invade the world, if, from beyond the final crest of its boundless rubbish heap, the street cleaners of other cities were not pressing, also pushing mountains of refuse in front of themselves. Perhaps the whole world, beyond Leonia's boundaries, is covered by craters of rubbish, each surrounding a metropolis in constant eruption. The boundaries between the alien, hostile cities are infected ramparts where the detritus of both support each other, overlap, mingle.

The greater its height grows, the more the danger of a landslide looms: a tin can, an old tyre, an unravelled wineflask, if it rolls towards Leonia, is enough to bring with it an avalanche of unmated shoes, calendars of bygone years, withered flowers, submerging the city in its own past, which it had tried in vain to reject, mingling with the past of the neighbouring cities, finally clean. A cataclysm will flatten the sordid mountain range, cancelling every trace of the metropolis always dressed in new clothes. In the nearby cities they are all ready, waiting with bulldozers to flatten the terrain, to push into the new territory, expand, and drive the new street cleaners still farther out.

Italo Calvino, "Le Città Invisibili", Einaudi, Torino 1977. "Invisible Cities", Harcourt, Brace & Jovanovich, New York 1974. Translated by William Weaver.

5. Toilet Bowl, *Vaso* / mod. Metha / des. Meregalli-Campi / prod. Pozzi-Ginori / 1982.
6. Bidet, *Bidet* / mod. Metha / des. Meregalli-Campi / prod. Pozzi-Ginori / 1982.
7. Bathroom-accessories, *Componenti da bagno* / mod. Snodo / des. F. Lenci-G. Talocci / prod. Guzzini / 1981.
8. Faucets, *Rubinetti* / mod. Le Nuvole / des. F. Bianchetti / prod. Zen / 1982.
9. Faucet, *Rubinetto* / mod. Calibro / des. D. Mercatali-P. Pedrizzetti / prod. Fantini / 1981.
10. Portable Radio, *Radio portatile* / mod. TS 502 / des. M. Zanuso-R. Sapper / prod. Brionvega / 1965.

DOVÈ LA LIBERTÀ

1954

ROBERTO ROSSELLINI

Totò

Giorgio Bassani
The Heron

Not immediately, but climbing with some effort up from the bottomless pit of unconsciousness, Edgardo Limentani stretched his right arm toward the bedside table. In the darkness the little traveling alarm clock that Nives, his wife, had given him in Basel three years before, on his forty-second birthday, continued emitting its shrill, insistent, but discreet sound. He had to silence it. He drew back his arm, opened his eyes and turned, his side supported by his elbow, as he stretched out the left arm; and at the very moment when his

fingertips reached the Jaeger's soft, already slightly worn doe-skin to press the alarm button, he read the time, marked by the position of the phosphorescent spheres on the dial. It was four o'clock: the time that, the night before, he had decided to be wakened. If he wanted to reach Volano an hour before daylight, he reminded himself, he hadn't a minute to waste. With one thing and another, getting up, going to the bathroom, washing, shaving, dressing, gulping down some coffee, and so on, he wouldn't be able to get into his car before five.
Finally, when he had turned on the light, sat up in bed, and looked slowly

around, he was seized with a sudden sense of dejection and was tempted to let the whole thing go, to stay home. Perhaps it was because of the chill in the room or the too-weak light that fell from the central chandelier; in any case, this bedroom where he had slept since childhood, except for a brief period just after his marriage and then, naturally, the year and a half in Switzerland, had never seemed so alien to him, so squalid. The dark wardrobe, tall, broad, potbellied (his mother had always called it the *armoire bombée*), which occupied a good part of the left wall; the heavy chest of drawers against the wall opposite, surmounted

by a little oval mirror, so opaque that it was useless, even for tying his tie; the little mahogany-and-glass gun case, there at the rear, tiny, next to the beige, vertical outline of the valance; the chairs; the clothes-stand on casters, where, yesterday afternoon, his mother had laid out in full view his woolen underwear, complete with long pants (the rest of his hunting clothes, boots included, she had put in the next room, the bath); the various picture frames – his diploma, the photographs, chiefly of mountain scenes – hanging more or less everywhere on the walls: each piece of furniture, each object which his eye fell on now jarred him,

---

Due of the re-scaling of houses, the rooms which had formerly been closed off for the visitor, were given a new look which bespoke much greater care and harmony of design in relation to the rest of the house.
In the case of the bathroom very little had been done to vary the forms of the sanitary fixtures, also because of the considerable technological difficulties involved in keeping within their extremely rigid limits. In the making of a sanitary fixture, indeed, one has to take into account the fact that the piece was designed as a function of the contraction it undergoes during the baking phase in the furnace, which is of the order of 11%. Also to be considered is the fact that sanitary fixtures in the housing sector in Italy constitute one of the most highly industrialized products in respect of the total number of pieces. It follows that it has a huge market which is for the most part traditional in taste.
The contribution of design has been fundamental in the achievement of all these results and of course the new forms and new colors have as a consequence led to a new concept of furniture and accessories, which have since been subjected to a radical transformation.
The old production of plate glass and chromium-plated brass formerly available to consumers was replaced by new materials.
Color came to play a leading role in the bathroom, with matching colors for tile, sanitary fixtures, faucets, furniture and accessories, and even towels. Bathtubs are no longer cast iron, they are shaped anatomically, and methacrylate plastic makes a great variety of shades of color available.
The bathroom, then, has been transformed and has become a status symbol.

Ambrogio Rossari

A causa del ridimensionamento delle abitazioni, anche i locali, che un tempo restavano chiusi all'occhio del visitatore, assumono una fisionomia diversa, più curata e armonica rispetto al resto dell'abitazione.
Nel caso del bagno si era fatto finora ben poco per variare le forme dei sanitari anche a causa delle difficoltà tecnologiche connesse che pongono dei limiti estrememente rigidi. Nell'esecuzione di un sanitario infatti bisogna sempre tener conto che il pezzo va progettato in funzione dei ritiri che dovrà subire in fase di cottura nel forno, il che sono sull'ordine del 11%, inoltre va considerato il fatto che il sanitario nel settore della casa in Italia è forse uno dei prodotti più industriali come numero di pezzi.
Raggiunge quindi un mercato molto vasto e perciò perlopiù tradizionalista e di questo bisogna tenerne conto durante tutto il processo progettuale al fine di non creare un oggetto bello e magari validissimo sotto l'aspetto estetico ma non venduto.
L'intervento del design è stato fondamentale per il raggiungimento di tutti questi nuovi risultati e naturalmente nuove forme e nuovi colori portano di conseguenza ad un concetto nuovo del mobile e dell'accessorio che subiscono una radicale trasformazione.
L'antica produzione di cristallo e ottone cromato, finora a disposizione dei consumatori, viene soppiantata da nuovi materiali.
Il colore diventa il protagonista del bagno con armonici accostamenti di piastrelle, sanitari, rubinetti, mobili e accessori fino alla biancheria coordinata. Le vasche non più di ghisa, hanno forme anatomiche ed il metacrilato consente svariate sfumature di colore.
Il bagno si è dunque trasformato, è diventato uno status symbol allo stesso modo della cucina superaccessoriata e del salotto con il mobile firmato.

Ambrogio Rossari

1

4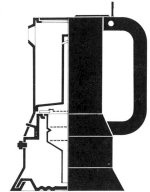

2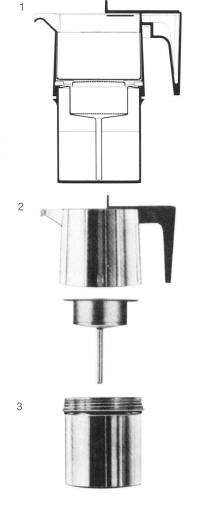

5

3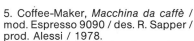

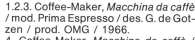

5. Coffee-Maker, *Macchina da caffè* / mod. Espresso 9090 / des. R. Sapper / prod. Alessi / 1978.
6. Multipurpose-Rack, *Portarobe* / mod. Portarobe / des. P. Polato / prod. Robots s.p.a. / 1978.
7.10. Clothes Rack, *Attaccapanni* / mod. Schiangai / des. J. De Pas-D. D'Urbino-P. Lomazzi / prod. Zanotta s.p.a. / 1977.
8. Vacuum Cleaner, *Aspirapolvere* / mod. Acqua Dry / des. Trabucco e Vecchi / prod. Alfatec / 1981.
9. Alarm clock, *Sveglia* / mod. Lucania / prod. Veglia-Borletti / 1938.

1.2.3. Coffee-Maker, *Macchina da caffè* / mod. Prima Espresso / des. G. de Gotzen / prod. OMG / 1966.
4. Coffee-Maker, *Macchina da caffè* / mod. Moka Express / des. A. e R. Bialetti / prod. Bialetti / 1945.

LA LUNA

1979

BERNARDO BERTOLUCCI

Jill Clayburgh
Mathew Barry

irked him. It was as if he were seeing it for the first time; or, to be more precise, as if only now he were able to see some base aspect of it, disagreeable, absurd.

He yawned. He ran his hand over his cheeks and chin, rough with beard, then pushed aside the blankets, and thrust his legs out of the bed. From a chair he took the camel-colored wool robe, put it on over his pajamas, stuck his feet into his slippers, and a few moments later he was at the window, looking through the panes and the half-closed shutters, down into the courtyard.

There was almost nothing to be seen.

The court was so deep in shadow that the well in the center could barely be distinguished. Still from the kitchen window of the Manzoli's, the concierge and his wife, came a strip of intense white light: it was so bright that it reached the top of the high wall opposite, toward Via Montebello, and touched the upper branches of the big climbing rosebush which, in summer, covered the wall almost completely. Gusts of sirocco stirred the branches, disheveled them. Dry and light, they moved in jerks, as if an electric shock ran through them at intervals. It wasn't raining: as long as this wind kept up, it wouldn't rain.

He turned to look toward the entrance. The door of the ground-floor apartment, occupied by the Manzoli family, had opened. From it came more light (much less bright than what filtered through the kitchen window): against it a bent, bundled-up form was immediately outlined.

— Romeo is already up, — he observed. Attentive and immobile, he then followed all the concierge's movements. He saw the man come forward, approach the wrought-iron gate that shut off the courtyard from the portico, open one wing of it a crack, step outside, examine, above his head, the dark sky, and finally, evidently seeing

his master, Romeo took off his cap and looked toward him.

He opened the double panes, flung the shutters wide (he was struck by a gust of damp, sticky, almost warm wind), then leaned out to fasten them to the wall.

He straightened up again.

"Good morning," he said, turning to the concierge. "Ask Imelde, if she's up, to make me some coffee, please."

Giorgio Bassani, "L'Airone", Mondadori, Milano 1976. "The Heron", Harcourt, Brace & Jovanovich, New York 1974. Translated by William Weaver.

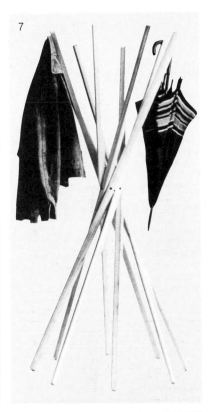

COFFEE MACHINES / *CAFFETTIERE*

1. mod. Moka Express / des. A. & R. Bialetti / prod. Bialetti / 1945.
2. mod. 9090 / des. R. Sapper / prod. Alessi / 1981.
3. mod. Carmencita Lavazza / des. M. Zanuso / prod. Balzano 1979.
4. mod. La Stella / prod. Metallurgica Lux / 1974.
5. mod. La signora / prod. D. Meazza & Masciadri / 1960.
6. mod. Stakbloc / prod. Girmi / 1970.
7. mod. Inox / prod. Bialetti / 1981.
8. mod. Nova Express / prod. Irmel / 1955.
9. mod. Nova Express / prod. Irmel / 1953.
10. mod. Napoletana / prod. Ruffoni / 1980.
11. mod. Napoletana / prod. Metallurgica Lux / 1981.
12. mod. Napoletana Delizia / prod. Vemi / 1979.
13. mod. Napoletana / prod. Irmel / 1975.
14. mod. Thermos Express / prod. Meazza e Masciadri / 1969.
15. mod. Thermos / prod. Meazza e Masciadri / 1969.
16. mod. Europiccola / prod. Pavoni / 1964.
17. mod. Cimbalina / des. R. Bonetto / prod. Cimbali / 1979.
18. mod. Baby / prod. Gaggia / 1979.

Today I find myself developing greater interest in the part of the operation of design that someone has called "designing the fantastic". It does not mean modifying a philosophy of design, especially in the case of someone like myself, for I have never held any ambiguous attitudes in practicing my profession as a designer. I have always tried to carry on the designing of industrial products in such a way as to achieve effective progress and qualitative modifications, without wrapping the work in a cloud of high-sounding theoretical statements. It is perhaps this very attitude which has now led me to seek renewed sensibility in the act of designing. Even in the case of a small object like the Cimbali electric coffee-maker for the home, which I designed after acquiring a certain experience in the sector of large coffee-makers for bars, the major aspect leading to my decision to produce an object for a special purpose was my sudden realization that there was a mass psychological phenomenon at work which would have us replace "home-made coffee" with the new ritual of "a good coffee at the bar". To reply to this tendency there had to be a change in the concept of the espresso coffee-maker as a small household appliance.

There are many other ways of making coffee, from the rudimental but perfect techniques of the people, such as I saw applied in Brazil, to the whole ancient Neapolitan tradition. Without disregarding all this, I consider the new object I designed a good compromise between the expression of a new ritual and the problems of an industrial product, for here we have a coffee-maker: that works properly, that is correctly defined ergonomically, and that has a simplified structural composition (in this case, only a few injection-forged pieces).

Rodolfo Bonetto

Mi trovo oggi a sviluppare un maggiore interesse per quella parte dell'operazione di design che qualcuno ha definito "progettare il fantastico": ciò non significa modificare una filosofia progettuale, soprattutto per chi come me non ha mai tenuto un atteggiamento ambiguo nell'esercitare il mestiere del designer: ho inteso infatti condurre sempre il disegno di prodotti industriali in modo di raggiungere effettivi progressi e modificazioni qualitative, senza sovrapporre a questo lavoro velleitarie dichiarazioni teoriche, ed è forse proprio questo atteggiamento che mi porta oggi alla ricerca di una rinnovata sensibilità nell'atto

progettuale. Anche in un piccolo oggetto come la caffettiera elettrica Cimbali per uso domestico, che ho progettato dopo una certa esperienza nel settore delle macchine da bar, l'aspetto più importante e che ha fatto nascere la decisione di produrre un oggetto "ad hoc" è l'accertamento di un fenomeno psicologico di massa, il sostituirsi cioè del nuovo rituale del "buon caffè del bar", al posto di quello del "caffè fatto in casa". Per rispondere a questo fenomeno si è operata una trasposizione dei concetti della macchina per caffè espresso in un piccolo elettrodomestico. Certamente esistono molti altri modi di fare il

caffè, dalle rudimentali e perfette tecniche popolari che ho visto usare in Brasile, a tutta l'antica tradizione napoletana: senza ignorare tutto questo, considero il nuovo oggetto da me disegnato una buona mediazione tra l'espressione di un nuovo rituale e i problemi di un prodotto industriale: il buon funzionamento, una corretta definizione ergonomica, una composizione strutturale semplificata (in questo caso, pochi pezzi stampati ad iniezione).

Rodolfo Bonetto

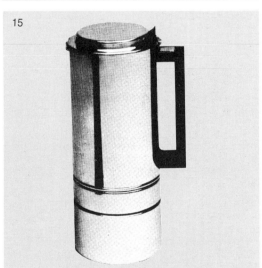

ON THE STREET
THE CITY COMES ALIVE

PER STRADA
LA CITTÀ RIVIVE

THE LOGIC OF LOCOMOTION.
PEDESTRIANS.
RED LIGHTS.
FOOTPRINTS IN THE WET CEMENT.
ANTHROPOLOGY OF COFFEE BARS.
THE PAIN OF PUNCTUALITY.
UP THE STEPS AND DOWN AGAIN.

LOGICA DELLA LOCOMOZIONE.
IL PASSANTE.
L'INTERDETTO SEGNALETICO.
L'ORMA NEL CEMENTO.
L'ANTROPOLOGIA DEI BAR.
IL DRAMMA DELLA PUNTUALITÀ.
SU E GIÙ PER GLI SCALINI.

Alberto Savinio
Automobile

In the chapter on mechanics from the treatise, *The Miracles of Art, Nature and Magic*, Roger Bacon states that soon there will be carriages without horses and machines to carry man around in the air. Clearly, the Franciscan scholar from Oxford was referring to the machine that the thoroughly modern and the brachyphonists call the car, and that flying apparatus that is spelled aeroplane and pronounced airplane. Incidentally, Gabriele D'Annunzio, who loved giving noble names to things he felt had ignoble names, proposed to call the aeroplane 'velivole', but had no success, the usual fate of those who through logic, aesthetics, or other things attempt to deviate the natural course of language. On that occasion, obscure philologists discovered that 'velivole' was not D'Annunzio own contrivance, but that of Chateaubriand, and recalled "le pêcheur napolitain dans sa barque vélivole", quoted in Volume VI, p. 164 of *Memoires d'outre-tombe*. The words of Roger Bacon can be elevated to the level of prophesy if you think that this lover of the Great Work which, as is well-known, was the search for the philosopher's stone, was born in 1214, died in 1294, and so

79% of Italian families own one car.
25% own more than one car.
Automobiles in circulation:

In 1946	149,650
In 1980	17,073,000

11% of the population own a motorcycle or motorbike.
Motorcycles and motorbikes in circulation:

In 1970	560,000
In 1980	6,200,000

(of which: 1,200,000 with license plates and 5,000,000 without plates)

Per capita transportation cost is 13% of total expenditures.

121,047 Coffee bars open directly on to the street.
There are a total of 119,487 barber shops and beauty parlors.
There is a coffee bar for every 472 inhabitants.

Distribution of Coffee bars in Italy:

North: a coffee bar every 460 inhabitants.
Central: a coffee bar every 391 inhabitants.
South and Islands: a coffee bar every 559 inhabitants.

Il 79% delle famiglie italiane possiede un'automobile.
Il 25% possiede più di un'auto.
Automobili in circolazione:

nel 1946	*149.650*
nel 1980	*17.073.000*

L'11% della popolazione possiede un ciclomotore.
Ciclomotori in circolazione:

nel 1970	*560.000*
nel 1980	*6.200.000*

di cui 1.200.000 con targa e 5.000.000 senza targa

Circa il 13% della spesa pro capite viene assorbita dai trasporti.

121.047 Bar si affacciano sulle strade italiane.
Sono aperti al pubblico 119.487 negozi di barbiere e parrucchiere per signora.
Esiste un bar ogni 472 abitanti.

Distribuzione dei bar in Italia:

Nord: un bar/460 abitanti.
Centro: un bar/391 abitanti.
Sud e Isole: un bar/559 abitanti.

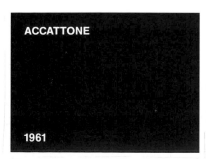

ACCATTONE

1961

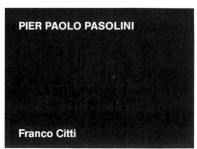

PIER PAOLO PASOLINI

Franco Citti

lived seven centuries before the discovery of the automobile and the aeroplane. In any case, it is not clear if Bacon garnered these ardent forecasts from his own divinatory faculties, or if they were suggested to him by that android he constructed in imitation of Albert Magne and which he taught to speak, in return for which the android revealed to him the secrets of the future. Be that as it may, Bacon was accused of sorcery and thrown into jail where he rested until he was freed by Clement IV, a great friend of the cabalists and a bit of a cabalist himself. In addition to the automobile and the aeroplane, Bacon also predicted the diving bell for submarine exploration and the suspension bridge. These visions are quoted in proof of his extraordinary genius, but the connection between genius and mechanistic thought remains to be established. For me, an infallible sign of non-intelligence (I'm speaking here in absolute terms), is this 'mechanistic' orientation of mind. I had a certain esteem for Roger Bacon as long as I believed him to be dedicated only to alchemy and magic, and lost it the moment I knew he was also concerned with the mechanical progress of the world. It always strikes me as peculiar, peculiar and disconcerting, that so much importance is given to the mechanical progress of the world and none to its moral progress. Is mechanization really so necessary to the health, the well-being, the happiness of man? We were happy, happy and proud that the automobile and aeroplane had penetrated our lives so profoundly that we believed we couldn't do without them. But the restrictions due to the state of war were enough to show us that we also can live without 'the car' and 'the plane'. There is a great difference between the way we travel and the way Plato traveled, but I don't find so much difference between the way a man of today thinks and the way Plato thought. I'd say, instead... the physiocrats argued that mental progress is a sacriligious delusion, a challenge to God. To me, that argument reeks of the most sordid moral cowardice.

Alberto Savinio, "Nuova Enciclopedia", Adelphi, Milano 1978. Translated by Robert Kleyn

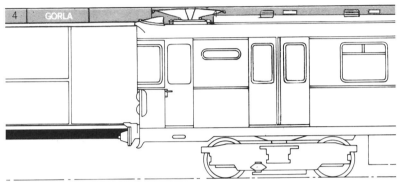

1. Motor scooter, *Ciclomotore* / mod. Vespa / des. C. D'Ascanio / prod. Piaggio / 1946-1982.
2. Car, *Auto* / mod. Panda / des. G. Giugiaro / prod. Fiat / 1980.
3. Pick-up, *Motofurgone* / mod. Ape P50 / des. Ufficio Tecnico / prod. Piaggio / 1969.
4. Subway signs, *Segnaletica metropolitana* / mod. Per Milano / des. B. Noorda / prod. Metropolitana Milanese / 1964.
5. Plastic can, *Taniche* / prod. Plastivalle / 1979.
6. Police call box, *Colonnina chiamata Polizia*.

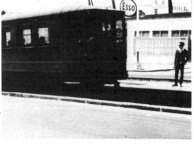

Luciano Mastronardi
A Southerner in Vigevano

I am walking to the office. It is Saturday. There is an open-air market in Market Square. The one in Vigevano is a silent market; no voices are raised. The vendors are sitting behind their stalls, their braziers alight, or they are standing warming themselves at fires glowing between one stand and another.

The post office hasn't opened yet, but old people are sitting outside the door with their pension books in their hands. There is a bar across from the post office building where I have my first cup of coffee. It is full of office workers at this time of day, breakfasting on *cappuccino* and sweet rolls, their noses buried in the newspapers. Behind the counter the owner is busy at the *espresso* machine, while a boy maybe twelve years old, scared and stiff like somebody on his first job, washes saucers and cups and spoons and waits on table.

There is a protective warmth here, even though the atmosphere is lugubrious. Every now and then, there are furtive glances at the clock followed by muffled sighs. Eight-twenty; a mute irritation is in the air.

"I said two lumps of sugar!"
"A spot of milk in the coffee!"
"The glass of water I asked for?"
"Are you sure this cup was properly washed?"

These remarks are addressed to the boy. He looks flustered and is doing all he can to bring second lumps of sugar, serve glasses of water, and bring coffee cups back to the owner for refills. Someone sends him to the tobacconist for a pack of *Nazionali*; somebody else hands him a jacket to remove a spot, a drop of coffee, kid, be careful with the spot remover, don't ruin the fabric.

The clerks all wear new shirts with splendid collars, ready-made suits ironed as neat as can be, socks just over the ankles revealing white skin when they cross their legs.

Several of them are having their first cigarette of the day.

There are office girls too, talking to the owner's wife, who is sitting at the cash register. They talk about their problems, always the same ones. One has a cleaning woman who is a monster, "I'm not exaggerating, madam, she's a monster." Every morning she reports the cleaning woman's latest monstruosity.

"Yesterday she tried to poison me," she says dramatically. "I realized just in time, it was the hand of God!"

Another clerk is telling with disgust

1.2.3. Street car, *Tram* / mod. Jumbo Tram / des. K. Koenig, R. Segoni / prod. GAI (Fiat/OM) / 1975.
4. Espresso Machine, *Macchina caffè* / mod. M20 CDV/3 / des. R. Bonetto / prod. La Cimbali / 1979.
5. Sugar bowl, *Zuccheriera* / mod. Bar / des. Ufficio Tecnico / prod. Alessi / 1965.
6. School uniforms, *Grembiuli scuola*.

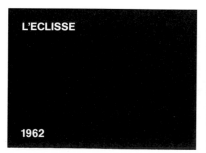

L'ECLISSE

1962

MICHELANGELO ANTONIONI

Monica Vitti
Alain Delon

about her relations with her mother-in-law.

"The good Lord should let her die, that mother-in-law of mine, if He is as just as He's supposed to be,"

The owner's wife has a very disappointing manner. She always says "yes, yes" at once, "of course, of course." Or as she did just now, while the office girl was telling her about the cleaning lady poisoning her, she seems totally taken by surprise.

"What ever do you say! Just think, think what kind of people there are in the world. What do you think of that!"

The owner of the cafe and his wife look strangely alike, at first glance you'd take them for brother and sister. They are southern Italians. First they had a news-stand. Then they opened up a little shoe factory. And now they've taken over this cafe.

The office workers are getting up. It is almost eight-thirty. While the wife makes change and wishes everybody a good day, a good day at the office, the owner and the boy are straightening out the newspapers, brushing crumbs off the tables, and cleaning the rings left by the saucers.

The office I work in is in the building next to the post office. The porter at the door has three different ways of greeting people, depending on the position of the bosses. For ordinary employees, he brings his hand up to his visor, and for trainees, he simply gives them a nod.

The porter's wife, instead, is more generous. She immediately strikes up an acquaintance with the employees and after a moment or two she is giving them an affectionate pat on the cheek. "I don't have children of my own, but I'm sure if I had a son, he'd be just as good-looking as you are, just as intelligent as you, and have the same brilliant career you do!" That's what she has said to all the men that work in the tax and mortgage offices, and there must be fifty ot them.

She has a good word for the trainees too.

"Cheer up, the last shall be first. That's what St. Paul said," she says with that touch of pride people have when they can quote from memory.

When she sees me, she says, "Well, sir, did you think about what I said? Hmm?... Remember there's no end of fine, good-looking girls here in Vigevano."

"I never doubted it for a minute!"

"Old-fashioned girls, like they used to be..."

When the porter and his wife manage to make a match they look so pleased you would take them for the bride and

---

The design of the transit stops for the Milan transit authority ATM, took into account that a number of tram lines were to become a surface extension of the subway system. The stops (marked by a "T" identical to that of the subway stations), have a platform at the same level as that of the subway cars and are protected by a roof. There is an automatic ticket machine at ground level. Ramps and underpasses allow pedestrians to cross the tracks.

At the rear of the stops, there is an illustration of the vehicles. The Jumbo-tram, divided into three parts, with a capacity of 300 passengers. This is the first car of its type, allowing passengers to enter and exit at platform level; since the front and rear doors project from the car body, the Jumbo-tram is highly asymmetric.

Given the current rebirth of interest in urban rail transit, this vehicle which is the largest and most modern in Italy, could have become the prototype for a unified surface-level urban transit system in Italy. But the failure to construct the stops with their raised platforms, as well as the necessity to isolate the lines from other traffic (a characteristic which differentiates surface rapid transit from normal tram lines), has aroused a strong negative reaction, fueled by the misunderstanding of the asymmetry of the vehicle.

Giovanni Klaus Koenig - Roberto Segoni

Il progetto di fermata tipo dell'ATM di Milano, fu fatto in previsione della trasformazione di alcune linee tranviarie in "metropolitane leggere di superficie". La fermata (il cui simbolo "T" ripete la segnaletica delle stazioni delle linee metropolitane) è rialzata a livello delle vetture, ha una pensilina con sedili e biglietteria automatica a terra, rampe di accesso e sottopassaggi pedonali di attraversamento.

Dietro la fermata è disegnato il veicolo articolato in tre spazi — detto Jumbo tram — capace di trasportare circa 300 persone. È il primo veicolo a sagoma tranviaria che, nonostante abbia due porte a sbalzo sui carrelli estremi, sia riuscito a mantenere parallele le fiancate, permettendo così l'accesso e lo sbarco diretto dalla vettura al piano della fermata. Le testate delle carrozze sono quindi fortemente asimmetriche.

Nella prospettiva del rilancio attuale del trasporto pubblico su rotaia, questo veicolo — il più lungo, il più moderno ed il più capace, fra quelli costruiti in Italia — poteva diventare il prototipo per una unificazione delle future metropolitane di superficie italiane, ma la mancata realizzazione delle fermate e delle banchine a livello nonché della necessaria protezione di linea (caratteristica che differenzia la metropolitana di superficie del tranvai) ha suscitato clamorose reazioni negative dal momento che non si comprende più l'asimmetria del veicolo.

Giovanni Klaus Koenig - Roberto Segoni

groom. And since almost all the civil servants in Vigevano come from southern Italy, the porter's wife has developed a kind of racial theory, based on arranged marriages and the children born of them, and at each new marriage, the theory is broadened and maybe modified. Children of mixed Calabrian and Vigevano parentage are brighter than they are beautiful. Children of Sicilians and Vigevanese are rather small. When it's people from Abruzzi and people from Vigevano the children are, well, so-so, but when it's someone from Vigevano and someone from Sardinia, the children they have, well, beautiful isn't the word for them.

Cross Tuscans and Vigevanese and you get overbearing children...
"When you decide to settle down, let me know," she says outside my office. When I went into the office, I felt that I'd come at the wrong moment. The office manager was sitting at a table and looking judgelike at Attilio the clerk, who stood in front of him looking confused. When Attilio saw me, he became even more confused.
There was a dusty silence in the room. The office manager was holding some papers in his hand. His eyes were fixed on Attilio, while Attilio's eyes wandered over the shelves in embarrassment.
I pretended not to notice anything and

sat down at my desk.
"I've told you several times, the rubber stamp has to be very clear and straight!" the office manager said.
"I didn't do it on purpose. My hand slipped," Attilio mumbled.
"What if a tax-payer got a form like this, what would he think of us?" the office manager continued talking through his teeth. He stopped for a moment and put the sheets of paper down on the desk.
"Do you realize?"
"What," Attilio mumbled.
"That this office isn't the place for you. You should be working for the post office. You can do anything you like

with rubber stamps there."
"But."
"Listen to me, apply for a job at the post office. Do it. I'll write you a recommendation. The Postmaster General was godfather to my daughter. A word from me and..."
"I'll have to talk it over with my wife," Attilio mumbled.
The office manager went to the window. After a moment he called Attilio. The window looked out on Market Square.
"There's your wife, see her?" the office manager said. "There, at the cornmeal stand, she's shopping. If you want to talk it over with her, you have my per-

1. Cement-Paver's shoes, *Pianelle per camminare sul cemento* / mod. Slippers / des. Ufficio Tecnico / prod. Ghelfi / 1982.
2. Dashboard, *Cruscotto auto* / mod. Veglia-System 3 / des. Ufficio Tecnico-R. Bonetto / prod. Veglia-Borletti / 1982.
3. Signboards for transport network, *Fermata mezzi pubblici* / mod. B. Noorda / 1964.
4. Motorcycle, *Motocicletta* / mod. RGS1000 / prod. Laverda / 1982.

SIGNORE & SIGNORI

1966

PIETRO GERMI

Virna Lisi
Gastone Moschin
Alberto Lionello
Olga Villa

mission to go," he went on in a sing-song voice. The office manager has an odd cadence when he speaks. Sometimes it's as if he were actually singing. After a few moments of silence, the office manager continued.

"It's not dignified for the wife of one of our employees to go to the market to buy cornmeal..."

"That's what I always tell her," said Attilio.

"It's different for someone who works in the post office. Our rules are very clear: an employee and his family must behave in such..."

"There's nothing actually wrong with it, though," Attilio said.

"Trust me, go to work in the post office!" the office manager said, and went into his private office.

Alone in the room, Attilio collapsed in front of his typewriter. He took one of the H 3 118 forms out of a drawer and began to recopy the poorly stamped form. The atmosphere was still charged with his nerves. Even the tap-tap of his typewriter was nervous.

When the sheets were finished, he put them on the table, and with tembling hand, a tense air, eyes attentive, he began to apply the rubber stamp.

"Are they stamped all right?"

"Very well!" I said.

He looked at me in an unfriendly way.

About noon the office manager's daughter came for her papa.

"Tell my employees who your godfather is," the office manager told her.

"My godfather is His Excellency, the Postmaster..." the girl said.

The boss looked at us with a superior air as if to say, "See who I know!"

He held out his arm to his daughter, and on the way out he said to Attilio, "Apply for a job at the post office, you loafer!"

When father and daughter had left, Attilio went to listen at the door, and when he heard their steps go down the hall, he took legal-size sheets and started stamping them, slamming the rubber stamp down so hard that the desks and tables in the room started to shake.

Luciano Mastronardi, "Il Meridionale di Vigevano", Einaudi, Torino 1964. Translated by Ronald Strom.

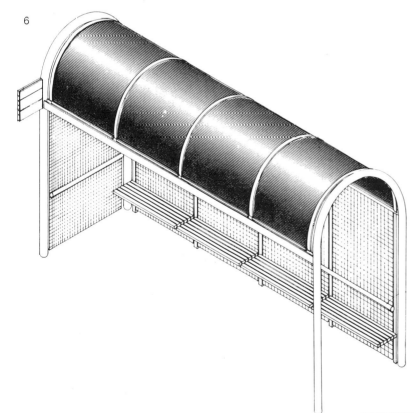

5.6. Bus stop shelter, *Pensilina fermata autobus* / mod. Duna System / des. Ufficio Tecnico D. Città / prod. D. Città / 1981.
7. Poster Hanger, *Attrezzatura affissione* / mod. Ape Car P2 / des. M.G. Marzuco / prod. ISIA / 1981.

MOTORCYCLES
CICLOMOTORI

1. mod. Firebird / prod. Malaguti / 1979.
2. mod. Pony / prod. MBM.
3. mod. Harvard Extra Lusso / des. P. Negrini / prod. Negrini / 1980.
4. mod. Sì / prod. Piaggio / 1979.
5. mod. CBA / des. Ufficio Tecnico Gilera / prod. Gilera / 1977.
6. mod. Gringo / prod. Cimatti / 1980.
7. mod. "Io" Vihks De Luxe / prod. Velomotor Testi / 1981.
8. mod. Chiù / prod. Moto Guzzi / 1975.
9. mod. Celisse / prod. Scalambra.
10. mod. Fantic "Lei" / prod. Fantic Motor / 1974.
11. mod. 50 GSA / des. P. Martin / prod. Gilera / 1982.
12. mod. Benelli S 50 / des. Centro Studi De Tomaso / prod. Benelli / 1980.

The esthetic look of a motorbike cannot be obtained by giving importance to its fairing and overlapping parts, not only because they compromise its slender line and increase its bulk, but also because they end by damaging the look of the bike when, as it grows old, these parts tend to be removed. What is essential is the architecture of the bike — that is, the layout of its various organs — and the proper choice of technical solutions, which can strongly condition the esthetic look. For example, incorporating the reduction gear in the back hub made it possible to conceal a bulky unit and eliminate the final chain, to the great advantage of the bike's architecture, cost, noise level, and wear.

To design a motorbike, keeping in mind the above-mentioned conditions, one must have a modern mass-production plant. In fact, this kind of planning reduces the possibility of having to use commercial parts, which therefore have to be specially made. This, however, is a positive point when it is made possible by the dimensions of the industry in question, since every detail can be optimized and given the most rational solution.

Besides the esthetic aspects, future

1

2

3

4

5

6

products will mainly have to take into account the varying costs in energy (not only in the manufacturing but in its use), greater riding comfort, and lowered noise level. In general, they will have to take into account the obvious consideration that while the overall features of this type of vehicle will remain the same, in time the product which has to embody it will have to adapt its structure, its look and its cost to developments in taste and to common sense.

Piaggio

Nel ciclomotore la caratteristica estetica non può essere ottenuta attraverso un uso importante di carenature e parti sovrapposte sia perché queste tolgono snellezza aumentando gli ingombri, sia perché finiscono con il danneggiare l'immagine del veicolo quando, nel corso dell'invecchiamento del mezzo, esse tendono ad essere asportate. È fondamentale invece l'architettura, intesa come disposizione degli organi, e la opportuna scelta delle soluzioni tecniche, in quanto l'estetica ne risulta fortemente condizionata. A titolo di esempio, l'incorporamento del gruppo riduttore nel mozzo posteriore permise nel "Ciao" di

nascondere un ingombro ed abolire la catena finale con vantaggi di architettura, oltre che di costo, rumorosità e usure.

Progettare un ciclomotore tenendo presenti le condizioni esposte presuppone una produzione in grande serie con impianti moderni. Infatti una tale progettazione riduce la possibilità di utilizzare parti di commercio, che pertanto devono essere fabbricate appositamente; questo è però positivo quando è consentito dalle dimensioni dell'industria interessata, in quanto ogni particolare può essere ottimizzato e realizzato in modo razionale.

Al di là degli aspetti estetici, i prodotti futuri dovranno tenere conto principalmente dei variati costi energetici, sia di fabbricazione che di utilizzo, di un migliore confort di marcia e minore rumorosità. Dovranno tenere conto, in generale, dell'ovvia considerazione che, ferma restando la prestazione complessiva di questo tipo di veicolo, il prodotto che deve assicurarla dovrà adeguare nel tempo la sua architettura, la sua immagine ed il suo costo all'evoluzione del gusto e del buon senso.

Piaggio

7

8

9

10

11

12

ON THE JOB
SLEEPLESS OBJECTS

AL LAVORO
GLI OGGETTI INSONNI

Paolo Volponi
My Troubles Began

I arrived at the factory gates the morning of June 26, 1946. One of the guards took me to the Personnel Department. We walked quickly through part of the ground floor, but I didn't have time to look around or understand exactly where we were. The hum of the work going on around me grew stronger. Inside the factory the noise was more distinct. It was the electric noise of many machines in action. The noise seemed to come from everywhere, even from the walls and floors of the factory. I couldn't see any work rooms during our walk, but just for a second through a half-opened doorway I saw a well lighted table, a glass table shining like the first light of morning. At one point I crossed an immense hall, a room roofed with enormous panes of glass bound in iron casings. Other hallways led from this room into still other rooms that seemed to dissolve the moment we left the light and walked toward the center of the building. The guard led me down the cleanest of the hallways, the only one painted white. We went up three steps to where the light glowed higher, and on each side of me I saw many doorways spaced at regular intervals. The end of

THE HAND IS THE TOOL.
EACH OFFICE A KINGDOM.
TIME AND SYSTEMS.

LA MANO ATTREZZO.
OGNI UFFICIO UN REAME.
TEMPI E METODI.

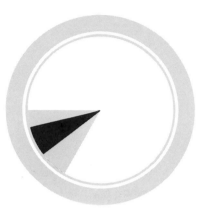

Officially employed	39.8%	*Ufficialmente lavora il*	*39,8%*
Unofficially employed	7 or 8%	*Non ufficialmente il*	*7 o 8%*
	47.7%		*47,7%*

Comparison with other industrialized countries:

Raffronto con altri Paesi industrializzati:

USA (officially employed)	47.6%	*USA (ufficialmente lavora)*	*47,6%*
Germany and France (officially employed)	43%	*Germania, Francia (ufficialmente lavora)*	*43%*

Composition of the work force:

Ripartizione lavoro:

Male	54.4%	*Lavoratori uomini*	*54,4%*
Female	26%	*Lavoratori donne*	*26%*

In the past ten years, the number of women working has increased from 21.7% to 26%.

Il lavoro femminile negli ultimi dieci anni passa dal 21,7% al 26%.

Division by sector:

Ripartizioni per settore:

Industry: 37.1% (with a tendency to decrease).
Artisans, white-collar workers, sales clerks and service workers: 49.8% (in expansion).
Agriculture: 13.1% (decreasing with a strong tendency towards mechanization).

Industria: 37,1% (con tendenza a decrescere).
Terziario (artigiani, impiegati, commercianti...): 49,8% (in espansione).
Agricoltura: 13,1% (con tendenza a decrescere ma con forte spinta verso la meccanizzazione).

45% of employed workers belong to trade unions.

Il 45% dei lavoratori dipendenti è iscritto al sindacato.

1. Drawing-board, *Tavolo da disegno* / mod. A90 / des. P. Parigi / prod. Heron Parigi / 1978.
2. Ski boot, *Scarpone da sci* / mod. Squadra Soft / des. I. Olivieri / prod. Caber / 1982.
3. Lamp, *Lampada* / mod. Parentesi / des. P. Manzù, A. Castiglioni / prod. Flos / 1970.
4.5.6. Sewing-machine, *Macchina da cucire* / mod. Logica / des. G. Giugiaro / prod. Necchi / 1982.
7. Lathe, *Tornio* / a) SAG 210 / des. G. Decursu / prod. Graziano / 1970 / b) traditional, *tradizionale*.

DESERTO ROSSO

1964

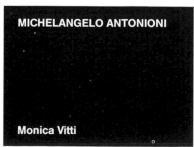

MICHELANGELO ANTONIONI

Monica Vitti

the hall led into a sort of waiting room. The guard left me with several other men who were also waiting. No one spoke, and the only noise was the sound of the factory which now seemed a little muted. Judging from the faces of those who were waiting, there were other things to listen to besides the sound of the factory. This was an enforced pause, and we waited in that bright white hallway with its linoleum floor.

During the five days that had passed since my first visit to the factory I had convinced myself that my call to work was a good thing, to my advantage. I wasn't afraid of being turned down because during those five days I had already felt myself present inside the factory. I had even dreamed about work, about having to perform a very exacting task constructing a complicated piece of machinery something like the mechanism of a clock. In the dream, just as I was about to finish, my machine would start clattering, while the machines of all the other workers busy doing the same type of work, lined up on either side of me, continued to function perfectly. I couldn't stop the clatter unless I removed one of the parts of the machine, thereby ruining the entire mechanisms. But suddenly the foreman, who reminded me of the young worker from Chivasso, would arrive, and he would tell everybody that according to the latest instructions all the machines were supposed to rattle just like mine.

Many years before, when I left France with my mother and father I had experienced that same feeling of emptiness together with a confidence in the future. With the stubbornness and determination of a thirteen-year-old boy, I refused to accept the idea of leaving. I didn't want to go back to Italy, and my father tried to convince me with grown-up arguments which completely disgusted me. My father said that he was tired and even a little sick and that he didn't feel secure in a foreign country. He said that Italy had changed and that Fascism had brought prosperity to the country. Now there were many opportunities for the worker and still more for a young boy's future. All this only made my last days in Avignon more painful and drained me of every thought and image of youth. As our trip drew near I was overpowered by an overwhelming desire to return to Italy, to Candia which my father had described as a beautiful village.

Paolo Volponi, "Il Memoriale", Einaudi, Torino 1981. "My Troubles Began", Grossman, New York 1964.

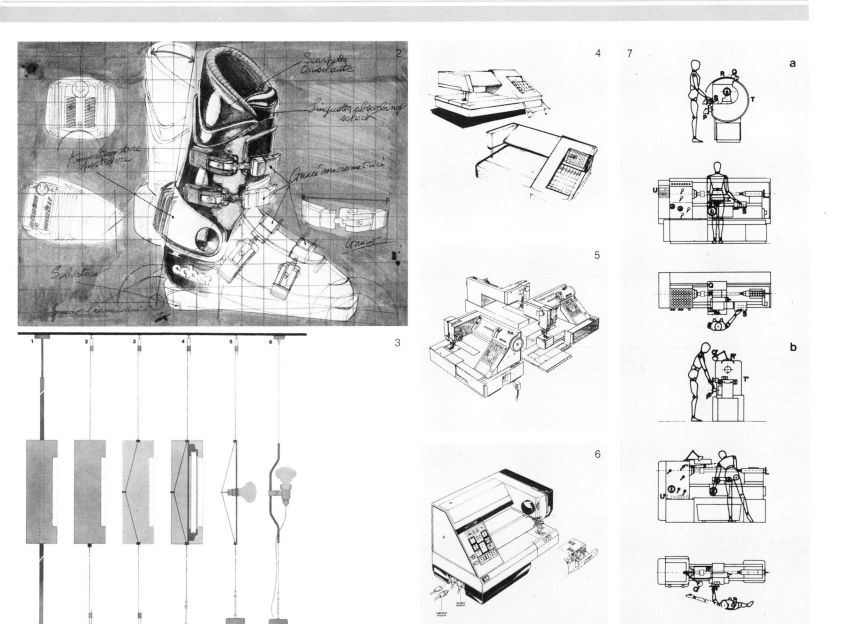

CONSTRUCTING THE PROTOTYPE OF THE FIAT PANDA
PROCESSO DI REALIZZAZIONE DEL PROTOTIPO PER LA PANDA

1. Making plaster casts of components, *Realizzazione componenti in gesso.*
2. Constructing a plaster model, *Costruzione del modello in gesso.*
3. Metrology department. Using the calculator to check the dimensions of the plaster model, *Reparto di metrologia. Controllo sul prototipo di gesso delle dimensioni al calcolatore.*
4. Aerodynamic tests of the plaster model, *Tests aerodinamici sul modello in gesso.*
5. Constructing the prototype in chassis sheet metal, *Costruzione del prototipo in lamiera.*
6. Crash tests with the chassis sheet metal, *Prove d'urto sul modello in lamiera.*
7. Beating sheet metal, *Battitura lamiera.*
8. Rough habitability manikin, *Manichino grezzo di abitabilità.*
9.10.11.12. First studies, *Prime ricerche.*
13. Diagram of mechanical components, *Geometrico della meccanica.*
14. Sketches, *Figurini.*

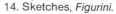

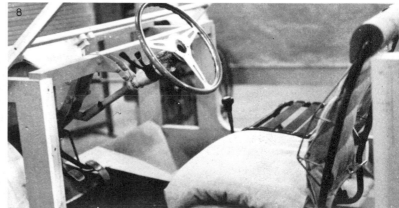

Drawing up a program of design for a widely-sold product involves a heavy investment of cognitive resources (aesthetic technological, and economic) in research, and demands close team work among experienced professional partners. I've always maintained that it was much more exhilarating to design the Fiat Panda than the four-door Maserati or a high-performance sports car. To compare it with mountain-climbing I would say that the design of a product for mass-production is like a summit to be scaled by a roped-party with 6th degree passages. To realize this you need only consider the commitment which creators, designers, and sheet-iron craftsmen put into the definition of a highly precise product with tolerances within 2/10 of a millimeter; here is a problem to be solved in every single detail, for the product is designed for big industry, which cannot afford approximations. Costs, weight, and international standards are all of the greatest importance in directing and conditioning research; but it is precisely within these limits and conditions that the creative spirit manifests itself and the results justify our appreciation.

Giorgio Giugiaro

Affrontare oggi un programma di design per un prodotto di largo consumo vuol dire concentrare nella ricerca risorse conoscitive (estetiche, tecnologiche, metodologiche, economiche) molto approfondite, e richiede un lavoro di équipe fra partners decisamente professionali. Ho sempre sostenuto che per me è stato esaltante progettare la Fiat Panda piuttosto che la Maserati Quattroporte o una granturismo sportiva. Per fare un paragone alpinistico direi che il disegno di un prodotto destinato alle altissime tirature è la cima da raggiungere con passaggi di 6° grado. Basti pensare all'impegno che devono sostenere creatori, progettisti, artigiani del legno e della lamiera nel definire un prodotto assolutamente preciso con tolleranze al di sotto di 2/10 di millimetro, risolto in tutti i suoi aspetti proprio perché destinato alla grande industria che non può lasciare spazi all'approssimazione. Costi, pesi, normative internazionali incidono in massima misura nell'indirizzare, nel condizionare la ricerca, ma proprio all'interno dei limiti e dei condizionamenti, la creatività ha modo di cimentarsi e il risultato ha più titoli per essere apprezzato.

Giorgio Giugiaro

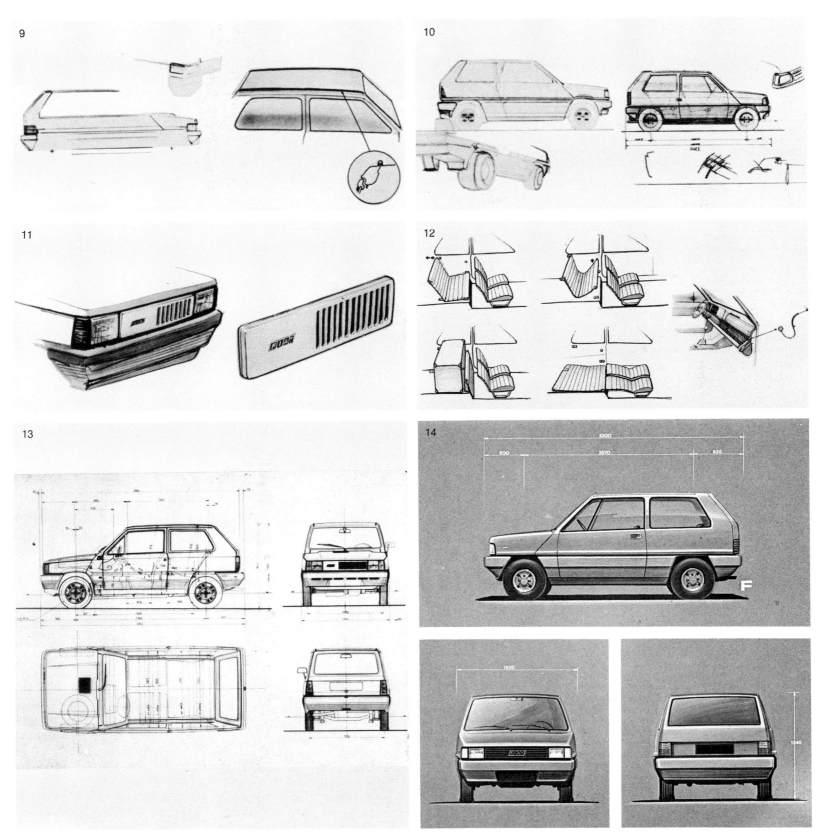

65

Primo Levi
Lilit and other Stories

After a few moments the whistling and the shivering went away and he found himself lucidly awake with the kernel of the poem sharp and clear; all he had to do was write it down, and, sure enough, the other verses didn't take long to crowd around it, in a docile but vigorous embrace. In a quarter of an hour the work was done: but even so this bolt from the blue, this lighting process, with conception and birth following one another almost like lightning and thunder, had only been granted to Pasquale five or six times in his life.

Luckily he wasn't a poet by profession: he had a quiet, boring job in an office. He first felt the symptoms just described after two years of silence, while he was sitting at his desk checking through an insurance policy. He felt them in fact with unusual intensity: the whistling was penetrating and the shivering was almost a convulsive shaking, disappearing quickly but leaving him dizzy. The key-verse was there in front of him, as if written on the wall, or right inside his head. His colleagues at neighbouring desks weren't taking any notice of him: Pasquale concentrated wildly on the sheet of paper in front of him, the kernel of the peom radiated

outwards in all directions like a growing organism, and soon it was there before him, seeming to shake like a thing alive. It was the most beautiful poem that Pasquale had ever written. There it was before his eyes, with no crossings-out, in a hand that was flowing, tall and elegant: it almost seemed as though the sheet of filmsy copy paper on which it was written had difficulty supporting the weight, like an over-slim column beneath the weight of a mighty statue. It was six o'clock; Pasquale locked it up in his drawer and went home. He thought he deserved a reward, and on the way he bought himself an ice-cream.

EACH OFFICE A KINGDOM.
OGNI UFFICIO UN REAME.

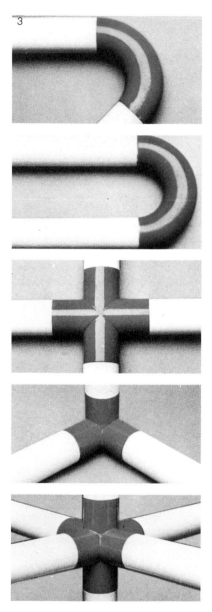

1. Calendar, *Calendario* / mod. Timor / des. E. Mari / prod. Danese / 1967.
2. Terminal system, *Terminale* / mod. TC 800 / des. E. Sottsass jr.-G. Sowden / prod. Olivetti / 1974.
3. Lighting system, *Illuminazione* / mod. Tondoluce 70 / prod. Sames / 1980.
4. Terminal components, *Componenti Terminale* / mod. TC 800 / des. E. Sottsass jr.-G. Sowden / prod. Olivetti / 1974.
5. Lighting system, *Illuminazione* / mod. Halley / des. P. King, S. Miranda, G. Arnaldi / prod. Arteluce / 1981.
6. Office furniture, *Mobili ufficio* / mod. Pianeta Ufficio / des. M. Bellini / prod. Marcatrè / 1974.
7. Clock, *Orologio* / mod. Dator N6 / des. Ufficio Tecnico / prod. Solari e C. Udine / 1979.
8. Light system, *Illuminazione* / mod. Sistema Atom Barra / des. E. Gismondi / prod. Artemide / 1982.

The following morning he rushed to the office. He couldn't wait to re-read it, knowing well how difficult it is to judge a work that has just been written: value and meaning, or the lack of value and meaning, only become clear the day after. He opened the drawer but couldn't see the filmsy sheet: and yet he was sure he'd left it on top of all the other papers. He searched through these, first furiously, then methodically, but he had to conclude that the poem had disappeared. He looked in the other drawers, and then he realized that the sheet was right there in front of him in the in-tray. That comes of not thinking of what you're doing! But how can you think about what you're doing when you're face to face with your life's fundamental work?

Pasquale was convinced that his future biographers would remember him for this alone: for this "Annunciation". He re-read it and was full of enthusiasm. He was about to take it to the photocopier when he was called by the manager; this tied him tup for an hour and a half, and when he got back to his desk the photocopier was out of order. The electrician had repaired it by four, but the special paper had run out. For that day there was nothing he could do about it; remembering what had happened the previous evening, Pasquale placed the sheet back in the drawer with great care. He closed it, had second thoughts, opened again, then finally closed it again and went away. The following day the sheet wasn't there. This was getting annoying. Pasquale turned out all his drawers, bringing to light papers forgotten for decades; while he rummaged, he was vainly trying to locate in his memory, if not the whole composition, at least that first verse, that kernel that had illuminated him. But to no avail: indeed, he had the clear feeling that he could never remember it. He was a different man, from that moment onwards: he wasn't the same Pasquale any more, he would never be able to go back, just as a dead person cannot return to life and the same water never passes twice under the same bridge. In his mouth he had a metallic, nauseating taste: the taste of frustration, of the nevermore. He sat down disconsolately on the office chair, and saw the sheet stuck to the wall, to his left, a foot or so from his head. Obviously some colleague had wanted to play a joke in bad taste, maybe someone who had watched him and discovered his secret.

Primo Levi, "Lilit e altri racconti", Einaudi, Torino 1981. Translated by Richard Dury.

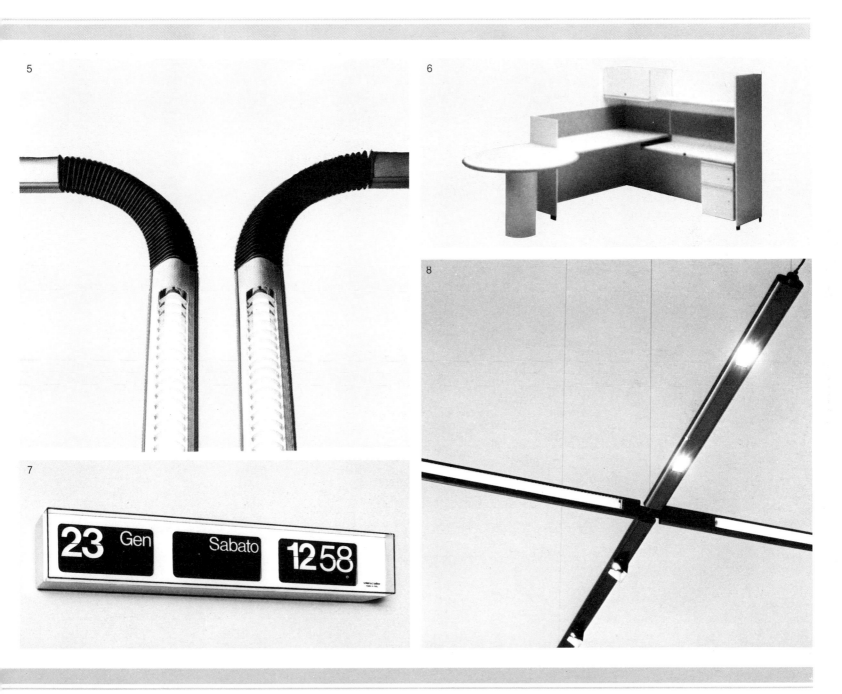

5

6

7

8

OFFICE SYSTEMS
SISTEMI PER UFFICI

1. Working positions, *Posti di lavoro* / mod. Pianeta Ufficio / prod. Marcatrè / 1974.
2.3. Examples of configurations, *Esempi di composizione* / mod. Pianeta Ufficio / prod. Marcatrè / 1974.

If, for reasons of economy, it is right to eliminate walls and doors (and so abandoning among other things an integral plan of rooms and corridors which is essentially rather squalid), we still cannot ignore the requirements of those working in offices. We must offer then an alternative structure which meets the needs we have mentioned elsewhere. The mistake committed by those who developed the philosophy of "Burolandschaft", or office landscaping which pushed beyond all limits what was above all a serious and rational mode of organization, was to delude themselves that they could sweep away a reactionary nostalgia for walls and doors, promoting new values which they were able to show as more modern and democratic, such as "opening up space", "light", "living together", etc. An initially obvious and not reassuring topological fragility of groups of tables, cupboards, screens and plants was replaced by a more "naturalistic arrangement of furniture. Even if this undoubtedly was an improvement over the oppressive rigidity of compact grid arrangements, there remained the feeling of being in a large furniture store or, to use an outdoor metaphor, a crowded camping site. No one has yet realised that if the furniture is the physical presence in the vast spaces of an office it is in fact there that one places those things that previously went on the walls and doors. This means that an open plan imposes a radical change in the traditional concept of furnishing understood as "a placing of objects to equip a space" instead, it must become "an organization of furnished space" which can reconstruct an architectonic organization of the surroundings which is more flexible than walls and will not be an obstacle to flows of information.

Mario Bellini - Giorgio Origlia

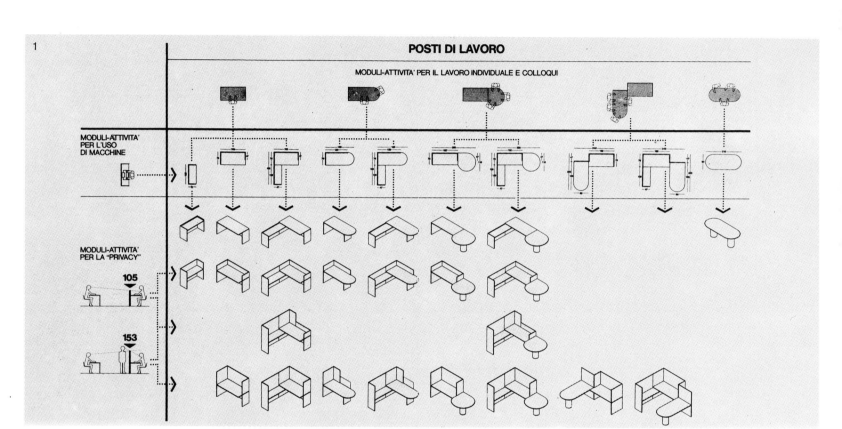

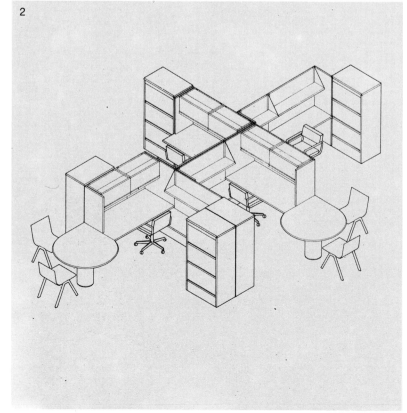

Se è giusto per ragioni economiche eliminare pareti e porte (abbandonando così tra l'altro uno schema aggregativo, quale quello a stanze e corridoi, di per sé piuttosto squallido), non si deve però ignorare la necessità di offrire a chi lavora in ufficio un supporto fisico alternativo ad esse, che risponda ai bisogni che abbiamo elencato. Questo errore è stato commesso da chi ha sviluppato e divulgato la filosofia del "Bürolandschaft" o "office landscaping": spingendo troppo oltre quello che era soprattutto un serio metodo di razionalizzazione organizzativa, ci si è illusi di poter spazzare via la nostalgia per muri e porte come

reazionarie, spingendo valori nuovi, abilmente presentati come più moderni e democratici: "apertura", "trasparenza", "comunanza", ecc. Così pure la evidente e poco rassicurante precarietà topologica delle aggregazioni di tavoli, armadi, schermi e piante verdi è stata contrabbandata per disposizione "naturalistica" dell'arredo. Questa, se costituisce un indubbio miglioramento rispetto alla rigidezza oppressiva dei ranghi compatti, non elimina la sensazione di essere in un magazzino di mobili, o, per mantenere la suggestione naturalistica, in un affollato campeggio. Non ci si era finora resi conto in modo chiaro che, se

l'arredamento rimane l'unica presenza fisica nei grandi ambienti d'ufficio, proprio su di esso tendono a depositarsi quei bisogni prima supportati da pareti e porte. Per la pianta aperta si impone una revisione radicale della tradizionale concezione di arredamento, inteso come "sistema di oggetti per attrezzare uno spazio": questo deve piuttosto diventare un "sistema spaziale attrezzato", in grado di ricostituire una organizzazione di tipo architettonico dell'ambiente, sia pure più flessibile delle pareti e non di ostacolo ai flussi delle informazioni.

Mario Bellini - Giorgio Origlia

OFFICE SYSTEMS
SISTEMI PER UFFICI

4.5.6.7.8.9.10.11. TC 800 Intelligent terminal system - studies of the modular units, *Sistema elettronico modulare TC 800 - studio delle unità modulari.*
12. TC 800 Intelligent terminal system, *Sistema elettronico modulare TC 800 / des. E. Sottsass jr.-G. Sowden / prod. Olivetti / 1974.*

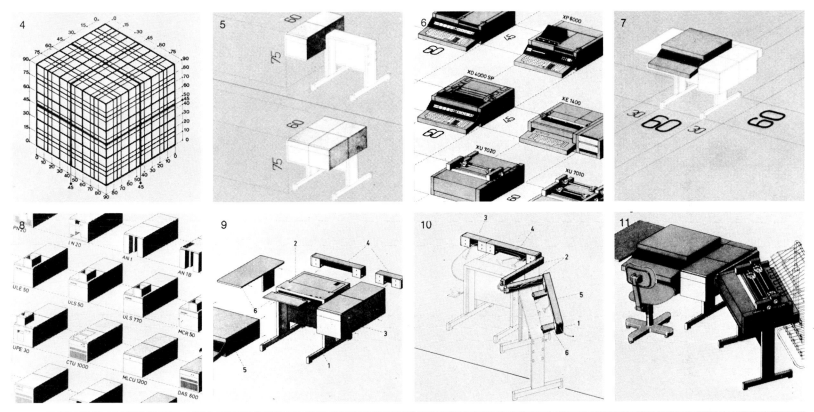

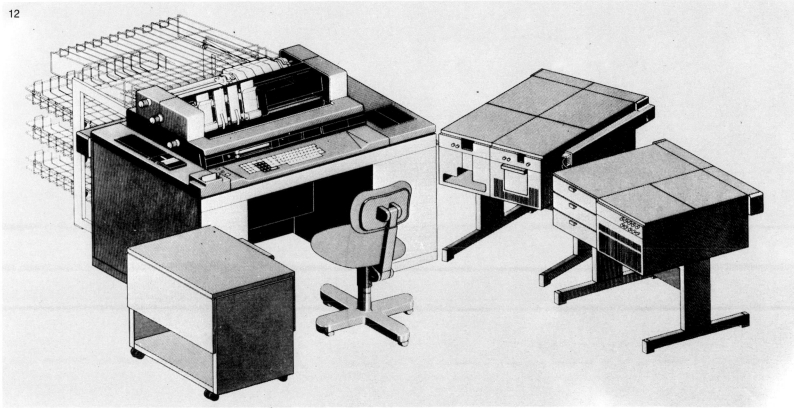

THE HAND IS THE TOOL.
LA MANO ATTREZZO.

Ercole Patti
A drop of oil

November 1969
In the morning these days there is soft, mild sunshine. In the early hours of the afternoon the sky becomes overcast and light rainfall comes down giving a glitter to the olive leaves, the Indian figs and the leaves of the jasmine which cover the high wall of pumice stone and the two small lemon trees beneath the olive trees. At sunset it stops raining and later the stars shine on the wet leaves drying in the night beneath the moon.

I have had the olives gathered from the few old trees surrounding my house to obtain a little oil. In the autumnal air, among the fresh young blades of grass still moist from the drops of rain from the day before, the olives fall, torn down by the hands of the peasant boy; they hit the nylon sheet stretched out underneath the trees, making a soft dead sound like small hailstones. Some of them have dark stains on one side but this, instead of ruining the resulting oil, from what the peasant says, seems to have a favourable influence on the quality. However, I am talking about the few liters of oil which will be sufficient on my occasional visits to this house by the sea. On the land, amidst the grass, here and there are some rocks covered with small flowering plants which have come out after the recent rain. In the grass near the rocks and beneath the trunks of the olive trees, thin wild asparagus are coming up from their thorny patch. Wandering around for a short while in the damp grass, one can collect a bunch sufficient to make a side dish. A youth with a small basket is picking up the fallen olives from the cracks in the rocks, in the fresh grass, from the cover on the well, on the pergola and among the small scattered plants of basil and wild herbs near the old walls and on the edges of the walls them-

1

2

3

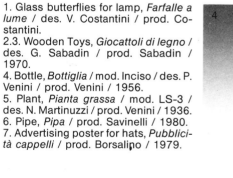

1. Glass butterflies for lamp, *Farfalle a lume* / des. V. Costantini / prod. Costantini.
2.3. Wooden Toys, *Giocattoli di legno* / des. G. Sabadin / prod. Sabadin / 1970.
4. Bottle, *Bottiglia* / mod. Inciso / des. P. Venini / prod. Venini / 1956.
5. Plant, *Pianta grassa* / mod. LS-3 / des. N. Martinuzzi / prod. Venini / 1936.
6. Pipe, *Pipa* / prod. Savinelli / 1980.
7. Advertising poster for hats, *Pubblicità cappelli* / prod. Borsalino / 1979.

4

5

selves. These simple peasant acts carried out in moments of fine weather in an uncertain season give a more pleasant taste to the small crop. At dawn we collected the olives together in two large sacks and took them to the oil mill in the nearby village (the ones collected yesterday were warm as if they had been placed near the oven and were beginning to ferment).

The car ran along the winding road which passed through the still drowsy lemon groves half asleep in the clear air. The cars that we encountered still had their headlights on in the pale light of a day about to begin.

In the oil mill in the shining brightness of the early morning lamps there lingered the strong smell of the crushed olives. The two enormous wheels of the press rotate on each other mincing the pulp and the stones. After the first pressing, the fragrant pulp is placed between thick flat discs of raffia which are then placed one above the other with a huge block of wood on top and then again placed under the powerful steel press. Beneath this strong pressure the first oil comes out little by little from a tube and goes slowly into a vat. When the odorous pulp is removed from between the discs of raffia it is put once more between the plates of the press. The large wheels press down once again, after which the pulp is returned between the discs and pressed again. The pressed olives are then reduced to dry solid blocks which are thrown away as something unusable.

The opaque yellow oil descends silently into the vat and from the vat is pumped up to a container placed high up from which it comes down through a long tube, passing through a small, very modern, shining, nickel-plated machine standing amidst the ancient things surrounding it. The machine, which has a centrifugal motor, separates the oil from the water. From one of the two mouths the opaque yellowish oil comes out and, from the other, water of almost the same colour, only slightly paler.

Ercole Patti, "Diario Siciliano", Bompiani, Milano 1975. Translated by Shane Hall.

6

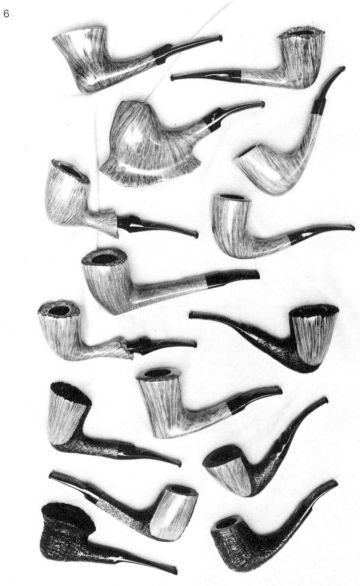

7

REALIZATION-SEQUENCE OF A BORSALINO HAT
SEQUENZA DI REALIZZAZIONE DI UN CAPPELLO BORSALINO

1. Fur-cutting, *Taglio del pelo.*
2. Forming, *Imbastitura.*
3. Sizing, *Calandratura.*
4. Felting, *Follatura.*
5. Blocking, *Informatura.*
6. Transportation to the drying process, *Trasporto verso l'essiccatura.*
7. Poucing process, *Raffinatura.*
8. Manual pressing, *Pressatura a mano.*
9.10. Mechanical pressing, *Pressatura a macchina.*
11. Lining-preparation, *Preparazione fodera.*
12. First cutting finish, *Rifilaggio di prima.*
13. Second cutting finish, *Rifilaggio di seconda.*
14. Flanging, *Sabbionatura.*
15. Morocco preparation, *Preparazione del marocchino.*
16. Packaging, *Imballaggio.*

There is woolen felt and hair felt. The Borsalino co. makes only hair felt hats, which are flexible and hard. The fur used is either domestic or wild rabbit's fur (skins come from Australia for the most part, but also from France, England, Belgium and Germany; Italian rabbits are not suitable). Also used are hare, beaver, nutria and muskrat. This fur is separated from the hide by special machines. The best fur is found on the animal's back. Divided up according to quality, the fur is passed on to the felt-making sector. Here, treatment is based on the quality of furs available: felt is formed as a result of the penetration of the microscopic cortical imbrications and scales found on the surface of the fur; each of these, in its way, sticks fast and indissolubly to the others. This goes on until, through successive operations based on carefully gauged applications of heat, water, and compression, a compact and resistant material is formed. The newborn felt, as stored in the hat factory, is bell-shaped. It is then dyed and, following this, made into a hat. The secret of Borsalino's 100 years will be found in the brains of its technicians and the hands of its workmen".

From "Omaggio al cappello"

C'è il feltro di lana e il feltro di pelo. La Borsalino fabbrica solo il cappello di feltro di pelo, flessibile e duro. Il pelo è di coniglio domestico o selvatico (le pelli vengono dall'Australia, per la maggior parte, e anche dalla Francia, dall'Inghilterra, dal Belgio e dalla Germania; non vi sono conigli adatti in Italia) oppure di lepre, di castoro, di nutria e di ratmusqué. Il pelo viene separato dalla pelle mediante apposite macchine. Il pelo migliore è quello del dorso. Diviso per qualità, il pelo passa alla fabbricazione del feltro. Questa si basa sulla caratteristica che i peli di quegli animali presentano: il feltro si forma grazie alla compenetrazione delle microscopiche embricature o squamette corticali che sono alla superficie del pelo, ciascuno dei quali si unisce in tal modo fortemente e quasi indissolubilmente agli altri, finché attraverso successive operazioni basate sull'azione pianificata del calore, dell'acqua e della compressione si giunge a formare una stoffa compatta e resistente. Il feltro appena nato ha, nella fabbrica di cappelli, la forma di una campana: viene tinto e poi con quello si fa il cappello. Il segreto da cento anni è il cervello dei tecnici, sono le mani degli operai.

Da "Omaggio al cappello"

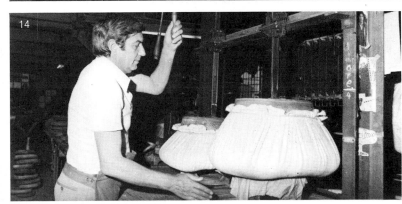

BACK IN THE STREET
CROSS-SOCIALIZING

DI NUOVO IN STRADA
SIMULTANEITÀ DEL SOCIALE

THE MARKET IS ALMOST OVER.
TIME OFF ON THE CONSTRUCTION JOB.
FRUIT AND VEGETABLE CARTS.
A TWIST OF LEMON IN VERMOUTH.
WHO'S PICKING UP THE CHILDREN AT SCHOOL?

MERCATO FINITO.
MERCATO INFINITO.
LAVORI IN CORSO.
L'ORTOFRUTTICOLO.
LA SCORZA DI LIMONE NEL VERMOUTH.
CHI VA A PRENDERE IL BAMBINO?

Corrado Alvaro
Empoli, People and Glass

One of the newest things about Italy today is the development of industry in old towns, take Tuscany for example. Far from defacing the townscape, industry adds something to the environment and the town, and rather than obliterate the old color of old life, industrial plants bring it out in relief. First of all there is the spectacle of how an Italian is transformed on contact with organized collective life, and that is not the least interesting aspect. He always keeps something of the craftsman about him, and after all the birth of industrialism in Italy is not that odd new development it was long considered. In the time of the great craft guilds and the old corporations, city centers grew up out of that structure and then they turned into museums of that very work. That is how we were accustomed to look at Italy; we regretted the passing of Europe's finest artisans and craftsmen, but we turned up our noses at factory smoke-stacks. And the Italy that was only agricultural and had given up civic ambitions was no longer the real Italy. That is why so many meaningless monuments were built, monuments that imitated the look of old loggias and old palaces of art. One thing

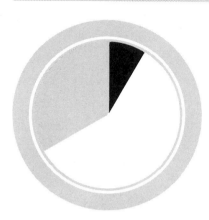

Retail outlets total 909,000, of which 417,909 handle foodstuffs (in the USA the total is 200,000).
Of the total, 227,000 are licensed peddlers (109,000 for foodstuffs, 118,000 miscellaneous goods). In addition there are 1,396 supermarkets and 786 department stores.

The percentage of Italians who at least once a week go to the following sales outlets is:

Wholesale	1.7%
Supermarkets	26.3%
Stores	13.4%
Groceries	54.2%
Bookstores	6.6%
Record stores	4.2%
Banks	14.3%
Perfumeries	2.7%
Boutiques	2.9%
Restaurants	7.3%

Market fragmentation means that stores tend to be small, so that 97% of Italians have a grocery store and bar within 2 Km of their residence.
Discount stores and mail order sales are rare.

Esistono 909.000 negozi di articoli vari di cui 417.909 di generi alimentari (gli USA ne contano 200.000).
Di questi 227.000 sono ambulanti (109.000 alimentari/118.000 vari) cui vanno aggiunti 1.396 supermercati e 786 grandi magazzini.

Percentuale di italiani che vanno almeno una volta la settimana nei seguenti punti di vendita:

ipermercati	*1,7%*
supermercati	*26,3%*
grandi magazzini	*13,4%*
alimentari/drogherie	*54,2%*
librerie	*6,6%*
dischi	*4,2%*
banche	*14,3%*
profumerie	*2,7%*
boutique abbigliamento	*2,9%*
ristoranti	*7,3%*

Risulta evidente la parcellizzazione del mercato, specie alimentare.
Su 100 Italiani, il 97% trova un negozio alimentare ed un bar a meno di 2 km. da casa.
Le formule di vendita del "discount" e "per corrispondenza", non sono quasi praticate.

IO LA CONOSCEVO BENE

1965

ANTONIO PETRANGELI

has not been lost, however, and that is the capacity of people who work to create their own monuments and bear witness to themselves the way the dyers and woolmen used to do. Elsewhere *tout finit par des chansons*, while in Italy everything ends up in architecture and art. All it needs is that a society organizes itself in a certain way and somehow recovers its natural aptitude, and that function will come back to life. They will not be art palaces as of old; it will be a tower, a summer camp, or a playing field, and life will take up the old thread. This faceless work, as industrial work used to be considered, will resume its former power. The entrepreneurs change, but the tendency is the same.

I happened to think of these things when I was standing outside the old cathedral in Empoli. Children were playing in the square, and women loitered with babies in their arms. A fountain commemorated the munificence of a gentlemen who endowed the city with drinking water. Below a marble basin overflowing with water stood four female figures smiling in marble. It was not the nakedness of times gone by, it was already a modern nudity reminiscent of bedrooms. People developed their own centers around them, nuclei of shops under the porticos, old cafés, wine shops, and signs that expressed something of the people artistically in painted zinc. And then the goods on the street, the daily market with its sense of life's immediacy and struggles, the countryside, and the markets. There is a way of arranging and displaying the things of the world that almost seems composed. You could spend hours here, who knows how far you might travel in response to this wine with its taste of old roses and old vases. Race matters. For people who hate the pretentiousness of a certain kind of modern living bent on seeming better than it is, there is a well-deserved rest about these taverns every so often that quench the thirst of the dusty street and the appeal of tripe and pigs' feet and any kind of simple food. Failing anything else, the people have provided their own decoration for daily life. There are saints on the corners of buildings, shop signs, and goods displayed; nothing is too heterogeneous for this atmosphere, which is one of hard struggle too. Even the mass-produced wares in the chain stores look like ornaments on a Christmas tree and take on some of the prestige that was childhood's. And what about the shop sign reading "Bazar Fantastico"?

Empoli lies in the plain. You can look

1.2. Umbrella, *Ombrellone* / mod. Da Mercato / prod. Scolaro / 1982.
3. Market scale, *Bilancia Stadera* / mod. Stadera / prod. Coba.
4. Electronic scale, *Bilancia elettronica* / mod. Mach SL2 / prod. Macchi.
5. Pricing scale, *Bilancia prezzatrice* / des. Ufficio Tecnico / prod. Santo Stefano.
6. Items counting scale, *Bilancia contapezzi* / mod. CP / des. Ufficio Tecnico / prod. Imba.
7. Scale, *Bilancia* / mod. BL / des. Ufficio Tecnico / prod. Imba.
8. Pick-up, *Motofurgone* / mod. Ape Car P2 ambulante / prod. Piaggio.

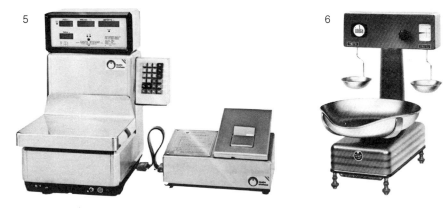

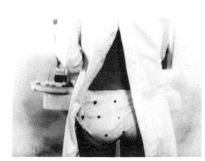

down its straight streets right out into the countryside, the glitter of bicycles mixing with that of elm leaves shaken by a long tremor as if they were throbbing. And the dust, the yellow fences of a playing field, hoardings that are larger and brighter, as if all of this were an announcement of a fair or an amusement park. The factory workers' neighborhood stretches out down there, because Empoli has at least fifteen glass factories. Wagonloads of flasks ready to be wrapped in straw are standing in front of the factory doors. The glassworks close down in the summer, but it was still cool when I arrived, and a few of them were still open.

At a certain point you reach the Arno River, with the same green color it has in Florence. The windows are open in the late afternoon, women are sitting on the balconies sewing, and the peasant in the neighboring field never finishes working. Children were playing on a dry river bank. The red sunset and the river disappearing in the plain reminded me of the sea. There was a man sitting looking on the river bank. He asked me if I had come to work in Empoli, and when I told him I lived in Rome, "oh," he said, "so you come from Rome. How fast does the Tiber run? I haven't been there since 1885,

and I always wondered whether the Tiber or the Arno ran faster. I was waiting for someone to ask." That is what a solitary man can think about when he is sitting on the bank of a river. He also asked me for news about Prato, since I was someone who travelled, but nothing further away. Then a shoemaker came along, out for a breath of air, with that philosophical manner that "cobblers" have all over the world, walking elbows out like someone pulling two ends of a string.

The great novelty that one of the glassworks was readying was a representation of a soccer game. The players were arranged on a table designed in

the form of a playing field. The figures of the players had colored shirts and white glass heads. The outstanding features were the noses and the team emblems. This was in a big store full of glass objects: roses, flowers and fruit of all colors, vases and lamps. You have to remember how fragile glass is every moment, we are so accustomed to being surrounded by things that are not fragile. At a certain point, the utter perishability almost panics you. These are things to be used and consumed, and yet there are objects of glass that are one or two thousand years old, dug up out of the earth where they have lain for centuries. Just think how many of

1. Lamp for works in progress, *Lampada per "Lavori in corso"* / des. Ufficio Tecnico / prod. Carattoni & Monti.
2. Street lamp, *Lampada stradale.*
3. Motor scooter, *Ciclomotore* / mod. Motorella GL / des. L. Bellini / prod. Benelli / 1968.
4. Street lamp, *Lampada stradale* / mod. A. Dal Lago / prod. Disano / 1979.
5. Street lamp, *Lampada stradale* / mod. Roma.
6. Taxi, *Tassì* / mod. Ritmo / prod. Fiat.

SIGNORE & SIGNORI

1966

PIETRO GERMI

Virna Lisi
Gastone Moschin
Alberto Lionello
Olga Villa

them, thousands, must have been broken for one of them to have survived. Suddenly all these glass objects seemed like humankind, going all around the world, running through life, travelling, and then stopping in some forgotten corner. Time passes, monuments of stone crumble, some of them leaving behind only a vague memory, the very plan of a city can disappear; yet this doll, this case, a memento of a past civilization, of life itself, survives on some piece of the earth.

Outside, stretching as far as the eye can see, are yards full of naked demijohns and flasks, low walls separating one warehouse from another. They look like kitchen gardens full of gourds; flasks in every shade of green are piled high, wall-like under awnings. It is an extremely precarious world. And then I thought, for example, of a hailstorm on all this glass. But in another warehouse, this one closed, there was an infinity of cruets and bottles, objects or forms in our homes, but here they took on the features of a tribe. At times those double cruets for oil and vinegar, like two little bags joined together, looked like an immense family of Siamese twins. Single cruets with stoppers looked like little girls, their heads poking out of starched collars. And you could follow this theme endlessly. Workers machine-smoothing glass edges, as if they were dealing with a whole world of babies or midgets, a world that had reproduced and multiplied like animalkind, generation after generation, and the different races were the different colors of the same kind of objects. The flower vases and bric-à-brac seemed to open monstrous mouths or resemble pieces of anatomy. I had fierce likes and dislikes. Everyone of those objects reminded me of some place, bedside tables, deep draughts of water in the middle of the night from a glass you fumble for, the water flask in a hotel room, a glass in an inn, breakages and new sets of glass at home, hospitals, and picnic baskets. And you could make out old shapes seen in childhood or countries you had visited, something seen in a museum, shapes that once belonged to the Phoenicians, and then repeated again and again over the years and over the centuries. All of it inspired by an unknown craftsman who found that first dimension for the emission of his breath into a blowpipe. Nowadays each of these factories turns out thirty thousands pieces of ordinary glassware every day, and three hundred pieces of fine glass.

7. Poster, *Manifesto* / Il Prodotto / des. P. Buttafava.
8. Trash box, *Cassonetto rifiuti* / 1981.

The job has something of the ordinary work of a schoolroom about it. The glass furnace is like an enormous inkwell that everyone dips into; the workers sit in a circle around it, each one with his own blowpipe. It looks as if they were tuning up musical instruments. Every breath has to be the same, after all every piece is alike, and the average variation in weight is not even 20 grams. The ceiling is very high, with beams and rafters, like an old factory or an old church. The workers are all clustered in the center, between the powerful fans and the windows. A board is hanging up where the workers chalk the "long lives" and the "down withs" of their daily passions. There is the solitude of individual work combined with the look of an old community intent on work that has something even playful about it, which is saying a lot for one of the hardest jobs there is. But this contrast may account for the whole charm of the sight. Alone yet together, each man with his own incandescent blob that passes through every color and form, ripens like hard green fruit, takes on color like a soap bubble, and gradually takes flame as more air comes in. The rhythm of the blowpipes between one man and the next, between one solitude and another, sets up a meeting of lines and a play of right angles like the converging rhythm of the ceiling rafters. It is like a grand concerto that manages to express nothing but rounded forms, something like the jazz cornet that looks as if it can barely blow a bubble out of its bell. Hanging down from a long blowpipe a big bottle swells like a bass note, and on the other side dinky little green quarter-liter bottles emit a sharper sound in this music. The glass blower is part of the volume that is born of his breath, like a plant watching the enormous growth of its fruit. In this orchestra of forms, where the only sound you hear is an occasional snap as the glass comes away from the pipe, the worker in fine glass is almost on his own. He has the privilege of a boy to help him, the aid of a wooden compass for measurement and for spreading and regulating corollas of glass. In his hands glass passes through every form from globe to cup, to plate, like a rapid summary of a whole family of geometric forms. The boy adds the foot, the boy removes the excess, the boy welds on an ornament, the boy stands by like an assistant during one of those perfect acrobatic numbers we see on the stage. And all around a whole choir is intent on feeling the great green bubbles quiver, settle, and marbleize under their breath. At inter-

1. Bus, *Bus* / mod. Autobus Inbus / des. Pininfarina / prod. ATM Milano / 1982.
2. Advertising, *Pubblicità* / prod. Cynar / 1952.
3. Shaker, *Agitatore* / mod. Programma 4 / des. L. Massoni e C. Mazzeri / prod. Alessi / 1956. Shaker, Agitatore / Boston / des. E. Sottsass jr. / prod. Alessi / 1979. Strainer and whisk, *Passino e frullino* / mod. Programma 5 / des. E. Sottsass jr. / prod. Alessi / 1979.

4. Streetcar turning sign, *Segnaletica ingombro tram* / 1975.
5. Coffee grinder and measurer for coffee counter, *Macina dosatore caffè per bar* / mod. MG / prod. Gaggia / 1981.
6. Advertising poster, *Manifesti pubblicitari* / mod. Punt & Mes / des. A. Testa / prod. Carpano / 1960.

vals the boys carry a long scorched pole with finished vessels at the top to be tempered in the furnace. The last little flame is still flickering and sparks shoot off the rod. The bottles are hardening in the oven, and they look like loaves of bread.

Corrado Alvaro, "Itinerario Italiano", Bompiani, Milano 1941. Translated by Ronald Strom.

6

PUNTₑMES
APERITIVO
un punto di amaro e mezzo di dolce

Italian graphic design is perhaps more open to renewal, more frivolous than that of the U.S., Poland, or Germany.

For many years, Italian graphic design followed two parallel roads, one destined for the masses (and therefore full of flashes and large letters spelling "new!"), the other reserved for disinfected graphic artists, with much purer images, sometimes even beautiful, but more often constipated.

The use of photography in advertising has had a lot to give in the past, and still has much to give in the future. But it's also given us a lot of banality. In the last decades of photography, people have forgotten how to draw. Or perhaps more correctly, illustrators have become even more obtusely realistic than photographers. When the real isn't transformed by a genial inspiration, by a clever stupidity, or by a contrived nastiness, it becomes a mere reality, that is, very little.

The return of free-style figurative painting which exploded during the 1980 Venice Biennale after years of conceptualism and servile politicization, will surely be able to inspire advertising design. Those who lead creative lives must be able to shrug things off after a number of years, for example, the cliches and mannerisms that have been produced in them. And the excess of marketing and research can itself limit creativity.

I think that today Italy is ready to take a leap forward to a freer figurative style less burdened by photography of by paraphotography. It's certainly something to hope for.

Armando Testa

Che cosa caratterizza la grafica italiana?
Forse il fatto che è più pronta, più frivola nei rinnovamenti di quanto non lo siano un'America, una Germania o una Polonia.
Per molti anni la grafica italiana ha permesso due strade parallele, una destinata alla massaia (piena quindi di annunci con flash e grandi scritte "nuovo!"), l'altra riservata ai grafici disinfettati, con immagini molto più pure, talora anche belle, ma il più delle volte stitiche.
La fotografia in pubblicità ha donato e molto potrà donare ancora, ma ha anche dato tanta, tanta banalità. In decenni di fotografia la gente ha disimparato a disegnare o meglio sono nati degli illustratori di un verismo ancora più ottuso della fotografia. Quando il vero non è riscattato da una trovata geniale, da una stupidità o da una cattiveria voluta, è solo vero qualunque, cioè poco.
Il ritorno ad un libero figurativo, scoppiato alla Biennale dell'80, dopo anni di concettualità e di servile politicismo, potrà sicuramente ispirare la pubblicità. Chi fa la vita del creativo dopo un certo numero di anni deve sapersi scrollare qualcosa di dosso: i clichés e le maniere che si sono prodotti in lui; lo stesso eccesso di marketing e di ricerche può limitare la creatività.
Penso che oggi l'Italia sia pronta per questo balzo in avanti: una figurazione più libera, meno piegata alla fotografia o al parafotograficismo, è senz'altro da auspicare.

Armando Testa

CAPSULA MODEL
MODELLO CAPSULA

1. Supporting chassis, *Pianale portante.*
2. Body components, *Elementi carrozzeria.*
3. Sedan, *Berlina.*
4. Holiday model, *Spiaggia-vacanza.*
5. School bus, *Scuolabus.*
6. Rescue truck, *Auto di soccorso.*
7. Pick-up truck, *Pick-up.*
8. Light truck, *Furgonetta.*
9. Fire fighting vehicle, *Per anti-incendio.*
10. Ambulance, *Ambulanza.*

With its "capsula" model, Giugiaro offers a decidedly unconventional vehicle consisting of a supporting platform, engine, driveshaft and related parts, gasoline tank, spare wheel, trunk, servobrake, heater, and wing and driving mirrors. The system promoted by "capsula" would enable industry to concentrate on the mass-production of the supporting platform, which would undoubtedly result in proportionately lower costs. Again, varying models of the transmission units made inside or outside the company would diversify the bodies according to market demand.

The mechanical system is based on integrated front-wheel drive, after a scheme invented and patented by Ital Design. What we have here then is a chassis that takes account of what has been going on in the world of motorbuses, a chassis fully equipped and self-sufficient onto which a body is fitted, a "capsule", in a word, designed to meet the particular requirements of the user: whether he needs a sedan for passengers, a commercial vehicle, an industrial vehicle, or whatever.

Thanks to the layout of the mechanical units and related parts on the supporting platform, out of dimensions that measure less than 4 meters

1

2

(3720 mm), an exceptional large useful load was obtained for the driver and passenger compartment: 80% of the total length of the vehicle is given over to space for passengers. Since this model is most decidedly designed for the road and not for "overland" use, Giugiaro was able to take advantage of the ample clearance between floor and road and employ it in expanding the housing for the service areas inside the chassis, setting the distance between the ground and the lowest level of the under-body at a point well within standards.

Italdesign

Col modello "capsula" Giugiaro avanza una proposta decisamente insolita di veicolo costituito da una pianale portante che include il motore, gli organi della trasmissione, il serbatoio del carburante, la ruota di scorta, il bagagliaio, il servofreno, il riscaldatore, i gruppi ottici anteriori e posteriori.
Il sistema promosso dalla "capsula" permetterebbe all'industria di concentrarsi sulla produzione in grande serie del pianale, beneficiando di indubbie economie di scala. Spetterebbe a unità di trasformazione — interne o esterne all'azienda — il compito di diversificare le carrozzerie secondo le richieste di mercato.

La meccanica ipotizzata è una trazione anteriore di tipo integrale secondo lo schema ideato e brevettato in Ital Design. Ispirandosi a quanto avviene nel mondo degli autobus, siamo dunque di fronte a uno chassis completamente attrezzato ed autosufficiente su cui si applica una carrozzeria — una "capsula" appunto — concepita per assolvere alle specifiche esigenze dell'utilizzatore: berlinetta passeggeri oppure veicolo commerciale, veicolo industriale, ecc. In meno di quattro metri di ingombro totale (3720 mm.) grazie alla sitemazione nel pianale degli organi e dei servizi, si è ottenuta un'area utile per la vita nell'ebitacolo

davvero eccezionale: l'80% della lunghezza totale del veicolo è adibita a spazio per l'uomo. Essendo nel nostro caso la destinazione del veicolo decisamente stradale e non "tutto terreno", Giugiaro ha potuto beneficiare dello stacco generoso del pavimento da terra per ricavare tutte le zone di servizio all'interno del telaio, fissando la distanza fra il piano terra e l'ingombro più basso del sotto-scocca a una quota che rientra negli standards.

Italdesign

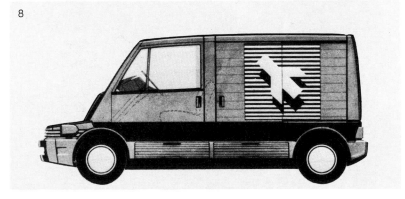

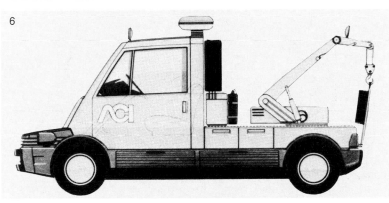

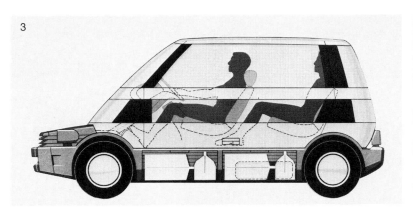

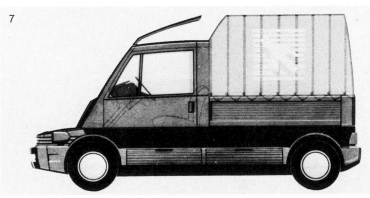

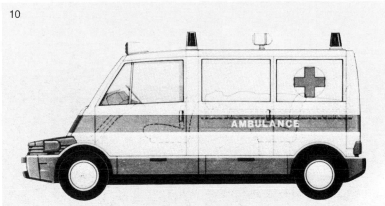

MIDDAY MEAL HOW MANY COURSES?

IF ANYONE CALLS SAY I'M UNAVAILABLE.
ELBOWS DOWN. ELBOWS ON THE TABLE.
CARBOHYDRATE, VEGETARIAN, MACROBIOTHIC, HIGH PROTEIN?
PASS THE PASTA.

A PRANZO LA TOVAGLIA E LE PORTATE

DI LORO CHE NON CI SONO.
GOMITI STRETTI. GOMITI SUL TAVOLO.
PROTEINE, VITAMINE...?
MANGIO LA PASTA.

Alberto Moravia
Two: a phallic novel

Elisa laid the table; and I followed her with my eyes, sinking back in my veneered, unpholstered hip-bath chair. First she covered the top of the table with a flannel undercloth. Then she spread the tablecloth and, as she leant forward, she raised her leg and displayed an unexpectedly round and fleshy calf. Incredible! And 'he' commented: 'I agree she's ugly. But, just for fun, and also partly to annoy your mother, I should like to see what would happen if, for instance, you put your arm round her waist.'

'Shut up, you idiot!'
Elisa opened the sideboard, took out plates, glasses, knives and forks and so on with her white-cotton-gloved hands, and laid two places at the table. Out came the old, well-known carafe of second-grade crystal, with its wide belly and long neck, half full of wine. And a bottle of mineral water, half empty too, with a plastic stopper. Here were the forks and knives and spoons with silver handles and the family initials in florid style, the gift of my grandparents who had in turn received them as a wedding present. The salt-container and pepper-pot of yellow majolica in the form of chickens with little holes in

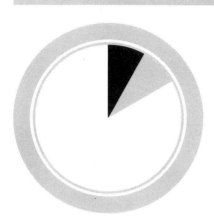

83% eat at home.
17% eat out (self service, etc.).

58% eat pasta every day.
There are many kinds of pasta, Every pasta factory produces 60 to 70 different kinds.

62% drink wine with their meals.
33% drink mineral water every day.

The consumption of mineral water is widely diffused and is the highest in Europe. There is a taste for mineral water similar to that for wine.
264 million pounds of pasta are consumed every year:
North: 115 lbs. each person/year
Central: 165 lbs. each person/year
South and Islands: 270 lbs. each person/year
Time spent on lunch and dinner:

	lunch	dinner
Less than 10 minutes	0.2%	0.2%
11-20 minutes	3.7%	2.7%
21-40 minutes	49.6%	59.2%
41-60 minutes	30,3%	19.4%
61-90 minutes	2%	0.3%
91-120 minutes	0.8%	0.2%

Young people tend to eat later and spend less time at the table. The opposite holds for those over 40. The midday meal remains the main meal.

83% pranza a casa.
17% pranza fuori (bar, mensa, ecc.).

58% mangia tutti i giorni pasta. La pasta è molto diversificata. Ogni pastificio produce in media 60/70 tipi di pasta.

62% beve sempre vino ai pasti.
33% beve acqua minerale tutti i giorni.

Il consumo dell'acqua minerale è il più alto d'Europa. Si registra un diffuso culto dell'acqua, un "palato dell'acqua minerale", analogo a quello, noto, per il vino.
Vengono consumati 12 milioni di quintali l'anno di pasta:
Nord: 55 kg. pro capite/all'anno
Centro: 79 kg. pro capite/all'anno
Sud e isole: 129 kg. pro capite/all'anno
Durata dei pasti di mezzogiorno e sera:

	pranzo	cena
fino a 10 minuti	*0,2%*	*0,2%*
11-20 minuti	*3,7%*	*2,7%*
21-40 minuti	*49,6%*	*59,2%*
41-60 minuti	*30,3%*	*19,4%*
61-90 minuti	*2,0%*	*0,3%*
91-120 minuti	*0,8%*	*0,2%*

La tendenza dei giovani è di ritardare ed economizzare il tempo del pasto.
Sopra i quarant'anni la tendenza è opposta. Il pasto di mezzogiorno resta quello principale.

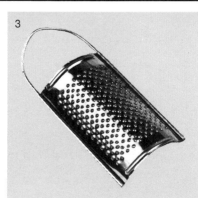

IL SEME DELL'UOMO

1969

MARCO FERRERI

Marco Margine
Anne Wiazenski

their heads. The salad oil-bottle in the same style as the wine carafe.

Elisa, without knowing it, was preparing the place and the instruments of a rite. For my mother was not religious, not in a 'practising' way, except from habit and social duty; her church-going was confined to Sunday mornings. But the rites of the family table, of the social visit, of the theatre, the cinema, the summer holiday and, indeed, of all the things that 'have to be done', constituted, for her, combined and linked together, a kind of bourgeois religion, entirely devoid of any sort of transcendency but not on that account any less carefully observed

and 'practised'. A religion, let me say in parenthesis, marvellously adapted to favour the particular type of sublimation that allowed my mother to keep me in a constant, irreversible state of inferiority.

My mother came in again. In silence she sat down, unfolded her table-napkin, corrected the position of the glasses. Then she raised her eyes and looked at me. At that precise moment I myself was also sitting down: innocently, I was holding a lighted cigarette in my fingers. My mother's eyes were directed, eloquently, at my cigarette. I did not take my place but looked round in search of an ashtray, and failed to

find one. 'Elisa', said my mother, 'give Signor Rico an ashtray.' Elisa did as she was told: I stubbed out my cigarette in the ashtray, sat down, and then, naturally, said the one thing that I ought not to have said: 'And Sabina – where is she?'

'I dismissed her.'

'Why? Wasn't she doing well?'

At this moment Elisa came in again, holding a small soup-tureen. My mother helped herself; then I did the same. A small tangle of yellowish spaghetti, shining with butter, lay at the bottom of the tureen. My mother had a delicate stomach; in her house, no sauce with the spaghetti. I put a couple

of forkfuls of this anaemic, nursing-home spaghetti into my bowl, sprinkled over it some cheese, also yellowish, taking it from the old-fashioned glass cheese-dish. My mother did not start eating, she was waiting until Elisa had left the room. Then, at last, she replied: 'Sabina – she was doing extremely well. But you wouldn't leave her alone. It was all very well to look at her; but to telephone her, to make appointments! And not outside the house, but here, in my own house, as you did this morning!'

'I never did such a thing. If it was Sabina who told you that, well, Sabina was lying.'

4

5

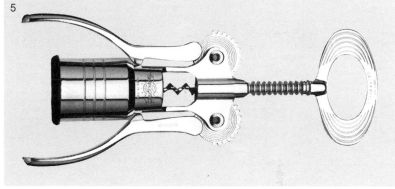

7

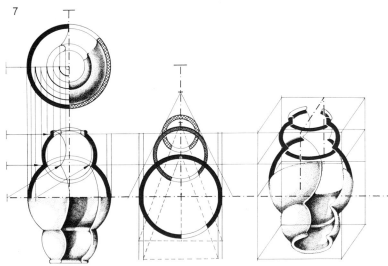

6

1. Cutlery, *Posate* / des. C. Scarpa / prod. C. Munari / 1977.
2. Oil-cruet, *Oliera*.
3. Grater, *Grattugia*.
4. Dining table, *Tavolo* / mod. Il Colonnato / des. M. Bellini / prod. Cassina / 1977.
5. Corkscrew, *Cavatappi* / mod. Big Miro / des. T. Campagnolo / prod. Campagnolo / 1978.
6. Flask, *Fiasco*.
7. Pasta, *Pasta* / mod. Conchiglia / drawing executed by G.P. Bodino.

'Sabina was *not* lying and she did *not* tell me.'

'Then how d'you come to be so sure?'

'It was present when you telephoned. Sabina handed me the receiver. I listened and heard you say you would come an hour early this morning on purpose to be with her. You thought you were speaking to Sabina, instead of which you were speaking to me. So I dismissed her, apologizing to her, and took on Elisa.'

Alberto Moravia, "Io e lui", Bompiani, Milano 1971. "Two: a phallic novel", Farrar, Straus & Giroux, New York 1972. Translated by William Weaver.

Carmelo Samonà
Brothers

It all begins with the way we move around the places we live, how we place ourselves.

When my brother moves through a space, it becomes larger and more hollow, stressed with uncertain rhythms. For him, a room can be a desert where he risks getting lost or, vice versa, a prison so close that he flounders like a crippled bird. Author of impulses which, at first sight, seem contradictory, he is subject to sudden shifts in mood which take him by surprise and then just as quickly abandon him to dissolve in periods of strange calm. He has two distinct rhythms and forms of behavior. In one, he leaps high up in the air, either whirling around over one spot, or else skirting the walls of the room, always in the same direction, describing the perimeter a hundred times or more, while with the backs of his hands or his finger-tips, he executes precise rituals on various parts of his face, particularly his eyes. In the second, he appears to be more concentrated and abstract, but he still moves around, mostly privileging a single object (usually meaningless to me) with countless, nearly imperceptible attempts to inspect it with his tactile, olfactory, and visual senses.

There doesn't seem to be any rule to these movements. Perhaps my brother is the occasional victim of a foreign presence which he bears patiently, at the same time interpreting its whims with his body. Watching him closely, however, I can see that his gestures are produced by a mysterious yearning. I suspect that his infinite repetitions, his leaping and whirling, his occasional words, sketch the air with cartoons which he animates all by himself. Maybe he does control his illness, making it conform to his will, humbling it into an uninterrupted performance. Through it all, there seems to be a firm,

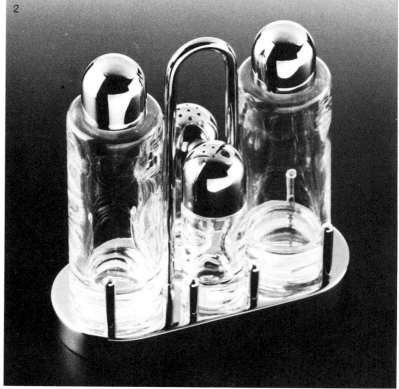

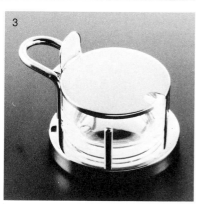

1. Coffee-pot, *Caffettiera* / prod. Bulgari / 1982.
2.3. Condiments server (oil, vinegar, salt and pepper), Grated Cheese server, *Servizio Olio-Aceto-Sale-Pepe, Formaggera* / mod. Programma 5 / des. E. Sottsass jr. / prod. Alessi / 1978.
4. Tea-Pot, *Teiera* / des. F. Albini-F. Helg / prod. San Lorenzo / 1972.
5. Carafe-Glasses, *Caraffa, Bicchieri* / mod. Casanova / prod. Venini / 1976.
6. Chair, *Sedia* / mod. Irma / des. A. Castiglioni / prod. Zanotta / 1979.
7. Chair, *Sedia* / mod. CAB / des. M. Bellini / prod. Cassina / 1977.

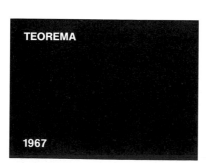

TEOREMA

1967

PIER PAOLO PASOLINI

Terence Stamp
Anne Wiazenski

feverish desire to replace something lost. His refusal of whatever I see as concrete corresponds to his own elaboration of an alternative reality. Provoked by a moment of rapture or concentration, his body sprouts little aleatory universes where he sometimes transfers himself for long periods of time, and where I sometimes have the privilege of joining him. We usually call these the Long Trips (to distinguish them from the normal movements between one point and another in the house, the Short Trips which, as opposed to the Long Trips, offer an immediate benefit, a profit). Even though the routes and the relative destinations don't change much, their variations are unpredictable and the ways of realizing them are infinite.

Our most common fantasies are of living underground or in the air. But not in airplanes or in elaborate bunkers. Instead, in huts suspeded in emptiness, casually furnished rooms between imaginary skies, and in shafts and holes which we can only have dug beneath us with our fingernails, with tenacity. You could say that, during the trip, my brother has no notion of the horizontal, nor of the plane over which we move, but only of an *above* or a *below*. These he conquers vertically, tracing elevations and the lines of precipices at certain points on the floor or in the air.

We live in these new spaces at intervals, immersed in a laborious solitude. It's like a house within a house, a time within a time. We have no common units of measurement, there's no short and no long, no minutes, no hours, no calculated understanding. We start out united but, naturally, our gestures are inspired by different intentions. Adhering to the earth is a continual effort for my brother. He moves to penetrate it, or he passes through air to reach the new headquarters he's decided to occupy. I pretend to encourage him so that I can study his behavior from close up.

Observing the sequence of his movements, I follow him at a distance. Sometimes I pull him to a stop and offer him concrete solutions in the hope that he'll return with me, to my horizontal world, stable and flat.

Carmelo Samonà, "Fratelli", Einaudi, Torino 1979. Translated by Robert Kleyn.

I think that a well-designed object should last indefinitely; it should become a prototype that can always be taken up again and not something subject to fashion.

A shortage of materials and the impossibility of providing maintenance will lead more and more to the abandonment of a tendency prevailing in the last two decades: the production of "throw-away", easily replaceable objects. Industry will be catering to an ever more impoverished but at the same time more sophisticated society. Though long used to enjoying highly sophisticated collective and scientific services, everyone in this society will know that he can no longer find this type of sophistication as a private citizen. Consequently, he will seek a striking image and great simplicity, so as to exclude or limit as far as possible the need for maintenance or for a replacement, which economically would be an impossible proposition. I think the moment has come for us to say: before, we used to think that what is useful is beautiful; now we know that what is beautiful is useful.

Vico Magistretti

Io penso che un oggetto di buon disegno debba durare sempre, debba poter diventare un archetipo sempre proponibile e non un oggetto di moda. Scarsa reperibilità dei materiali ed impossibilità di manutenzione porteranno sempre più all'esclusione di una tendenza dei due decenni passati, quella del throw-away, dell'oggetto deperibile perché facilmente sostituibile. Ci si rivolgerà ad una società sempre più povera e, contemporaneamente sempre più sofisticata.

Questa società, abituata a fruire di servizi collettivi o scientifici di grande sofisticazione e tecnologia saprà di non poter ritrovare nel privato lo stesso tipo di sofisticazione e vorrà oggetti di forte immagine e di grande semplicità tali cioè da escludere o limitare al massimo la necessità di una manutenzione ormai impossibile o di una rapida sostituzione economicamente improponibile. Credo sia forse arrivato il momento di dire: prima pensavamo che è bello ciò che è utile, ora sappiamo che è utile ciò che è bello.

Vico Magistretti

6

7

GLASSES
BICCHIERI

The glass came into being immediately after the use of the hands in the shape of a cup and the invention of the wooden bowl as an answer to the essential problem of drinking.

A fundamental stage in the history of the glass was passed only in the second half of the 18th century: an extremely light glass was invented. It was blown and completely made by hand. This was a glass hot-decorated with garlands, flowers, and colored tracings. With the end of the 18th century, and the advent of the earliest mechanical processes in glass-making, a product came about whose cost enabled all social classes to enjoy it, for it was priced at several levels in accordance with the finishing and general quality. Today a glass made of crystal or of plain glass can be considered a generally used article with no more mysteries about it. Even today, a glass can be manufactured in various ways. It can be pressed or produced with an automatic blowing process, starting with a continuous tank of glass, with multiple die machines producing thousands of pieces an hour with, of course, only a limited possibility of producing variants. Glasses can also be made by hand, using rather complex and highly advanced types of dies, or semi-

automatic burn — off machines with either machine or hand — made finishings. In this way an average-level product can be made in which one can still find strangely-shaped decorative embroidery and even individually decorated glasses. High quality products are thus produced displaying a creative variety which is both striking and repeatable. Then there are glasses which are made literally "by hand". Unfortunately, glassblowers using this technique are becoming rare; they can be found chiefly at Murano and in artisan settlements.

Ludovico de Santillana

Il bicchiere nasce subito dopo l'uso delle mani a coppa e delle ciotole in legno per risolvere il problema essenziale del bere. È dapprima in legno, poi in pietra. Come spesso accade agli oggetti essenziali, di base, il bicchiere verrà anche adoperato come oggetto celebrativo, prezioso, come dono e simbolo.

Una tappa fondamentale nella storia del bicchiere è superata solo nella seconda metà del XIII secolo: viene inventato il bicchiere leggerissimo. Soffiato e realizzato interamente a mano. È un bicchiere decorato a caldo con ghirlande, fiori e fili di colore.

L'avvento infine alla fine dell'ottocento delle prime lavorazioni meccaniche, ripropone un prodotto il cui costo permette oramai a tutte le classi sociali la sua utilizzazione a diversi livelli di prezzo per finitura e perfezione qualitativa. Oggi il bicchiere in vetro e in cristallo rappresenta un prodotto senza più misteri e di uso totalmente universale.

Peraltro ancora oggi il bicchiere si può produrre in vari modi. Si fanno bicchieri in pressatura o in soffiaggio completamente automatico, a partire da bacini di vetro a fusione continua, con macchine a stampi multipli che realizzano migliaia di pezzi all'ora con naturalmente una limitata possibilità di varianti. Si fanno anche bicchieri a mano con l'uso di stampi anche complessi e perfezionati, di scalottatrici semi-automatiche, e con finiture a macchina o a mano — realizzando quel prodotto medio in cui può ancora essere ricamata la forma strana, la decorazione individuale. Vengono così realizzati dei prodotti di qualità spesso eccellente, di una varietà creativa vivace e rinnovabile. Si fanno infine dei bicchieri interamente "a mano". Purtroppo questa tecnica è sempre più rara: concentrata essenzialmente a Murano e nelle zone artigiane.

Ludovico de Santillana

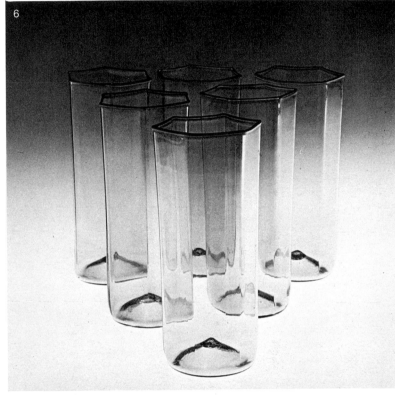

THE PIAZZA
OBSESSIVE FOUNTAINS

SHOP FRONTS METAL SHUTTERED.
TRAFFIC TRUCE... BUT NOT FOR
LONG.
PIGEONS SCAN THE PAVEMENTS.
CHIAROSCURO.
MAPS ARE UNFOLDED AT STREET
CORNERS.

PIAZZA
LE FONTANELLE OSSESSIVE

SARACINESCE GIÙ.
TRAFFICO... BREVE INTERMEZZO.
L'INDAGINE DEL PICCIONE.
CHIAROSCURO.
LA CITTÀ IN TESTA LA MAPPA IN TASCA.

Guido Piovene
Voyage in Italy

Turin
"When you get to the big street, call out." Who said that? A clown? No, he's an ordinary man in the streets of Turin. I asked him for directions. The 'big street' is Corso Roma, and 'call out' means ask somebody there. If I had to describe Turin in only a few words, I'd say it was French, Jesuitical, riverain and mountaineer. As a paradox, I'd add gracious, mannered, and affected. The Piemontese are said to be polite liars, but this is completely untrue, they are sincere. This saying could stem from a sharp, thorny side to their character. French is the order of the streets, squares, porticos, dominated by the grace, reason, and fussiness of the seventeen hundreds. The Jesuitical element brings along something that isn't quite Spanish, but proud. I'm thinking of the churches and that the most beautiful of them houses the Holy Shroud. The baroque of Turin is just and secure, welthy but not intoxicated with its wealth, it's not whimsical, theatrical, or foolish. It's a formal style honoring God, the sign of a religion intended as a serious public duty, but always discreet, convinced, and well-behaved. In these Turin churches, I

All stores close from 12.30 to 3.00 p.m. Coffee bars and restaurants stay open later or throughout the day. Otherwise, when the population stops work, stores close.
The traditional fragmented structure of retailing with its large number of small speciality stores has prevented the development of large-scale retail centers.

Average time of midday intermission in different occupational categories
hours

	hours
Businessmen, professional men, executives, managerial staff	2.30
Store owners, sales clerks, artisans	1.44
Office workers	1.20
Factory workers	1.24
Self-employed farmers	1.23
Agricultural workers	1.15
Miscellaneous workers	1.34

Dalle ore 12,30 alle ore 15,00 tutti i negozi sono chiusi.
Fatta eccezione per i bar, i ristoranti e le trattorie che adottano un orario più lungo o continuato. Quando la popolazione non lavora l'attività commerciale si ferma.
La struttura distributiva è parcellizzata in punti di vendita specializzati, di piccole dimensioni, capillarmente dislocati negli aggregati urbani.
Tali condizioni non hanno favorito lo sviluppo dei centri di vendita pluricommerciali, ad alto livello di concentrazione, come in altri paesi industrializzati.

Durata media dell'intervallo di mezzogiorno nelle diverse attività professionali
ore

	ore
Imprenditori, liberi professionisti, dirigenti, impiegati di concetto	*2,30*
esercenti, negozianti, artigiani	*1,44*
impiegati non di concetto	*1,20*
operai specializzati, operai generici	*1,24*
agricoltori in proprio	*1,23*
agricoltori dipendenti	*1,15*
condizioni non professionali	*1,34*

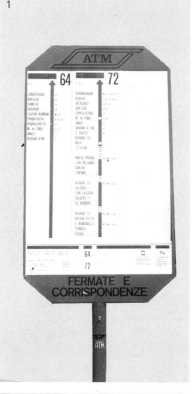

1

2

3

LE OCCASIONI DI ROSA

1981

SALVATORE PISCICELLI

Marina Suma

experienced that special narcosis associated with a dazzling neatness. The tomb of the Savoia family in Superga is like a tiny convent, narcotically funereal with its gold, its marble, its statues. It radiates a magnificent *cupio dissolvi*, a religious nihilism that, during the ultimate phase of this royal family, has become shrunken and secular, cynical and mean in its realism. But the panorama from Superga counteracts this feeling. The last time I was there, an orange sunset glowed behind the crown of mountains. The city's domes and the mountains in the background were flat black silhouettes against that fantastic color and appeared to be equally far away. The River Po shone at me, the slopes were sprayed with snow, and the entire landscape expressed a modesty characteristic of mountain people, the rustic mixed with the elegant. Turin could well be the most hybrid of all Italian cities.

The hybrid character, however, doesn't depend on external forces, but comes from an innately rigid and contradictory character. Turin is more modern than Milan in its industrial and social development. But some of its museums are so strictly kept that they seem almost private collections rather than public endowments. The Egyptian Museum in particular is run like the property of a selfish man more interested in keeping his collection to himself than in showing it to the public. Even in the streets you can see the hybrid character of Turin. The stores full of mannequins and orthopedic devices reach a conspicuous strangeness (you could call it surrealistic), in the context of that regular, right-angled unity. Some of the barber shops with their wood paneling, never redecorated, look exactly like drugstores. And like the drugstores of the nineteenth century, they are sanctuaries for gossip. The pastry shops which have made Turin famous for over two centuries, tend to look like drugstores (or funeral parlors) in their elegant austerity. Often, I've stood enraptured before those windows in their heavy wood frames decorated in gold, gold writing on the glass. Displayed behind those mournful windows were precious pastries shining like jewels, flaky baskets of candied fruits, food fit for a king, golden cones filled with whipped cream and dusted with cocoa! Then, turning around, I saw a thin mist blowing through the streets, a mist that must be called by the French name *voile*, a mist that softens faces and sweetens the lights. But the people of Turin are also slow, heavy, as thoughtful as book-keepers, alien in

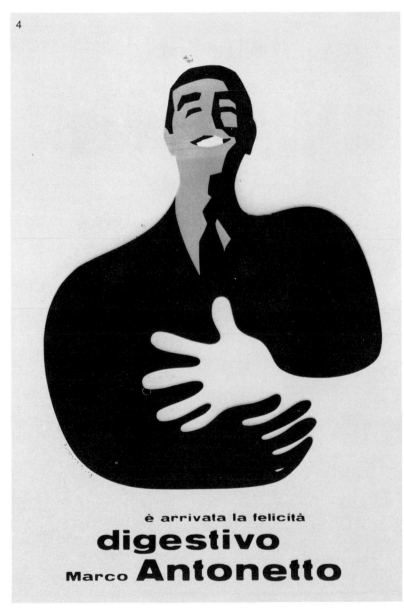

è arrivata la felicità
digestivo
Marco **Antonetto**

1. Bus schedule, *Fermata mezzi pubblici* / prod. A.T.M.
2. Telephone booth, *Cabina telefonica* / prod. SIP / 1960.
3. Coffee machine, *Macchina caffè* / mod. Prestige P6 / prod. Faema / 1974.
4. Advertising poster, *Pubblicità* / mod. Digestivo Antonetto / des. A. Testa / prod. Antonetto / 1961.
5.6. Lock, *Antifurto* / mod. Tuo / des. Ufficio Tecnico / prod. Viro Innocenti / 1981.
7. Motorcycle parking, *Parcheggio motocicli* / des. D. Città / 1981.

their gestures and abstractness, religious in a strictly private way, lacking theatricality, resistant to the opinions of others, stingy by consensus. And if they feel admiration for something, they'd rather keep it to themselves instead of expressing it in applause. Turin has more opinions than ideas, as opposed to the rest of Italy which is thick with ideas while opinions are sparse. They prefer their meat boiled, many kinds of meat, as long as it's lean. The French despise this regional dish which is at the same time the most rustic and refined of foods, the true food of critics, since its very sincerity doesn't allow for any pretense, and a fine palate can distinguish a hundred degrees of perfection. Not really of the Po region, the people of Turin are pushed towards the French, the rococo, towards face powder. Some areas are famous for their thin, wiry men of inflexible opinions, intransigence, and moral consistency, notoriously touchy, intractable and irascible, men who mince, wheedle, smile and blush coyly, eccentric as nuns or little ladies. And everywhere you go, boiled meat and cream-filled pastries dusted with cocoa. That hybrid (but never false) character is reflected in the vision of the city, endowing it with the attraction of those little Chinese boxes one inside the next, an attraction not found elsewhere in Italy.

Piemonte, as everyone knows, is the home of Italian unification. Even more than in Lombardy where nationalism is no less strong, the unification of Italy has created a curious conflict in the soul of Piemonte. Mentor to the rest of Italy, it supplied the model civil service. The Piemonte bureaucracy was like a father who controls the accounts, keeps inexperienced and ambitious sons from straying, demands honesty, sets limits, and correctly evaluates the existing realities. Because of this, Piemonte possesses all the virtues so disliked by those who lack them, the virtues of the military officer, the public official, the teacher, the virtues of age. Not to forget honesty, competence, the sense of duty understood as service and so never questioned or subject to personal opinions, tastes, or the prestige to be gained, obeying the demands of principles, and demanding to be obeyed.

Naples

The only way left to see a living metropolis of the ancient world is to plunge into the heart of Naples, Spaccanapoli, the poor part of the city, for example. Not even Rome offers such a striking example. I mean, of course, life rather

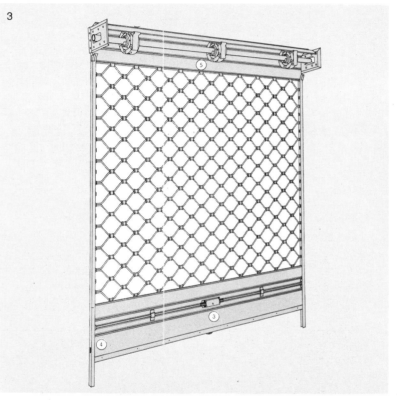

1. Pneumatic air pump, *Pistola gonfiaggio pneumatici* / mod. 25E / prod. ANI / 1979.
2. Water fountain, *Fontanella Acea* / mod. Roma / prod. Fonderia Carnevale.
3. Store Shutter, *Serranda* / mod. Onda / prod. Pastore / 1982.
4. Flagstone, *Sampietrini* / prod. Lombarda Graniti.
5.6.7. Bar table, *Tavolo bar* / mod. Cumano / des. A. Castiglioni / prod. Zanotta / 1979.
8. Ferry Dock, *Pontile traghetti* / des. G. Cittato / prod. Azienda Trasporti Venezia / 1977.

GLI ITALIANI SI VOLTANO

1953

ALBERTO LATTUADA

than style. Everything is strangely fore-shortened, as if seen through a telescope – oblique stairways, shrines, churches, baroque obelisks. There are even shrines set back in the courtyards of apartment buildings, decorated by the laundry hung out to dry. As is wellknown, the people of Naples place their trust in the holy, and one of the obstacles to the restoration of monumental churches is the many houses built right onto the churches themselves, against the chapels, sometimes even on the roofs. Here you buy octopus or octopus broth, the cheapest of all hot drinks since it costs only ten lire. Here you'll find fried food

shops and stands where you can pass the time with crunchy morsels. Some girls piece together artificial flowers in their dingy groundfloor room while an antique dealer watches from the door of his shop. Those with money to spare are eating pizza, breadsticks with pasta inside, cheese, omelettes, beans. Children swarm everywhere, poor little things. Even most people who can afford to eat in restaurants are surrounded by their children. Naples is a maternal city suckling its children, continually pregnant. For the common people of Naples, love is a demigod that redeems itself through procreation. The city's poverty has its vices,

but one vice that's always missing there is incest, the scourge of other cities. In Naples, love of the family and its blood run too deep.

You can only guess how many people live in this teeming city, maybe around 300,000. The upper classes long ago emigrated to the waterfront and the hillsides, leaving their empty, desolated homes behind them. Much has been written about the 'bassi', the homes of so many poor people. Entire families live in these dwellings, crowded into a single ground-floor space which serves them as living room, bedroom, workshop, and store. The crowded conditions and the lack of

bathrooms means that everything is thrown into the streets which is also where the laundry is hung up to dry. Sleeping only a few hours, staying outside as much as possible both night and day, that perpetual street life so important to Naples, is often the result of these awful living conditions. But it will take time to rebuild Naples, and Draconian measures won't help.

Guido Piovene, "Viaggio in Italia", Mondadori, Milano 1957. Translated by Robert Kleyn.

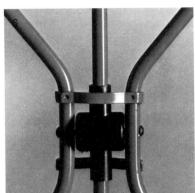

Thinking about a plan for the urban environment today implies a rejection of all hedonistic rhetoric regarding an "improvement in the quality of living" and the negation of the plan as a way to solve the esthetic problems of urban society. Planning the urban environment means to accept the notion that it involves everything that one sees of the city itself, the whole of its construction units. The types of constructions concerned in the project are: those to be considered of historical interest, and as such subject to preservation programs; those which it is still possible to use but which, for productional reasons, it is no longer possible to carry on and which, as such, should be kept up only until their productive cycle runs out; those which are in general no longer suitable and therefore should be eliminated; and those with characteristics generally suitable for the varied requirements of the town and which as such, should be expanded and planned in respect to their cycles of production, use, and maintenance. From this type of census/card-indexing it is possible to derive a list of overall requirements which could guide one in the planning of new products.

Enzo Mari

Pensare oggi al progetto dell'arredo urbano implica il rifiuto di ogni retorica edonistica sul "miglioramento della qualità della vita", la negazione del progetto come risoluzione ai problemi estetici della realtà urbana. Al contrario progettare arredo urbano significa acquisire la nozione che esso è tutto ciò che si vede della città stessa, l'insieme dei manufatti.
Le tipologie dei manufatti interessati al progetto sono: quelli da considerare come persistenze di interesse storico, e come tali soggetti ad un'opera di conservazione; quelli di cui è ancora possibile l'utilizzazione ma che per ragioni produttive non è più possibile perpetuare, e come tali vanno mantenuti finché non si esaurisca il loro ciclo produttivo; quelli complessivamente inadeguati e quindi da eliminare; infine quelli con caratteristiche generali adeguate alle diverse esigenze, e come tali da estendere e da pianificare nel loro ciclo produzione-uso-manutenzione. Da questo tipo di censimento/schedatura è possibile derivare anche l'elenco dei requisiti complessivi che facciano da guida nella progettazione di nuovi prodotti.

Enzo Mari

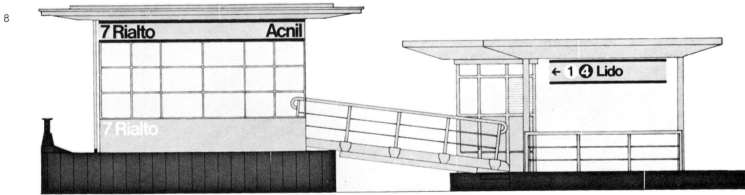

BACK AT WORK JUST AS IT WAS

POMERIGGIO DEL LAVORO

PERSISTENZA DEGLI OGGETTI

Carlo Emilio Gadda
Moonlit night

THE HAND IS THE TOOL.
EACH OFFICE A KINGDOM.
TIME AND SYSTEMS.

LA MANO ATTREZZO.
OGNI UFFICIO UN REAME.
TEMPI E METODI.

Some are wearing broad trousers of homespun, almost a rough velvet, which then taper at the ankles; others are in shorts, with leggings or heavy stockings well and maternally made, and they dart off on their bicycles, head bowed, as if thinking: "and to hell with those who can't stomach me." Those who proceed on foot wear a poor little jacket on their back, sweating still in the evening: thirsting miners, breakers of the ancient rocks. The hands of the former are yellow, or earth-color, and, inside, callused. The hands of the latter are pink, as if an acid had skinned the palm: it's lime, the stone. The dyers, thanks to the chloride, and the apprentice butchers, to the salt, have swollen hands that sweat perennially in the palm. In some gaunt faces, bronzed, amid the hairs of a beard, on the wrinkles of the not-yet-pensionable skin, a spatter of lime, a white mole, has remained. The smiths, the mechanics, the drivers sometimes wear an overall of blue duck, but now blackened by soot and filings, with broad grease-stains; and their face is grimmer than the foremen's. But it is less thin, and obviously when washed, it may reappear fuller. Youths descend-

The Italian economy is based on a network of small and middle-size industries which are extremely versatile and productive.
There are:
63,000 small businesses (11-100 employees)
6,000 medium-sized businesses (100-500 employees).
These account for 51.4% on the GNP.
Over half of the output of Italian industry comes from small and medium-sized firms.

L'economia italiana è massicciamente sostenuta ed alimentata da un fitto tessuto di piccole e medie imprese estremamente vitali e dinamiche. 63 mila piccole imprese (tra gli 11 e i 100 addetti), 6 mila medie imprese (tra i 100 e i 500 addetti) producono il 51,4% del prodotto nazionale lordo industriale. Oltre la metà del prodotto dell'industria italiana è appannaggio della piccola e media industria.

Occupational distribution:

		Distribuzione percentuale della popolazione sul lavoro:	
Businessmen, managers, professionals	1.3%	imprenditori, dirigenti, liberi professionisti	1,3%
Office workers	8.8%	impiegati	8,8%
Sales clerks, artisans, store owners	9.8%	commercianti, artigiani, esercenti	9,8%
Farmers	3.4%	agricoltori	3,4%
Teachers	2.7%	insegnanti	2,7%
Students	7.2%	studenti	7,2%
Factory workers	19.9%	operai	19,9%
Farm labourers	2.3%	braccianti	2,3%
Housewives	26.4%	casalinghe	26,4%
Unemployed and pensioners	18.2%	altri non occupati e pensionati	18,2%

IL CASO MATTEI

1962

FRANCESCO ROSI

Gian Maria Volonté

ed from the scaffoldings and catwalks, face all whitened by the dusting of plaster, are like Pierrot in the pallor of the moon, like befloured millers. You rarely encounter obese, chubby masons. In the adolescents, when you look at them, the length and thickness of forearm and wrist are amazing, compared to the still-frail chest. Suspenders, rare, mostly prove rather old, and sweaty; or wrinkled, scrofulous; and they are affected by reparatory complications of strings and laces, which have fairly complex relationships with surviving buttons. But there are those who, like the well-off, like a favorite of Fortune, have quite broad, rubber suspenders, new, taut as a slingshot, which usually adhere in every movement, in every instant, to the warm and vigorous committment of the chest to the toil of the job.

Heavy shoes! the masons and the country workers, with spikes in the heel and all around the sole, which screech on the pavement and on the stones; and some are lost along the way, to puncture the cyclists's tires. Because each, as he goes on, happens to leave some testimony of his going and his being, and he is unaware of it. Good shoes, or sometimes less good, or shabby; and if the sole is worn, a bit of flesh then replaces that patch of sole that is lacking. The mechanics wear little cyclists's shoes, light and slim as slippers, but held up by leather thongs. Others are without heels: it is a known fact that their footwear, once shined, at the outset performed the happy Sunday duties, in the display of the festival, or in the brief pomp of the dance; then, as the feast day is followed by the working days, so in approaching and attacking work, their heavy, rough-muscled feet have distorted the original elegance of the sheath. The heel has dwindled to nothing, and at the level of the little toe, the tip has come loose from the upper, as if through a hernia of the horny foot.

Women and girls go by; and for some of them, on occasion, the men or youths turn and murmur among themselves what they think or what it seems their duty to desire. They walk and laugh; and, turning, the boldest stumbles. Now and then one may cast a glance that a girl meekly collects; and then, walking on he admits to his spirit a kind of hope and a consoling sweetness, after the tired hours.

Carlo Emilio Gadda, "L'Adalgisa", Einaudi, Torino 1974. Translated by William Weaver.

1. Racing-saddle, *Sella da corsa* / mod. 300 gr. / prod. Pariani / 1906.
2. Jug, *Caraffa per liquidi* / mod. Umbro.
3. Water pitcher, Orcio per acqua / mod. Marchigiano.
4. Vase, *Vaso* / mod. argento e Rodonite / des. G. De Vecchi / prod. Calderoni.
5. Silver vase, *Vaso d'argento* / des. G. De Vecchi / prod. De Vecchi.
6. Jug with plate, *Brocca con piatto* / des. B. Gambone / prod. Gambone / 1970.
7. Bicycle, *Bicicletta* / mod. Laser / des. Gabella / prod. Cinelli / 1982.

1. Bottom bracket shells in cast steel, *Scatole movimento microfuse in acciaio* / prod. Cinelli.
2. Handle bends, *Curve manubrio* / prod. Cinelli.
3. Saddle, *Sella* / prod. Cinelli.
4.5. Handle bar attack, *Attacco manubrio* / mod. Domino / prod. Cinelli.
6. Racing bicycle shoe and pedal junction, *Scarpetta bici e attacco al pedale* / prod. Cinelli.

In the beginning it was a matter of mutual attraction. On the one hand a man who loved bicycle riding, on the other a bicycle that gave everything it could. In the middle, the limts of the mechanical object. And it is precisely at this point that attraction turns into passion. Once we have discovered the limits, we immediately want to eliminate them, get rid of them and to make this well-beloved mechanical object a thing of perfection. What about the wheels? Too big. There are no cobble-stones to negotiate with every push of the pedal. Let's make the wheels smaller, that way they'll be sturdier. And while we're at it, let's fix up the line of these tubes, make this bicycle a little more maneuverable and maybe a little lighter, too. But once the front has been touched up, its the turn of the details; of each piece examined by itself and then fitted back into the whole, because while each item works by itself, it's also got to work with all the others. It's high technology that plays the main role. Its turn has come. To get where no one else has ever been before, thanks to materials of great purty worked like precious objects. In the life of every Cinelli handlebar, saddle, frame, fork, and microfused component there comes an essential moment never to be repeated. It is moment when instruments and machinery are finally put aside and two hands take command of all those parts, thereby carrying out the last act of the metamorphosis. For in those two hands, the mechanical "piece" achieves perfection. It is a gesture at once old and new each time, something full of love and yet severe; it is either a victory or a defeat. Above all, it is an irrevocable judgement. Time after time those two hands make a Cinelli bicycle a splendid piece of craftsmanship.

Antonio Colombo

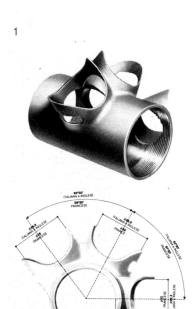

MODELLO	38		39		40		42				B	C
MISURA (mm)	A	D	A	D	A	D	A	D	A	D		
MOD. 63 *Campione del mondo*	380	220			400	240					147	76
MOD. 64 *Giro d'Italia*	380	220			400	240					142	78
MOD. 65 *Criterium*	380	120			400	140					147	77
MOD. 66 *Campione del mondo*	380	210			400	230	420	250			156	90
MOD. 67 *Pista*			390	108							163	83

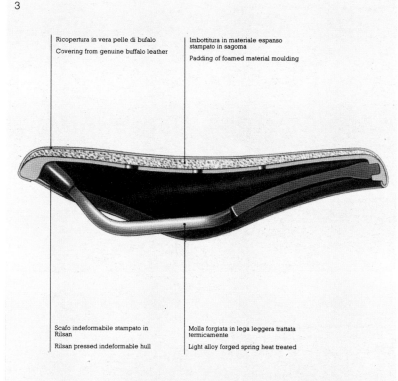

Ricopertura in vera pelle di bufalo
Covering from genuine buffalo leather

Imbottitura in materiale espanso stampato in sagoma
Padding of foamed material moulding

Scafo indeformabile stampato in Rilsan
Rilsan pressed indeformable hull

Molla forgiata in lega leggera trattata termicamente
Light alloy forged spring heat treated

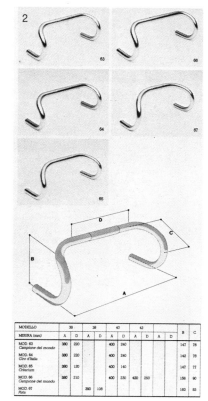

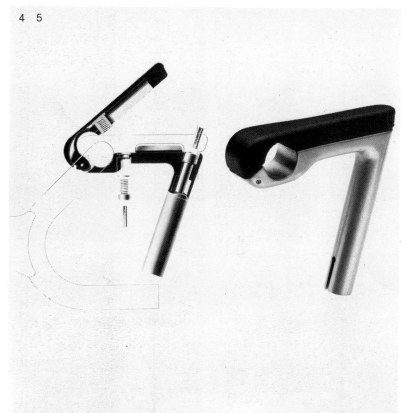

All'inizio è stato un fatto di reciproca attrazione. Da una parte un uomo che amava andare in bicicletta, dall'altra una bicicletta che dava tutto quello che poteva. In mezzo, i limiti dell'oggetto meccanico. È proprio a questo punto che l'attrazione si trasforma in passione.

Una volta scoperti i limiti, nasce la voglia di cancellarli, di toglierli di mezzo e di fare dell'oggetto meccanico così amato un oggetto perfetto.

Le ruote? Troppo grosse queste ruote. Non c'è più l'acciottolato da affrontare ad ogni pedalata. Facciamole più piccole queste ruote, così sono anche più robuste. E già che ci siamo ridiamo una sistemata anche all'angolatura dei tubi, facciamola più manovrabile questa bicicletta e magari anche più leggera. Ma una volta rifatta la faccia, arriva il turno dei particolari; del mezzo esaminato singolarmente e poi rimesso nel tutto, perché ogni cosa funzioni sì da sola, ma soprattutto insieme alle altre. È l'alta tecnologia che gioca il ruolo principale. È il suo turno. Arrivare dove mai nessuno è arrivato prima grazie a materiali purissimi lavorati come oggetti preziosi. Nella vita di ogni manubrio, sella, telaio, forcella, componente microfuso Cinelli c'è un momento essenziale e irripetibile. È il momento in cui, messi finalmente da parte strumenti e macchinari, due mani si appropriano di loro e compiono l'ultimo atto della metamorfosi. Fra quelle due mani, il "pezzo" meccanico diventa il "pezzo" perfetto. È un gesto vecchio e nuovo ogni volta, amoroso e severo, è una vittoria oppure una sconfitta. È soprattutto un giudizio irrevocabile. Queste due mani fanno ogni volta di un pezzo Cinelli un pregiatissimo pezzo d'artigianato.

Antonio Colombo

WORKING PHASES
FASI DI LAVORAZIONE
7. Milling of the frame's tubes, *Sgolatura dei tubi del telaio*.
8. Working of the lugs, *Lavorazione delle giunzioni*.
9. Fork-blades bending, *Curvatura foderi forcella*.
10. Bottom bracket shell brazing process, *Brasatura scatola movimenti*.
11. Frame-control, *Controllo del telaio*.
12. Leather-cutting for the saddle, *Taglio della pelle per la sella*.
13. Handle-bar bending, *Curvatura del manubrio*.
14. Balancing the wheels, *Centraggio delle ruote*.

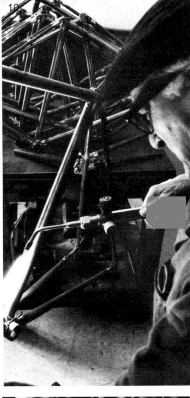

Ottiero Ottieri
The man at the gate

Tuesday

"Oh, no one ever comes here, Doctor. You're much better off in the administration wing," grinned the foreman of the cellulosing section; and at once ready to conduct me – his colleague, guest, superior: he seemed uncertain which – round his department.

We watched the little frames of the calculators, like tiny motor-cars, sliding along the conveyor on their complicated course, during which they are cellulosed, coated with enamel, dried, recellulosed and finally dried again by the heat of very powerful lamps.

We passed the ovens; we went round the inferior work of a non-mechanical kind; and paused at the electrolytic vessels into which the parts are plunged for plating with nickel of chromium. My guide bestowed on them a slight grimace of contempt, although he was careful to explain them to me, being proud of the chemical complexity of the processes.

For a while we stopped behind the men who were preparing small parts for immersion in the vats. Each part had to be slipped on to the wire dipping-frames, and the men, seated before them, worked at a great rate, hooking one after another on to one row after another, from left to right and from the top downwards, as though filling a page with writing. The foreman glanced at me. He was aware that these workers do not find their job interesting, but this does not worry him overmuch; whereas we, of the personnel office, are accustomed to regard it as one well suited for psycho-social study and research.

When one frame is finished, it is lifted off, packed and jingling with parts, and another begun. Nowadays, the frames are moved vertically by a pedal, in other words they can be raised and lowered in such a way as to keep the

EACH OFFICE A KINGDOM.
OGNI UFFICIO UN REAME.

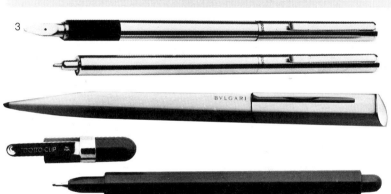

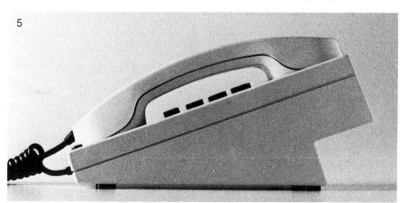

1. Typewriter, *Macchina da scrivere* / mod. Praxis 35 / des. M. Bellini / prod. Olivetti / 1981.
2. Calculator, *Macchina da calcolo* / mod. M 20 Personal / prod. Olivetti / 1981.
3. Pen, *Penna* / mod. Hastil / des. M. Zanuso / prod. Aurora / 1969.
Pen, *Penna* / mod. Tratto Clip / des. Design Group Italia / prod. Fila / 1978.
Ball point pen, *Penna* / mod. Eccentric / prod. Bulgari / 1981.
4. Telephone, *Telefono* / 1+ / des. P. Polato / prod. SAIET / 1981.
5. Telephone cost calculator, *Telefono-Budget* / mod. Telebudget / prod. Sime Brondi.

line that has to be filled at arm-level; formerly the workers had to bend down for the lower lines; a back-breaking job. The movable frame has been a technical and social conquest.

Each worker, like a child with his abacus, was threading each piece by means of a little hole in the hook, in one movement of the arm; then another piece; then another. When one row was finished, the process was repeated.

Among them was an elderly man who had been taken on because he was disabled. He heard us behind him, but did not turn round. He lifted his arms slowly to find the hooks, one by one, while the others could now do it without looking. He stumbled on, with the meticulous care of the old, his thin back bent over his work.

"The others are getting on well," said the foreman. "Not this one. You'll have to remove him."

But who would have him?

"It's work for women, really. If it weren't that we have always to give priority to the men, because of the unemployment here..." I paused.

His eyes narrowed, and he said stiffly: "Anyway, our women in the south wouldn't come and work here. We aren't in Northern Italy, Doctor..." There was silence.

Nearby, other workers, the most shabbily clad in the factory and wearing clogs, were putting the frames into vats of steaming acid. They all lifted their caps to us, pleased at the notice taken of them. But the foreman wanted to hurry me away, unwilling to let me stop – out of all his department – precisely with those who were dressed in rags. He was anxious to show me the work at the benches, of which he was particularly proud: three men hammering the chassis to straighten them out, and filing the join between frame and cover in order that it should fit well. Although they work at the mass-production machines their job is an individual one.

They have to trust their intuition, their eyes, their artistry, as in wrought ironwork; and the final result varies in quality and in the time it takes. There is nothing that a worker enjoys more. He had wanted to present this group to me, but they slipped away, having no time to spare. All the workers at the benches are independent, and rather conceited.

Ottiero Ottieri, "Donnarumma all'assalto", Bompiani, Milano 1959. "The man at the gate", Gollancz, London 1962. Translated by L.M. Rawson.

6
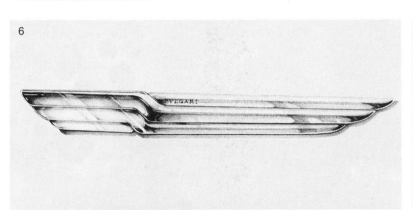

7

8
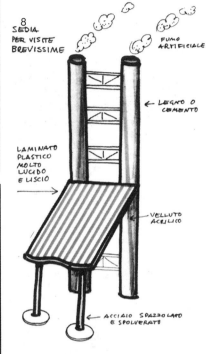

9
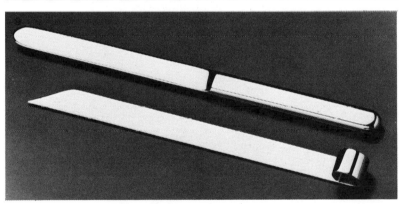

10
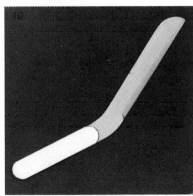

11

12

6. Letter opener, *Tagliacarte* / mod. Wings / prod. Bulgari / 1982.
7. Interoffice telephone, *Interfonico* / mod. Multicom / prod. Dial / 1981.
8. Chair, *Sedia* / mod. "Per visite brevissime" / des. B. Munari / 1982.
9. Letter opener, *Tagliacarte* / des. A. Piva / prod. San Lorenzo / 1973.
10. Letter opener, *Tagliacarte* / mod. Boomerang / des. L. & M. Vignelli / prod. San Lorenzo.
11. Agenda, *Agenda* / mod. Impatto 7 / des. H. Waibl / prod. Nava / 1980.
12. Telephone book, *Rubrica telefonica* / des. G. Confalonieri / prod. Nava / 1981.

OFFICE CHAIRS
SEDIE DA UFFICIO

1. mod. Executive 80 / des. A. Mangiarotti / prod. Skipper / 1980.
2. mod. Mix / des. A. e T. Scarpa / prod. Unifor / 1978.
3. mod. 236 Cassia / des. De Pas, D'Urbino, Lomazzi / prod. Zanotta / 1975.
4. mod. AZ / des. Archizoom, G. Corretti, P. Deganello / prod. Planula / 1978.
5. mod. Grinta / des. J. Colombo / prod. Zanotta / 1968.
6. mod. Pluralis / des. L/O / prod. Alfeo / 1977.

7. mod. Dattilo / des. H. Von Klier, G. Arnaldi / prod. Olivetti Synthesis / 1980.
8. mod. Polo / des. P. Parigi / prod. Heron Parigi / 1975.
9. mod. Davis / des. V. Magistretti / prod. I.C.F. / 1978.
10. mod. Modus 5 / des. Centro Progetti Tecno / prod. Tecno / 1972.
11. mod. Vertebra / des. E. Ambasz, G. Piretti / prod. Castelli / 1979.
12. mod. Mix / des. A. e T. Scarpa / prod. Unifor / 1978.

13. mod. Sedile / des. De Pas, D'Urbino, Lomazzi / prod. Marcatre / 1975.
14. mod. AZ / des. Archizoom, G. Corretti, P. Deganello / prod. Planula / 1978.
15. mod. Dress / des. P.L. Molinari / prod. Vallio / 1980.
16. mod. S8 / des. T. Ammannati, G.P. Vitelli / prod. Brunati / 1980.
17. mod. Edys / des. H. Von Klier / prod. Olivetti Synthesis / 1980.
18. mod. Direzionale / des. Ufficio Tecnico / prod. Marcatre / 1975.

It may seem somewhat presumptuous to set ourselves the problem of how to create a chair, one of the oldest and most thoroughly established elements of the material culture preceding ours, a culture with which we are expected to compare ourselves every time we proceed with the creation of a new product. Consequently we shall have to set ourselves clearly identified objectives: first of all, the improvement of the product's features; for example, when Castelli created the "Plia" chair, there were of course other folding chairs on the market, but with this model Castelli attained much higher levels in light-

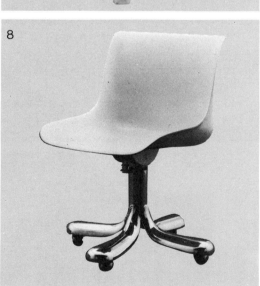

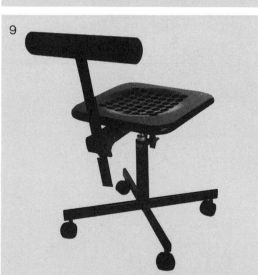

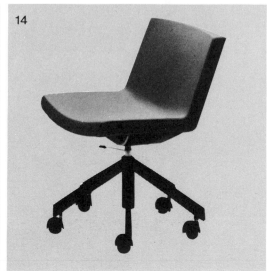

ness and practicality, it being easily folded up and manageable, as well as being far better suited to the human body in the sitting position than any previous model in the same category. The same objective should be set in regard to the problem of form: designed to accompany us for a considerable portion of our activities in life and work, an object like a chair should be so defined esthetically as to be pleasant and acceptable also to avoid rapid obsolence with the first change in fashion.

Lastly, in defining the level of quality a judicious mean should be struck between the features of the object and the price at which they are to be made available to the final user. For this reason, in the present productional system, it is indispensable to have a truly industrial conception of design and of the production of a decorative element, so as to make feasible mass-production, without which it is impossible (and will always be in the future) to create a chair of better quality at a reasonable price.

Leonida Castelli

Può sembrare un atto di presunzione porsi il problema di creare una sedia, uno degli elementi più antichi e stabilizzati della cultura materiale a noi precedente. Per questo è necessario darsi degli obiettivi ben identificati: innanzitutto il miglioramento delle prestazioni; ad esempio quando la Castelli ha realizzato la sedia "Plia" esistevano certamente già altre sedie pieghevoli, ma con essa si sono ottenuti livelli superiori di leggerezza, praticità e adattamento alle caratteristiche del corpo umano nella posizione seduta, mai raggiunti fino ad allora nella stessa tipologia. Lo stesso obiettivo va posto per il problema formale:

un oggetto come la sedia deve avere una definizione estetica che lo renda gradevole e accettabile così da non divenire rapidamente obsoleto con il variare delle mode.
Infine, nella definizione di un livello di qualità va stabilita una giusta mediazione tra le caratteristiche dell'oggetto ed il prezzo per questo, nell'attuale sistema produttivo è indispensabile una concezione veramente industriale del disegno e della realizzazione di un componente d'arredo, che ne renda attuabile la produzione in grande serie.

Leonida Castelli

Beppe Fenoglio
The Factory

On the corner on the square which previously had borne the King's name he met Baracca, the invalid, on his wheel chair drawn by two dogs. He crossed the square with him.

"I have never seen you around at this hour of the morning" Baracca said to him and Ettore bent down to stroke the red haired dog and then on rising replied "I am going to work this morning".

Baracca was a little surprised and asked him where.

"At the chocolate factory".

"I'm pleased for you because it's a good job".

Ettore didn't want Baracca to carry on about his work and for this reason asked him where he was going.

Baracca went and placed himself in front of the station and made the two dogs lie down and waited for the trains to arrive. He spent pleasant mornings waiting for the trains because strangers were moved by the two dogs. Leaving the station Baracca made the two dogs walk towards the Cassa di Risparmio and settled himself in the entrance beneath the porch where he collected money because people who had come out of the bank after dealing with their business almost always left some change with Baracca.

When he had left, Ettore thought that Baracca had worked out a good system. He had put his ruined legs to good use and lived well: many would have liked to be able to keep themselves in that way. Baracca deserved it because one day he had known how to make up his mind. The whole town knew that he had been a good worker and that he had had an accident but nobody had expected him to go begging and that one day he would be seen in the city in a wheelchair drawn by two dogs holding a bunch of leaflets telling one's fortune, which were multi-coloured, in

TIME AND SYSTEMS.
TEMPI E METODI.

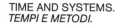

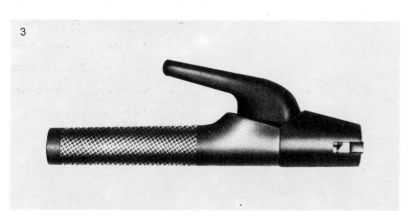

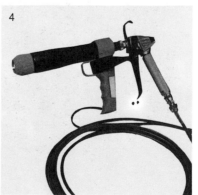

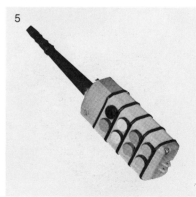

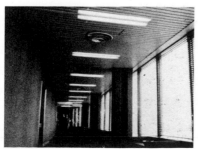

one of his hands. That day had been a difficult one for Baracca and the people but then they had both become accustomed and since then he has been living better than before.

— I, too, must organize things in such a way that people become accustomed to something decided by me. I must make up my mind, I ought to today, because, if not, I run the risk of getting myself into the habit of working for other people. —

By now he was walking down a side street and his only thought was that his steps were taking him nearer work. As he walked, he thought of his father whom he had seen a quarter of an hour before at the door of his shop. He had been touched when he saw him leaving the house to go to work with eyes like those of a sporting dog. His father stretched out his hand and he shook it and while shaking it stared at him as if he didn't recognize him – and he thought:

— Are you my father? Why aren't you a millionaire then? Why wasn't I born the son of a millionaire? — That man there in front of him had done him a great wrong making him born the son of a poor man, the same as if he had let him be born stunted or with his head bigger than the rest of his body.

Then he thought of the person who would be beside him within a quarter of an hour to teach him how to write a consignment note.

— Christ — he said.

Walking along he had seen a workman in his workshop and he hadn't got a sad face, even though fumbling with a lathe. Then the workmen from the Electricity Board passed by on their lorry. They looked almost military in their blue uniform with the small copper discs on their caps as well as the orderly way they sat at the sides of the lorry. They too seemed neither sad, nor tired, nor surly but instead appeared to be extremely proud.

He shook his head on both occasions and then arrived in front of the chocolate factory.

There were already more than a hundred workmen and women and whichever way they looked they all seemed to be turned towards the large metal entrance door to the factory as if they had been magnetized. He didn't go near. In fact he moved away and went towards a public lavatory and from there he looked at the group of workers and the large, still closed entrance door.

Beppe Fenoglio, "La paga del sabato", Einaudi, Torino 1972. Translated by Shane Hall.

1. Welding tool, *Saldatrice statica* / mod. Thytronic 115 / des. Ufficio Tecnico / prod. CEA / 1982.
2. Time and motion calculator, *Marcatempo* / mod. Tempor / des. Ufficio Tecnico / prod. Solari / 1979.
3. Non-slip grip, *Impugnatura antiscivolo* / mod. Urania 500 / prod. Sacit / 1980.
4. Spray gun, *Pistola elettrostatica* / mod. Spray-Wrap / prod. Larius / 1979.

5. Remote Control, *Pulsanteria pensile* / prod. Giovenzana / 1980.
6. Protective goggles, *Occhiali* / mod. Montreal / prod. Sacit / 1973.
7. Protective goggles, *Occhiali* / mod. Sparta / prod. Sacit / 1973.
8.9. Welding masks, *Caschi per saldatura* / prod. Sacit / 1980.
10.11. Fork-lift, *Carrello elevatore* / prod. Incab.

AGRICULTURAL MACHINES
MACCHINE AGRICOLE

1. Tractor, *Trattrice* / mod. 95 RS / des. Ufficio Tecnico / prod. Ferrari / 1980.
2. Combine Harvester, *Mietitrebbia* / mod. M182 / des. Ufficio Tecnico / prod. Laverda / 1981.
3. Tractor, *Trattrice* / mod. R 235 / des. Ufficio Tecnico / prod. Lamborghini.
4. Tractor, *Trattrice* / mod. 1556 DT / des. Ufficio Tecnico / prod. Lamborghini.

In certain respects the seventies have marked a return of interest in agriculture and everything connected with it. There has been a continual drain of farm workers (with an average drop of 2.5-3% per year), but there has been a growth of interest in more highly specialized crops closely connected with processing industries.

This picture has become more complex and at the same time more organic. One need only consider the policy of reappraising our vine-growing and wine-producing and our fruit and vegetable industries, which has only recently been launched.

At the same time, as a result of a proc-ess initiated several years ago, there has been an upsurge in the metallurgical and mechanical industries concerned with agricultural machines. Considering the level it has reached in Italy, nothing comparable can be found in other ountries in what has been called small-scale mechanization.

Scaling down these machines, and therefore the expenses, to the farm-owner's investment capabilities, and fully exploiting medium-sized Italian farms has opened the way for a new type of equipment.

Small, general-use, highly reliable and easily maintained, these

1

2

machines, whose chief production center is located in Emilia Romagna, have conquered the world market. Total sales in this sector have risen from 95 millions dollars in 1974 to 440 millions dollars in 1980, with a number of employees estimated today at about 10000.

Schumaker, an american economist, gave his famous book the title, "Small is Beautiful": which is a perfect description of our farm-machine industry.

Aurelio Picco

Gli anni settanta segnano, per alcuni aspetti, un ritorno di interesse per l'agricoltura e tutto ciò che ad essa si ricollega.

Continua l'esodo della forza lavoro dei campi (con un calo medio del 2,5/3% annuo), ma ci si avvia a colture più specializzate, strettamente connesse con l'industria di trasformazione.

Il quadro si fa più complesso e nel contempo più organico; basti pensare alla politica di riqualificazione della nostra vitivinicoltura e ortofrutticoltura che prende un deciso avvio solo in questo periodo.

Parallelamente, con un processo già avviato negli anni precedenti, si ha un

forte sviluppo dell'industria metalmeccanica per la meccanizzazione agricola.

È un fenomeno che non ha riscontro, nelle dimensioni che ha raggiunto in Italia, in nessun altro paese se riferito a quella che viene definita la piccola meccanizzazione.

Dimensionare le macchine, e quindi i costi, alle capacità di investimento, impiego e pieno utilizzo per la media proprietà agricola italiana ha aperto la strada ad una nuova tipologia di attrezzature.

Piccole, multiuso, affidabilissime e di facile manutenzione queste macchine, che hanno il loro maggiore centro

di produzione in Emilia Romagna, hanno conquistato il mondo. Il fatturato di questo settore è passato da 130 miliardi di lire nel 1974 a 600 miliardi nel 1980, con un numero di addetti valutabile oggi intorno ai 10000.

Un economista americano (Schumaker) ha intitolato un suo famoso libro "Small is beautiful": un'affermazione più che esatta anche per la nostra industria meccano-agricola.

Aurelio Picco

3

4

TWILIGHT STREETS
WINDOW SHOPPING

STRADE AL CREPUSCOLO
LA VETRINA INCANTATA

Nanni Balestrini
Violence illustrated

ON STAGE IN THE LATEST FASHION.
RENDEZ-VOUS AT THE CORNER.
THE LAST SHAVE AT THE BARBER'S.
AFTER HOURS PEDESTRIANS ONLY.
CHATTERING RISES.

LO STRUSCIO.
IL SISTEMA DELLA MODA.
APPUNTAMENTO ALL'ANGOLO.
LA SEDUTA DAL BARBIERE.
ZONA PEDONALE.
CRESCENDO DI VOCI.

The busy life of Milan was rocked yesterday afternoon by a sudden wave of violence and fury unprecedented even in the darkest hours of the city's recent history. All afternoon and well into the evening the main streets were the scene of bitter, fierce, and ferocious conflict between police and dense groups of demonstrators belonging to extreme left groups. There were dozens of wounded on both sides. Barricades. Cars overturned and burned. Officers hauled from the cars and badly beaten. Showers of Molotov cocktails. Waves of acrid tear gas. Barricades. Lines of streetcars with shattered windows.

Once again guerrilla warfare has broken out in the streets of Milan. For more than three hours the center of the city was turned into a battlefield. On one side the forces of order intervened with extreme violence, and on the other leftist extremists, presumably according to plan, devastated everything that stood in their way. It was a very rough exasperating attack. For more than three hours guerrillas armed with iron bars, stones, iron and glass pellets, and rockets set fire to automobile and swung buses sideways to barricade

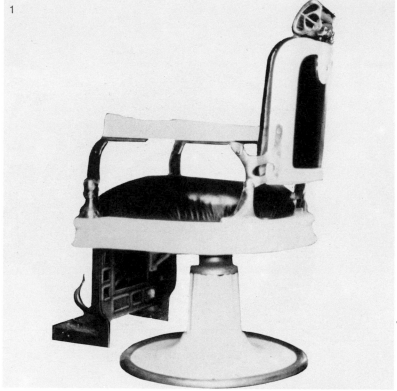
1

The trade surplus of the Italian fashion industry is the highest of any sector. The turn-over of the fashion industry totals approximately 10,000 million dollars per year.
61% of production is absorbed internally.
Exports, or 39% of production, amount to 3,500 million dollars.
Imports are estimated at 639 million dollars.
The trade surplus for 1981 is thus 3,261 million dollars.
For each person clothing is the third most important item of expenditure, accounting for 10% of the total.

A comparison of the three basic items of expenditure shows clothing to be the third item of importance in the family budget.

Consumption:

food	31%
housing (rent, maintenance)	13%
clothing	9%

41% of Italians dress traditionally
38% of Italians wear sports clothes
21% of Italians dress casually.

La moda italiana è la prima voce del saldo attivo della bilancia commerciale italiana. La produzione nazionale matura una cifra d'affari di 13.500 miliardi di lire.
Il mercato interno assorbe il 61% del prodotto.
L'esportazione il 39% del prodotto, pari a 5.280 miliardi di lire.
L'importazione si aggiudica 863 miliardi di lire.
Il saldo commerciale (1981) risulta di + 4.417 miliardi di lire.
Circa il 10% della spesa pro capite viene assorbito dall'abbigliamento.
Nel confronto tra le voci fondamentali della spesa, l'abbigliamento si situa come la terza voce del bilancio familiare.

Consumo:

alimentare	*31%*
casa (affitto, condominio)	*13%*
abbigliamento	*9%*

41% veste in modo classico tradizionale
38% veste in modo classico sportivo
21% veste in modo informale casual.

2

I VITELLONI
1953

FEDERICO FELLINI
Alberto Sordi

the streets, hundreds of Molotov cocktails were hurled by the demonstrators, They applied the techniques of urban guerrilla warfare. They would suddenly assemble one place, attack the police, and then disperse into the side streets and meet up later.

The demonstrators brought guerrilla warfare into the streets of the historic center of Milan. Violent clashes with the police continued for more than four hours. There were 49 wounded among the forces of law and order: 25 carabineers, 5 officers, 3 NCOs, and 19 patrolmen. Civilians continue to be admitted to various hospitals, some of them demonstrators. Many of them preferred to go to private doctors, instead. The police and the carabineers have arrested 82 demonstrators. Damages are now being estimated. The *Corriere della Sera* building was seriously hit. Dozens of automobiles were set fire to.

The mob exploded in Milan today. A mob limited to a few groups of leftist extremists, but enough to provoke very serious incidents, and only numbers can give the exact extent. A bystander is near death. It seems he was hit in the head by a rock or a tear gas canister, he fell against the iron pole of a traffic sign, and then had a heart attack in the ambulance. He is in critical condition in the hospital. Dozens of injured, cars burned, Molotov cocktails thrown all over, stores broken into and smashed, and streetcars damaged.

Never before perhaps had urban guerrilla warfare in Milan reached such a peak of bitterness, ferocity, and organized violence as it did yesterday. The city was rocked by the clashes, the rocks, clubs, police charges, and tear gas canisters, as well as by the Molotov cocktails, the fires, and the barricades of cars and buses set up in dozens of streets. There were dozens and dozens of police vehicles and jeeps and streetcars half destroyed by clubs and rocks and the firebombs. Widespread damage was caused in a vast area of the city, where the guerrillas kept the forces of law and order busy for hours and hours with sudden rapid raids.

There were serious cases of provocation this afternoon in the heart of Milan. In the course of extended clashes the police violently attacked groups of extremists. An old man passing by was hit in the forehead with a tear gas canister and is lying near death in the polyclinic. Bands of provocateurs belonging to so-called leftist extra-parliamentary organizations committed acts of delinquency in various parts of the city and at the *Corriere della Sera*. One of the bloodiest episodes of urban

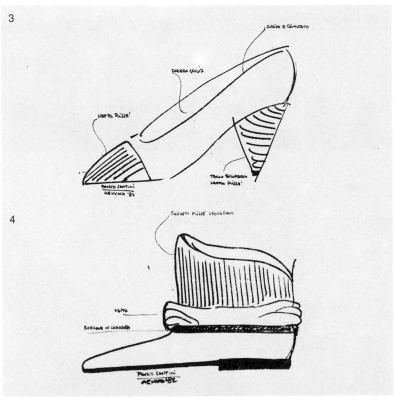

1. Barber chair, *Sedia barblere*.
2. Shopping bag, *Sacchetto* / prod. Versace / 1980.
3. Woman's shoe, *Scarpa da donna* / des. F. Santini / prod. Santini & Dominici / 1982.
4. Man's shoe, *Scarpa da uomo* / des. F. Santini / prod. Santini & Dominici / 1982.
5. Street sign, *Segnaletica* / prod. Ministero dei Lavori Pubblici / 1979.
6. Wrist watch, *Orologio* / des. G. Bulgari / prod. Bulgari / 1979.
7. Street scale, *Bilancia stradale* / prod. Salus / 1956.

guerrilla warfare ever to occur in Milan. It lasted several hours and spread like wildfire. There were dozens of hot spots. It is impossible to give a logical account of the course of events, but they seem to have followed a carefully thought-out plan of provocation.

A few minutes after four p.m. the procession of the extra-parliamentary left came up Via Cusani, evidently from Corso Garibaldi. The police blocked the way into Largo Cairoli by closing off access at the level of Foro Bonaparte. There was a brief meeting between police officials and the organizers of the march, and then the two groups stood face to face for a few minutes without anything happening. All the evidence was that the marchers had decided not to go any farther and just occupy the area around Largo Cairoli. At about four p.m. 5,000 people crowded into the street around Via Ponte Vetero, one of the old quarters of Milan. But when they wanted to go on to Largo Cairoli there was a meeting between the organizers of the demonstration and the chief of police, who demanded that the participants give up their flagpoles and any thing else that could be used as weapons. The organizing committee did not accept this. They did not want body searches. In the meantime, the head of the procession had stopped awaiting decisions from Via Cusani, but the rear of the procession had gone off down Via Broletto. The organizers claimed that they wanted to reach Via Dante and then Largo Cairoli by taking a longer route. When the demonstrators had almost reached Piazza Cordusio, they were driven back by police who launched several tear gas bombs.

The first incidents took place about 4 p.m. in Piazza Cordusio. According to the official version, police on duty in the area noticed a group of demonstrators with helmets and flagstaffs heading towards Largo Cairoli and asked them to desist. According to the official version, the demonstrators responded by suddenly hurling rocks. It was then that the police attacked and chased the extremists who were now turning back down Via Broletto. A few minutes earlier another group of demonstrators had reached Largo Cairoli out of Via Cusani. they too were wearing helmets, kerchiefs, and had wooden flagstaffs. At this point you could hear the sound of the tear gas bombs that the police were exploding in Piazza Cordusio. Soon after, the two groups of extremists joined up.

Small groups of the extra-parliamentary left had started joining up on their way to Largo Cairoli. But Via Dante was

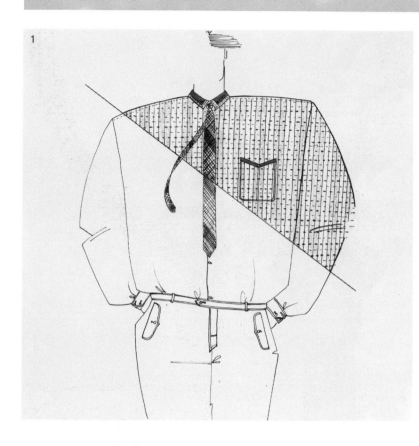

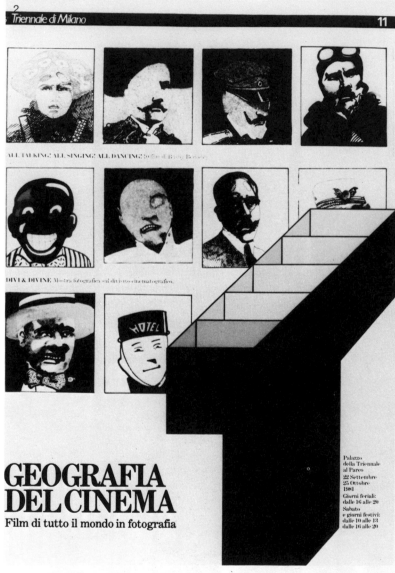

GEOGRAFIA DEL CINEMA
Film di tutto il mondo in fotografia

GLI ITALIANI SI VOLTANO

1953

ALBERTO LATTUADA

blocked off by the police. Several of the demonstrators wore motorcycle helmets and carried flagstaffs. After brief skirmishing they dispersed into the side streets and tried to reach largo Cairoli. The first violent clashes occurred at the corner of Via Cusani and Corso Garibaldi, where the police had set up a cordon of men and vehicles. The first tear gas bombs were thrown, and the demonstrators responded with stones and Molotov cocktails.

The leftist groups stationed at the corner of Via Dante and Via Giulini threw the first stones at the police cordon that kept them from reaching Largo Cairoli. In itself it seemed an almost negligible episode, but it was the spark that set off the violence. The first incendiary bomb exploded in Piazza Cordusio at the end of Via Dante, where the end of the procession stationed in Via Cusani had arrived. Disturbances broke out here too, where the guerrillas had already set up barricades by hauling a host of private cars into the middle of the street. Police jeeps, their sirens blaring, a dozen vehicles at full speed left Largo Cairoli.

The demonstrators pulled back, but in their flight they began dislodging cobblestones from the street and making barricades with parked cars. A few minutes later a second disturbance broke out in Via Cusani, where the street widens at the junction of Via Broletto, Via Ponte Vetero, and Via dell'Orso. The extremists threw rocks and iron pellets, and the police responded with tear gas bombs. This was the moment that guerrilla warfare started. Barricades, cobbles torn out of the streets, rocks hurled. All of this under the black smoke of the canisters shot off by the police to disperse the demonstrators.

The first incidents broke out far from Via Cusani, in Piazza Cordusio where the police charged a group of extremists. This was the beginning of the disturbances. There were extremely violent police charges along Via Broletto, Via Dante, Via San Tommaso, and Via Rovello. In no time at all the clashes had spread throughout the area, with points of particular violence in Via Cusani, where the main body of the demonstrators was. Hundreds of tear gas bombs were shot off, almost all of them point blank. Some of them damaged streetcars and buses that had been blocked. Provocateurs set about destroying several parked cars. A cry rose from the square, the first rocks and the first tear gas bombs criss-crossed through the air, and the two sides clashed with frightening

3

5

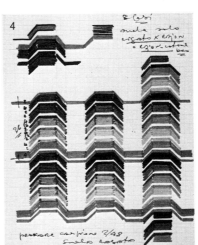

4

1. Man's suit, *Abito da uomo* / prod. Punch / 1982.
2. Films poster, *Manifesto cinema* / des. I. Lupi, A. Marangoni / prod. Triennale di Milano / 1981.
3. Man's suit, *Abito da uomo* / prod. Basile / 1982.
4. Knitting, *Maglia* / des. Missoni / 1982.
5. Coin necklace, *Collana con moneta* / mod. Alexander the Great / prod. Bulgari / 1981.

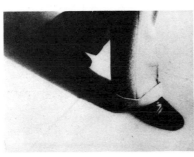

rage. Rifle butts and clubs swung to a sinister accompaniment of exploding tear gas bombs and the muffled sound of the incendiary bombs. The battle quickly turned into furious hand-to-hand combat after the front rows of demonstrators had been overwhelmed by the first police charge in a series of fierce and intense struggles with no holds barred. The air was full of iron lugs, bolts, pellets, and porphyry cobbles that filtered through the gray volutes of the tear gas and the bonfires of the first cars. Dozens of cars caught fire when they were hit by Molotov cocktails. Many of the cars had been turned sideways to form barricades.

From 4:00 p.m. on, the main streets were rocked by extremely serious disturbances. Groups of extra-parliamentary left demonstrators clashed with the police. It was veritable guerrilla warfare in the streets, flooded with the acrid fumes of tear gas bombs, while people on the streetcars and bystanders ran for any cover they could find. The guerrillas struggled for a long time with the police, and the police responded vigorously, sometimes gripping their rifles by the barrel and using them as clubs. More than once the police and the carabineers had to pull back in the face of guerrilla tactics as the terrorists pressed forward. Many

bystanders lived through moments of panic, while others took refuge in doorways. Janitors in several buildings closed the outside doors.
The disturbances started in the maze of alleyways around Largo Cairoli, across the way from Castello Sforzesco, and they spread rapidly as far as Via Solferino, where the *Corriere della Sera* offices are. Some hundred extremists got there before the police squads, and they attacked the few patrolmen on duty. A dozen Molotov cocktails were hurled at the newspaper's windows, especially the newsroom on the ground floor. Flames and smoke spread inside. Bricks and metal

pellets were thrown as high as the first floor and smashed the windows of the editorial room and the teletype room. When the police arrived, charges and raids continued in nearby streets. The police took their rifles by the barrel end and charged again, driving the extremists back. The extremists then headed towards Piazza del Carmine and nearby streets. The blocked streetcars gave the extremists cover, and they continued to pepper the police with rocks, and steel pellets and occasionally tossed back unexploded tear gas bombs. At this stage the police stopped hosts of people, chiefly young people and children, and some of them

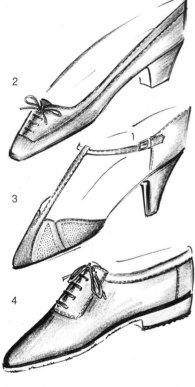

1. Woman's dress, *Abito da donna* / mod. Cristalli Liquidi / des. C. Ruggeri / prod. Bloom / 1982.
2. Woman's shoe, *Scarpa da donna* / mod. Rotary / prod. Ferragamo / 1982.
3. Woman's shoe, *Scarpa da donna* / mod. Rischio / prod. Ferragamo / 1982.
4. Man's shoe, *Scarpa da uomo* / mod. Heros / prod. Ferragamo / 1982.
5. Woman's dress, *Abito da donna* / des. Versace / prod. Versace / 1981.
6. Man's suit, *Abito da uomo* / des. Versace / prod. Versace / 1982.
7. Evening overall for woman, *Tuta da sera per donna* / des. Krizia / prod. Krizia / 1982.

8. Evening bag, *Borsa da sera* / des. Bulgari / prod. Bulgari / 1981.
9. Woman's dress, *Abito da donna* / mod. G.F. Ferré / prod. Ferré / 1982.
10. Man's jacket, *Giacca da uomo* / prod. Zegna / 1982.
11. Necklace, *Collana* / mod. Tubogas / des. Bulgari / prod. Bulgari / 1981.

DOVE LA LIBERTÀ

1954

ROBERTO ROSSELLINI

Totò

were chased into building hallways. Boys and girls were taken to the police station with swollen faces. It wasn't 5 o'clock yet. It looked as if the incidents were coming to an end. Instead that was when extremely serious incidents suddenly broke out again.

Nanni Balestrini, "La violenza illustrata", Einaudi, Torino 1976. Translated by Ronald Strom.

9

It is of some importance to define first the relationship between medium and large-scale production on the one hand, and elite production on on the other. To the latter category belong the "griffes" of a small but effective group of Italian creators who may be included in what I would call the international avant-garde. Elite production is the one that least suffers from the ups and downs of the market, the one that avails itself of affluent national resources and enjoys the stylistic variations typical of all creative artists. Its influence on production for a far wider range of consumers comes about directly in production catering to licensed dealers, or indirectly, through mediators. As for the matter of style, it can never be divorced from the reality of the times and from the slow social and environmental transformations taking place, which turn out to be constant elements of analysis. My function, and my commitment, bring to bear real plans and elaborations of formal research onto products connected with dressing, with a strong intention of respecting the human body and with a need to express its creative contents.

Gianfranco Ferré

10

Ritengo importante premettere una definizione dei rapporti tra la media e grande produzione e la produzione elitaria alla quale appartengono le griffes di pochi ma incisivi creatori italiani che rientrano in quella che chiamerei avanguardia internazionale. La produzione elitaria è quella che meno subisce oscillazioni di mercato, è quella che si avvale di agevolate risorse nazionali e fruisce delle elaborazioni stilistiche tipiche di ogni creatore. La sua influenza sulla produzione a più largo consumo avviene in modo diretto, con le progettazioni per i licenziatari, o indiretto, indotta dai media. Le proposte stilistiche non possono essere mai slegate dalla realtà dei tempi e dalle lente trasformazioni sociali ed ambientali, che risultano quindi costanti elementi di analisi. Il mio metodo di lavoro, la mia funzione, il mio impegno, è quello di intervenire con reali progettazioni ed elaborazioni di ricerca formali sul prodotto legato al vestire, con decisi intenti di rispetto del corpo e con necessità di espressione di contenuti creativi. Tali intendimenti devono essere precisi e di facile lettura, e ciò fa sì che il rapporto tra forma ed espressione si sviluppi in modo sempre più determinante.

Gianfranco Ferré

11

HOME
THE HOUSE IS YOU

CASA
L'IO ILLUSTRATO

RENAISSANCE REVIVAL.
MILANESE HIGH-TECH.
ROMAN SOUVENIRS.
BAROQUE STANDING LAMPS.
TERRACE JUNGLES.
FROM THE CREDENZA THE TV
LIGHTS THE ROOM.

STILE RINASCIMENTALE.
TECNOLOGICO MILANESE.
RICORDI ROMANI.
ARREDO BAROCCO.
LA GIUNGLA IN TERRAZZA.
SULLA CREDENZA GUARDA IL
TELEVISORE.

**Giuseppe Tomasi
di Lampedusa
Two Stories and a Memory**

First of all, our home. I loved it with utter abandon, and still love it now when for the last twelve years it has been no more than a memory. Until a few months before its destruction I used to sleep in the room where I was born, five yards away from the spot where my mother's bed had stood when she gave me birth. And in that house, in that very room maybe, I was glad to feel a certainty of dying. All my other homes (very few, actually, apart from hotels) have merely been roofs which have served to shelter me from rain and sun, not homes in the traditional and venerable sense of that word.

So it will be very painful for me to evoke my dead Beloved as she was until 1929 in her integrity and beauty, and as she continued after all to be until 5th April 1943, the day on which bombs brought from beyond the Atlantic searched her out and destroyed her.

The first impression that remains with me is that of her vastness, and this impression owes nothing to the magnifying process which affects all that surrounds one's childhood, but to actual reality. When I saw the area covered by the unsightly ruins I found they were

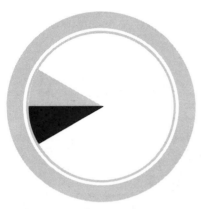

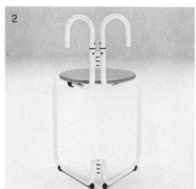

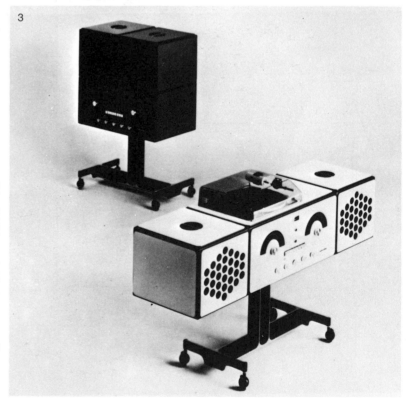

56% of the population own their own home.
The average number of rooms per dwelling is 3.8.
the average numer of residents per dwelling is 3.5.

Il 56% della popolazione possiede la casa in cui abita.
3,8 è la media del numero di stanze per abitazione.
3,5 la media di abitanti per abitazione.

Which spouse should...

	M%	W%	C%
Support the family	32.9	1.0	66.1
Buy household appliances	6.8	20.0	73.2
Buy the car	33.3	0.5	66.1
Select the apartment to live in	2.9	6.9	90.3
Prepare meals	1.5	72.0	26.5
Pay the taxes	47.6	7.1	45.3
Get up at night when children cry	1.7	42.0	56.4
Clean the house	0.8	71.4	27.8
Wash the children	1.4	70.2	28.4
Do the shopping	17.0	55.5	42.9

In una coppia chi dovrebbe...

	U%	D%	C%
Mantenere la famiglia	32,9	1,0	66,1
Acquistare gli elettrodomestici	6,8	20,0	73,2
Acquistare l'auto	33,3	0,5	66,1
Scegliere l'appartamento	2,9	6,9	90,3
Preparare i pasti	1,5	72,0	26,5
Pagare le tasse	47,6	7,1	45,3
Alzarsi di notte quando piangono i bambini	1,7	42,0	56,4
Pulire la casa	0,8	71,4	27,8
Lavare i bambini	1,4	70,2	28,4
Fare la spesa	1,7	55,5	42,9

The average Italian watches television 4 hours per day (as compared to 6 hours for Americans).
Approximately 72 minutes per day are dedicated to the preparation of meals.
Women perform 90% of the housework.

Televisioni risultano accese una media di 4 ore al giorno (USA 6 ore).
Circa 72 minuti al giorno sono impiegati per la preparazione dei pasti.
La donna svolge il 90% del lavoro domestico.

IL SEME DELL'UOMO

1969

MARCO FERRERI

Marco Margine
Anne Wiazenski

about 1600 square yards in extent. With only ourselves living in one wing, my paternal grandparents in another, my bachelor uncles on the second floor, for twenty years it was all at my disposal, with its three courtyards, four terraces, garden, huge staircases, halls, corridors, stables, little rooms on the *mezzanine* for servants and offices – a real kingdom for a boy alone, a kingdom either empty or sparsely populated by figures unanimously well-disposed.

At no point on earth, I'm sure, has sky ever stretched more violently blue than it did above our enclosed terrace, never has sun thrown gentler rays than those penetrating the half-closed shutters of the "green drawing-room," never have damp-marks on a court-yard's outer walls presented shapes more stimulating to the imagination than those at my home.

I loved everything about it: the irregularity of its walls, the number of its drawing-rooms, the stucco of its ceilings, the smell from my grandparents' kitchen, the scent of violets in my mother's dressing-room, the stuffiness of its stables, the good feel of polished leather in its saddle-rooms, the mystery of some unfinished apartments on the top floor, the huge coach-house in which our carriages were kept; a whole world full of sweet mysteries, of surprises ever renewed and ever fresh.

I was its absolute master and would run continually through its vast expanses, climbing the great staircase from the courtyard to the loggia on the roof, from which could be seen the sea and Mount Pellegrino and the whole city as far as Porta Nuova and Monreale. And knowing how by devious routes and turns to avoid inhabited rooms, I would feel alone and dictatorial, followed often only by my friend Tom running excitedly at my heels, with his red tongue dangling from his dear black snout.

The house (and I prefer to call it a house rather than a palace, a word which has been debased in Italy, applied as it is nowadays even to blocks fifteen storeys high), was tucked away in one of the most secluded streets of old Palermo, in Via di Lampedusa, at number 17, the uneven number's evil omen then serving only to add a pleasantly sinister flavour to the joy that it dispensed. (When later the stables were transformed into storerooms we asked for the number to be changed, and it became 23 when the end was near; so number 17 had after all been lucky).

The street was secluded but not so very narrow, and well paved; nor was it

1.2. Stool, *Sgabello* / des. L. Leonori / prod. Pallucco / 1981.
3. Stereo set, *Stereo set* / mod. RR126 / des. A. e P.G. Castiglioni / prod. Brionvega / 1967.
4. Armchair, *Poltrona* / mod. AEO / des. P. Deganello - Archizoom / prod. Cassina / 1973.

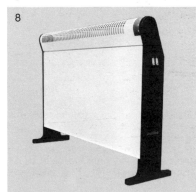

5. Television set, *Televisore* / mod. Alta Fedeltà / des. M. Bellini / prod. Brionvega / 1979.
6. Sewing machine, *Macchina da cucire* / mod. Logica / des. G. Giugiaro / prod. Necchi / 1982.
7. Electric fan, *Ventilatore* / mod. Ariante / des. M. Zanuso / prod. Vortice / 1975.
8. Radiator, *Termoconvettore* / mod. Scaldina / des. L. Bonfanti / prod. BCS / 1981.

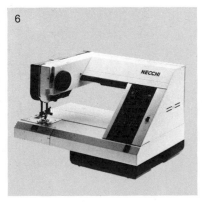

dirty as might be thought, for opposite our entrance and along the whole length of the building extended the old Pietrapersia palace which had no shops or dwellings on the ground floor, its austere, clean front in local white and yellow punctuated by numerous windows protected by enormous grilles, conferring on it the dignified and gloomy air of a old convent or state prison. The bomb explosions later flung many of those heavy grilles into our rooms opposite, with what happy effect on the old stucco work and Murano chandeliers can be imagined. But if Via di Lampedusa was decent enough, for the whole length of our

house at least, the streets into it were not; Via Bara all'Olivella, leading into Piazza Massimo, was crawling with poverty and squalor, and depressing to pass along. It became slightly better when Via Roma was cut through, but there always remained a good stretch of filth and horrors to traverse.

The façade of the house had no particular architectural merit: it was white with wide borders round windows of sulphur yellow, in purest Sicilian style of the seventeenth and eighteenth centuries in fact. It extended along Via di Lampedusa for some seventy yards or so, and had nine big balconies on the front. There were two gateways

almost at the corners of the building, of enormous width as they used to be made in older days to allow carriages to turn in from narrow streets. And in fact there was easy room even for the four-horsed teams which my father drove with mastery to race-meetings at La Favorita.

Just inside the main gate which we always used, rose the stairs, faced by a colonnade of fine grey Billiemi stone supporting the overhanging *tocchetto* or gallery. Beyond this gate in fact lay the main courtyard, cobbled and divided into sections by rows of flagstones. At the far end three great arches, also supported on columns of Billiemi

stone, bore a terrace which linked the two wings of the house at that point. The main staircase was a very fine one, all in grey Billiemi, with two flights of fifteen steps or so each, set between yellowish walls. Where the second flight began there was a wide oblong landing with two mahogany doors, one facing each flight of stairs, with bulging little gilt balconies above.

Just past the entrance to the stairs, but on the exterior, in the courtyard, hung the red cord of a bell which the porter was supposed to ring in order to warn servants of their mistress's return, or the approach of visitors. The number of rings, which the porters gave with

1

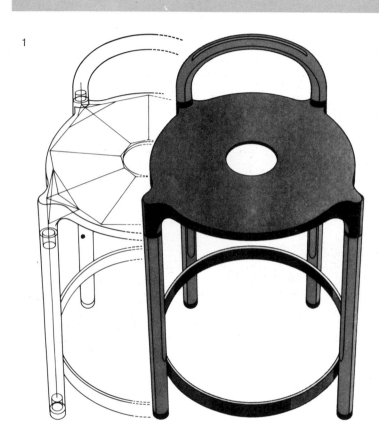

2

3

4

GRUPPO DI FAMIGLIA IN UN INTERNO

1974

LUCHINO VISCONTI

Silvana Mangano
Burt Lancaster
Helmut Berger
Claudia Marsani

great skill, obtaining, I don't know how, sharp separate strokes without any tiresome tinkling, was rigorously laid down by protocol; four strokes for my grandmother the princess and two for her visitors, three for my mother the duchess and one for her visitors. But misunderstandings would occur, so that when at times my mother, grandmother and some friend picked up on the way entered in the same carriage a real concert would ring out of four plus three plus two strokes which were never ending. The masters, my grandfather and father, left and returned without any bell ringing for them at all. The second flight of stairs came out on to the wide luminous *tocchetto*, which was a gallery with the spaces between its columns filled in, for reasons of comfort, by big windows with opaque lozenge-shaped panes. This contained a few sparse pieces of furniture, some big portrait of ancestors, and a large table to the left on which were put letters on arrival (it was then I read a postcard addressed to my uncle from Paris, on which some French tart had written: *"Dis à ton ami qu'il est un mufle"*). Opening out of this was an immense hall flagged in white and grey marble, with three balconies over Via di Lampedusa. To my parents' great regret, its decoration was entirely modern, as in 1848 a shell had destroyed the fine painted ceiling and irreparably damaged the wallfrescoes. For a long time, it seems, a fig tree flourished in there. The hall was done up when my grandfather married, that is in 1866 or '67, all in white stucco with a *wainscot* of grey marble. It was in this great hall that the footmen waited, lounging in their chairs and ready to hurry out into the *tocchetto* at the sound of that bell below.

A door with green hangings gave on to the antechamber, with six portraits of ancestors hung above its balcony entrance and its two doors, walls of grey silk and other pictures. And from there the eye fell on a perspective of drawing-rooms extending one after the other for the length of the façade. Here for me began the magic of light, which in a city with so intense a sun as Palermo is concentrated or variegated according to the weather, even in narrow streets. This light was sometimes diluted by the silk curtains hanging before balconies, or heightened by beating on some gilt frame or yellow damask chair which reflected it back; sometimes, particularly in summer, these rooms were dark, yet through the closed blinds filtered a sense of the luminous power that was outside; or sometimes at certain hours a single ray

1. Stool, *Sgabello* / des. A. Castelli Ferrieri / prod. Kartell / 1979.
2. Pressure cooker, *Pentola a pressione* / mod. HE / des. Ufficio Tecnico / prod. Lagostina / 1959.
3. Spaghetti pan and drainer, *Cuocispaghetti e colaspaghetti* / des. R. Sambonet / prod. Sambonet / 1979.
4. Tray set, *Vassoi componibili* / des. Centro Kappa / prod. Kartell.
5. Grids, *Trafile* / mod. Pastamatic
6. Pasta machine, *Macchina per la pasta* / mod. Dalia / prod. IMB / 1962.
7. Oil cruet, *Oliera*.
8. Pasta machine, *Macchina per la pasta* / mod. Pastamatic / des. A. Cavalli / prod. Simac / 1980.

would penetrate straight and clear as that of Sinai, populated with myriads of dust particles and going to vilify the colours of carpets, uniformly ruby-red throughout all the drawing-rooms: a real sorcery of illumination and colour which entranced my mind for ever. Sometimes I rediscover this luminous quality in some old palace or church, and it would wrench at my heart were I not ready to brush it aside with some "wicked joke."

After the ante-chamber came the *"lambris"* rooms, so called because its walls were covered half-way up by panelling of inlaid walnut; next the so-called "supper" room, its walls covered with dark flowered orange-coloured silk, part of which still survives as wall-coverings in my wife's room now. And to the left was the great ballroom with its enamelled floor and its ceiling on which delicious gold and yellow twirls framed mythological scenes where with rude energy and amid swirling robes crowded all the deities of Olympus.

After that came my mother's boudoir, very lovely, its ceiling scattered with flowers and branches of old coloured stucco, in a design gentle and corporeal as a piece of music by Mozart.

Giuseppe Tomasi di Lampedusa, "Racconti", Feltrinelli, Milano 1980. "Two Stories and a memory", William Collins Sons & Co., Pantheon Books, 1962. Translated by Archibald Colquhoun.

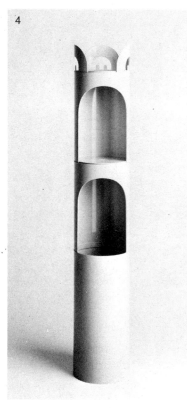

1. Container, *Contenitore* / des. Centro Kappa / prod. Kartell / 1975.
2. Sofa, *Divano* / mod. Girasole / des. Gregotti associati / prod. Casanova / 1981.
3. Bed, *Letto* / mod. Abitacolo / des. B. Munari / prod. Robots / 1970.
4. Container and clothes rack, *Contenitore e appendi-abiti* / mod. Kerguelen / des. E. Mari / prod. Danese / 1968.
5. Child's cutlery, *Posate per bambino* / prod. Chicco / 1980.
6. Clothes rack, *Appendiabiti* / des. E. Mari / prod. Danese / 1980.
7.8. Toy-magnetic constructions, *Giocattolo-costruzioni magnetiche* / mod. Compongo / prod. Embi.

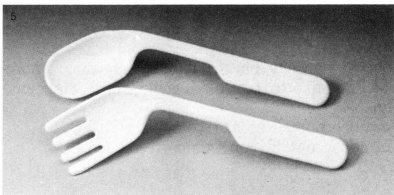

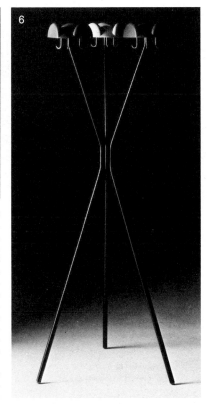

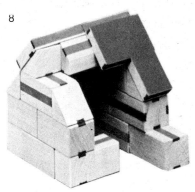

What is an interior compartment? Called a cockpit in single-seater airplanes, it is the pilot's cab containing all the instruments of command; a space which in airliners becomes the flight deck. In automobiles of all kinds it is the space which houses passengers and it is called the passenger compartment. In space ships it is the space where the astronauts sit and work, and is called a space capsule; it contains everything necessary for living and for controlling navigation. The interior cabin is habitable space *par excellence*. In a figurative sense it is also a cosy individual recess, the interior place where one finds everything that fills his world.

In the houses of adults not all children have their own "interior compartments". The more fortunate of them have a room of their own that they can transform and decorate as they like. Many others have only a bed, a table, a chair, a place for their books, and their clothes in their travelling bag, as i myself had for a long time. They have no "compartment" where they can be alone, study, think, read, listen to their own music, read, sleep, and talk with their friends.

Bruno Munari

Che cos'è un "abitacolo"? Negli aerei monoposto è il posto del pilota contenente comandi e strumenti, spazio che nei grandi aerei diventa la cabina di pilotaggio. Negli autoveicoli di ogni tipo è lo spazio che accoglie le persone. Nelle astronavi è lo spazio che accoglie gli astronauti con tutto il necessario per vivere e controllare la navigazione. Abitacolo è lo spazio abitabile in misura essenziale. In modo figurativo è anche l'intimo recesso individuale, è il luogo interno dove è situato tutto ciò che forma il proprio mondo. Nelle case degli adulti, non tutti i ragazzi hanno il loro abitacolo. I più fortunati hanno una camera tutta per loro che possono trasformare e arredare a piacere. Molti altri hanno solo un letto, un tavolo, una sedia, un posto per i libri, gli abiti in una valigia come ho avuto io stesso per parecchio tempo. Non hanno un abitacolo dove potersi isolare, dove potere studiare, meditare, scrivere, ascoltare la propria musica, leggere, dormire, conversare con gli amici.

Bruno Munari

SOFAS
DIVANI

1. mod. Strips / des. Cini Boeri, L. Griziotti / prod. Arflex.
2. mod. 150 Grand'Italia / des. De Pas, D'Urbino, Lomazzi / prod. Zanotta.
3. mod. Capitolo / des. A. Rossi, L. Meda / prod. Molteni.
4. prod. Cinova.
5. mod. Carrera / des. De Pas, D'Urbino, Lomazzi / prod. Bonacina Meda.
6. mod. Squash / des. P. Deganello / prod. Driade.
7. mod. Sindbad / des. V. Magistretti / prod. Cassina / 1981.
8. mod. Ouverture / des. P.L. Cerri / prod. Poltrona Frau / 1982.
9. mod. Small Wave / des. G. Offredi / prod. Saporiti.
10. mod. Paros / des. T. Ammannati e G.B. Vitelli / prod. Brunati / 1981.
11. mod. Le Bambole / des. M. Bellini / prod. B&B Italia.
12. mod. Anfibio / des. A. Becchi / prod. Giovanetti.

One lives with families of forms which, like those of relatives, multiply, quarrel, grow old, and now and then die. The memory of one's adolescence, of one's parents' family; the austerity of the post-war years, the austerity of functionalism, armchairs with all their bones in sight, wooden bones, bones of black iron, jutting out and (who knows why?) aerodynamic; grey suits, earnest and hard-working people; few but deeply venerated masters. Sitting down to talk, decide, analyze. Then our youth and our family, folk and pop music, assemblies, a lot of us sitting around just to be together, and often lying down; the yearning for something soft, round, low, something to embrace, shift around, pile up; one's physical relationship with his armchair-companion / or daughter / and or mother; conceal the bones, make them disappear, polyurethane that grows and covers, a metaphor for making by shaping; air, wadding, feathers, colors, hopes and creation, a lot of design, with all of it amusingly lumped together, fathers that grumble but follows one, grandparents that write and encourage one. Maturity and reflux; puzzled we watch our children grow; correct forms (a bit), seriousness (a bit), industry, supplies, marketing (a bit); durable mate-

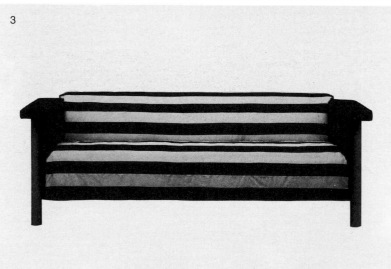

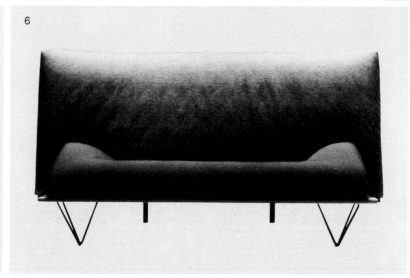

rials, high quality cloth and consoling and (a bit) reassuring armchairs; celebrations, exhibitions, retrospective reappraisals. The armchair gladly becomes a divan and exhibits itself, sure of its form: you know what you're sitting on; take it from me, you'll be properly supported and shown to good advantage. But look out! Groups of younger brothers and a few old codgers are moving about distributing padded forms at once simple and original, covered with bright colors and with improbable decorations.

Jonathan De Pas - Donato D'Urbino - Paolo Lomazzi

Si vive con famiglie di forme che, come quelle di parenti, si moltiplicano, litigano, invecchiano, ogni tanto muoiono. Ricordo d'adolescenza, famiglia dei genitori; austerità del dopoguerra, austerità del razionalismo, poltrone con tutte le ossa ben in vista, ossa di legno, di ferro nero, scattanti e (chissà perché) aereodinamiche; abiti grigi serietà e impegno; pochi maestri molto venerati. Sedersi per parlare, decidere, analizzare. Poi la gioventù e la nostra famiglia, il folk e il pop, assemblee, sedersi in tanti e in ogni modo per stare assieme, sdraiarsi spesso; e la voglia del morbido, del tondo, del basso, da abbracciare, spostare, am-

mucchiare; il rapporto fisico con la poltrona compagna/o, figlia/o e mamma; nascondere le ossa o farle sparire, il poliuretano che cresce e copre, metafora del fare formando; l'aria, l'ovatta, la piuma, il colore, speranza e creazione, tanto design, tutti assieme divertentemente, i padri brontolano ma seguono, i nonni scrivono e promuovono. Maturità e riflusso; perplessi guardiamo crescere i figli; forme corrette (un poco), serietà (un poco), l'industria, la fornitura, il marketing (un poco); materiali duraturi, tessuti pregiati e poltrone consolanti e un poco rassicuranti; celebrazioni, mostre, rivisitazioni. La poltrona

diventa volentieri un divano che si esibisce sicuro della sua forma: sappi su cosa ti siedi, comunque credimi sarai degnamente sostenuto e valorizzato. Ma, attenzione: gruppi di fratelli più giovani, qualche vecchio scapestrato trascorrono qua e là distribuendo forme imbottite tanto semplici quanto inaspettate, coperte da vividi colori e da stoffe dalle decorazioni improbabili.

Jonathan De Pas - Donato D'Urbino - Paolo Lomazzi

7

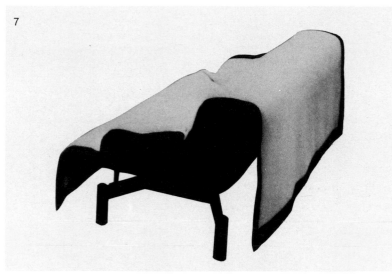

8

9

10

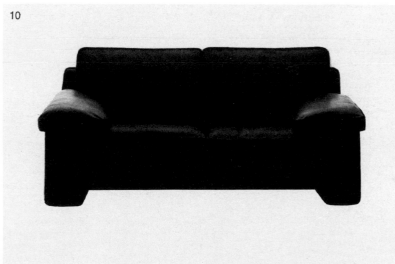

11

12

NOCTURNE
CITY LIGHTS

A SERA
LUCI DELLA CITTÀ

HONK AND HUM RESUME.
WHO'S DRIVING?
KEYS UNDER FLOWER POT.
LATE FOR THE MOVIE.
THE SPECIFIC GRAVITY OF ICE
CREAM.
THERE IS ALWAYS A LAST
STREETCAR.

MOTORI E FRASTUONO.
FRASTUONO E MOTORI.
CHI GUIDA?
L'ALLARME HA LA CHIAVE.
INIZIO SECONDO TEMPO.
GELATO GRAVITAZIONALE.
L'ULTIMO TRAM.

Pier Paolo Pasolini
Fragments of the Roman night

During the nights of March, the waters of the Tiber don't yet absorb the light cast by the thousands of lamps stretching from Ponte Milvio all the way to San Paolo where they fade out. A thin layer of cold air separates the water and the light. Some nights when it's prematurely warm, you can catch a glimpse of the agreement that the breeze and the river will reach in the purity of the spring. The dark landscape of water and air is punctuated by countless lights following curved lines in the arabesque of a night that's thicker than the city trees... And when that cold layer has vanished, the light, impalpable air circulating between the river and the lamps will be transformed completely into odor. And this enormous shambles pierced by the thousand odors that make it what it is, settles on the banks of the Tiber like an enchanting gas that poisons you inadvertently, so that everyone, taken unawares, wishes for death, just for a moment, in that perfume of distant asphalt streets (the Pincio, Corso Trieste, the Città Giardino, the southern quarters...), of garbage, of sweet grasses, and of urinals. The tram tracks sinking beneath

59% of the population goes to the movies (12% goes at least once a week).
21% attends concerts (5% at least once a month).
26% goes to the theater (6% at least once a month).
11% goes to the opera and the ballet.
27% attends conferences and debates.
36% goes to art exhibits.
25% goes to museums.
21% goes to libraries.

Il 59% della popolazione va al cinema (il 12% va al cinema almeno una volta la settimana).
Il 21% va al concerto (il 5% almeno una volta al mese).
Il 26% va al teatro (il 6% almeno una volta al mese).
L'11% va all'opera e al balletto.
Il 27% assiste a conferenze e dibattiti.
Il 36% visita mostre d'arte.
Il 25% visita musei.
Il 21% frequenta biblioteche.

Entertainment expenditures breakdown:

Movies	42%
Sport events	16%
Theater, opera, concerts	5%

The percentage of expenditures on movies shows a tendency to decrease. Expenditures on sport events, theater, opera and concerts are increasing.

Spesa per gli spettacoli:

Il cinema assorbe il	42%
Le manifestazioni sportive il	16%
Il teatro, l'opera, il concerto il	5%

La spesa per il cinema tende a ridursi. In aumento la spesa per le manifestazioni sportive, per il teatro, l'opera, la danza, i concerti.

1. Woman's evening dress, *Abito da donna da sera* / des. Valentino / prod. Valentino / 1982.
2. Play bill, *Locandina* / prod. Piccolo Teatro di Milano.
3. Play bill, *Locandina* / prod. Teatro alla Scala / 1921.
4. Steering-wheel-movements, *Movimento volante* / mod. Orca / des. G. Giugiaro / prod. Italdesign / 1982.
5. Steering-wheel-movements, *Movimento volante* / mod. Medusa / des. G. Giugiaro / prod. Italdesign / 1980.

DOV'È LA LIBERTÀ

1954

ROBERTO ROSSELLINI

Totò

118

the small, hard gravel of the pavement begins to take on a mute expressiveness, tragically nostalgic and severe. Look, there's the city with its new suburbs and its afternoons when the white sun is deadening in its monotony, everything pervaded by a depressing normality, like a mild tubercular fever. Along those tram tracks, along those sidewalks, along those parapets flanking the feverish river banks, on those stairways that lead to the water down steps smeared with feces, across those bridges silhouetted against that seventeenth century sky of Rome – corrupted and magnificent but never pure, grandiose without

being infinite – over those fields where the green is devoured by an insane emerald, against those stucco walls aged by the sun, walls that will never be restored, as if consecrated to a desolating eternity, in all these places the perfume of the first premature spring nights moves like an animal roused from hot sleep, stretching freely, shaking sleep out of its brain. This marvellous breath, so anonymous and infernal, reconstructs last year's "fragments of the Roman night" with pitiless precision.

The landscape along the Tiber from Ponte Sisto to Isola Tiberina is a rustic one. To the left, the Ghetto sings at the

top of its voice, from Piazza delle Tartarughe to the Theater of Marcellus, from Piazza Campitelli to the maternal forest of Trastevere to the right. From here, the horizons are filled with the paved yards of the slaughter-house, the central market and, further away, Saint Paul's Basilica with its Sunday-best Tyrrhenian airs become hardened and dirty. Going still further, you have the Monteverde district, the enormous storage depot of an eternal altar, between massive papal walls and junk yards, until you reach Ponte Bianco, a construction zone crusty with useless refuse. This is the source of those supremely aphrodisiac odors, those

odors that tempt you to surrender yourself to your vices, even at the risk of sacrificing your life. It's the haunt of masochists, long-loaders and light-loaders and impotents. Throughout the normality of everyday pretenses and traffic like an immense Gordian knot whose solution has been lost to the secret past and must be untied a strand at a time – a sumptuous, brilliantly bourgeois and scrupulous syndrome – the perfume of last summer's warm nights spreads like a disinfectant spray.

Pier Paolo Pasolini, "Alì dagli occhi azzurri", Garzanti, Milano 1965. Translated by Robert Kleyn.

3

4

5

The ornamental function is considered ephemeral, yet Italians have succeeded in making it a lasting element of their way of life. Ornamental objects may not be considered the highest form of creativity, yet the way in which they have been conceived could witness a sophistication reflecting the wider horizon of all formal arts. The ornamental function has mainly a symbolic purpose; therefore relating objects, having the sole aim of beautifying, are often signs of a dreamlike world not otherwise expressed. After world war II Italians became affluent enough to indulge more widely in the ephemeral world; they soon became great goldsmiths, recognized masters in the art of everyday ornaments. Taking advantage of their cultural background, which made them protagonists of all formal arts since ancient times, they have expressed through these crafts their passion for the symbols of that aesthetic monument that is their everyday life.

Gianni Bulgari

La funzione ornamentale è generalmente considerata come facente parte dell'"effimero". Gli italiani, grandi cultori di esso, l'hanno sublimata rendendola parte integrante del proprio modo di essere e promuovendola a grande protagonista della loro stessa vita. Gli oggetti ornamentali possono non essere considerati come la più alta espressione della creatività e tuttavia il modo con cui vengono concepiti può essere la testimonianza di un sofisticato processo creativo che ha fatto ricorso al più vasto bagaglio di tutte le arti formali. La funzione ornamentale ha un carattere soprattutto simbolico e l'oggetto ornamentale, non avendo altra funzione che quella di "ornare", costituisce il simbolo di sogni spesso non altrimenti espressi. Gli italiani negli anni del dopoguerra, diventati più facoltosi, si sono potuti permettere di indulgere nell'effimero, diventando i maestri incontestabili, dell'ornamento quotidiano. E, dando fondo al grande retaggio culturale che quasi senza soluzione di continuità li ha resi protagonisti delle arti formali dall'antichità ad oggi, hanno espresso con questa, che è pur considerata un'arte minore, la loro passione per i simboli di quel grande monumento estetico che è la loro vita di tutti i giorni.

Gianni Bulgari

STEERING-WHEELS
VOLANTI

1. mod. A112 / des. Abarth / prod. Autobianchi.
2. mod. 127 Super / prod. Fiat.
3. mod. 208 Turbo / prod. Ferrari.
4. mod. Navajo / des. N. Bertone / prod. Alfa Romeo 33 / 1976.
5. mod. Orca / des. G. Giugiaro / prod. Italdesign.
6. mod. Capsula / des. G. Giugiaro / prod. Italdesign / 1982.
7. mod. Cingolo / des. N. Bertone / prod. Mazda / 1982.
8. mod. Sibilo / des. N. Bertone / 1978.
9. mod. Countach / des. N. Bertone / 1971.
10. mod. Athon / des. N. Bertone / 1980.
11. mod. Medusa / des. G. Giugiaro / prod. Italdesign / 1980.
12. mod. Trevi / des. M. Bellini / prod. Lancia / 1978.

At Bertone we believe that the purpose of the bodywork should not only be limited to the research of car form and styling but should extend to the development of new ideas, even difficult mechanical and technical solutions, that might stimulate the firms and component manufacturers. For this reason an unquestionably original tracked steering wheel was created. It is a band, made up of small, flexibly united plastic dowels, which runs around the main part of the dashboard. The toothing on the inside of the track drives a pulley that is connected to the power steering system by a small shaft. Besides offering a very interesting and pleasing new driving sensation this solution minimizes obstruction, resulting in total instrument display visibility. Although this solution may seem to embody some science-fiction, let's not forget that it has already been in use in the field of avionics for some years. In our opinion it is the "final solution" as far as the instrumentation of the cars of the 90's is concerned.

"All the visible control functions that until now were dealt with by single instruments, even if advanced in design and technology, are now condensed in a cathode-ray tube: a small, colour monitor that is situated on the

1

2

3

4

5

6

inside of the tracked steering wheel. With this system it is possible to increase the car's command possibilities and supply the driver with excellent graphic representations fo every piece of information; calculator, digital, three-dimensional, in colour, and so on.

Paolo Caccamo

Noi della Bertone pensiamo che la funzione del carrozziere non si limiti alla ricerca formale dello stile dell'auto, ma si estenda allo sviluppo di nuove idee, anche se di difficile soluzione meccanica e tecnologica, tali da stimolare le Case e i produttori di componenti. Proprio per questo motivo è stato realizzato un volante a cingolo assolutamente originale. Si tratta di un nastro formato da piccoli tasselli in materia plastica e uniti tra di loro in modo flessibile, che ruota attorno al corpo principale del cruscotto. Questo cingolo possiede internamente una dentatura che comanda una puleggia collegata, tramite un alberino,

al sistema di sterzo servoassistito. La soluzione presenta, oltre ad una interessante e piacevole nuova sensazione di guida, un ingombro molto contenuto e una visibilità totale del quadro strumenti. Anche per questo particolare abbiamo scelto una soluzione che, pur se oggi ha del fantascientifico — ma non dimentichiamo che in avionica è già utilizzato da alcuni anni — è a nostro avviso la "soluzione finale" per quanto riguarda la strumentazione delle autovetture degli anni 90". "Tutte le funzioni visive di controllo che finora erano svolte da strumenti singoli, pur se avanzati come tecnologia e design, sono ora condensati in

un tubo a raggi catodici: un piccolo monitor a colori che trova la sua naturale collocazione all'interno del volante a cingolo. Con questo sistema non solo è possibile ampliare le possibilità di controllo della vettura e dare di ogni dato la rappresentazione grafica più gradita al guidatore — analogica, digitale, tridimensionale e a colori.

Paolo Caccamo

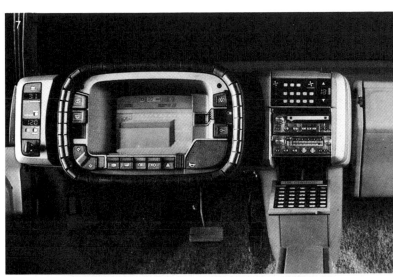

SLEEP
THINGS OF THE DAY FADE AWAY

TAKE A BOOK TO BED.
THE NEIGHBOURS LOVE MUSIC.
A CUP OF CAMOMILLE TEA?
MOTORCYCLES ARE POPULAR.
VELVET IS THE NIGHT.

IL SONNO
DAL SEGNO AL SOGNO

SI LEGGE A LETTO.
LA MUSICA DEI VICINI.
UN CANARINO IN TAZZA?
PASSANO LE MOTO.
NOTTURNO FELPATO.

Luigi Malerba
A Dreamer's Diary

Settecamini, December 30-31, 1978 (My decision to write down my dreams everyday during 1979 is starting to disturb my sleep so that I'm dreaming tomorrow night's dreams.)
I have the same mute dream every night. It's a like a painting that calls for some minor retouching. The painting is nothing other than the front page of a newspaper whose name I can't make out. In protest, I don't bother reading the headlines, but just the same, they provoke my comment: "This is a dream I would have preferred to have tomorrow, since tomorrow I'm starting to write down my dreams."

Rome, January 25-26
I get out of bed and go to open the window, but the handle comes loose in my hand. I realize that the wood of the frame is rotten inside, and that only the outside layer is still healthy. Pushing my finger against the wood, it gives like a sponge, soft, damp, and dark. I go to the chest of drawers and discover that it's also rotten inside. Again I push my finger against the surface of the wood, and again it gives and my finger penetrates into the rot. I quickly check everything wood in the room and realize

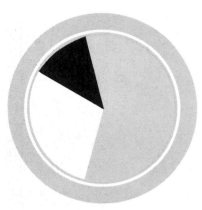

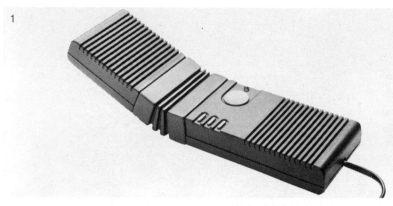

Relaxing at home after dinner:
36% read
26% watch television
12% knit or embroider
 6% listen to music

The average bed-time on week-days is 10.30 p.m.
The length of sleep per night averages 8 hours.
Men sleep an average of 7.54 hours per night, while women sleep an average of 8.22 hours per night.

Average length of sleep per night according to age and occupation:

Businessmen, executives, professionals, managers	7.59
Store owners, Sales clerks, artisans	8.51
Office workers	8.03
Skilled workers and unskilled workers	7.55
Farmers	7.45
Agricultural workers	8.00
Miscellaneous workers	8.31

Lo svago in casa dopo cena:
36% leggono
26% guardano la televisione
12% lavorano a maglia, ricamano
 6% ascoltano musica

Nei giorni feriali l'ora del riposo notturno della popolazione inizia mediamente attorno alle ore 22,30.
La durata media del riposo notturno si aggira attorno alle 8 ore.
Rilevata secondo il sesso: uomini 7,54; dinne 8,22.

Durata media del riposo notturno secondo le attività professionali:

imprenditori, liberi professionisti, dirigenti, impiegati di concetto	7,59
esercenti, negozianti, artigiani	8,51
impiegati non di concetto	8,03
operai specializzati, operai generici	7,55
agricoltori in proprio	7,45
agricoltori dipendenti	8,00
condizioni non professionali	8,31

IL DESERTO ROSSO

1964

MICHELANGELO ANTONIONI

Monica Vitti
Richard Harris

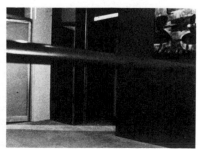

that *all the furniture has the same disease*. Even the doors. Worried, I go into the bathroom and look in the mirror. I'm very pale. I push my finger, against my cheek and am horrified to realize that it sinks into the flesh just like the wood.

Rome, January 26-27
I discover that my burnished steel rule measures time. I can measure the time, but only during the daytime, because the rule is black at night. I say to myself, "The time for clocks has run out."

Settecamini, January 27-28
Thieves have broken into my Rome house again. I inspect it carefully and am forced to admit that *they've stolen the same things they stole last time*. I accept this contradiction without difficulty, annoyed as I am by their new intrusion.

Rome, January 29-30
I'm at the theatre. Each spectator holds a string tied to one of the actors on the stage. I have a string to a young actress, and once in a while I give it a slight tug in order to "correct" her performance. The other people in the audience do just the same.

Rome, January 30-31
There's a part of Rome I've been dreaming about for years now, but only at long intervals, and I always find it the same, just as if it really existed. It's a concave piazza paved with blocks of stone, somewhere near a bridge over the Tiber, surrounded by low, ancient houses that face two different streets, one of which could be Via Giulia, although it isn't, while the other is a narrow street, much poorer. All the buildings are asymmetrical in shape, façades with roofs sloping sideways, French windows and normal windows, little windows irregularly spaced, doors to one side rather than centered. On the ground floor of the building in the middle of the two streets there are two bar-restaurants with tables outside, very discreet, frequented by quiet people. Cars don't pass here and I like to come on foot, sit down at one of the tables and smoke a cigarette or have a drink. Here I can hope to meet friends. Not far away there's a cross street where a woman sells paintings by famous artists (I recognize a de Chirico). Next to her lies a small chest of drawers, abandoned. It has a pebbled glass door which I open to hide a roll of bills which have a de Chirico drawing in an oval on one side. It could be a million lire, maybe more. After hiding the money, I follow a guide wearing a visored cap who's been waiting for me

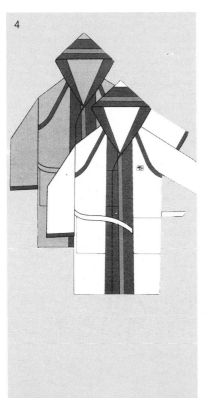

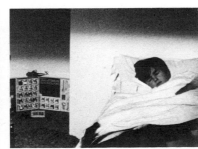

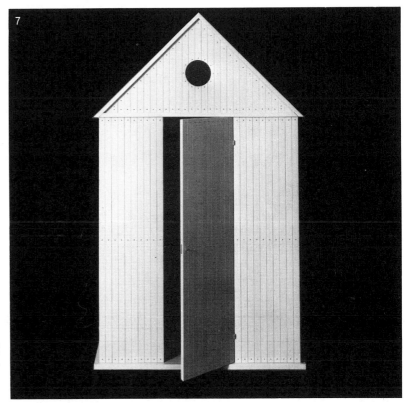

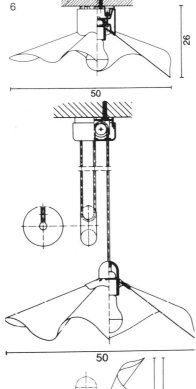

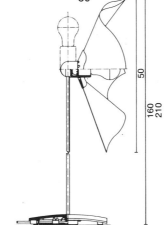

1. Intercom, *Radiocitofono* / des. Centro kappa / prod. Perry Electric s.r.l. / 1981.
2. Sofa, *Divano* / mod. Siglo 20 / des. F. Soro / prod. ICF De Padova / 1982.
3. Television set, *Televisore* / des. C. Casati / prod. Voxson / 1981.
4. Bath-robe, *Accappatoio* / mod. New Comfort / prod. Superga / 1982.
5. Clock, *Orologio* / mod. Arcobaleno / des. A. Leclerc / prod. Lorenz / 1966.
6. Lamp, *Lampada* / mod. Area / des. M. Bellini / prod. Artemide / 1974.
7. Wardrobe, *Cabina armadio* / mod. A. Rossi / prod. Molteni / 1980.

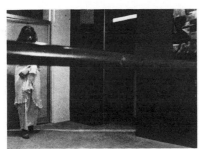

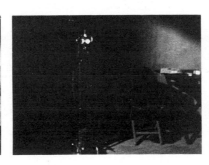

on the corner of the street. We enter an underground gallery, recently discovered, passing beneath the Tiber. I'm surprised by the large number of Roman statues in the gallery entrance, placed in niches in the wall according to their height. I express my wonder and admiration, but then quickly realize that all the statues are plastic. I'm ashamed of my clumsy mistake and continue down the gallery which is beginning to look like a long corridor with a vaulted ceiling, very high, decorated with stuccos and frescos. Are these fake like the statues? The display of Roman statues along the walls continues, all fakes, placed, in niches

lined with shining gold. The gallery continues, curving slightly, the floor sloping like a street. Despite the fake statues, the discovery of this gallery is astonishing, if only for its grandiose dimensions. I finally step out into the light together with my guide, passing through a small door, half-hidden, leading to a small garden. The guide points to the river-bed where a surface of bricks has been worn smooth by the water and partially covered by sand. This is the roof of the gallery. I go back to the street where I hid my money. The chest of drawers is no longer there. I'm very upset. I see a woman, not the same one as before, at the corner of a

street, next to a pile of furniture, and I notice the chest of drawers where I hid the bills. I open it, but it's empty. I don't say anything, knowing it's useless. I have to resign myself to losing the money, even though it disturbs me greatly. I wander around the streets without purpose, with the vague suspect that *I'm waiting to wake up.*

Settecamini, February 3-4
The Sahara Desert. I'm surprised it's not as hot as I'd heard. I don't feel the heat, but I'm sweating abundantly. It's a cold sweat. An airplane appears in the sky, circles around to draw an O (or a zero?) and then disappears again. I'm

alone, but over there towards the horizon, I see a screen with images from *Casablanca.* I walk towards the screen. When I get there, I'll become part of the film.

Rome, February 10-11
Near Piazzale Clodio, there is an elevator built against a stone wall, its pulleys, steel cables, guides, well-oiled gears, all exposed. This elevator takes you up to Monte Mario. It's large enough to hold a car, almost like a freight elevator. A girl with an American accent tells me she wants to trade her near new Porsche for the old Alfa Romeo belonging to A.M. But why is she asking

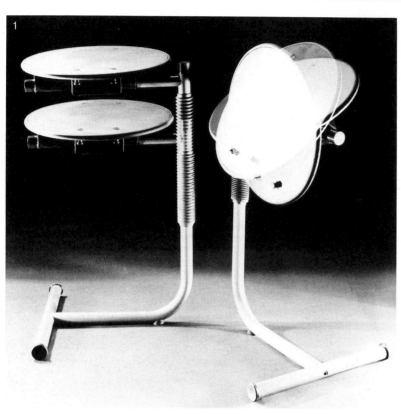

Normally when one thinks of books one thinks of writings of various kinds: literary, philosophical, historical, essayistic, and so on, writings to be printed on paper. Very little attention is paid to the paper, the binding of the book, the color of the ink, and all the things that contribute to making a book as an object. Very little interest is aroused by the type and still less by the blank spaces, margins, pagination and the rest of it.

Can the book as an object, independent of the words printed in it, really communicate anything? And if so, what?

Normally books are made with only a few types of paper and bound in two or three different ways. Paper is used as a support for the writing and illustrations and not in order to "communicate" something. If we want to explore the possibilities of visual communication offered by the materials of which a book is made, then we should try with all types of paper, all kinds of formats; and with different bindings, die-cuts, sequences of forms (of sheets), and paper of different materials, as well as with their natural colors and textures.

Bruno Munari

Normalmente quando si pensa ai libri si pensa a dei testi, di vario genere: letterario, filosofico, storico, saggistico ecc., da stampare sulle pagine. Poco interesse viene portato alla carta e alla rilegatura del libro e al colore dell'inchiostro, a tutti quegli elementi con i quali si realizza il libro come oggetto. Poco interesse viene dedicato ai caratteri da stampa e ancora meno agli spazi bianchi, ai margini, alla numerazione delle pagine, e a tutto il resto.

Il libro come oggetto, indipendente dalle parole stampate, può comunicare qualcosa? E che cosa?

Normalmente i libri vengono fatti con pochi tipi di carte e rilegati in due o tre modi diversi. La carta è usata come supporto del testo e delle illustrazioni e non come "comunicante" qualcosa. Se si vuole sperimentare le possibilità di comunicazione visiva dei materiali con i quali è fatto un libro allora dovremo provare con tutti i tipi di carta, tutti i tipi di formati; con rilegature diverse, fustellature, sequenze di forme (di fogli), con carte di materie diverse, coi loro colori naturali e le loro texture.

Bruno Munari

LA DOLCE VITA
1960

FEDERICO FELLINI

Anita Ekberg
Marcello Mastroianni

me? She should tell A.M. who is a friend of mine. Fine. You can go up to Monte Mario whenever your want, you can do as you like. The elevator goes up silently. The girl pulls me into a dark corner and begins to strip. "Just like that, standing?" "I prefer it standing," replies the girl. I decide not to go up to Monte Mario but to go to the U.S., leaving the relationship with the girl "suspended".

Rome, February 11-12
A new system for mailing letters. I open the window, place the sealed envelope on a current of air, and the letter takes off for its destination. It's a nice inven-tion, finally they've invented something useful. I close the window and sit down to write another letter.
(This dream has no dimensions. no space, and lasts a very brief time before I slip back into the dark of sleep.)

Rome, February 12-13
A street in Rome near San Salvatore in Lauro. Alongside the street, on the sidewalks, there are gigantic irides-cent vases filled with colored facial powder. People walk along the street, someone takes the lid off a vase and covers himself with the powder using a feather duster.

Second dream. I find myself in the Tri-tone tunnel and climb the stairs to reach a bar on Via Crispi. I get to the street, but then I climb more stairs, then I go down other stairs, then I climb up again, always a new stairway. I'm lost in a labyrinth of stairways and don't find the bar.

Settecamini, February 18-19
A snake's head appears around the corner of a building, above the roof of a house, among the trees in Villa Bor-ghese. It's a head which fades like a greenish cloud, with glasses, and has the features of a famous Italian politic-ian. Everyone sees it and recognizes its but no one reacts, no one speaks. I'm worried and shocked. This is the head of the Mafia who's organized right-wing vandalism and left-wing ter-rorism, he's behind every scandal, and now he wants to become *president of everything*. I look over a bridge across the Tiber and this time I see the head of the snake pulling down a soft body which occupies the entire river bed.
(This dream seems to contain an inverted metaphorical process, since the metaphor is translated into a "real" image within the dream.)
Luigi Malerba, "Diario di un sognatore", Einaudi, Torino 1981. Translated by Robert Kleyn.

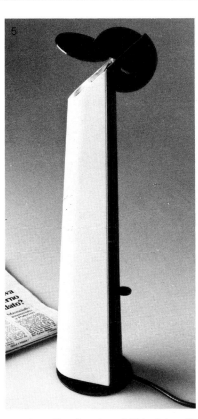

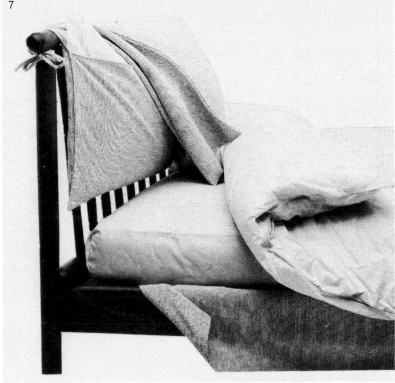

1. Table, *Tavolino* / mod. Trio / des. R. Lucci, P. Orlandini / prod. Magis / 1981.
2. Lamp, *Lampada* / mod. Minibox / des. G. Aulenti, P. Castiglioni / prod. Stilnovo / 1982.
3. Lamp, *Lampada* / mod. Valigia 20073 / des. E. Sottsass jr. / prod. Stilnovo / 1977.
4. Candle holder, *Candelabro* / mod. Magritte / prod. Bulgari / 1982.
5. Lamp, *Lampada* / mod. Ginigiana / des. A. Castiglioni / prod. Flos / 1981.
6. Books, *Libri* / prod. F.M. Ricci-Adel-phi-Einaudi.
7. Bed, *Letto* / Andreij / des. V. Magi-stretti / prod. Flou / 1980.

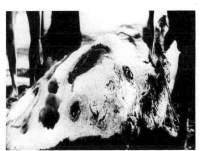

1. mod. Jill / des. King, Miranda, Arnaldi / prod. Arte Luce / 1979.
2. mod. Ciclope / mod. J. Colombo / prod. Bieffeplast / 1969.
3. mod. Bipip / mod. A. Castiglioni / prod. Flos / 1976.
4. mod. Albatros 393 / mod. V. Magistretti / prod. O'Luce / 1976.
5. mod. Crisol / mod. King, Miranda, Arnaldi / prod. Arteluce / 1981.

6. mod. Frisbi / mod. A. Castiglioni / prod. Flos / 1978.
7. mod. Area Sospensione / mod. M. Bellini / prod. Artemide / 1974.
8. mod. Lampiatta / des. De Pas, D'Urbino, Lomazzi / prod. Stilnovo / 1978.
9. mod. Plutone / des. D. Puppa / prod. Fontana Arte / 1981.
10. mod. Nemea / des. V. Magistretti / prod. Artemide / 1979.

In studying the problem of artificial lighting in a constructed area, criteria will depend on what, how, and how much one wishes to see.

The quantity of light, its provenance and quality depend on the type of use to be made of the premisses and on the need to give prominence to particular zones and elements.

The variability of light and the alternative of artificial light have exerted a more and more important influence on ambient architecture, to the point of modifying even spatial values.

Lighting apparatus can be classified according to five main models of illumination: direct lighting, and intense direct lighting. All these possibilities of distributing light throughout the area are at our disposal in dealing with the problems of lighting the home.

As various activities can be carried out in the living-room we need diffused light in the parlor area for conversation, a more intense light at another point for reading purposes, and a concentrated light on the surface of the dining table, without dazzling the diners; then, an even more concentrated light on a small writing-desk or working table so that one can carry out necessary work. Entrance halls will only need a diffused or reflected

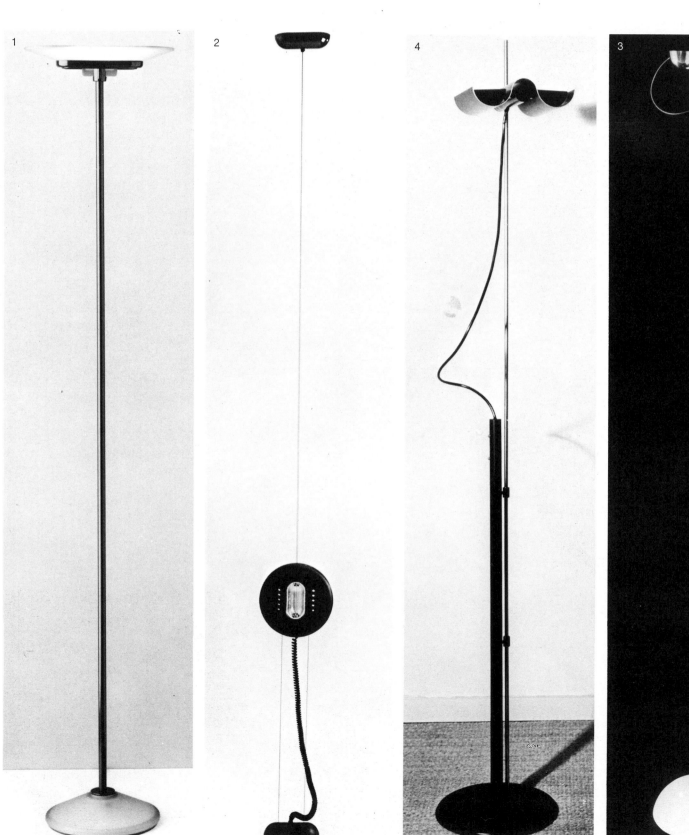

light, as will the bedroom, with a spot of light on the bedside table corresponding to an eventual wardrobe or dressing table. Corridors, too, can be illuminated by diffused or reflected light. Bathrooms should have diffused lighting with more intense light by the mirror.

In the process of designing lighting apparatus the form should be defined as a function of use and the type of lighting desired. The esthetic effect of the object is obtained by progressively eliminating everything superfluous.

Achille Castiglioni

Nello studio del problema della luce artificiale nell'ambiente costruito, i criteri di illuminazione dipendono da cosa, da come e da quanto si vuole vedere.

La quantità di luce, la sua provenienza e la sua qualità dipendono dal tipo di uso che si fa dell'ambiente e dalla necessità di mettere in evidenza zone ed elementi particolari.

La variabilità e l'alternativa delle luci artificiali incidono sempre più notevolmente nella architettura dell'ambiente mutando perfino i valori spaziali.

Le apparecchiature illuminanti si possono classificare secondo questi cinque principali moduli di illuminazione: illuminazione a luce diretta, illuminazione a luce indiretta, illuminazione a luce diffusa, illuminazione a luce diretta-riflessa, illuminazione a luce diretta concentrata.

Per risolvere i problemi della luce nella casa, noi abbiamo a disposizione tutte queste possibilità di illuminazione da distribuire nell'ambiente.

In un soggiorno potremo svolgere attività diverse; quindi avremo la necessità di luce diffusa nella zona salotto per conversare, di luce più intensa in un punto per poter leggere, di luce concentrata sul piano del tavolo da pranzo, evitando l'abbagliamento dei commensali; di luce ancora più concentrata su un iccolo scrittoio o tavolo di lavoro dove si possano svolgere particolari attività.

Nel processo di progettazione di un apparecchio illuminante la definizione della forma è in funzione dell'utilità e del tipo di illuminazione che si vuole ottenere. Il risultato estetico dell'oggetto è ottenuto per progressiva eliminazione del superfluo.

Achille Castiglioni

6

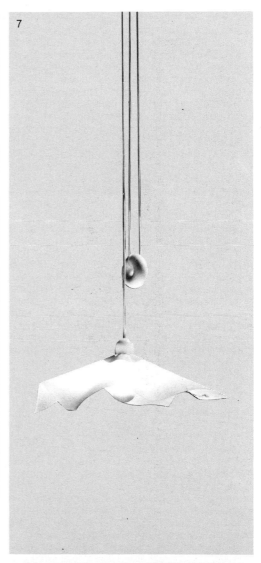
7

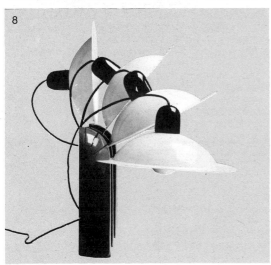
8

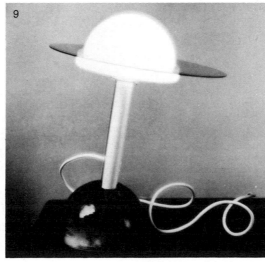
9

10

PHENOMENA OF THIS SORT MUST ALSO BE INCLUDED IN ANY PANORAMA OF ITALIAN DESIGN. OTHERWISE IT IS HARD TO GRASP AN IDEA OF ITALY ITSELF OR OF DESIGN

UMBERTO ECO

1. We are surrounded by artificial objects, or artifacts. The notion of artifact covers a wide range of things, from the house to the screw. A great Italian architect and theorist of architecture, Ernesto Rogers, formulated the following slogan as the designer's ideal: *from the spoon to the city*. Artifacts are *designed*. The English term "design" is richer and more comprehensive than the Italian term "disegno", and indeed an expression such as "industrial design" cannot be exactly translated by what would appear to be the Italian synonym *disegno industriale*. *Disegno* in Italian gives the idea of a profile, an outline, something that has more to do with the outer shape than with the organic form of an object. *Disegnare* is the verb you would use to describe what a draughtsman does when he draws (in English it would be better to say "sketches"), the shape of a horse, but a horse is really designed in as much as it is an object of nature, that is to say, it is designed according to a relationship between the inside and the outside, between form and function.

Let us talk then about design, but not only about industrial design: between the second half of the last century and the first half of the present one various thinkers came to the conclusion that design already existed before the industrial world did, indeed, before the time of the eighteenth-century mechanical looms. Neolithic woman (apparently it was a woman: men went out hunting, and women invented objects in the village), when she dampened the clay and turned it on a wheel to produce a vase (the perfect, functional, revolutionary shape), she was acting as a designer.

We have thus established two points: design concerns the vase as much as it does the city; and design is a form of human activity that precedes the industrial revolution.

2. However we still have to distinguish three types of design:

a) Identified Design, which is the outcome of an expressed theory and of a practice in which the object aims to exemplify explicitly its author's theory; the Seagram Building and Pininfarina's belong to this category, but so do the submarine and the war machine designed by Leonardo da Vinci.

b) Anonymous Design (or design that does not seem to have an author that anyone can remember, even if there was one originally); design of this sort has no explicit theory, or if it does, it does not claim to exemplify it; the author, famous or anonymous, only wanted to resolve a practical problem; this category includes the various coffee machines that can be seen in Italy, those produced industrially for coffee bars and the hand-made ones once used in people's homes.

c) Non-conscious Design: I use this term in order to avoid the term "savage" or *selvaggio* currently used in Italian, which does not seem quite right; this category includes farmers' and blacksmiths' tools and many other devices that can be found in industrial society; the people who made these objects did not think of themselves as designers, were not aware of demonstrating any theory and certainly did not think their names would be handed down to posterity: their concern was only to produce an object that would work; this is how the inventor of the first plough or rudder worked; this is how the anonymous inventors of many (perhaps hundreds) of different kinds of pasta used in the Italian peninsula approached their task; let us, then, not talk about savage design, even in Lévi-Strauss's sense of the "savage mnd", because these objects rely on technical knowledge that is very similar to that of anyone who conceives of and constructs an industrial object today.

These three types of design are present in any civilization: in archaic society, we can think of a pyramid or the sarcophagus of a mummy as examples of identified design, weapons of war as an example of anonymous design, and agricultural tools as an example of non-concious design. In the United States, the Seagram Building is identified design, a gas station is anonymous design, and a lollipop is non-conscious design. New York's Towers are identified design; uptown apartment buildings are anonymous design; Manhattan and especially Wall Street as an almost casual result of "savage" planning, are non-conscious design and, seen from the sea, Manhattan is more beautiful than the Statue of Liberty, which is an examle of identified design.

3. In each of the three cases that we have given the person who designs an object does so for three reasons:

ANCHE QUESTI FENOMENI DEBBONO FAR PARTE DI UN PANORAMA DEL DESIGN ITALIANO, ALTRIMENTI NON SI CAPISCE NÉ COSA SIA L'ITALIA NÉ COSA SIA IL DESIGN

UMBERTO ECO

1. Siamo circondati da oggetti artificiali o artefatti. Quella di artefatto è una nozione abbastanza vasta che comprende sia la casa che la vite. Un grande architetto e teorico dell'architettura italiano, Ernesto Rogers, nel proporre l'ideale del designer. aveva elaborato il seguente slogan: Dal cucchiaio alla città. Gli artefatti sono disegnati. Il termine inglese design è più ricco e comprensivo del termine italiano "disegno", e infatti una espressione come "industrial design" non viene tradotta con esattezza dall'apparente sinonimo italiano "disegno industriale". Infatti l'italiano "disegno" suggerisce l'idea di un profilo, di una outline, di qualcosa che riguarda più la forma esterna che la forma organica di un oggetto. Un disegnatore "disegna" (in italiano, ma in inglese sarebbe meglio dire sketches) la shape di un cavallo, ma un cavallo come oggetto di natura è designed, progettato secondo un rapporto tra interno ed esterno, e secondo una corrispondenza tra forma e funzione.

Parliamo dunque di design, ma non solo di industrial design: le riflessioni, condotte tra la seconda metà del secolo scorso e la prima metà di questo secolo sull'idea di design nel mondo industriale, hanno portato a riconoscere che c'era del design anche prima del mondo industriale, anche prima dei telai meccanici del secolo XVIII. La donna del neolitico (pare che fosse una donna: l'uomo era a caccia, e la donna inventava oggetti nel villaggio) che per prima ha bagnato della creta e l'ha fatta girare su di una ruota, inventando la forma del vaso (forma perfetta, funzionale, rivoluzionaria) ha fatto del design. Abbiamo dunque stabilito almeno due cose: che il design riguarda tanto la città quanto il vaso; e che il design è una attività umana che precede la rivoluzione industriale.

2. Tuttavia dobbiamo ancora distinguere tre tipi di design:

— il design firmato, effetto di una teoria espressa e di una pratica in cui l'oggetto vuole anche esemplificare esplicitamente la teoria del suo autore; appartengono a questa categoria il Seagram Building, la macchina disegnata da Pininfarina, ma anche il sottomarino o la macchina da guerra progettata da Leonardo da Vinci;

— Il design non firmato (o di cui nessuno ricorda la firma, anche se c'è stato un autore individuale); questo design o non ha teoria esplicita o, se ce l'ha, non pretende di esemplificarla; l'autore, noto o anonimo che sia, voleva solo risolvere un problema pratico; appartengono a questa categoria, per esempio, le varie macchine da caffè che si vedono in Italia, sia quelle prodotte industrialmente per i bar, sia quelle prodotte artigianalmente e usate nelle famiglie di un tempo.

— il design inconscio; uso questo termine perché non mi pare giusto parlare, come si fa, di design "selvaggio"; rientrano in questa categoria gli attrezzi da contadino o da.fabbro e molti strumenti che circolano nella società industriale; chi costruiva questi oggetti non pensava di essere un designer, né di dimostrare alcuna teoria, né immaginava che il suo nome potesse passare alla storia: si preoccupava solo di produrre un oggetto capace di funzionare; così ha lavorato chi ha inventato il primo aratro, o la prima nave con timone posteriore cernierato; così hanno lavorato gli anonimi inventori delle decine e decine (forse centinaia) di tipi di pasta usati nella penisola italiana; non parleremo dunque di design selvaggio, neppure nel senso in cui Lévi-Strauss parla di "savage mind", perché dietro a questo oggetti c'è una sapienza tecnica molto affine a quella di chi costruisce oggi un oggetto industriale.

Questi tre tipi di design sono presenti in ogni civiltà: in una società arcaica possiamo pensare alla piramide o al sarcofago della mummia come esempi di design firmato, alle armi da guerra come esempio di design non firmato, agli attrezzi agricoli come esempio di design inconscio. Negli Stati Uniti, il Seagram Building è design firmato, una gas station è design anonimo e un lollipop è design inconscio. Le Towers di New York sono design firmato, gli apartment buildings di uptown sono design anonimo, Manhattan e specialmente Wall Street, come risultato quasi casuale di una pianificazione selvaggia, è design inconscio e, vista dal mare, è più bella della Statua della Libertà, che era design firmato.

3. In tutti e tre i casi che abbiamo elencato, chi progetta un oggetto lo fa per tre motivi:

(i) Anzitutto si vuole che l'oggetto serva, e cioè che permetta a chi lo usa di farlo funzionare nel modo giusto. L'idea sembra elementare, e

a) First of all the object is meant to be *useful*, in the sense that whoever uses it should be able to make it work the right way. The idea seems elementary, and certainly whoever built the first plough had an idea of this sort in mind.

In this sense we could say that the first theorists of design included thinkers of the past who posed the problem of the relationship between beauty and utility. For example, St. Thomas Aquinas wondered if a saw made of crystal could be considered beautiful and answered in the negative because a crystal saw cannot perform the function proper to a saw. Thus Sullivan's formula "form follows function" must refer not only to the shape of objects but also to the choice of materials. An object must be shaped so that it serves the purpose it was conceived for; this condition is necessary for the concept of design, but it is not sufficient.

b) indeed, an object should show what its purpose is and how it should be used. In a word, the object has a *communicative* aspect, and this is part of its design. A pair of scissors is a perfect example: the shape makes it quite clear where the fingers go, even to someone who has never seen scissors before. Scissors are a masterpiece of design: not only do they cut, but they show how they have to be handled. This aspect of design is fundamental, although it is not always borne in mind. Indeed, there is no denying that non-conscious "savage" design is often considerably wiser than identified design, because the latter often bows to "aesthetic" demands and comes up with new forms that tell the user nothing useful at all.

c) Finally, design has *symbolic* functions: by this I do not mean those primary functions that the object must allow for, but a host of further meaning that allow the object to be used as a mark of social status, power, and so on. These symbolic functions should not be thought of as something extraneous to the object; far from it, they are part of its functions, and it would be wrong to imagine that, if "form follows function", the form should not follow symbolic functions as well. The clearest example is the Rolls Royce. Obviously, if the purpose of car is to cover a certain distance at a certain speed, then we can buy a Fiat or a Ford Rather than a Rolls Royce. But if the ornamental and symbolic aspects of the Rolls Royce have an important social function, one that is as important as its mechanical functions, such that even in the case of the Rolls it can be said that form follows function, then the form is exactly what it should be if the Rolls Royce is to be used as a Rolls Royce. The Rolls Royce continues to perform its social functions when it is parked motionless outside the office or the Hilton Hotel.

4. It would be interesting to write a history of Italian design from the time of the Roman empire to the present. We would discover marvelous examples of identified design, of anonymous design (think of the acqueducts) and of non-conscious design. And we would find some marvelous examples of objects that serve their purpose, that declare and communicate their functions and at the same time communicate symbolic meanings: the first thing that comes to mind is something you can still see in Italian trattorias, the wine flask. It serves its purpose because it holds wine and stands upright on the table; it clearly communicates how it has to be held and how the wine is to be poured, and if the wine drips down the side it is absorbed by the straw covering and does not stain the table; it also communicates ideas and feelings of authenticity, happiness, and simple living. But this analysis would take us too far, and it is probably better to begin our history with the industrial era, when Italian design became well known in America, where it is represented by objects in the Museum of Modern Art in New York (for example, the Olivetti Lettera 22 typewriter). We will start out with this type of "high" design, because Italy is perhaps the country in which the idea of design has been most highly cultivated even in connection with political and social problems. If other countries have had a theory of design, Italy has had a philosophy of design, maybe even an ideology.

In 1972 MOMA in New York organized an exhibition of Italian design that differed from this one, because it stressed identified design and its philosophy. It was a good opportunity, even for Italians, to review the entire history of the dreams, the utopias, and the crises of the design idea. Let us try to identify the most interesting period in the history of "high" design in Italy. I would place it between 1950's and

certamente chi ha costruito il primo aratro aveva in mente una idea del genere. In questo senso tra i primi teorici del design possiamo porre quegli antichi pensatori che si sono posti il problema del rapporto tra bellezza e utilità: per esempio St. Thomas Aquinas si chiedeva se una sega fatta di cristallo potesse essere ritenuta bella, e rispondeva negativamente, perché una sega di cristallo non riesce a svolgere la propria funzione. Quindi, la formula di Sullivan "form follows function" deve essere riferita non solo alla shape degli oggetti, ma anche alla scelta dei materiali.

L'oggetto deve essere shaped in modo che serva a ciò per cui è stato concepito: questa condizione è però necessaria per il concetto di design ma non è sufficiente.

(ii) Infatti occorre anche che l'oggetto mostri a cosa serve e come deve essere usato. C'è insomma un aspetto comunicativo dell'oggetto, che fa parte del suo design. Un esempio perfetto è dato dalle forbici: la loro forma indica, anche a chi non le abbia mai viste, dove si debbono infilare le dita per farle funzionare. Le forbici sono un capolavoro di design: non solo tagliano, ma dicono come debbono essere manovrate. Questo aspetto del design è fondamentale ma non sempre viene tenuto in considerazione. Anzi, bisogna riconoscere che spesso il design inconscio e selvaggio è ben più sapiente del design firmato, dove (per esigenze "estetiche") sovente si inventano nuove forme che non dicono nulla a chi deve usare l'oggetto.

(iii) Infine il design ha funzioni simboliche: intendo per funzioni simboliche non le funzioni primarie che l'oggetto deve premettere, ma tutta una serie di comunicazioni ulteriori che permettono di usare l'oggetto come segno di status sociale, di potere, eccetera. Non bisogna pensare che le funzioni simboliche siano qualcosa di aggiunto all'oggetto, anzi, fanno parte delle sue funzioni e sarebbe sbagliato pensare che, se "form follows function", la forma non debba seguire anche le funzioni simboliche. L'esempio più chiaro è quella della Rolls Royce: evidentemente se un automobile serve a percorrere una strada a una data velocità, allora potremmo acquistare, invece di una Rolls Royce, una Fiat o una Ford. Ma gli aspetti ornamentali e simbolici della Rolls Royce hanno una importante funzione sociale, altrettanto importante della funzione meccanica, e pertanto anche della Rolls Royce si deve dire che la forma segue la funzione. La forma è esattamente quello che deve essere perché una Rolls Royce possa essere usata come una Rolls Royce (le funzioni sociali della Rolls Royce rimangono anche quando la macchina è ferma e parcheggiata sotto l'ufficio o davanti allo Hilton Hotel).

4. Sarebbe interessante fare una storia del design italiano, dai tempi dell'Impero Romano ai giorni nostri. Scopriremmo meravigliosi esempi di design firmato, di design anonimo (si pensi agli acquedotti) e di design inconscio. E troveremmo degli esempi meravigliosi di oggetti che servono allo scopo, manifestano e comunicano la propria funzione e al tempo stesso comunicano significati simbolici: il primo oggetto che mi viene in mente è il fiasco, che ancora oggi si vede nelle trattorie italiane. Serve allo scopo, perché contine il vino e sta ritto sulla tavola; comunica in modo chiaro dove deve essere impugnato e come si può far scorrere il vino, che deborda, lungo la paglia per non macchiare il tavolo; e comunica anche idee e sentimenti di autenticità, allegria, popolarità. Ma questa analisi ci porterebbe troppo lontano, e forse è meglio che iniziamo la nostra storia dal design dei tempi industriali, quello per cui l'Italia è conosciuta in America, quello i cui oggetti sono ormai conservati al Museum of Modern Art di New York (si pensi alla Olivetti Lettera 22). Partiamo da questo tipo di design "alto" perché l'Italia è forse il paese dove l'idea "colta" di design è stata elaborata in modo più approfondito, anche in riferimento ai problemi politici e sociali. Se in altri paesi c'è stata una teoria del design, in Italia più che altrove c'è stata una filosofia del design, forse una ideologia.

Nel 1972 il Moma di New York aveva organizzato una mostra del design italiano, che si differenziava da questa perché poneva maggiormente l'accento sul design firmato e sulla sua filosofia. Era stata una buona occasione, anche per gli italiani, per rivedere la intera storia dei sogni, delle utopie, della crisi di questa idea di progettazione. Cerchiamo di individuare l'epoca più interessante della storia del design "alto" in Italia. La fisserei tra gli anni cinquanta e gli anni sessanta, nel clima di rinascita economica, politica e civile dopo la fine della guerra, anche se venivano discussi problemi che erano già stati

the 1960s, in the climate of economic, political and civic rebirth after the end of the war, although some of the problems discussed had already been faced before the war During the course of the 1950s architects (and designers) were in a privileged position in Italy: they personified a Leonardesque dream, that is, they tried to give new life to a renaissance image of man interested in all aspects of life. While Italy was industrializing and distinct specializations developed in all sectors, the architect tried to be a sort of intellectual interested in politics, art, literature, philosophy, and sociology. The architect wanted to produce a way of living by means of the objects he built, and he wanted these to reflect the ideas and the ideals that were being worked out in literature, art, politics and philosophy, and sociology. In those days, at the center of Italian design, that is to say, in Milan (for centuries a center of European culture, a cross-roads between France, Germany, Switzerland, the Slavic countries and Italy), it was easy to come across architects talking about contemporary philosophy, the psychology of perception, aesthetics, the organization of labor, social planning or economy. When Rogers said, as already mentioned, that designers should concern themselves with everything, from spoons to cities, he meant that the modern architect's dream was to influence life in all its aspects through his proposals. Designing meant being engaged in politics and helping to solve social problems. It was a time when an industrialist of great culture and sensitivity to social problems, such as Adriano Olivetti would gather researchers from various disciplines around him, and in particular the best designers; not only to produce functioning objects that would sell, but also to project through industry itself a more just and humane society. I am not trying to give my political judgement of that project here; I am just registering a fact that should make understandable the atmosphere in which design developed in those years (basically industrial design, of course). Architects and designers wanted to "build society". The great ideas of Walter Gropius and Frank Lloyd Wright found a new climate in which to grow and develop. Designers expressed faith in culture as an independent power that could influence politics, The crisis of that ideal came in the years when architects and designers realized that this was not at all possible, because the laws of economy and politics often frustrated their good intentions.
To summarize, we might say that the drama of the designer was that of an intellectual who had decided to use the power of industry to educate the masses for a better life and to do so had decided to leave the artist's or thinker's ivory tower and to make compromises with economic power. These intellectuals suddenly realized that they had modified the form and several of the technical functions of radios, watches, typewriters (and sometimes even buildings) and had certainly invented more beautiful objects, but had in no way modified or conditioned political or economic power.
I am not saying that this utopia turned out to be a failure or that designers have completely abandoned those ideas; I am saying that the utopia of the 1950s has been cut down to size and that designers now tend to have a more critical and prudent attitude. In some cases this utopia generated cynicism (and the designers produced what industry asked for); in others, designers answered the crisis with ironic and provocative programs (radical design).
5. But what is interesting in this exhibition is that it shows how many of the projects of identified design have produced a civilization of anonymous design over and above the crisis and disillusionment of the defeat of utopia. This civilization of anonymous design is contradictory, in that it includes kitsch objects and objects that are useless or that do not serve their pupose as well as modest ones that look good and work well, that do what they are supposed to do and make it quite clear how they should be used, that tell symbolically how the average Italian lives, works or amuses himself.
This is an interesting outcome, one that would seem to indicate that in Italy there is a widespread style that is expressed in the anonymous work of small industries and artisans and that helps to maintain a certain "quality of daily life" despite political and economic crises.
We shall not be so naive as to think that the "average" beauty of Italian objects can save Italians from other and far more serious problems. But when we say that good anonymous (or non-conscious) design is

affrontati prima della guerra. Nel corso degli anni cinquanta gli architetti (e i designers) hanno occupato in Italia una posizione di privilegio: essi incarnavano un sogno "leonardesco", ovvero cercavano di far rinascere una figura di uomo rinascimentale interessato a tutti gli aspetti della vita. Mentre l'Italia si industrializzava e in tutti i settori nascevano specializzazioni molto precise, l'architetto cercava di essere un tipo di intellettuale interessato alla politica, all'arte, alla letteratura, alla filosofia, alla sociologia. L'architetto voleva produrre un modo di vivere attraverso gli oggetti che costruiva e voleva che questi oggetti riflettessero tutte le idee e gli ideali che venivano elaborati nella letteratura, nell'arte, nella politica, nella filosofia. In quell'epoca era facile trovare nel centro del design italiano e cioè a Milano (città che da secoli è un centro di cultura europea, posta al crocevia tra Francia, Germania, Svizzera, paesi slavi e Italia) architetti che discutevano di filosofia contemporanea, di psicologia della percezione, di estetica, di organizzazione del lavoro, di pianificazione sociale, di economia. Quando Rogers, come si è detto all'inizio, diceva che il designer deve occuparsi di tutto, dal cucchiaio alla città, voleva dire che l'utopia dell'architetto moderno era di influenzare, attraverso le sue proposte, la vita in tutti i suoi aspetti. Fare design era fare politica, era aiutare a risolvere i problemi sociali. Era l'epoca in cui un industriale di grande cultura e sensibilità sociale come Adriano Olivetti, radunava intorno a se studiosi di varie discipline e in particolare i migliori designers: non solo per produrre oggetti funzionanti che si vendessero bene, ma anche per progettare, attraverso l'industria, una società più giusta e più umana. Io qui non sto cercando di dare un giudizio politico su quel progetto: registro un fatto affinché si capisca in quale atmosfera viveva in quegli anni il design (che era naturalmente anzitutto industrial design). L'architetto e il designer volevano "costruire la società". Le grandi idee di Walter Gropius o di Frank Lloyd Wright trovavano un nuovo clima in cui maturare ed espandersi.
I designers esprimevano una fiducia nella cultura come forza autonoma che poteva influenzare la politica. La crisi di questo ideale venne con gli anni, quando architetti e designers si accorsero che questo non era del tutto possibile, perché le leggi dell'economia e della politica spesso frustravano le loro buone intenzioni.
A voler sintetizzare il problema, diremo che il dramma del designer è stato quello di un intellettuale che aveva deciso di usare il potere dell'industria per educare a una vita migliore le masse, e per far ciò aveva deciso di uscire dalla torre d'avorio dell'artista o del pensatore, per compromettersi col potere economico. Questi intellettuali a un certo punto si sono accorti che avevano modificato la forma e molte delle funzioni tecniche delle radio, degli orologi, delle macchine da scrivere (e talora degli edifici), e avevano certamente inventato degli oggetti più belli, ma non avevano modificato o condizionato il potere economico o politico.
Non dico che questa utopia si è risolta in un fallimento o che i designers abbiano abbandonato del tutto quelle idee: dico che l'utopia degli anni cinquanta si è ridimensionata, e l'atteggiamento dei designers è diventato più critico, più prudente. Talora l'utopia ha generato il cinismo (e il designer ha prodotto ciò che l'industria gli chiedeva) talora il designer ha risposto alla crisi elaborando programmi ironici e provocatori (radical design).
5. Ma se c'è un aspetto interessante di questa mostra è che essa permette di capire come molti dei progetti del design firmato hanno prodotto, al di là della crisi e della delusione per la sconfitta dell'utopia, una civiltà del design anonimo. Questa civiltà del design anonimo è contraddittoria, ospita oggetti kitsch, inutili, inadatti alla loro funzione, ma anche oggetti umili e belli al tempo stesso, efficaci, che fanno quel che debbono fare, e dicono a tutti come debbono essere usati, e dal punto di vista simbolico raccontano come l'Italiano medio vive, lavora o si diverte.
È un risultato interessante, per cui si potrebbe dire che in Italia esiste uno stile diffuso, che si realizza nel lavoro anonimo di piccole industrie e di artigiani, e contribuisce, attraverso le crisi politiche ed economiche a mantenere una certa "qualità della vita quotidiana". Non saremo così ingenui da pensare che la bellezza "media" degli oggetti italiani salvi un popolo da altri e ben più gravi problemi. Ma quando si dice che un buon design anonimo (o inconscio) continua a popolare il nostro paese, non si dice solo che esistono tanti piccoli e ignoti "artisti" che

1. Tailor's scissors, *Forbici da sarto* / prod. Donagemma.
2. Scissors, *Forbici* / prod. Scissy / 1981.
3. Scissors, *Forbici* / des. Cini & Nils.
4. Cutlery, *Posate* / des. A. Piva / prod. San Lorenzo / 1970.
5. Cutlery, *Posate* / des. G. Ponti / prod. Krupp-Milano / 1951.
6. Cutlery, *Posate* / des. A. e T. Scarpa / prod. San Lorenzo / 1981.
7. Wine bottle, *Fiasco* / prod. Chianti.
8. The hands talk, *Le mani parlano* / Bruno Munari / 1981.

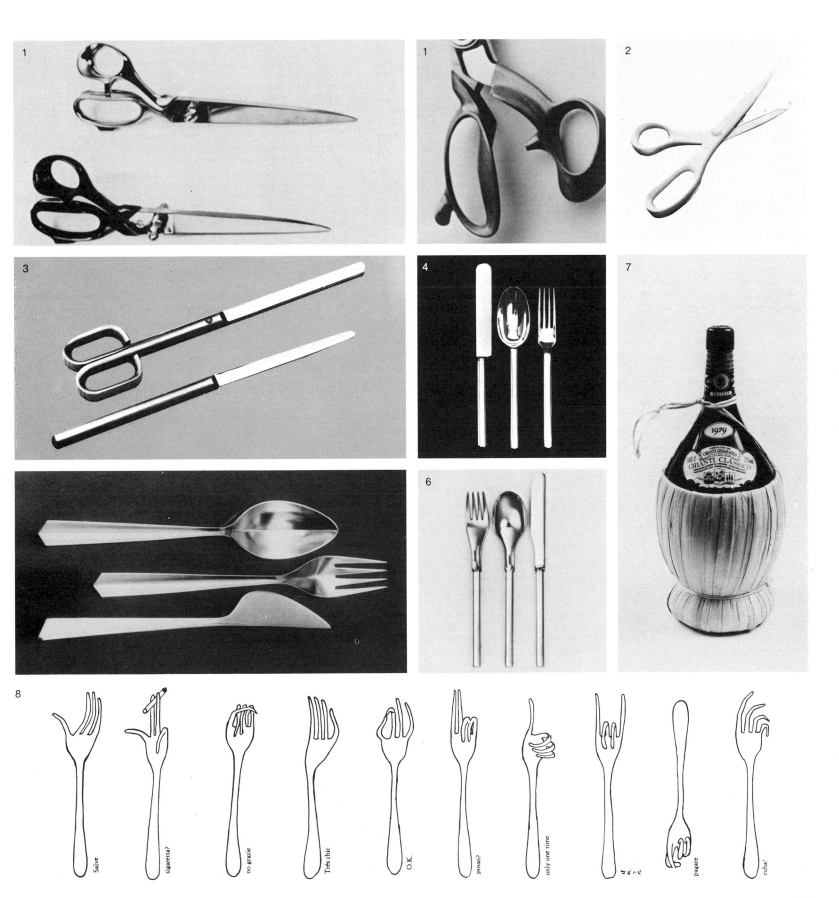

still present in our country, we are not saying only that it is still full of minor and unknown "artists" who continue to produce even as economic crisis knocks at the door or terrorists shoot in the street. We are also drawing attention to a phenomenon that helps explain how it is that economic crisis, terrorism and bad government do not reduce Italy to a state of ruin. There is a term that is used in our country, it is "submerged economy". The term refers to a wide range of economic activities involving small and medium industry that flourish in every small Italian city and that prosper, even when large national industries face periods of crisis. This submerged economy is said to be what saves Italy. Well, anonymous and non-consciuos design is the external façade of this submerged economy. Behind the "good" form of a coffeee machine, of a pair of shoes, of an article of clothing, there is human labour, creative intelligence and economic productivity that are never completely in a state of crisis

And this is why an exhibition that includes anonymous and non-conscious design alongside identified design does not tell two different stories or merely deal with a purely "aesthetic" history that has little to do with the real life of the country. They are not different stories, because there are influences and adaptations that connect identified design to the success of anonymous design (just as non-conscious design has often inspired identified design). This is not a purely "aesthetic" history because, as I have said, behind these objects there is the creativity and optimism of a society that continues to produce and produce efficiently.

6. One aspect of the exhibition that may surprise visitors is the large number of objects related to leisure time. All things considered, even the Italian bar with its coffee machines, glasses and sugar bowls is a fundamental aspect of free time in Italy. Italians do not go away for long weekends, but they interrupt the working day (or continue to work) by going to the bar, and the bar is a social mechanism of great importance. The list of leisure time objects also includes sports cars, seaside and mountain holiday equipment, sports equipment, even the bicycle.

It would be wrong to suggest that all this only concerns free time. In fact, behind this phenomenon there is a civilization of work time, and it is the liveliest and sanest part of an economy.

7. Finally I would like to say that anonymous design often corrects the errors made by identified design. Indeed, among the causes of the crisis of the design utopia during the 1950s was undoubtedly an unconscious betrayal of the true functions of objects. Paradoxically, in aiming to make functional objects, designers tried to accentuate the communicative functions of these objects; and instead of producing objects that communicated the way they could be used, they produced objects that communicated the design philosophy. That is, the object did not say "I can be used like this" but rather said "I am a perfect design object". Let me try to give a very simple example. In anonymously designed Italian cutlery there is the long-pronged fork. It is a fine object, it looks like a hand, and Bruno Munari, once did a whole book in which the forks "talked" by moving their prongs as though they were the fingers of a hand. (Italian forks can do this sort of thing because, as everyone knows, the Italians often express themselves with hand movements.)

At certain point designers sought to make more beautiful, more functional forks that were inspired by the ones designed by the Danes, and they produced beautiful forks with short prongs.

For many people, buying these forks meant being up-to-date. The fork said "I am a modern fork".

Unfortunately the Italian eat spaghetti, whereas the Danes eat a lot of peas. Now short-pronged forks also work as spoons, that is, they can be used for spearing meat as well as for scooping up peas. But this kind of fork is no good for eating spaghetti, because spaghetti can only be twirled around a long pronged fork, which the eater plunges into the spaghetti perpendicularly to the surface of the dish and then rotates in such a way as to roll up the spaghetti. So the designers' forks were all right in rich people's houses where more meat and less spaghetti were eaten, but not in poor people's houses. What's more, they weren't even any good in restaurants, because even rich people usually eat spaghetti in restaurants, because each restaurant has its own speciality.

continuano a produrre mentre batte alle porte la crisi economica o mentre i terroristi sparano per strada. Si sta indicando l'esistenza di un fenomeno che permette di capire perché le crisi economiche, il terrorismo, o il cattivo governo non conducano del tutto l'Italia verso la rovina. C'è un termine che viene usato nel nostro paese, ed è "economia sommersa". Questo termine indica una serie vastissima di attività economico e industriali di piccolo e medio formato che crescono in ogni piccola città italiana, e che crescono bene, anche quando le grandi industrie nazionali affrontano momenti di crisi. Si dice che questa economia sommersa salvi l'Italia. Ebbene, il design anonimo e inconscio è la facciata esterna di questa economia sommersa. Dietro alla forma "buona" di una macchina da caffè, di un paio di scarpe, di un prodotto d'abbigliamento, c'è del lavoro umano, della intelligenza creativa, della produttività economica che non entrano mai completamente in crisi.

Ecco perché una mostra che raccoglie, accanto al design firmato, anche il design anonimo e inconscio, non sta raccontando due storie diverse né sta raccontando una storia puramente "estetica" che non ha nulla a che vedere con la vita reale del paese. Non sta raccontando due storie, perché ci sono influenze e adattamenti che legano le proposte del design firmato alle riuscite del design anonimo (così come il design inconscio ha sovente ispirato il design firmato). Non sta raccontando una storia puramente "estetica", perché come si è detto dietro a quegli oggetti c'è la creatività e l'ottimismo di una società che continua a produrre, e in modo efficiente.

6. Un aspetto della mostra che può colpire il visitatore è la grande quantità di oggetti che riguardano il tempo libero. In fondo anche il bar italiano, con le sue macchine, i suoi bicchieri, le sue zuccheriere, è un aspetto fondamentale del tempo libero in Italia. L'italiano non fa lunghi week ends, ma interrompe la giornata lavorativa (o continua a lavorare) al bar, e il bar è una macchina sociale di grande importanza. Ma potremmo aggiungere a questa lista di oggetti per il leisure time le automobili sportive, gli attrezzi per la vacanza al mare o per la vacanza in montagna, gli oggetti sportivi, la stessa bicicletta. Sarebbe sbagliato parlare di fenomeno che riguarda solo il leisure time. Infatti dietro a questo fenomeno c'è una civiltà del tempo di lavoro, e l'aspetto più vivo e più sano di una economia.

7. Direi infine che spesso il design anonimo corregge gli errori del design firmato. Infatti tra le cause della crisi della utopia del design degli anni cinquanta c'è stato anche un tradimento inconscio delle vere funzioni dell'oggetto. Paradossalmente, nell'intento di realizzare oggetti funzionali, i designers hanno cercato di accentuare le funzioni comunicative di questi oggetti; e invece di produrre oggetti che comunicavano il modo in cui potevano essere usati, hanno prodotto oggetti che comunicavano la filosofia del design. Cioè, l'oggetto non diceva "posso essere usato così e così" ma diceva piuttosto "sono un perfetto oggetto di design".

Cercherò di fare un esempio molto semplice. Tra le posate italiane, effetto di design anonimo, c'è la forchetta a punte lunghe.

E un bell'oggetto, sembra una mano, e una volta Bruno Munari ha disegnato un intero libro in cui le forchette "parlavano" muovendo i loro denti come se fossero le dita di una mano (le forchette italiane possono fare queste cose perché gli italiani si esprimono molto, lo si sa, col movimento delle mani).

Ad un certo punto i designers hanno cercato di fare forchette più belle, più funzionali, ispirati dal modello del design danese, e hanno prodotto forchette bellissime a denti corti.

Comperare queste forchette significava per molti essere à la page. La forchetta diceva "io sono una forchetta moderna".

Sfortunatamente gli italiani mangiano spaghetti, mentre i danesi mangiano molti piselli. Ora la forchetta a denti corti serve anche come un cucchiaio, cioè, da un lato i denti corti servono a infilzare la carne, dall'altro la forchetta serve a raccogliere i piselli. Ma questa forchetta non può avvolgere gli spaghetti, perché per fare questo serve una forchetta a denti lunghi, che si infigge negli spaghetti, perpendicolarmente alla superficie del piatto, e poi la si fa ruotare in modo che avvolga gli spaghetti.

Le forchette dei designers servivano nelle case delle persone ricche, che mangiavano più carne e meno spaghetti, ma non nelle case delle persone povere. Non solo, non serviranno neppure al ristorante,

I imagine that some designers made this choice on purpose, in that they tried to introduce new feeding habits into a more affluent society through the design of forks. But it wasn't up to the designer to decide who should eat more meat, so he ended up by producing fine museum pieces but terrible ones for restaurants.

In this sense anonymous design has taken its revenge, has corrected the errors of the identified designer utopia and has repopulated the country with good "normal" forks. Normal means more efficient, more understandable, and thus more beautiful and more human.

8. I think that the history of Italian design should not be seen as a linear history, but as a development that contains these contradictions, that arises from a trial-and-error process, and in this sense it is interesting story even for non-Italians. And I believe that this exhibition can supply the elements necessary for reading the history of Italian design in this way; a way that is free, I hope, in which everyone will try to compose his or her own story.

This aspect of Italian life may call for some further observations. These observations may appear to have little to do with design and more with ways of living. In a highly departmentalized university they wouldn't concern the Dept of Architecture but the Dept of Cultural Anthropology. This would be a mistake: the only way to understand the nature of non-conscious design in a given society is to understand the needs that this society expresses. We were on the subject of coffee bars. In Paris a bar is a *café terrasse*, an easy-going meeting place where people sit at tables, where Sartre wrote, where lovers decide on their adulteries, where cinema producers meet actors. In New York bars like this don't exist. There are places where you can drink an orange juice standing up beside a cocaine pusher and a tramp, and there are cosy little coffee shops where you can eat and talk in peace. The Italian bar is something different again, perhaps more like a French café than an American coffee shop, but that is not all. In Italian bars most people stand up. You can sit down too if you want to, but you don't have to. You go in, you order a coffee and get it in two minutes, you drink it and you go out. But in this space of time, standing up at the bar, all sorts of things get done. Business is discussed, real estate is bought and sold, the candidacy of politicians or the end of a love affair is decided. You drink a coffee, an aperitif, you eat a croissant, a toasted sandwich, maybe even a steak.

The bar no more belongs to work than it does to leisure time; it's a no man's land, half way between leisure and the job. People go there to fill out football pool coupons, so it's also a sort of gambling saloon where people discuss sport. It's a classless place: except for a few areas of the city (there are blue collar bars and white collar bars), the bar is a place where the chairman of a corporation discusses the fate of ten thousand workers alongside an accountant who chats with a friend about what he's going to do on the weekend.

This is cultural anthropology, and it has its effects on design. The bar is a place where you order something but where you also *choose* or *take* something with your hands (a sandwich, a lottery ticket, a package of chewing gum). So everything in the bar has to be "legible". Each object has to be so designed that it can be quickly, immediately, easily and independently used. Without an anthropological background of this sort, even the espresso coffee machine would be hard to understand. Espresso coffee is a symbol of Italianness throughout the world, but real Italian coffee is Neapolitan coffee, and this is made in little handmade machine with religious care and love: there is no haste and the balance between water, flame and time has to be perfect. In a wonderful scene in Eduardo De Filippo's play *Questi fantasmi*, the rite of coffee-making is described to perfection. Thus the espresso coffee machines you find in bars are Italian in the sense meant by Malinowski when he said that certain bicycles, used in Africa countries but manufactured in Japan for the African market, were no longer objects of European civilization but were new autochthonous objects of African civilization. Espresso coffee is coffee plus the civilization of the bar. And the same can be said of the cups, the sugar bowls and the glass cupboards with their sliding doors that the pastries are kept in.

The second subject is the bicycle. Do Italians use bicycles for work or for sport? It's hard to say where one begins and the other ends. Of course, in 1940 the bicycle was a work tool. In the fifties and sixties,

perché al ristorante anche i ricchi ordinano di solito un piatto di spaghetti, la specialità del locale.

Immagino che per qualche designer la scelta sia stata volontaria: ha cercato, disegnando forchette, di introdurre nuovi usi alimentari, per una società più affluente. Ma il designer non poteva decidere da solo chi avrebbe mangiato più carne, e il suo progetto ha prodotto dei bei pezzi da museo, ma dei pessimi pezzi da ristorante.

In questo senso il design anonimo si è vendicato, ha corretto gli errori dell'utopia del designer che firmava, ha ripopolato il paese di buone forchette "normali". Normali vuole dire più efficienti, più comprensibili, dunque più belle e più umane.

8. Credo che la storia del design italiano non debba venir vista come una storia lineare, ma come la vicenda di queste contraddizioni, di questi trial-and-error processes. E in questo senso è una storia interessante, anche per chi non è italiano. E credo che questa mostra possa offrire gli elementi per leggere la storia del design italiano in questo modo: un modo libero, spero, in cui ciascuno cercherà di comporre la propria storia, di vedere la società italiana da diversi punti di vista.

Questo aspetto della vita italiana merita forse qualche osservazione in più. Sono osservazioni che apparentemente non riguardano il design, ma il modo di vivere. In una università molto dipartimentalizzata, esse non riguarderebbero il Dpt of Architecture ma il Dpt of Cultural Anthropology. Sarebbe un errore: non si può capire cosa sia il design inconscio in una società se non si capisce quali bisogni questa società esprime. Dicevamo, il bar. A Parigi il bar è un café terrasse: luogo di incontro disteso, ciascuno seduto a un tavolino, Sartre vi scriveva le sue opere, gli amanti vi decidono i loro adulteri, i produttori cinematografici vi incontrano gli attori. A New York il bar non esiste: ci sono posti dove si beve in piedi un Orange Juice, accanto a un venditore di cocaina e a un tramp, e coffee shops molto comodi dove si mangia e si parla in santa pace.

Il bar italiano è un fenomeno a sé, più simile al café francese che al coffee shop americano, certo, ma non basta. Nel bar italiano si sta per lo più in piedi. Volendo ci si siede, ma non è necessario. Si entra, si ordina un caffè, lo si ha in due minuti, si beve, si esce. Ma in questo spazio di tempo, in piedi al banco, al bar si fa tutto. Si discute di affari, si decide la compravendita di un edificio, la candidatura di un uomo politico, la fine di un amore. Si beve un caffè, un aperitivo, si mangia un croissant, un toast, persino una bistecca.

Il bar non appartiene né al tempo libero né al tempo di lavoro: è una terra di nessuno, a metà tra tempo libero e attività professionale. Vi entra gente che decide di giocare a totocalcio e quindi è anche luogo di scommesse e di discussioni sulle scommesse e sullo sport. È un luogo interclassista: salvo certe zone della città (ci sono bar per lavoratori e bar per impiegati) il bar è un luogo dove il presidente di una corporation discute sul destino di diecimila operai, accanto a un ragioniere che chiacchiera con un amico sul modo di impiegare il week end.

Questa situazione di antropologia culturale ha i suoi riflessi sul design. Il bar è un luogo dove si ordina qualcosa ma anche un luogo dove si sceglie e si prende qualcosa con le proprie mani (un panino, una scheda per scommettere, un chewing gum). Quindi tutto nel bar deve essere "leggibile". Ogni oggetto deve essere disegnato in modo da permettere un uso rapido, immediato, facile, autonomo. Senza questo background antropologico non si comprenderebbe neppure la macchina per il caffè espresso. Il caffè espresso è il simbolo di italianità in tutto il mondo, ma il vero caffè all'italiana è caffè napoletano, e lo si fa con piccole macchinette artigianali lentamente, con cura religiosa, con amore e senza fretta, dosando l'acqua, il fuoco, il tempo. C'è una splendida scena di "Questi fantasmi" di Eduardo De Filippo che descrive il rito del caffè. Quindi la macchina espresso dei bar è italiana nel senso in cui Malinowski aveva deciso che certe biciclette, usate in paesi africani ma prodotte in Giappone per il mercato africano, non erano più oggetti della civiltà europea, ma nuovi oggetti autoctoni della civiltà africana. Il caffè espresso è il caffè più la civiltà del bar. E così si dica per le tazze, le zuccheriere, le teche di vetro a sportello scorrevole in cui sono custodite le "paste".

Secondo argomento, la bicicletta. Gli italiani usano la bicicletta per lavoro o per sport? È difficile dire dove cominci una attività e finisca

with the automobile boom, the bicycle practically disappeared. I remember Rogers back in 1962 seeing a mutual friend, a rich industrialist, arrive one evening by bicycle and saying: "He's a lucky man to be able to come by bike!" In those days going by bicycle was a luxury, or worse, an oddity, like going by balloon, an oddity that only a millionaire could allow himself. Nowadays, what with the oil crisis, ecology and urban overcrowding, bicycles have come back as a means of transport. But those who use them not only aim at getting around quickly. Alright, they're moving around for work, but the're also getting the same sort of exercise that Americans get with jogging. It's a question of cholesterol. This has influenced the shape of bicycles. Before the war bicycles came in two shapes; normal and racing models. The normal ones were for normal people, straight up and down jobs without extra bits and pieces; the racing ones were for those who had to get everything possible out of a bike. Today the bicycle is a centaur, a thing that is both functional and symbolic at the same time; it's used for getting around on, for keeping muscles in tone and for showing everyone that its rider has chosen the ecological option (the bicycle is thus a vehicle and a philosophical declaration). And what does the bicycle look like? Its shape becomes ambiguous, functional elements unite with symbolic elements, and it's no longer clear which bits are supposed to make the wheels go round (to lessen the effort), which are supposed to keep the legs moving (to increase the effort), and which bits are supposed to keep the mind and the imagination going. What does "form follows function" mean for a bicycle nowadays? What is its function? These questions have to be borne in mind if we are to understand the design of the contemporary Italian bicycle.

Another important aspect of Italian life is the concept of space. Proxemics scholars studying the social meaning of spatial distance have distinguished between centripetal spaces and centrifugal ones. Centripetal spaces tend to put people in contact, centrifugal ones to separate them. The classic Italian city, with its houses surrounding the square and its network of roads converging towards the square in diminishing circles, is the sort of space that deliberately encourages people to meet each other (whether to socialize or fight is neither here nor there). The structure of the American city, with its main street lined with shops and its residential areas away from the city centre, deliberately ensures individual privacy and thus tends to separate. Much has already been said about the structure of urban space. But these problems have to be taken into consideration when thinking about the structure of a restaurant or a café in Italy. They're centripetal structures that tend to promote contact between people.

Suffice it to think of the typical structure of train compartments in Italy. The American train is like a bus, a long corridor with seats one behind the other so that each person can see only the back of whoever is sitting in front: this train defends privacy. Compartments in Italian trains on the other hand are divided up like little sitting-rooms in which passengers have to sit *facing* each other. This sort of a compartment favours socialization and conversation. In an American train the most important thing is to have a little pull-down table in front of you, like in airplanes, so that you can put something to eat or drink down on it (what else is there to do?). Italian trains have few of these pull-down tables, not one per passenger, because this isn't considered to be an important problem. In American trains the lights are usually individual spots, as they are in airplanes, whereas in Italian trains the lights help create a collective ambience. In American trains the colours are dark and isolating, in Italian trains they are light and conducive to socialization.

Understanding this Italian conception of space means being able to understand not only the design of small objects but also certain recent decisions regarding the restructuring of space in cities. During recent years Italy has suffered from a phenomenon that has grown widespread in large industrial civilizations: urban violence, and the temptation that people then feel to stay home or stick to a few suitably "fortified" places where everyone is checked at the entrance. In many American cities there are public spaces that are only open for a few hours in the day for a whole range of activities: Washington Spare, for instance, or Central Park in New York, for as long as there's daylight. As soon as it's dark the city is deserted, except for the part of town

l'altra. Certo, nel 1940 la bicicletta era strumento di lavoro. Negli anni cinquanta e sessanta, con il boom dell'automobile, la bicicletta era quasi scomparsa. Ricordo che Rogers, nel 1962, vide una sera arrivare un comune amico, ricco industriale, in bicicletta, e disse: "beato lui che può!". A quei tempi andare in bicicletta era un lusso, peggio, una bizzarria, come andare in pallone, una bizzarria che si poteva concedere solo a un milionario. Ora, con la crisi del petrolio, l'ecologia, il sovraffollamento della città, la bicicletta si è riaffermata come mezzo di trasporto. Ma chi la usa non intende solo muoversi in fretta: si muove, e per lavoro, ma al tempo stesso ottiene quello che un americano otterrebbe con lo jogging. Una questione di colesterolo. Questo ha influenzato la forma delle biciclette. Prima della guerra le biciclette. Prima della guerra le biciclette erano di due forme: normali e sportive. Le normali erano per la gente normale, diritte, senza fronzoli e strumentazioni speciali; le sportive erano per chi doveva trarre dal veicolo il massimo rendimento possibile. Ora la bicicletta è un centauro, una entità funzionale e simbolica al tempo stesso: deve servire a muoversi, a tenere in esercizio i muscoli e a dichiarare simbolicamente la propria scelta ecologica (la bicicletta è un veicolo e una dichiarazione filosofica). Quale forma assume la bicicletta? Una forma ambigua, dove elementi funzionali si uniscono a elementi simbolici, non è chiaro che cosa veramente serva per far muovere le ruote (per diminuire la fatica), cosa serva per tenere in esercizio le gambe (per aumentare la fatica), e cosa serva per tenere in buon esercizio la mente, l'immaginazione. Cosa vuol dire per una bicicletta attuale che "form follows function"? Quale è la sua funzione? Tutte queste cose vanno tenute presenti per capire il design della bicicletta italiana contemporanea.

Un altro aspetto importante della vita italiana è il concetto dello spazio. Gli studiosi di prossemica, e cioè della scienza che studia il significato sociale delle distanze spaziali, hanno distinto tra spazi centripeti e spazi centrifughi. Lo spazio centripeto tende a porre le persone in contatto, lo spazio centrifugo a separarle. La città italiana classica, con le case intorno alla piazza, e le vie disposte a cerchi concentrici o a spirale che converge verso la piazza centrale, è uno spazio studiato per consentire alla gente di incontrarsi (se si incontrano per socializzare o per lottare, è irrilevante). La struttura della città americana a main street, con i negozi lungo l'arteria principale e le abitazioni decentrate, serve a garantire a ciascuno la propria privacy, a separare.

Molto si è detto su questa struttura dello spazio urbano. Ma questi problemi vanno tenuti presenti nel considerare anche la struttura di un ristorante o di un caffè in Italia. Strutture centripete, tendono a mettere la gente in contatto.

Si pensi alla tipica struttura di uno scompartimento ferroviario in Italia. Il treno americano è come un autobus, un lungo corridoio con sedili affiancati, in modo che ciascuno veda solo la schiena, o la nuca, di chi gli sta davanti: il treno difende la privacy. Il treno italiano è diviso a scompartimenti, come tanti piccoli salotti, in cui la gente deve stare di fronte *una all'altra*. Lo scompartimento ferroviario favorisce la socializzazione, la conversazione. In un treno americano la cosa più importante è avere davanti a se una tavoletta ribaltabile, come sull'aereo, per riporvi qualcosa da bere o da mangiare (altrimenti cosa si fa?). Il treno italiano dispone di poche tavolette ribaltabili, non necessariamente una per ogni sedile: il suo problema è un altro. Nel treno americano le luci sono come sugli aerei, puntate sul singolo. Nel treno italiano le luci debbeno creare ambiente collettivo. Nel treno americano i colori sono scuri, isolanti, nel treno italiano sono chiari, socializzanti.

Capire questa concezione italiana dello spazio significa capire non solo il design degli oggetti minuti ma anche certe recenti decisioni per la ristrutturazione dello spazio urbano. L'Italia ha sofferto negli ultimi anni di un fenomeno consueto alle grandi civiltà industriali: la violenza urbana, e la tentazione dei cittadini a ritirarsi in casa, a frequentare solo alcuni locali dovutamente "fortificati" con controllo all'ingresso, evitando gli spazi pubblici. In molte città americane ci sono spazi pubblici aperti per alcune ore del giorno alle attività più varie: si pensi a Washington Square o Central Park a New York, ma solo sino a che splende il sole. Dopo la città si spopola, meno che nei quartieri dello spettacolo (Broadway). L'Italia stava svviandosi ad assumere queste

where the shows are (Broadway). Italy began to move in this same direction a few years ago, but the structure of Italian cities simply couldn't cope with temporal and spatial divisions of this sort. The Italian city was built to be lived in *all* day and *centrally*.

In recent years many interesting proposals have been made for the revival of the historic old centres of towns by means of festivals, collective shows, events of one sort and another; these amounted to attempts to rescue the city as a place for "living in together". These efforts have involved design, particularly the design of amusements (processions, shows, masquerades) and the revival of objects and situations (archaic design such as the sweetmeats stall, the soft drinks kiosk, temporary sales points). These are not new inventions but the recovery of old traditions that once belonged to country fêtes and have now turned up again in the city. They cannot be said to be purely commercial attractions but part of an overall policy (much discussed and perhaps questionable, but nevertheless interesting and important). Phenomena of this sort must also be included in any panorama of Italian design. Otherwise it is hard to grasp the idea of Italy itself or of design.

abitudini statunitensi, ma la struttura delle città italiane non sopportava queste divisioni temporali e spaziali. La città italiana è fatta per essere vissuta tutto il giorno e in modo centrale.

Negli ultimi anni ci sono state interessanti proposte di ricupero dei centri storici attraverso feste, manifestazioni collettive, spettacoli: un nuovo tentativo di far rivivere la città come luogo per "stare insieme". Queste iniziative hanno implicato altre decisioni di design, design del divertimento (cortei, spettacoli, mascherate) e la riscoperta di oggetti e situazioni (design arcaico come la bancarella dei dolciumi, il chiosco delle bibite, il luogo di vendita provvisorio ed effimero). Non si trattava di una invenzione nuova, si trattava del ricupero di antiche tradizioni della festa di paese, ma riproposta nella grande metropoli. Non si è trattato di pure iniziative commerciali e spettacolari, ma di decisioni "politiche" (discusse e discutibili, ma proprio per questo significative e importanti). Anche questi fenomeni debbono far parte di un panorama del design italiano, altrimenti non si capisce né cosa sia l'Italia né cosa sia il design.

JUST STROLLING.
GREEN OLIVES.
GREEN BOTTLES.
NEWSPAPERS CROSS THE VIEW
FULL SAIL.
THERE IS A TABLE IN THE SUN.

GIRONZOLANDO.
VERDE OLIVA.
VERDE BOTTIGLIA.
GIORNALI A VELE SPIEGATE.
UN TAVOLINO AL SOLE.

Goffredo Parise
Cinema

One Sunday in January 1942, a single lady of a certain age, her frizzy red hair tied back in a bun, decided to go to a movie. She'd been to the movies only a few times in her life, and always to take the children to see cartoon features (she was a governess to a very elegant family), except when she saw *Salvator Mundi* with the family on the Easter Sunday of a year she couldn't remember. Movies weren't thought of very highly at home, but that Sunday she had decided to go alone without telling anyone.

It was a rainy day. The dense yellow smoke coming from the chimney of a factory that toasted barley wrapped around her and her umbrella, solitary voyagers along an endless brick wall. It was windy as well. The lady reached the city center, walked smartly in her loden to the Edison theater, stopped to look at the publicity photographs for *The City of Gold*, one of the first German color films of the period, then noticed that the front of the box office was crowded with soldiers and men in general. The lady knew that that film was considered racy, and she also knew that the director wasn't one of the best, but she didn't want to let this inf-luence her. (She'd been raised in a boarding school run by poor nuns, but she spoke perfect German and had been an interpreter.) Her heart beat slightly faster. Unwilling to push her way through that crowd of men, she forced herself to ask a boy selling candy (his mouth black from chewing liquorice) to buy the ticket for her. She bought five pieces of candy to thank him and went inside. She realized immediately that it was a working-class theater, that there were very few women among the audience, except for some scattered blondes and an occasional wife with her husband. She saw an empty seat, a bad one in the

Since eating is a linguistic process — in which linguistic stands for the visual transformation of signs — and also a cultural fact, it is somehow suject to creative action — that is, there is no eating without there being a creative process. In this sense it may be considered part of the designer's province. Not even fruit is excluded. Let us take an apple, for example: it is grown, peeled, cleaned, and subjected to a transformation. The same standrds apply to packaging. The kinds and forms of food are determined by their presentation and probably also by their packaging. In the beginning we were served particular foods on banana leaves which, if you like, are also a kind of packaging. As I see it, packaging is an integral part of foods. Today we mostly eat canned or boxed food. So we tend to see food through its packaging. I absolutely refuse to express any moral judgements in the matter of packaging and presentation. For me banana leaves and boxes are the same thing.

Ettore Sottsass

Poiché il mangiare è un processo linguistico — dove linguistica sta per trasformazione visiva di segni — ed un fatto culturale, è soggetto in certo qual modo ad un'azione creativa e, cioè, non esiste mangiare senza un processo creativo. In questo senso rientra nelle competenze di un designer. Persino la frutta non ne è esclusa. Prendiamo, ad esempio, la mela: viene coltivata, sbucciata, ripulita e sottoposta a trasformazione. Per il confezionamento degli alimenti valgono gli stessi criteri. Il genere e la forma degli alimenti sono determinanti per la presentazione ed eventualmente il confezionamento. Prima ci sono stati serviti determinati alimenti su foglie di banane che, se si vuole, sono pur sempre una forma di confezione. A mio parere la confezione è parte integrante degli alimenti. Oggi mangiamo per lo più cibi in scatola. Li percepiamo, quindi, tramite la loro confezione. Non vorrei assolutamente esprimere un giudizio morale sulla confezione e sulla presentazione. Per me foglie di banane e scatole sono la stessa cosa.

Ettore Sottsass jr.

IL POSTO

1961

ERMANNO OLMI

Sandro Panzeri

middle of a gang of young toughs, and she was about to cross to it when someone in a black uniform stepped in front of her saying, "It's taken." The house lights went out and she found herself standing against the wall, right beneath the projection booth. A strong smell of acetone seeped down to her and this unexpected smell was already enough to fill her with a sense of mystery. Images of Alpine soldiers en route to who knows where and fashion shows in Rome passed across the screen, followed by a commercial with a diva sipping at a coffee known as 'astragalo'. The house lights came back on, and the lady wandered around searching for a seat, becoming more and more uneasy. (She was wearing a Tyrolese hat with a little badger-hair brush stuck in the ribbon.) Finally a large hand, swollen and strong, grabbed her by the arm. She turned around, frightened but aggressive, and saw an old man wearing a short overcoat with wide red fur lapels. He smiled at her and pointed to an empy seat next to his.

The lady said, "Thank you," and passed in front of him bumping against his legs which felt very hard, then sat down. A blast of heat struck her face (the theater was filled with smoke), she unbuttoned her loden, untied her shoelaces, and then the lights went out and the movie started. The lady immediately fell in love with the heroine, a beautiful young German girl playing a pure country maid, but then she began to realize that the movie was much more risqué than she possibly could have imagined. She just knew that the hero and heroine would end up kissing, if not worse. For a moment she was going to leave (where to go?) but then she abandoned herself to a certain internal weakness, a result of the heat in the thater and the very hard and inert leg of the man beside her, the leg she'd have to climb over if she left. Her heart was beating fast. And then, from behind, a woman tapped her on the shoulder with a finger smelling of mandarin oranges to say, "Excuse me, could you move a bit to the left?" The lady moved to the left, but very soon that orangy finger returned with the voice of the woman asking, "Maybe you could move to the right instead." The lady obeyed. "Like this?" she asked, and the woman replied, annoyed, "Like that."

More time passed and the same woman said, "Listen here, I can't see." A man who was with her muttered something, the lady didn't know what to do, and the people nearby were saying, "Enough, quiet!" At this point, the

1. Packaging, *Confezione* / mod. Pandoro / prod. Alemagna / 1974.
2.3. Espresso machine, *Macchina da caffè* / mod. DP 9 Automatica / des. Ufficio Tecnico / prod. La Pavoni / 1975.
4. Packaging, *Confezione* / mod. Colomba / prod. Motta / 1973.
5. Packaging, *Confezione* / mod. Panettone / prod. Motta / 1968.
6. Packaging, *Confezione* / mod. Pandoro / prod. Motta / 1974.
7. Bottle, *Bottiglia* / mod. Etichetta Nera / des. A. Sassoli de Bianchi / prod. Buton / 1939.

8. Chocolate eggs packaging, *Confezione uova di cioccolata* / mod. Gallina / des. Gruppo creativo Robots / prod. Perugina / 1981.

fat man in the fur lapels made his move. With more than a little effort, he lifted himself up only slightly and banged his hard leg against the wooden seat which made a musical sound. A brief squabble followed, in a dialect which the lady couldn't understand, although she did hear the word, 'manners'. Finally, the woman said in a loud voice, "How could anybody think of going to the movies wearing a hat like that?" The lady's temper flared up and with a quick, precise movement, she lifted the hat from her head, pulling her bun free so that some tangled locks of red and grey hair fell around her ears. She put the hat on her lap, holding it with

both hands, and turned her attention back to the screen, where the pure blonde maid was sprawled on a bed covered by a large eiderdown, her lips swollen and trembling, her face flushed with heat, her roughly-woven nightgown stretched tight by her frantic breathing. Panting in desperation, the lady drank in the image.
"I'm going to leave, no I'm not, I'm staying, how disgusting, don't get worked up, you're above this, how disgusting..." These thoughts ran through her mind, but they must have escaped from her lips as well, because the man beside her glanced at her and said softly, "What? What did you say?" He

smiled at her with that large mouth of someone who likes to eat. The lady didn't reply and concentrated on the screen. Then she heard a noise, a noise he was making with his inert leg, a tapping. The tapping was transmitted directly to her leg. It reminded her of knocks on a door. She glanced down to her right two or three times, very quickly, and saw that the man had one of his large hands on his leg and was tapping it with his fingers. The terrified lady couldn't understand how a leg could make such a sound (the man was now knocking hard with his knuckles, exactly like you knock at a door). She sat immobile, looked back

to the screen where the seduction was well underway, and she moaned. It was like a brief scream. Her heart was pounding.

Goffredo Parise, "Sillabario n. 1", Einaudi, Torino 1972. Translated by Robert Kleyn.

1. Advertising, *Pubblicità* / mod. Vov / des. G. Pin / prod. Pezziol / 1980.
2. Advertising, *Pubblicità* / mod. Bitter / prod. Campari / 1971.
3. Bottle, *Bottiglia* / mod. Bitter Analcolico / des. Ufficio Tecnico / prod. Sanpellegrino / 1962.
4. Weekly magazines, *Settimanali* / prod. Panorama, L'Europeo, L'Espresso, Il Mondo, Amica.

A CAR, A BUS, A TRAIN, A BOAT,...
A HOME AWAY FROM HOME.
CYPRESSES BREAK STEP WITH
UMBRELLA PINES.
THE VIEW IS AN ANCIENT
MONUMENT.

*UN AUTO, UN PULLMAN, UN TRENO,
UNA BARCA,... LE CASE MOBILI.
CIPRESSI IN FILA E PINI A
OMBRELLO.
LA VEDUTA È UN MONUMENTO
ANTICO.*

Raffaele La Capria
The Mortal Wound

Gaetano crossed the street and paused to look from the parapet at the sea, grey in the heavy heat, like dish water. Below street level the reddish rectangle of the tennis court, and the players in their white shorts, fat and ridiculous trotting after the ball. A slimming cure, the fat dissolves, a little exercise prescribed by the doctor for the sake of the paunch. On either side of the tennis court the squares of the Nautical Club's two terraces. Members lying in deck-chairs chatting, others stretched out on the ground naked and motionless, like a row of corpses. How hard they worked at their sun-tan! Would Massimo be at the Club? It was always tiresome to arrive at his home when he wasn't there. What would he talk about with his mother? Better prepare a topic of conversation. Or else go down into the club rooms and ask for Massimo De Luca. It seemed easy enough. But there was always that sense of shame, of embarrassment, as soon as he set foot there... *Why shame, why embarrassment? Don't you know what they are? Eaters of macaroni, they adore Scarfoglio, and as for reading, at most they leaf through the illustrated magazines. Fluent and prolific, they still prefer – and always will – vulgarity to genius. The wanton manufacture of images has made them dream of lands beyond the sea; the partisans of Crispi and the Libyan wars eulogized lyric combat and the Fascists the blitzkrieg. In the great sandbox we've twice defecated blood in honour of big business concerned for the stability of its income. Moderates, men of honour, worthy and high-minded spirits: founts of wisdom. This is where the picture begins to fall apart. So then, I know who I am, and therefore there's absolutely no need – And yet: 'Is Signor Massimo De Luca here?' And inquisitive eyes will look you up and down from out of his*

5

45% of the population does not go on holiday during the year.
38% takes one holiday a year.
19% takes more than one holiday a year.
The average length of holidays is 20.5 days a year.

14% of the Italians own a second house.

4% of the population engages in a sport on Sundays.
Sports mostly engaged in:

Jogging/running	7.5%
Swimming	7.3%
Soccer	7.1%
Tennis	6.9%
Hunting/fishing	5.3%
Skiing	4.8%
Gymnastics	3.6%

*Il 45% della popolazione non fa mai vacanza nel corso dell'anno.
Il 38% fa un periodo di vacanza l'anno.
Il 19% fa più di un periodo di vacanza.
La media è di 20,5 giorni di vacanza per anno.*

Il 14% degli Italiani è proprietario di una seconda casa.

*Il 4% della popolazione pratica uno sport la domenica.
Sports maggiormente praticati:*

Footing/corsa	*7,5%*
Nuoto	*7,3%*
Calcio	*7,1%*
Tennis	*6,9%*
Caccia/pesca	*5,3%*
Sci	*4,8%*
Ginnastica	*3,6%*

6

8

7

9

5. Pullman bus, *Pullman* / mod. Spazio Gran Turismo / des. P. Salmoiraghi, A. Barrese, I. Hosoe, A. Torricelli, A. Locatelli / prod. Carrozzeria Orlandi Gruppo Iveco / 1977.
6. Gasoline pump sign, *Marchio distributore benzina* / mod. Agip / des. Guzzi / prod. Agip / 1952.
7. Street signs, *Segnaletica stradale* / mod. Ministero dei Lavori Pubblici / 1979.
8.9. Pneumatics, *Pneumatici* / mod. Cinturati P3-P7 / prod. Pirelli / 1974.

world, intuition and animal flair will smell out in you neither dog nor wolf, but the ambiguous victim of their absurd scale of values, ambiguous because of an atavistic predisposition to submit to it while rejecting it – all this, and the inability not to care, to lie down as they do, naked in the sun. Instead you feel ashamed and embarrassed, there's a sticky clot of sensibilities and obscure social resentments, petty but justified even when you let them off on Massimo, your friend. These invitations to Sunday dinner, for instance. I could do without them. Nini's lessons too, for all he's ever got out of them – justifiable on the ground of friendship, yes, – but when you're the sort of friend who'd hesitate to take off your jacket in his house even if it's hot? I'll tell him I'm leaving, that I'm going to Milan – it doesn't yet seem true – far from all this waste of time...

He started walking slowly along. The façade of the large decrepit Bourbon edifice hid the sea from view. On the promenade the usual coming and going of bathers, a stream pouring out from the interior of the Neapolitan continent, it swelled on Sundays and overflowed the pavement.

Barefoot children of all sizes, sunburned, cheery and undernourished; and their glances, the eye-whites like cloves of garlic. You saw one, you turned away for a moment and when you looked again there were two or three; parthenopian parthogenesis. Grazed by the unnerving passage of motor-scooters, buses with clusters of human beings hanging from the footboards, by cars, under the July sun – and what a sun!

After the strawberry-red building had been left behind, a vague noise burst from below: under the promenade the sea again, in the pleasant arc of the beach, shut in a forest of pile embankments, overcrowded as the Borgo San Lorenzo – one and a half kilometres square, 125 thousand inhabitants, with a density of 840 inhabitants per hectare; allowing for the streets, the thickness of the walls and the other unutilizable space, you obtain, water-closets included, a density of 2.5 inhabitants per room. and there are fourteen churches, which further diminishes the space.

He leaned over the parapet: the fierce noise rose up, they were shouting themselves hoarse, covered with sand up to the chin, making epileptic gestures in the shallow water before the pure, soul-stirring light of the sea. Each time that troublesome sense of promiscuity, even a little while ago on the bus. A sort of vertigo that drew you

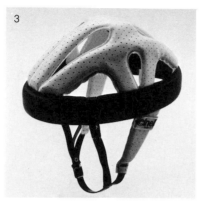

1.2. Cycling gloves, *Guanti ciclismo* / prod. Cinelli / 1981.
3. Cycling helmet, *Casco ciclismo* / prod. Cinelli / 1981.
4. Bicycle tandem, *Tandem* / mod. Tandem Super Corsa Uomo-Donna / des. Ufficio Tecnico / prod. Cinelli / mod. 1979.
5. Sports car, *Auto decapottabile* / mod. Duetto Spider 1600 / des. Pininfarina / prod. Alfa Romeo / 1966-1981.

towards the overheated mass of bodies and faces marked by the wear and tear of the back alleys. A single glance of sympathy given or received, a single gesture of recognition, the least trifle, would be enough to make one feel strangled by the human effluvium like a tree by lava, destroyed, one's selfhood lost, sucked into the enveloping psychological unity, overwhelmed by, yet privy to, historical forces. The priests and friars aroused these people with the powerful stimuli of religion. Without love of party, but for the sake of profit and robbery, they swore allegiance to the throne. Aniello, Totonno, Ciccillo, greedy hordes of

Holy Church, galvanized by the promise of plunder, were moving up the peninsula. The Virgin Forest advancing, with cardinals in the van, moving slowly to give the ruins of the Republic the opportunity to expand, and hearsay the chance to tell the tale. Adorers of Yellow Face and brazen face still dream of bread, circuses and gallows, a thieving king, the waste, banquets and luxuries of '44, they still get along on a gamble, hidden from God, in the windings and turnings of the back alleys: the last debris of the dissolution.

Feeling giddy he turned his eyes away from the little Chinese ant-heap on the

beach below. Beyond the last row of cabins, stretched out into the sea like a barrier against the encroachment of all those bathers, mirrored in quieter waters, the crumbling and noble mass of the Palazzo Medina dominated the bay.

There the sounds of the beach would be deadened by the overhanging immensity of the day, like the hum of insects among the geraniums or that of an aeroplane that has passed in the sky leaving a thin trail of vapour. From the terrace Signora De Luca would be casting a housewifely eye over the panorama as though to assure herself that everything was in place: Vesuvius

over there, dusty violet on top; farther down, the heat, fallen like a tulle curtain, merging the colours into a shade of blue-grey; and far away on the coastline, ragged edges of pastel pink, a cluster of houses or a village. 'Sundays in summer are impossible,' she would be saying, 'They shout louder on Sundays.'

Massimo's uncle lying in the deck-chair: – 'Last Sunday they ate three missionaries!' – on the terrace waiting for dinner hour. Signora De Luca would not take note of the pleasantry, would not understand it, her gaze would continue to rove, filled with disapproval, over the Sunday sea thick with sails,

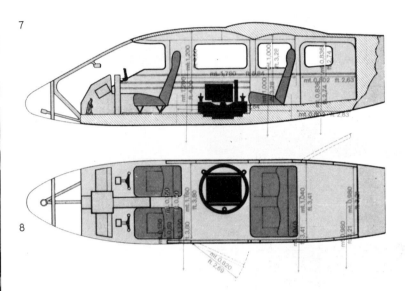

6.7.8. Airplane, *Aereo da turismo* / mod. Bimotore / des. Pascali / prod. Partenavia / 1972.
9. Car, *Auto* / mod. 308 GTS / des. Pininfarina / prod. Ferrari / 1981.
10. Saddle, *Sella* / mod. Olympic / prod. Pariani / 1968.

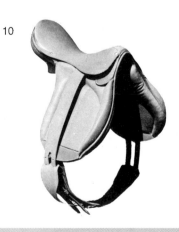

rowboats, bathers, shouts, all in disorder, she would think, and would come to rest on a point beyond the cabins, beyond the crowd of bathers on the beach, beyond the Bourbon building, where the Nautical Club stood in its bleached whiteness. 'I say, are we having trifle?' The voice from the deckchair would prevent her from formulating the thought which had caused her eyes to rest on that point, and the thought, hiding there, in a corner of her brain, without making up its mind to come out, would accentuate that futile nerve strain, that overstrung absentmindedness, which you so often found in Massimo too. 'I say, are we or aren't

we?' the voice from the deck-chair would insist and, receiving no reply, would begin a monologue: 'Today Mamma is coming and you know she likes a sweet on Sundays. Besides, you have a guest, I've seen the place laid, not to mention myself who might be regarded as a guest too, though I notice that with me you don't stand on ceremony. But anyhow with all these people it doesn't seem right not to have a sweet.' Finally the thought would make its way into the centre of the Signora's brain and would reveal itself: 'he's quite capable of staying at the Club the whole day, but I ask you, what does he do there all day long

without giving any sign of himself, without remembering that he's got a family, without letting me know; at certain moments in life you've got to be punctual, otherwise what will we all come to?' She would go to the telephone guided by this thought, dial the number and wait with the receiver to her ear for the waiter at the club to call Nini, Massimo, her husband, anybody. From the terrace there would come back to her, together with the distant noise of the beach, a song of protest: 'No, you don't eat broccoli, Cabbage of stock-fish... You feed on gardenias; Lilacs are your dish...'

'Is it possible for a man of fifty-three, and I mean fifty-three,' Signora De Luca would think referring to her brother singing to himself out there, and would leave this thought incomplete too, like all the others. Forgotten there, holding the receiver, the ill-mannered brutes, it was a habit of theirs! And she would hang up in annoyance. 'She always has a thought at the front of her head and a thought at the back of it,' Massimo was saying as if for the first time.

... Assume the vaguely amused air called for by the circumstances, by the rather special atmosphere of comedy to be found at Sunday dinner with the

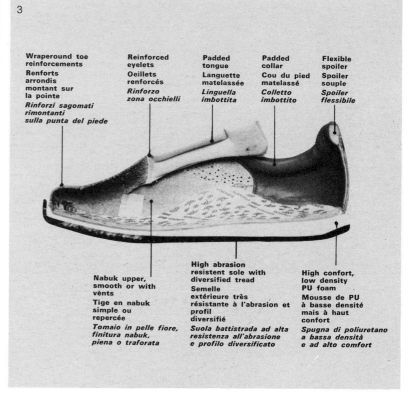

1. Roller skates, *Pattini a rotelle* / mod. X-Line Turbo / des. I. Olivieri / prod. I. Olivieri / 1982.
2. Rubber boots, *Stivaletti in gomma* / mod. Happy / prod. Superga / 1982.
3. Running shoes, *Scarpe da corsa* / mod. Dual Power / prod. Superga / 1982.
4. Basket ball shoes, *Scarpe da basket* / mod. Pressing / des. Ufficio Tecnico / prod. Lotto / 1982.

5.6. Walking canes, *Bastoni da passeggio* / prod. Ravarini Castoldi.
7. Sporting gun, *Fucile* / mod. Automatico A 302 / prod. Beretta / 1981.
8. Sporting guns, *Fucili*: a) mod. Carabina Olimpia / prod. Beretta / 1963 - b) mod. Parallelo 424 / prod. Beretta / 1963 - c) mod. Automatico A 302 / prod. Beretta / 1981.

De Lucas, knowing in advance everything that will be said and done, without understanding why Massimo lends himself to it. At times it can be irritating. For example how can you draw him aside and tell him, 'Massimo, I'm going to Milan, it's settled now.'

He's continuing, 'Let's say, the thought at the front is "I must to the dressmaker's at five." And the thought at the back, "Will Nini have bought a pair of shoes?" Nini comes in: "Have you been to the dressmaker's to buy a pair of shoes?" she asks him, and Nini answers, "I'll go as soon as I work up a bit of an appetite." They go on like this for a while and she doesn't notice anything—'

At this point one should laugh.

'Well, what is there to laugh about? Perhaps I was a trifle absent-minded.'

'For her, people are divided into two categories, *dears* who are *ladies and gentlemen*. And *boors*, who are all the others, those you meet in the street, on the bus or at the Club. As a matter of fact there are also two intermediate categories, the *decent souls* and the *impossibole people*. Her friends, for example, are dears, Papa's friends and customers are boots, her dressmakers are decent souls, if they're late with the delivery they become boors. The Communists are boorish and vulgar, the Monarchists gentlemen, and so on—'

The uncle: 'How am I classified?'

'Vulgar and impossible.'

Here another burst of laughter.

'I knew it, I knew it. and you're a scamp, but coutside the discussion, because she doesn't classify her sons.'

'Gaetano is a decent soul, but he reeks of Communism, Grandma is impossible but a lady.'

'Why am I impossible?'

Signora De Luca: 'Why do you listen to him?'

Grandma: 'Do you know whom I was thinking about today? The Marchese Solino Belmonte, In Rome, when your grandmother was one of the reigning beauties of the capital, received by all the nobility—'

'And by the Black Aristocracy,' puts in Uncle Umberto.

'Received by Popes and Cardinals, receptions such as you, poor boy, have never dreamed of! Ah well, you all belong to another era, and anyway you, poor child, I can't think which side of the family you take after!'

'I take after the plebeian side.'

'You certainly don't take after me, nor after your sisters. What was I saying?'

'About the Marchese Solino Belmonte,' says Massimo.

'Oh yes, at that time this Marchese was paying court to your grandmother.

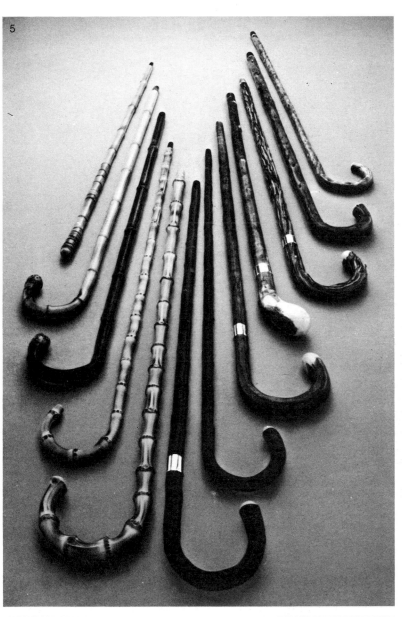

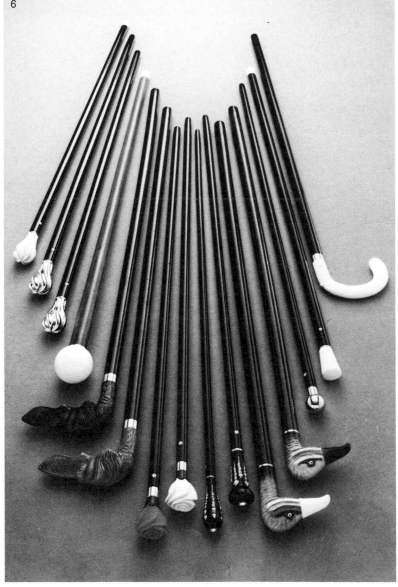

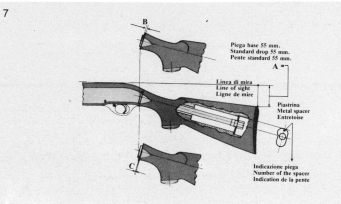

Those were the days—'

And she turns to me. – The days, she'll explain, when in the Villa Borghese King Umberto, passing in his carriage, had his horses turned about in order to fling her a regal glance. – What if I talked to her about the riots in Milan in '98? An almost irresistible temptation. The soldiers of the Good King firing on the crowd, Turati and Anna Kuliscioff arrested, a different side of it altogether.

'–this Solino Belmonte was immensely wealthy, magnificent home, princely, servants in livery, gold plate, tapestries, indescribable! And one evening, hearing me sing Tosca – *Vissi d'Arte Vissi*

d'Amore – he lost his head, poor man. At that time your grandma was a real beauty, not the old hag you see now, and with a voice, – a voice!'

As foreseen. She sings, *'Viiii-ssiii, d'Aaa-rte, Viii-ssiii d'Aaa-more!'* with great conviction for an entire minute, from an imaginary stage, a broken soprano voice, and at the finale an arm warding off applause, the phantoms of the past, kings, marquises – Assuntina spellbound, with the macaroni timbale, followed by Mississippi with his tail erect.

'Put that cat out!' says Signora De Luca, 'I hate cats.'

The uncle, in the silence that follows

the first concentrated forkfuls: 'For me eating is of no importance,' and waits for the rejoinder. 'That's abvious.'

'On Sundays I make an exception.'

'Then why do you ask me every time we meet, "What did you have for dinner today?"'

'The family intellectual has spoken.'

'Massimo dear, leave him alone. He's a trifle *grossier*, understands nothing but football.'

'Sorry, Grandma, but wouldn't you say *grossier* was too refined a word to apply to Uncle Umberto?'

'You're right, even the name is wasted, a noble name for a king.'

'And the Marchese Solino Belmonte?'

'That's right dear, tease me. If I were to make a little expedition to Rome, senile as he is, I'd refresh his memory, he'd leave us something—'

Now for the tapestry.

'A single one of those tapestries the old dodderer keeps hanging on his drawing-room walls would be enough to change our style of life!'

'But he's alive and flourishing!'

'Alive? Of course he's alive! Even the dying are alive. We'd go to Paris, you're invited too, yes, because you must be a fine young man, modest, isn't that so?' on the *modest*, Massimo winks at me. Shame and embarrassment.

'—and there, my dear, in spite of my

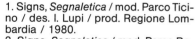

1

1. Signs, *Segnaletica* / mod. Parco Ticino / des. I. Lupi / prod. Regione Lombardia / 1980.
2. Signs, *Segnaletica* / mod. Parco Regionale La Mandria / des. B. Benenti / 1980.

seventy-two years, yes seventy-two, I'd show you the meaning of *verve*! Oh! Paris!'
Massimo laughs encouragement, in a blue pullover, suntanned like the lot of them. An answering smile from the pale friend to the bronzed one.
'Pa-a-rigi, o-o cara, noi-rì-veremo...!'
Nini! Late as usual, he waltzes in singing the aria from *La Traviata*, on his grandmother's last words, impersonating Violetta with an imaginary champagne goblet overflowing.
Raffaele La Capria, "Ferito a morte", Bompiani, Milano 1975. "The Mortal Wound", Farrar, Straus & Giroux, New York. Translated by William Weaver.

FLIGHTS OF IMPECCABLE CYCLISTS. DOGS POINT.
SPEARING INKY SQUID.
SEARCHING SEA URCHINS.
VIEW ON THE GULF.

ORDE DI CICLISTI.
I CANI PUNTANO.
CACCIARE LE SEPPIE, CERCARE I RICCI.
SI VEDE DAL GOLFO.

Raffaele La Capria
The Mortal Wound

What water that day! It made you feel jubilant. Whitish rock starred with black sea-hedgehogs and split by long crevices, shady hollows and thick boulders between reaches of dazzling sand, and there among sand and rock, in a slowly whirling motion, the colonies of bream. Occasionally two or three would detach themselves from the round-dance and chase after one another, striped bream, flat with a little pointed mouth, and white bream, big with the bisons' heads and a single black ring at the narrow part of the tail.

Quick! Goggles, tube, gun – the new gun, on its first try-out, just arrived from Genoa – and the leap into the water, the icy splash, the gurgling tube, the body down among myriads of tiny bubbles run wild, the hands larger than life through the glass of the goggles fixed on the luminous gun, and the startled space expanding, swallowing me... then the upward push, like two delicate hands at your waist bringing you back to the surface, the pressure diminished, and that gliding stroke in the absolute quiet. All this was still new to me. And at every dive the precipitate flight of the bream back to their crannies in the cliff, the motionless after-

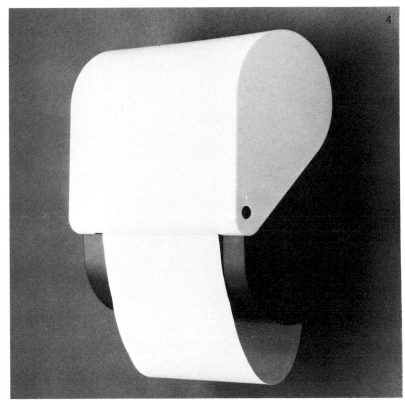

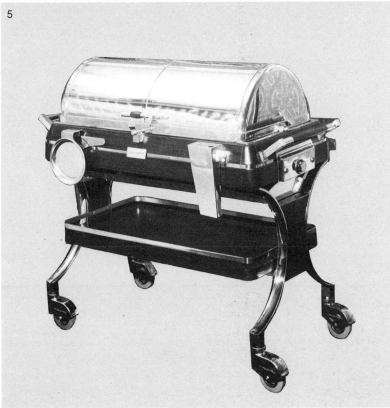

3. Advertising, *Pubblicità* / mod. Ferrarelle / des. M. Rizzi & Ass. / prod. Ferrarelle / 1981.
4. Towel dispenser, *Distributore automatico asciugamani* / mod. F 80/Visio 80 / des. A. Macchi-Cassia / prod. DI.W.S. / 1982.
5. Restaurant cart, *Carrello ristorante* / mod. PD 490 / prod. Giga.
6. Wine-carafe, *Caraffa vino* / mod. Litro.

noon light, in which the contours of a rocky ledge stood out as sharply as a whetted blade. Before the glass of the goggles a lock of my hair kept falling and every now and then I had to push it aside like a curtain. Three mullets, three little leaden torpedoes always the same distance ahead of me, out of reach but near. I was swimming above a slab of sloping rock that finished in a sort of sandy valley and one of the mullets stopped to graze above a cone-shaped boulder. Separated from the others he felt the thing that was I arriving, clumsily on top of him, and darted off an instant before I discharged the gun, flurried, with frantic zig-zag seek-

ing his companions, and then safely back in their midst. At that moment – how huge it seemed! – the bass swam by, and I found myself powerless with the gun still unloaded looking at it. It seemed a bomber plane, a Flying Fortress, such as I had previously seen appear all of a sudden outlined against the sky of Naples. Reloading the gun in furious haste, regulating the string, I turned but the bass was too far away, had disappeared. The sandy valley, encased like a river-bed between two steep banks of rock, ended in a funnel-shaped opening, and oyster-shells lay whitening on the sand like the bones of animals in front of a cave. Little bream

translucent like glass were moving there. Indolent as fans, they still delayed before entering the darkness, of the crevice. I swam towards the bottom, my stomach grazing the sand, following the gulley as far as its opening: it was wide enough. I thrust in my arm with the gun, then my whole head, while with the free hand I held on to a spur of the rock. I saw them at once, two bream, large, luminous inside the lair, motionless and tranquil in the dark. The larger one in profile, within reach. Instead of the bream the glitter of a silver plate, the spear shaken by a tremor, the sand of the bottom shifted. A hit. I rose again, the spear came away

without hindrance: only grazed, too bad. I reloaded, and swam in the direction of the nearby reef. Then there was an upheaval at the bottom; from between the rocks of the reef a wave rose, a mist of sparkling water which enveloped them for a moment, and from that luminous mist emerged a grey shadow, solitary, which came towards me like a metallic instrument. The bass again! It seemed even larger, it hadn't seemed so big at first, heavens! The water remaining in the crook of the tube was grating, I hardly breathed but swam slowly, delicately, to bring myself into its orbit without alarming it. It was calm and indifferent, but perhaps I would not

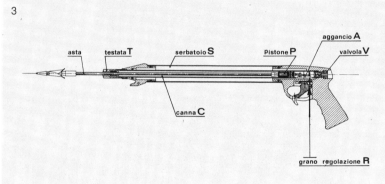

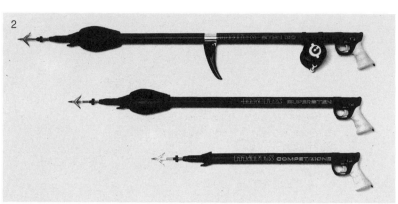

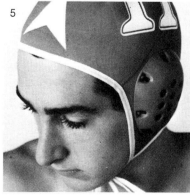

1. Flippers, *Pinne* / mod. Plana / des. Ufficio Tecnico / prod. AMF Mares Sub / 1980.
2.3. Spear guns, *Fucili subacquei* / mod. Sten 130, mod. Supersten, mod. Competizione / des. Ufficio Tecnico / prod. AMF Mares Sub / 1967.
4. Diving mask, *Maschera subacquea* / mod. Formula 2 / des. Ufficio Tecnico / prod. AMF Mares Sub / 1980.
5. Water polo cap, *Calottina water polo* / prod. Diana Sport / 1981.

6. Racket case, *Portaracchette* / prod. Elmex / 1981.
7. Sun glasses, *Occhiali da sole* / mod. Alitalia-Sport Frames / des. Kuno Prey de Meyo / prod. G.d.S. / 1980.
8. Sun glasses, *Occhiali da sole* / mod. Pieghevolissimo / des. Rally Delta / prod. I. Cremona / 1981.
9. Tennis outfit, *Completo tennis* / mod. Borg / des. P. Rolando / prod. Fila / 1981.

IL SEME DELL'UOMO

1969

MARCO FERRERI

Marco Margine
Anne Wiazenski

succeed in cutting off its route, it was approaching too quickly. So I changed my tactics, expelled the rest of the water from the tube and swam rapidly. As I had foreseen, the noise alarmed it, diverting it towards the reef. They rarely do an about-face. The one danger: its getting beyond the necessary point of passage between my gun and the reef before I came within shooting distance. Now I saw it well in every detail: the sulky look of the mouth bordered with fleshy white, the corners turned down, the fixed eye, the scales in relief, the smoky gold shagreen along the body already vibrating with alarm. And behind it rose the mass of boulders that formed the reef. The decisive instant – aiming vertically at the thickest part of the fish where the body swells – and I felt the spear enter the body. Transfixed, it rolled over on to its side, all shining silver, with the fin erect on its back, the mouth open in a spasm, the body in a crescent and as if paralyzed. The weight of the spear dragged it to the bottom, on to a smooth white rock, and the blood rose from the wound like a thread of rosy smoke in the water. Then the spear began to clink against the rock, the cord jerked taut in my hands, the bass with the spear piercing its body resisted, struggled frantically. But the wing of the harpoon had opened wide, there was no escape. I rose to the surface, took two or three deep breaths, my ears were humming, and then came that call, Nini's childish voice: 'Maaa...ssimo! Maaa...ssimo!' The gun tight between my legs, I pulled on the cord, grasped the spear with one hand, with the other the viscid silvery quivering flesh which was still trying to escape, thumb and forefinger like pliers in the red opening of the gill, and thus I held it, alive. At that moment again Nini's voice...

As now: 'Maaa...ssimo! Maaa...ssimo!'

Raffaele La Capria, "Ferito a morte", Bompiani, Milano 1975.

6

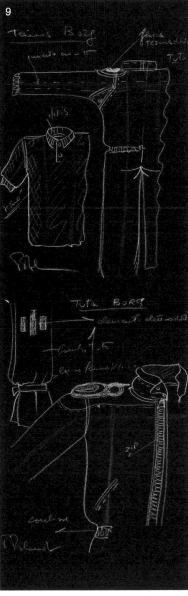

9

7

8

Sportswear develops on the basis of the equation: technology, life, fashion. It the last six or seven years everything has been revised, and as a result of sports practically everything has been sold to everybody.
While it is true that Fashion always considered itself the filter of the times, on this occasion it has ended up at the end of the line in this respect, or at least it has taken second place to the new fashion of sports. In fact it is hard to understand how a tennis player can be a sportsman in the active sense if he wears pure cotton Bermuda shorts designed for sailing as he takes off for the Wimbledon finals, or how a skier can face the poles of a slalom with a parachutist's outfit, only because these items of sportswear happen to be "fashionable".

Pier Luigi Rolando

L'abbigliamento sportivo si sviluppa sulla base dell'equazione — tecnica, vita, moda —.
In questi sei o sette anni si è rifatto tutto, e attraverso lo sport si è venduto tutto a tutti.
Se è vero che la moda ha sempre tradotto come sua espressione il filtro dei tempi, questa volta è venuta un po' in coda in questa considerazione, o perlomeno è venuta seconda ad una nuova moda quella sportiva. In effetti non si capisce come potrebbe essere sportivo nel senso di active, un tennista che indossi i bermuda di tessuto a navetta in puro cotone, per una finale di Wimbledon, o di uno sciatore che affronti i paletti di uno slalom con una tuta da paracadutista, solo perché tali capi di abbigliamento sono di moda!

Pier Luigi Rolando

PLAY CARDS, PLAY BOCCE, PLAY BEACH BALL.
CHANGING GEARS.
ROADS AND TRACKS, ASPHALT AND SNOW.

SCOPONE, BOCCE, PALLA A MANO.
CAMBIO MARCIA.
STRADA E PISTA, ASFALTO E NEVE.

Tommaso Landolfi
The Stolen Hand

"In my opinion," he said "it's time for poker."
"Why poker?" someone asked wearily. He continued. "We'll play elimination, dropping players every hand, until only one winner is left."
"And then what?"
"The winner keeps his clothes on, at least that's his right, while everyone else will have to take theirs off, to undress completely. What do you think?"
"It's not such an original idea, is it?" replied a sculptor, a marquis and son of an ex-cabinet minister. The women shouted musically, letting their voice be heard.
"I know. But just the same, it could be fun."
"Really?"
"It's worth a try."
"Well then, let's do it," the other concluded indifferently. But no one moved, no one seemed particularly interested in getting the thing underway. This was enough to push Marcello into action. "Well then?" he insisted, "you don't really want to play?" Then, moving over to Gisa and looking her straight in the eyes, he added, "What do you think?" Of course, the girl had understood from the start that Marcello's idea concerned her personally, although she couldn't have guessed how furiously single-minded his desire was. She still hadn't so much as blinked. Now she was directly involved, but she used her normal calm as a shield to keep from getting upset. In any case, she stared at the young man for a long time without replying. As if naked, Marcello stood there in front of her during this short pause, and he suddenly saw in its true light the dangerous adventure into which he had thrown himself so blindly. In fact, the proposed game also meant that he might have to strip naked in front of her while she remained fully clothed, a prospect that

1. Portable electronic organ, *Organo elettronico portatile* / mod. G. Giugiaro / prod. Bontempi / 1982.
2. Ice-cream counter, *Bancone per gelato* / mod. Canguro / des. Ufficio Tecnico / prod. COF / 1981.
3. Ice-cream machine, *Macchina per gelati* / mod. L 12 C / des. Ufficio Tecnico / prod. Carpigiani / 1982.
4. Accordion, *Fisarmonica* / Gran Concerto / des. Ufficio Tecnico / prod. P. Soprani / 1982.
5. Folding bicycle, *Bicicletta pieghevole* / mod. Graziella BS 16 / des. Ufficio Tecnico / prod. Carnielli / 1963.
6. Playing cards, *Carte da gioco* / mod. Napoletane / prod. Modiano.
7. Gas lamp, *Lampada a gas* / mod. Asta-Estensione / prod. Plein Air International / 1980.
8. Picnic set, *Servizio per picnic* / mod Trapper / des. A. Boghetich / prod. Selar / 1980.
9. Camping tent, *Tenda da campeggio* / Air Camping / prod. Gabbiano / 1982.
10. Bowls, *Bocce* / mod. Unicolor (1937), Bicolor, Metalfab (1952) / prod. Fabra.

made him shiver with worry.

"I don't see why you're asking me," she replied at last, still staring at him.

"I have to ask somebody."

"Well, I'm not going to spoil your fun," she answered, a certain tone of challenge in her voice.

"You see? She accepts. Bring out the cards. Who wants to deal?" Marcello shouted artificially. Actually, he was hoping that something else would come up and put a stop to it all.

But the hostess, although unwillingly, produced a deck of cards. They began to discuss the rules, the system of elimination, etc. Meanwhile, Marcello's embarrassment, or rather his anxiety, grew. It's true that, on the one hand, the longed for naked girl was shining at him, the prize of victory in the coming game. But on the other hand, he could easily picture what would happen if he lost. He would be naked and trembling before her and everyone else, and there was no doubt as to which prospect weighed more heavily upon him. But what to do? To withdraw after having suggested the idea to begin with would amount to a public confession of his own timidity, his own cowardice. He'd be confessing it, oh God, to the girl. After she had played her part so well! It was exactly the wrong thing to do! Well, what then? His fantasy, his will, seemed to be failing, to be pulling back, pulling him along onto a street with only a single exit. And even that exit was a dangerous one. The losers had to have an alternative. They had to have the choice of stripping naked or doing something else. So, if he should happen to fall among their number... He was just about to suggest this lucky variation when the same marquis said jaggedly, "Look here. The game as it stands now doesn't seem very promising. It's just too literal, so to speak. One person wins and the others strip. An interesting moment, then everyone will put their clothes back on and it'll be all over. What the heck? Is it worth all this trouble just to end up with such a banal effect? No. I suggested, instead, that the losers be given an alternative. If it's well-structured, etcetera, it would at least give us some indication of each person's pride."

"How's that?" asked a woman's voice.

"Don't worry about it, darling," replied one of the painters. "It's a bit too complicated for you. But anyway, as to my noble colleague's idea, I agree. So lets decide on an alternative."

"Why bother," said someone else. "The winner will decide as he pleases."

"No, no!" Marcello interrupted excitedly. "What are you saying? We have to decide beforehand so that we'll all

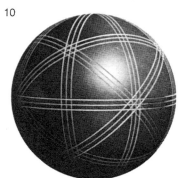

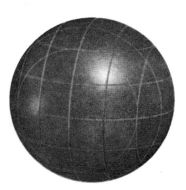

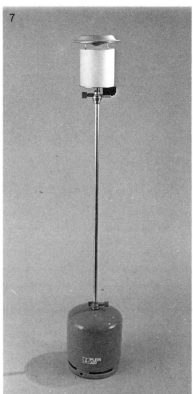

know what we're up against."

At first our young man had been pleased by that unexpected and almost divinely inspired assistance, but now, late as always, he saw how uncertain the situation really was. The alternative couldn't be unacceptable (since it would have been harmful to Marcello himself), but it couldn't be acceptable either (since Gisa, if she lost, would certainly choose it.) And so he was again torn between two possibilities and didn't know what to think. "Well, let's get on with it," someone suggested in the meantime. "Let's decide on this alternative. So? What's it to be?"

They discussed various proposals, not very seriously, and without reaching any agreement. Finally someone else said:

"Damn it all, listen here. You decide, Marcello. After all, it was your idea to begin with. Just tell us what it's to be, and we'll accept your proposal without further discusion."

"You want me to decide on the alternative?"

"Yes," several people replied together. It was the moment of decision. He had to choose, right then, between cowardice and confidence, between renunciation and the will to conquer, between the mean and the dirty and furi-ous passion. This time passion won. But there was yet another problem for Marcello to take into account. If he proposed something totally unaccep-table, something extreme or danger-ous, wouldn't that have spelled the failure of his whole project? They wouldn't even have taken him serious-ly. But Marcello had already made up his mind and, as often happens with shy people, he had outdone himself. The room was silent. And in this silence, Marcello said:

"Fine. The alternative should be... death."

"What? What?"

"How's that?"

"Death!"

"Nothing less!"

"Yes," he went on, "death, or let's say suicide. Anybody who doesn't want to strip naked is free to commit suicide instead. Immediately, in our presence."

"Interesting," commented the prince of the blood, whimpering like a phony connoisseur.

"Not in the least," disagreed the mar-quis sculptor. "The alternative doesn't strike me as well chosen. Nor is it fertile in any way. In fact, I'd say it's complete-ly futile. In fact, I'd say it isn't an alterna-tive at all. Who would possibly consider committing suicide when they could take their clothes off instead?"

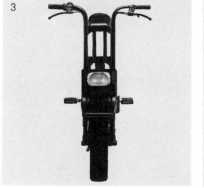

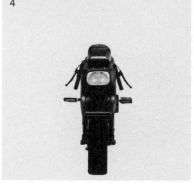

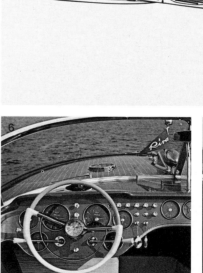

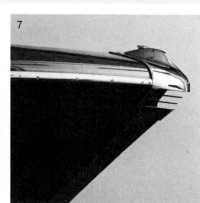

DESERTO ROSSO

1964

MICHELANGELO ANTONIONI

150

"You never know!" answered Marcello, exasperated and vaguely anxious.

"You've got to be joking."

"Could be. Just the same, you appointed me the referee and promised there'd be no discussion, if I remember correctly. Do you agree or don't you? That's all you have to tell me."

"We agree. Of course," said the hostess a moment later.

"Yes, yes, we agree, if that's how it's got to be," several people confirmed.

"And you, what do you think about it?" Marcello asked Gisa.

"Look here," she laughed, but without any apparent emotion. "Do you have to interrogate me on each point? I didn't think my opinion was so important. Sure, all right, it's fine with me. Why would you doubt it?"

"So we're all agreed and we can begin," Marcello added gravely. This ready and general agreement was easily explained. Each one of them had already decided that they could always drop out of the game and leave. If Marcello wanted a joke, that was his business. If the joke wasn't very funny, maybe the next time. And anyway, it was only a matter of stripping naked, and that didn't cost anyone anything. Just the same, in their midst and unknown to them, there were two people very worried about being naked in public, whatever their spurious motives. and the struggle had to end up between these two desperate and invisible people.

The elimination didn't work smoothly at all. One hand followed another, some losing out each round, until most of them were finally out of the game. It was getting late. An occasional person livened up under the influence of some more alcohol, but it dulled the minds of most of the others. Not accidentally, Marcello ended up next to Gisa and, surprised at the sound of his own voice, suddenly said to her:

"Together we'll conquer the world."

"I know," was her simple and surprising answer.

Almost everyone else was bored. In the previous hand, it had been Marcello's deal. Just to be precise, both he and his girl had already lost a hand each, but on the basis of the cavillous rules established by a writer who was a specialist in these things, they had the right to appeal and continue the game. One of the painters had dominated the last three or four hands, and he was now the obstacle that Marcello and two others were forced to overcome.

He had to win right to the last. First, however, he had to win this hand. His anxiety had been appeased temporarily, but it rose up within him once again,

8

11

1.2.3.4. Folding motorcycle, *Motorino pieghevole* / mod. Pack 2 / des. Tartarini / prod. Italjet / 1982.
5.6.7. Motor boat, *Motoscafo* / mod. Aquarama Special / des. Riva / prod. Riva / 1961.
8. Hydrofoil boat, *Aliscafo* / RHS 160 / prod. Rodriquez / 1970.
9.10. Rubber boat, *Gommone* / Alcione America / des. Ufficio Tecnico / prod. Callegari / 1982.
11. Floating glasses case, *Astuccio occhiali galleggiante* / mod. Boat / des. Ufficio Tecnico / prod. Salice / 1981.

9

10

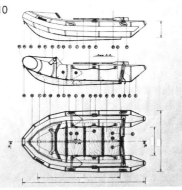

convulsively.

The cards were dealt face down and each player turned them up. Then they discarded in turn, called out their hands and, finally, the winner of the hand was proclaimed. Waiting for his cards, Marcello strained his will-power in an attempt to influence fate. The others were hesitant, raising the corners of their cards with the sides of their faces almost touching the table. Instead, he exposed his with a single movement. And what he saw stunned him. Five hearts lined up before him. A flush. But his excitement was dampened when he saw the other hands which included two with three of a kind, while the fourth hand could become at most a full house. Marcello was in a cold sweat. Until the two players with three of a kind drew new cards and remained with their threes of a kind.

He'd won. But what about the coming rounds? There were still many trials ahead... In any case, to be dealt a flush was already something of a sign – maybe fate had decided to declare herself. Keep calm, keep calm, it's too soon to sing of victory. It would be dangerous to let himself be swept away by a sense of security or by euphoria. It could be dangerous. (And why? Cards could change because of feelings, or maybe just out of spite. They do change, too, with the feelings of the people who hold them.) Marcello won again, easily, with his pants down, so to speak. Then he won again. And again with the next group. And again and again. He was sure of himself and could no longer hold off his feeling of euphoria, etc. He had luck within his reach!

Finally, it was time for the last hand, the decisive one. To lose it would have meant that all his previous efforts (and so he thought of them, instead of as the generosity of fate), would have been wasted. In this last hand, he had to play against, among others, his real opponent. He had almost forgotten her; suddenly he saw her before him, and all his sureness evaporated. Here, here was the real test. Here his luck would have to show itself solid.

The cards were dealt. Again, too excited to wait, he turned all his cards up at once. Two tens, the stiff hooks of two sevens, and a fifth card (the Queen of hearts!), clearly useless. How was this possible? Was it possible for fate to betray him in this final moment? He looked at the other players' hands: two of his opponents already had better cards, although the game wasn't over yet. Still, that didn't mean anything. Let's not lose our head. So. Two pairs

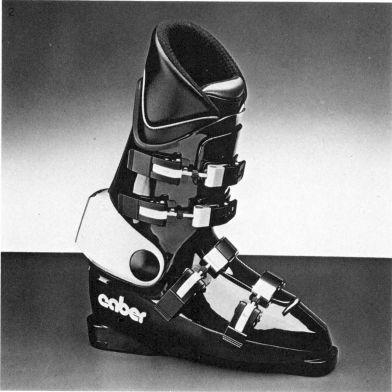

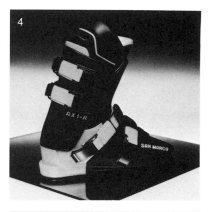

20% of the population engages in a sport.
By regions:

Northern Italy	24%
Central Italy	21%
Southern Italy	12%

By sex:	
Men	29%
Women	12%

Il 20% della popolazione pratica uno sport.
Secondo regione:

Nord	*24%*
Centro	*21%*
Sud	*12%*

Secondo il sesso:	
Uomini	*29%*
Donne	*12%*

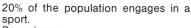

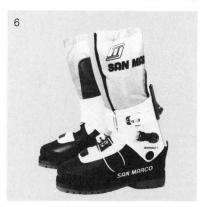

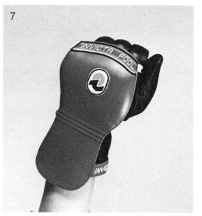

152

higher than mine, but the danger probably isn't there, because winning with a full house is much harder than it seems. In fact, the danger is really in her hand, in that straight open at both ends. It's so easy to go straight when you can pull both ends. Look at that straight! What a cold, narrow, miserable straight! Or at least opening to one. But when these nasty little straights close in the flush of victory, they'll beat even three splendid aces (and, frankly, that's unfair)... The impulse to drop three cards tempted him. He'd keep the pair of tens and, if he managed to get three of a kind, and if no one else got a full house... If, if,

how stupid. Just the same, his full house would be higher than the others possible... Oh, it's crazy to think in these terms, to give in to confusion... The others discarded. The two pairs remained just that, but then again, her hand, her straight, turned into a straight flush just as was to be expected. Closed from below with a miserable seven. But that seven was now in her hand, and that made it much less likely for him to get a full house... At this point the game had become a single battle. It was only a matter of beating that straight or not neating it, it was really a matter of stripping naked in fronted of her, fully dressed, or to be fully dressed

in front of her, naked.
Marcello, who had decided to play it safe, got his new card. But he didn't have the courage to turn it face up. His cowardice was stronger than his anxiety, and he asked permission to go slowly. Picking up his four exposed cards – the two tens and the two sevens – he stacked them neatly and turned them over. Then, still face down, he placed the unknown card, the card of destiny, on top and flipped the whole little stack around, gripping it firmly. Since this was the hand that would decide the outcome of the game, everyone was standing around the table. She was sitting there, never tak-

ing her eyes off him, seemingly interested only in observing his plight.

Tommaso Landolfi, "Tre racconti", Vallecchi, Firenze. Translated by Robert Klein.

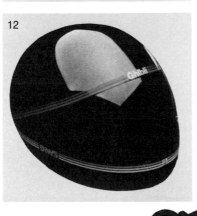

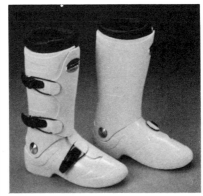

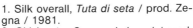

1. Silk overall, *Tuta di seta* / prod. Zegna / 1981.
2. Ski boots, *Scarponi da sci* / mod. Squadra Soft / des. I. Olivieri / prod. Caber / 1982.
3. Ski helmet, *Casco da sci* / mod. Racing / prod. Boeri.
4. Ski boots, *Scarponi da sci* / mod. AX 1-R / des. G. Conte / prod. San Marco / 1981.
5. Ski boots, *Scarponi da sci* / mod. Competition SV / des. M. Santor / prod. Nordica / 1981.
6. Alpinism ski boots, *Scarponi da sci per alpinismo* / mod. Modulo 1 / des. G. Conte / prod. San Marco / 1980.
7. Hand protection for special slalom, *Protezione mano per slalom speciale* / mod. Hard-Top / prod. Invicta.
8.9. Motorcycle helmet, *Casco per moto* / mod. Emme 85 / des. L. Parissenti / prod. MPA / 1980.
10. Motorcycle helmet, *Casco per moto* / mod. Superspecial / des. L. Parissenti / prod. MPA / 1978.
11. Motorcycle helmet, *Casco per moto* / mod. 7001 B Bicolor / des. M. Miele / prod. Bieffe / 1980.
12. Motorcycle helmet, *Casco per moto* / mod. Ghibli / des. Cini & Nils / prod. Plastic Screen / 1982.
13.14.15. Theftproof, *Antifurto* / mod. MPA / prod. MPA / 1978.

COLUMNS STANDS, THE MULTITUDE
KNEELS.
A BLESSING FROM THE HIGH
WINDOW FOLLOWS A
MULTILINGUAL HOMILY.

*SI ERGE IL COLONNATO, S'INCHINA
LA FOLLA.
ALLA FINESTRA.
L'OMELIA È POLIGLOTTA.*

Giorgio Manganelli
The Vault of Angels

The façade of Santa Maria Novella fascinates me not for the grace, lightness and inspiration of its decoration; but rather for the fact the grace is too overcrowded, the lightness belied by undisguished pleasure and voluptuous enjoyment in line movement, the inspiration undetermined by an innocent rashness.

The façade of Santa Maria Novella doesn't fascinate because it is in some way perfect, but because it is openly and exquisitely wrong, permits itself an excess totally absent elsewhere in Florence, apart from the odd Baroque feature where we have a decidedly sophisticated break with the rest of the city. But this façade is not sophisticated, it's artful and astute. Just look at the cheerful restlessness communicated by the arches along the bottom, interrupted by the rapid vertical movement of the two side doors and by the deafening boom of the centre door. And it is impossible not to enjoy, as accomplices, that alliance between rectangles and half-arches, that ordered but farcical line of squares above the first entablature, the huge and closely decorated volutes that curl on the level above, leading the eye to the vaguely mitre-like pediment. It is a delightfully excessive façade, as crowded as the tiny sitting room of a comfortably off and happily plebean family. But there are more games in store; and game is the right word for the addition below of two sixteenth century astronomical instruments: an armillary sphere – a three dimensional model of the movement of the spheres – and a gnomon – the rod which casts the shadow on a sundial. The game is astutely played, seeming to indicate the cosmic parentage of this accidental delight, this exquisite and seemingly distracted design.

But there is no doubt that the suprm-

Nowadays — and rightly — when one talks about the Church, one always specifies "before the Council" or "since the Council". The Second Vatican Council lasted from 1962 to 1965. It was called by Pope John XXIII in order to bring the Church up to date. What followed was rather the bringing up-to-date of practically everything, including ecclesiastic design. There were a number of liturgical reforms before the Second Vatican Council. Patristic and liturgical studies had shed light on the rationale and the functions of various rites. It was explained how the rites had developed (why, for example, was the Easter Sepulchre of Jesus held on Holy Thursday, before his death on Friday? Why did liturgy have him rise on Saturday instead of Sunday?). It was explained what was more essential and what was "added", owing to considerations of history, culture, or even fashion. In the fifties Pope Pius XII reformed the liturgy of Holy Week — that is, the week before Easter, restoring the rites of those days to the original structures they had in the earliest centuries of Christianity. The final document sanctioned by the Council, the one concerned with Liturgy, decreted among other things that liturgical rites could be celebrated in the local language. But if the Mass was to be read in Italian, it was soon seen that of necessity a great many other things would have to change. Now that everyone understood what was being said at Mass, the Priest would have to speak directly to the faithful and not turn his back to them. This led to a new architecture, because the altar had to be shifted. And in shifting the altars, the authorities had to revise all church spaces, and then its objects (it was difficult to use Renaissance chalices in XX century spaces), its tabernacles, paintings, sculptures... giving them new forms, a new kind of design. Evidently, to try to attribute all these transformations to the use of Italian instead of Latin would be to oversimplify things: the factors leading to any change or development are almost always highly numerous. In this case, various Churches in various countries, encouraged by the Council's reforms, introduced elements of their own culture or the culture of the moment into their liturgies. These novelties soon spread from one country to another, and from one Church to another, and church liturgy gradually moved out of the stereotypes of the last 200 years. This process is still going on, and little by little subjects and models are being established which express the perennial and joyous novelty of the Church.

Pierre Riches

Ormai — giustamente — quando si parla di cose di Chiesa, si parla sempre di "prima del Concilio" o di "dopo il Concilio". Il Concilio Vaticano II durò dal 1962 al 1965. Fu desiderato da Papa Giovanni XXIII per "aggiornare" la Chiesa. Ne conseguì un po' l'aggiornamento di tutto, anche del design ecclesiastico. Ci furono delle riforme liturgiche prima del Concilio Vaticano II. Studi patristici e liturgici avevano fatto capire meglio le ragioni e le funzioni dei vari riti. Si vide come i riti si erano sviluppati (perché, per esempio, si facevano i "sepolcri" di Gesù, il Giovedì Santo, prima della sua morte il Venerdì? e perché la liturgia lo faceva risorgere il Sabato invece che la Domenica?); si vide quello che era essenziale e cosa invece erano aggiunte dovuto a fatti storici, culturali o addirittura di moda. Pio XII, già negli anni '50 riformò la liturgia della Settimana Santa, cioè quella che precede la Pasqua, riportando i riti di quei giorni alle loro strutture originali dei primissimi secoli del cristianesimo. Il primo documento sancito dal Concilio, quello sulla Liturgia, decretava fra l'altro che si potevano celebrare i riti liturgici in lingua volgare. Ma se si diceva la Messa in italiano, si vide ben presto che tante altre cose dovevano per forza cambiare. Ora tutti capivano quello che si diceva alla Messa, e bisognava che il Sacerdote che parlava ai fedeli li guardasse invece di girare loro le spalle. Questo portò ad una nuova architettura giacché bisognava spostare l'altare. E spostando gli altari, bisognava rivedere tutti gli spazi, e poi gli oggetti (era difficile usare calici rinascimentali in spazi del secolo XX) spostare i tabernacoli, i quadri, le sculture dando loro anche forme nuove — un nuovo design. Evidentemente attribuendo tutte queste trasformazioni all'uso dell'italiano invece che al latino, sto semplificando molto le cose; le componenti di qualsiasi cambiamento e sviluppo sono sempre numerosissime. In questo caso, varie Chiese in diversi paesi, incoraggiate dalle riforme del Concilio, introducevano nella liturgia elementi della loro cultura o della cultura del momento. Queste novità si travasarono presto da un paese all'altro, da una Chiesa all'altra e si uscì dallo stereotipo degli ultimi duecento anni. Questo stà ancora accadendo, e pian piano si stanno stabilizzando dei temi e dei modelli che esprimono la perenne ed allegra novità della Chiesa.

Pierre Riches

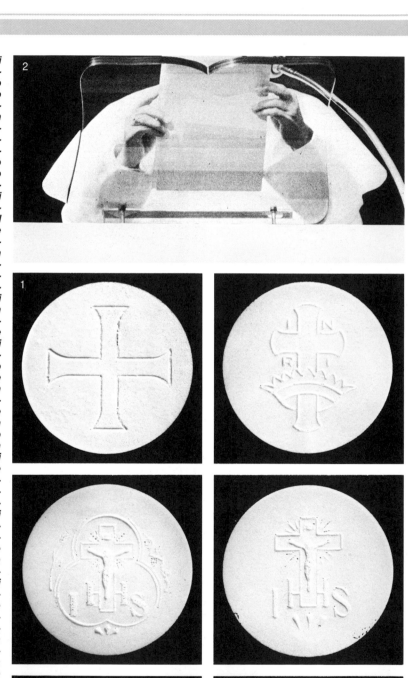

ely astute move, the great playful feature of the façade, is the addition made by Leon Battista Alberti.

Not far from Santa Maria Novella stands one of the most intense and singular building complexes in Florence, San Lorenzo. San Lorenzo is one of those churches that was never allowed to find a peaceful conclusion in an outer façade. It is a place that gathers within itself some violently conflicting places; it is a battlefield of the mind. The interior is a delight of air and stone, the kind of thing Brunelleschi did, but its ultimate and decisive points are elsewhere: the Old Sacristy, by Brunelleschi, and the *Cappella dei Principi*

and the New Sacristy, by Michelangelo. San Lorenzo is a kind of princely, courtly cemetery of the Medicis, from the fifteenth-century Cosimo, "father of his country" and the richest banker in Europe, to the soft and bizarre Gian Gastone, grand duke and *postremus*, the last of the dynasty into which the wealthy and ambitious family had transformed itself. (It was Gian Gastone who left the stern and bellicose Medici Palace for the subtle and seductive charm of the Pitti Palace.) Nevertheless San Lorenzo is not a mausoleum. The Old Sacristy is what one would expect from Brunelleschi, the man who conceived Santo Spirito and the Pazzi

Chapel. He was mathematical, but his mathematics is airborne: his numbers are angels and by some miracle they breathe. The walls are weightless, and the dome irresistibly draws one upwards. There is something delicately cool and chaste, an impossible mix of abstraction and grace that supports and holds together this minute and exact "place." something with the *terribilità* of absolute discretion.

Outside San Lorenzo stands the building that houses the crypt of the Medicis – those delicately tragic tombs of the little princes who died in the cradle – the *Cappella dei Principi*, and the New Sacristy. The Chapel, they say, is

the greatest stone structure in the world. And here stand those gigantic sarcophagi, with their statues, crests, and mottos, the magnificent but unfinished mausoleum of the Medicis. This myth of the great mausoleum long troubled the imagination of the grand dukes. Francesco I, an excentric and subtle man, had helped gather the stones; and his brother and successor, Ferdinando I, put his hand to the work, following the plans of another Medici, Don Giovanni. Therefore this chapel is a kind of idea of themselves that the Medicis proposed, as a race of dead sovereigns. Inside this chapel there is something rare for the mental make-up

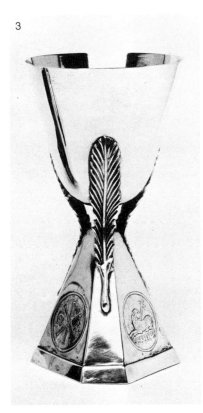

1. Hosts, *Ostie* / prod. Suore di S. Giuseppe / 1982.
2. Lectern, *Leggio* / mod. Antiproiettile / 1981.
3. Chalice, *Calice* / des. G. Muzio.
4. Mitre, *Mitra* / mod. per Papa Giovanni Paolo II / des. Ass. Orefici d'Italia / prod. Ass. Orefici d'Italia / 1982.
5. Mitre, *Mitra* / mod. per Papa Giovanni Paolo II / des. L. Scorselli / 1981.

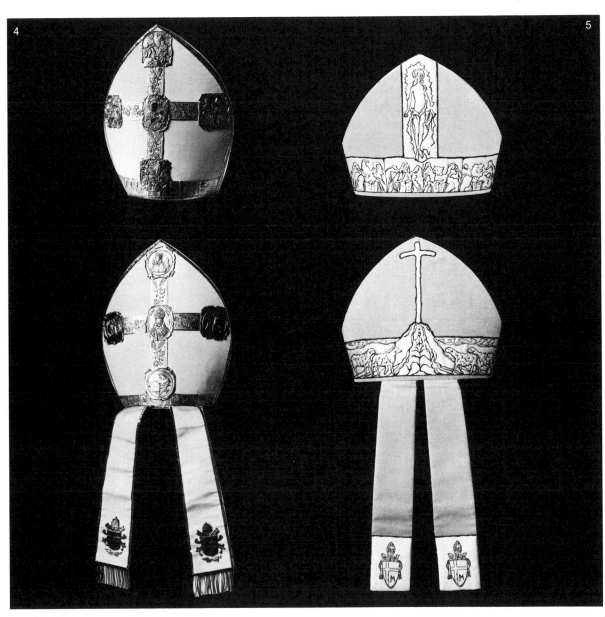

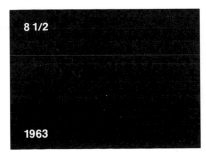

of Florence: luxury. The Medicis' bourgeois origins were well known, and it took great effort for them to join Europe's dynastic nobility. They had an ornate, pompous, and exhibitionist idea of their own eternitiy. This pomp did not celebrate the glories of one of Europe's most singular families but was rather an adornment of the disappearance of that family. These splendid stones are courtier stones uttering a highly charged and unfinished farewell address, unfinished because at a certain point the courtier stones themselves were assimilated in the ceremony of death. This chapel is not an ornament to dead Medicis; it is an adornment of the death, the end, and the silent dust that once were the Medicis of Florence.

Near the Chapel, at the end of a short passageway adorned with two mysterious statues that are monstrous and enigmatic but altogether pertinent, is the entrance to Michelangelo's New Sacristy. It is altogether obvious that this sacristy has always been at war with the other one, insofar as it is possible to make war on an elusive and fugitive design by Brunelleschi. The black and white walls remove all sense of illusion; these walls do not aspire to the quality of air. The mighty statues of Day and Night and Dusk and Dawn, stone flesh, and the two images of the princes, stand guard over a motionless catastrophe, a murder mimed in stone. If you look up at the dome you see at once where the secret mathematical point of the challenge lies. The coffered dome is the exact opposite of Brunelleschi's dome. It does not embrace and entice the air, it rejects the air; perhaps it captures the air and turns it into stone, in this place where all metamorphosis is in the direction of defeat. Michelangelo constructs, situates, and defines, and his power lies in this cohabitation of tyranny and defeat. This theologian of stone is an inventor of tombs and allegories of downfall, a motionless defeat from which the clash of battle has disappeared. In this geometric melee, the myth of the Baptistery could not transcend this argumented catastrophe, which is counterpointed, only a few feet away, by the mild, aery desertion of another geometry, that of the Old Sacristy. No other building in Florence narrates the ferocity, the grandeur, and the imperative consistency of conflict with such clarity, and it is a conflict that is fought out around a race of sumptuous ghosts.

Florence is literally a sacred city, totally enveloped within the circle of Christian myth, and I have no dount that one

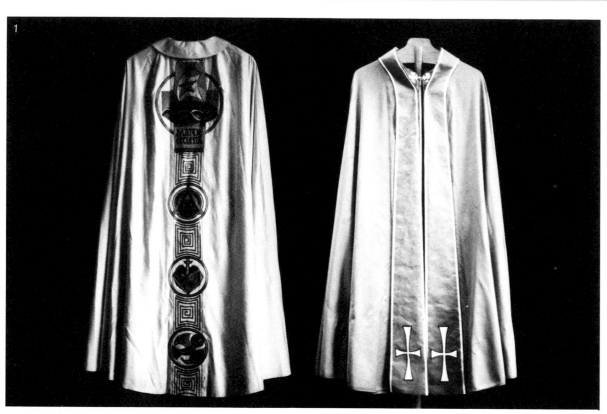

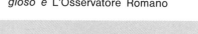

1A. Cape, *Manto* / mod. per papa Giovanni Paolo II / 1982.
1B.2. Cape, *Manto* / mod. per Papa Paolo VI / 1964.
3. Astronomical clock, *Orologio astronomico* / mod. per Palazzo Comunale - Alessandria / prod. Capanni.
4. Newspapers stand, *Edicola giornali*.

There are 1,391,018 clergymen and women, of whom:

Parish priests (of whom 21,957 secular and 2,183 regular)	24,140
Bishops	448
Priests (of whom 157,733 monks and 258,603 diocesans)	416,336
Nuns	974,682
Other members of the clergy	73,891

There is a parish priest for every 1,800 inhabitants.
55,500,000 Italians have been baptized, which is 97% of the population.
48% of the population claim to be practicing Catholics and always to attend Mass. 35% frequently attend.
87% of wedding are church weddings.
9 out of 100 marriages end in separation, and 3.3 in divorce.
The leading and almost the only daily newspaper dedicated to religion is *L'Osservatore Romano* edited by the Vatican City.

Il corpus religioso comprende 1.391.018 religiosi ed è composto di:

Parroci (di cui 21.957 secolari e 2183 regolari)	24.140
Vescovi	448
Preti (di cui 157.733 religiosi e 258.603 diocesani)	416.336
Religiose	974.682
Altri religiosi	73.891

Vi è una parrocchia ogni 1800 abitanti.
55.500.000 sono battezzati, il 97% della popolazione.
Il 48% della popolazione si professa praticante e frequenta sempre la Messa. Il 35% frequenta spesso.
L'87% dei matrimoni avvengono con rito religioso.
Su 100 matrimoni si registrano 9 separazioni e 3,3 divorzi.
Il primo e quasi unico quotidiano religioso è L'Osservatore Romano

could give a strictly theological reading of this impossible city. Florence may have known this itself, because there is a fifteenth-century manuscript of St. Augustine's *City of God* with a miniature depicting the features of that city: and the city is Florence. This sacred quality, this scent of something eternal and conclusive stains even those buildings we call civic. I should like to close this catalogue of arbitrarily favorite places with a few lines about a place I love: Alberti's Rucellai Palace. Alberti starts out with an overall idea of the building that might well have ended up in a triumph of mathematical menace, but he avoids this with his

incredible delicacy of touch and constructs an endlessly and minutely varied façade that is both stable and restless. And he invents a stone construct that seems sensitive to the wind, that carries in itself a constant tendency to metamorphosis, and a rapid play of references in the three architectural orders, but the reference is sited in an unlikely context, as it already had been in the façade of Santa Maria Novella. The Rucellai family crest in the second entablature of the palace had also made its appearance in the church façade, a brisk heraldic design of sails.

PIAZZA, SQUARE, ROUND, RECTANGULAR OR OVAL, THE CENTER HOLDS.
CLOCKS AND KIOSKS.
OLD BRONZE SCULTURE, ENAMELLED CARS.

IN PIAZZA... VESTITA DI GIORNALI. LA FACCIATA SEGNA L'ORA. CARROZZERIE SMALTATE E ANTICHI BRONZEI.

Giorgio Manganelli
"Discovery"
in the Center of Town

Last year I discovered Finland; I began this year by discovering Florence. After all, it's just a matter of alphabetical oreder. It suits my personal neurosis, a combination of encyclopedic ambitions and rigorously methodical obsessions. France must come before Jamaica. I won't deny that it seems more natural to use the verb "discover" for Finland, peripheral home of birch trees and aurora borealis, that for Florence. Florence, unlike Helsinki, is not at the end of the longest non-stop flight

3

4

IL CASO MATTEI

1962

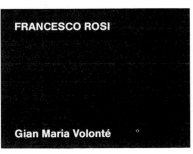

FRANCESCO ROSI

Gian Maria Volonté

within the continent of Europe; it's less than three hours from Rome, where I live, and little more than that from Milan. Every year I pass more than once through Florence station. Yet I had to walt till a mature age and for something like a late passion in order to get to know Florence. When, last September I went to Florence to do honour to Pinocchio, it was the first time in years I'd set foot in the place. Certainly, if it hadn't been for love of Pinocchio, that infantile psychopomp, I wouldn't have accepted. But for the sake of Pinocchio I put up a front against my anxiety and cowardice, and the piece of firewood that is Pinocchio

gave me Florence in return; as always, Pinocchio can't do his sums, his mathematics belong to the realm of fables.

But, you ask, or anyway I ask: why had I kept Florence at arm's length for so many years? Why did it need Pinocchio to make me start thinking that one of the most unusual experiences of my life was a few minutes by train from my home? Oh, I know why, that's no problem. I know why I know Lucca, Pistoia, Modena and Ascoli Piceno better than Florence.

For years, I believed blindly in the official view of Florence. Florence is a beautiful city, bellissima, wonderful; it's

a masterpiece, a collection of masterpieces, a lived-in museum, an eighth wonder, an exclamative city, a city to shout from the rooftops, a city to swoon over, a summary of art history. Florence, a highly aesthetic city. It's funny how you take literally the tritest kind of tourist propaganda, rubbish. It's strange how long it took me to realize that a city like Florence "cannot" be judged "beautiful" or even "a masterpiece"; because these were for me the two prohibitive words, they summed up the prohibition I felt against discovering Florence.

Let's look at the two words. In the first place, I don't think that there are any

cities that you could define as "beautiful". Whatever it is, a city won't let itself be judged with a word that is only just tollerable for a sonnet or a quartet. If a coty is "beautiful" there must be something rotten about it. I refuse to go there. A city is a network of places, routes, resting places, corners, buildings and absence of buildings; it contains all the possible cities that are designed before our eyes as we follow different routes within it. I've seen Calcutta; Calcutta isn't "beautiful" and shows how an aesthetic definition becomes fatuous when faced with one of the key places needed for the interpretation of our planet. Calcutta is a

1

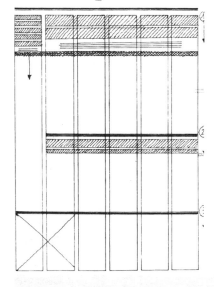
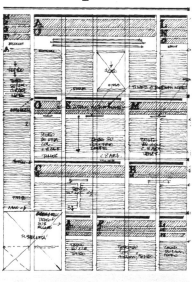

La Repubblica **was born in 1976, the first major newspaper in tabloid format, quite different from the traditional model in form and content. Is a newspaper which emphasizes synthesis, but without eliminating analysis, its raster original for the absolute rationality of its graphic structures and its compelling functionalism.**
La Repubblica **was a gust of new ideas during a time which, cultural and politically, was only waiting for a correct interpretation of the situation to begin a new phase in the renewal of journalism.**

Sergio Ruffolo

Nasce La Repubblica *nel 1976, il primo quotidiano in formato tabloid, diverso dal modello tradizionale nella fisionomia e nel contenuto. Un giornale che esalta la sintesi senza bandire l'analisi, originale nella gabbia per l'assoluta razionalità delle strutture grafiche e per la stringente funzionalità.* La Repubblica *è stata una ventata di novità in un momento politico e culturale che aspettava solo una corretta interpretazione della situazione per una svolta di rinnovamento giornalistico.*

Sergio Ruffolo

In Italy there are:

Daily newspapers	121
Weeklies	525
Bi-monthlies	556
Monthlies	2,500
Pluri-monthly periodicals	2,863

The most widely-read newspaper, *Il Corriere della Sera*, has a distribution of 575,000 copies a day.
The percentage of people reading one or more newspapers is fairly high, while it is very high for weeklies.

Sono stampati in Italia:

Quotidiani	*121*
Settimanali	*523*
Quindicinali	*556*
Mensili	*2.500*
Pluri-mensili	*2.863*

Il Corriere della Sera, *primo quotidiano d'Italia, ha una diffusione di 575.000 copie al giorno.*
La lettura del quotidiano non è molto alta, mentre elevatissima risulta la lettura dei settimanali.

total place where the mythical essence of the city is concealed and revealed; the city presents itself as a symbolic, magic place, a page to be interpreted, an interweave of meanings, allusions and fantasies; a city is a mysterious place, where a crumbling wall, a dilapidated building, an unending unpaved piazza punctuated by puddles and tufts of tough grass, all tell a secret story, a fable in which horror and splendor insist on living together. Go through the darkest quarters of an Eastern city. Don't tell me they're "characteristic". Those agglomerations of clearly unstable places are propositions, significant images, most of all they are hypotheses about the world, microcosms. No-one would dare to call them "beautiful"; I don't mean that they're "ugly", which is saying the same thing in a different way; I'd simply say that looking at them as places of aesthetic relaxation, as parking places for our cultivated and refined souls, means seeing nothing. And here we actually touch with our hand something that we often suspect: I mean, the idea that so-called aesthetics is a materialist trick to avoid contact with the mythical, violent and dionysiac matter that is within an object. This proposition is deliberately ambiguous: the word "object" can be either object or subject, like the phrase "dionysiac matter". Let's get back to Florence. If the adjective "beautiful" is pertinent to Florence, it might mean that Florence is a city totally identifiable with its personal aesthetic vocation, a place that consumes itself with its own "beauty"; or it could mean that the aesthetic interpretation has been imposed on a place of extremely tich meaning, so that the place stays put, doesn't shift around, so it's reduced to material for educated recreation, so, as we said before, it's just an exclamation place. In short, "beautiful" Florence is an exorcised city; it's harmless, it's just an unending spring of intellectual joy, it knows no demons, it doesn't mean anything, it does not allude, it is not an allegory of the world. Either Florence is actually like this, or someone has tried to drain the blood from Florence, to persuade the world that Florence isn't like Calcutta. If Florence is a place that is highly or exclusively aesthetic, then something else follows: we're incited to contemplate it as a crazy concentration of art history. With relief I notice I wrote "crazy". The madness that led Francesco I, Grand Duke of Tuscany, to found the Uffizi Gallery can be used as interpretative yardstick for the whole city. The city is a gallery of famous buildings, each one with its own label

1. Newspapers graphic project, *Progetto grafico giornale* / mod. Repubblica / des. S. Ruffolo / 1975.
2.3. Car, *Auto* / mod. Countach LP 500 / prod. Lamborghini / 1982.
4. Motorcycle, *Motocicletta* / mod. Guzzi 850 Le mans III / prod. Guzzi / 1982.

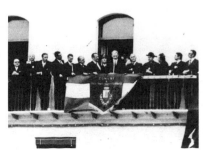

showing date and architect. A city has a history, and in this case it's an art history. But is this so true? I doubt it.

I live in Rome, a city that exhibits objects from a period of over two thousand years. Still, when I walk through this remarkable city, I can only "use" this endless temporal dimension on a cultural level. For me, Rome is simultaneously the Colosseum, St. Peter's, Piazza Navona, Piazza Bocca della Verità, the Torre delle Milizie, the Arch of Titus, Bernini's St. Teresa and Rome Termini station. The result is an impossible fabric, if we expect a city to be a calm place; but it's up to us to experience this urban discourse for what it

allows itself to be, for the readings it stimulates, for the hypotheses about the world included within its map. A city is all and always contemporary; it's made up of elements which, taken one by one, are incompatible, but which have a lot to tell us if we act as messengers between one and another; and while carrying the messages, we secretly read them, naturally.

If I refuse to grant the city I contemplate its character deriving from historical formation, or rather if I refuse to read it according to historical layers, the result is that I no longer see the buildings in relationships of reciprocal dialectic; but it is an immobile dialectic

without development, never reaching a conclusion; and this is not where we will find the ultimate fascination of a city. And I believe that in Florence, which seems to want to impose a reading through art history, this refusal of history is essential. Everything is contemporary, everything is non-temporal, and conflicts will go on for ever. Once we realize this, the city advertised as a place of perfect delight and a home of absolute beauty becomes the place where conflicts remain immobile, unresolved and unresolvable, where various hypotheses of the world pull down and build up each other: a tragic city, a city of meaning, a city like Calcutta.

"Masterpiece": a word which kept me away from Florence for so many years, since, quite reasonably, I detest the concept of the masterpiece, and in Florence it seems that everything is or ends up by becoming one. The word "masterpiece" has something odious and dishonest about it. If a work is presented to me as a masterpiece, there is a presupposition that I won't make any objection to it; instead, I will fall into a state of stupor, exclaiming "oh!" and "ah!", joining my hands in an act of supplication as if to say "have pity on me"; I may even hold my breath and roll my eyes. The masterpiece is not open to discussion; it deserves no less than

1

2

1.2. Car, *Auto* / mod. Countach LP 500 / prod. Lamborghini / 1972.
3.4.5. Camera, *Macchina fotografica* / mod. Camera / des. J. Colombo / prod. Fatif / 1970.
6.7. Structure, *Struttura* / Gondola.
8. Stern row-lock, *Forcola di poppa* / Gondola.
9. Prow iron profile, *Ferro di prua* / Gondola.
10. Construction drawings, *Disegni di costruzione* / Gondola.

3

4

5

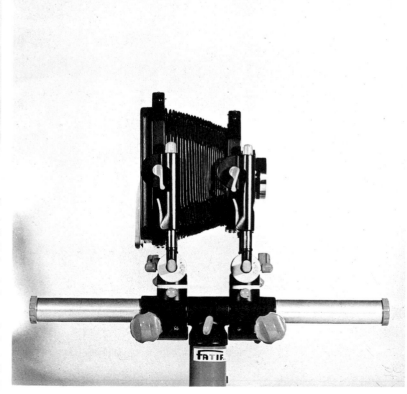

In sexual affairs the initiative is most often taken by:

Men	62%
Women	4%

52% of sexual relations occur on weekends.
36% of young people (from 18 to 24 years of age) use the car for their relations.

Men are by far the more active sex in extra-marital affairs:

Men	41%
Women	14%

Chi prende più spesso l'iniziativa nel rapporto sessuale:

Uomo	62%
Donna	4%

Il 52% dei rapporti sessuali avvengono in giorni festivi.
Il 36% dei giovani (dai 18 ai 24 anni) consuma il rapporto sessuale in macchina.

La media dei rapporti extra coniugali è fortemente a vantaggio del sesso maschile:

Uomini	41%
Donne	14%

a "personality cult". It is tyrannical; it restricts the freedom of the press and of opinion. Just think of Leonardo da Vinci's Mona Lisa and the amount of rubbish, some of it in fine prose, written about that "masterpiece".

Or the Parthenon: yes, one dady I'd like to talk about the Parthenon. If Florence is a masterpiece of a city it doesn't interest me. Instinct makes me look for minor places, controversial objects, peripheral worlds, forms that are unthinking of undemonstrative. I don't want the exact image, but the image that also has experience of error.

It's strange that it was the trip to Florence that showed me the mistake in my argument, the appalling mistake. I must believe a little in anthropomorphism but not without reason I believe. A work, an object, an hour of light become "masterpieces" and then hide themselves away. If a place is central, once it is transformed into a masterpiece it is concealed, shifted, it becomes peripheral and acquires the privileges of error; what I mean is that the masterpiece becomes something unknown, it's something one doesn't talk about, it becomes the object of elusive and erratic discourse. There's no more perfect disguise than that of the "masterpiece".

So, if a city cannot be "beautiful", if it should not be a milestone in the "history of art", if a necessary consequence of its becoming a "masterpiece" is that it hides itself and makes the itinerary of discovery more complicated, how should we talk about Florence , or rather, of any city at all? What is a city? I would like to reply with a quotation from a delightful book recently published in Italy: *L'idea di città* by Joseph Ryckwert (Einaudi). Ryckwert says of the city: "more than anything else it resembles a dream". It is in this way that I will try to speak of Florence.

Translated by Richard Dury.

WAVES OF PASSION.
SEND FLOWERS, SEND CHOCOLATES, SEND KISSES.
I GIFT-WRAP THE OBJECT OF MY AFFECTIONS.

ONDE DI AMORE.
FIORI, BACI, E CIOCCOLATINI.
L'INVOLUCRO DELLA MIA PASSIONE.

6
7
8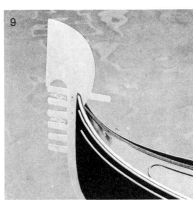
9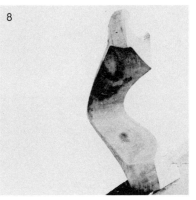

10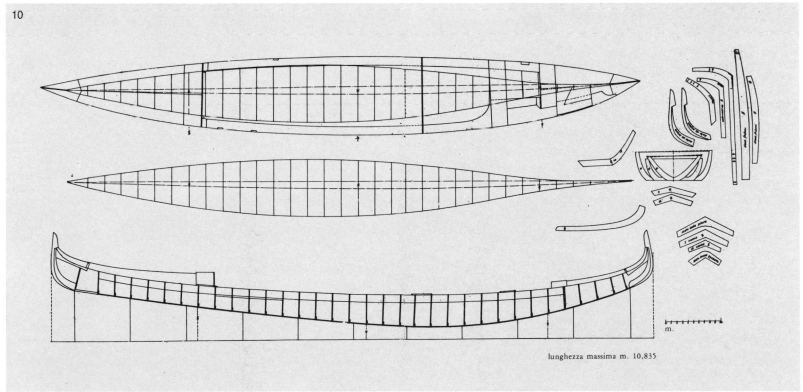

lunghezza massima m. 10,835

DESERTO ROSSO

1964

MICHELANGELO ANTONIONI

Monica Vitti

Alberto Savinio
Love

Who can claim to have experienced love "totally"?

Only a monster of multiplicity, a squid man with a host of tentacles, one for each of the countless desires that give our life a semblance of sense and an illusion of necessity, and that all go together to make up the great deception that is life.

And what sort of love is being referred to?

A general consideration of the matter would leave us all at sea, and only a detailed examination of each kind of love might be able to provide us with some illumination: man's love of God and vice versa, children's love for their parents and vice versa, fraternal love, love of glory or wealth, love of the arts, sexual love, Platonic love, love for animals, love of nature in the raw or manufactured nature, self-love, etc., etc.

But even a "specialist" examination of each kind of love would probably leave us with a handful of dust.

There is an ineluctable reason that precludes any possibility of encounter between us and love; it is that at the very point at which love is about to be born, love dies. (What an ugly union these two words make: two pieces of half-melted candy stuck together.)

Is it only sensual love that dies? Unfortunately we know about that. No, any love, even the love of riches dies in the very act of acquiring wealth.

The only enduring loves are ones that are never consummated, loves that *cannot possibly achieve love*, that is to say, that can never possess the object of desire.

Like the love of a spinster for her Pekingese, because, except for cases of superacute sadism, even in her blindest fits of passion and hysteria, she never carries the affectionate caressing of her Pekingese beyond the point at which she would crush the animal between her loving hands to make it hers, at which point the fit of passion and hysteria would begin: love.

Another thing that precludes the fulfillment of love, i.e., the achievement of one's desire in an amoric sense so to speak, is that at the moment in which we take possession of the beloved object, our love for the loved one loses its transitive character, it gets confused with self-love and is absorbed by it. Women are surprised that at the moment men should be at their most amorous, they turn back into uncommunicative egoists.

Even in the greatest loves, sublime love, the love of Petrarch for Laura, the

1

lover loves himself.
And in the case of Petrarch, indeed, the intransitivity of love is demonstrated by his becoming a poet; he is crystallized in the state of intransitivity *par excellence*.
So what about love? Love does not really exist.
It is an hypothesis, a great immeasurable hypothesis. By an error of concept as much as of expression, the origin of which is lost in the dawn of language, love is confused with the "preparation of love," that is to say, with desire. Love is used to describe the effect of a natural inclination and a passion aroused by the attraction of exter-nal form rather than the result of choice and reflection, what the Romans expressed with the word *diligere*, a compound of *legere*, meaning "to choose." And a good thing that it is. Desire is the limitless, the infinite.
Love is death. (This is a new meaning to give to the binomial love-death.) Now I should turn to the matter of desire, that is, the matter of what is in effect love. But here indeed I lack the experience, or rather I am beginning to lack it. Desires hold us fast to life, the way cables hold a ship in port.
But desires gradually die, the cables snap without our noticing, and tomorrow our ship will set sail serene and free of desire. Will the "great hypothesis" then become an actuality?

Alberto Savinio, "Nuova enciclopedia", Adelphi, Milano 1978. Translated by Robert Kleyn.

You unload pots, cans, and four-sided styrofoam containers which have been unsparingly worked on by lithographic or serigraphic inks destined to last as long as a midsummer night's dream.
Future collectors will be ecstatic over the hand-made straw covers of wine flasks, or the skins of Negronetto salami, or again, true walnut shells. This kind of fossilized garbage dump might enrich someone who manages to localize it, and anyone who contrives to decipher the myth of Dash detergents is sure to win a place in history. The next revival will see even Bacon on boxes of candied chestnuts, while some children will learn about bananas only from the illustrations of their superseded primers.
Similarly, just as the horse of the Gondrand shipping company gradually disappeared along with the blue-papered packages of export pasta, the leading figure during the blackout years, we shall lose our interest in Ferrochinabisleri bottles and the color of Ginevroni candy. This, however, when women again cover themselves down to their ankles, even during the summer, so that they can surrender themselves much more slowly. Quite acceptable as an exchange.

Giancarlo Iliprandi

Le discariche sono piene di barattoli, lattine, tetrapac e styroform sui quali si sono accaniti inchiostri litografici, destinati a durare come il sogno di una notte di mezza estate.
I collezionisti futuri spasimeranno per i fiaschi impagliati a mano, la pelle del Negronetto ed i veri gusci di noce. Una discarica fossilizzata potrà rendere ricco chi la saprà localizzare e qualcuno passerà alla storia per avere decifrato l'enigma di Dash. Al prossimo revival anche Bacon finirà sulle scatole di Maron Glacées, mentre certi bambini conosceranno le banane soltanto dalle illustrazioni del loro sorpassato abbecedario.
Così come sono scomparsi i cavalli da tiro della Gondrand ed i pacchi di pasta avvolti nella carta blu oltremare, protagonista degli anni d'oscuramento, perderemo il gusto della bottiglia Ferrochinabisleri ed il colore dei Ginevroni di zucchero. Questo quando le donne avranno ripreso a coprirsi sino alla caviglia, anche d'estate, per potersi concedere più lentamente. Un baratto accettabile.

Giancarlo Iliprandi

2

3

4

5

1. Chaise lounge, *Dormeuse* / mod. Paolina / prod. Poltrona Frau / 1926-1980.
2. Packaging, *Confezione* / mod. Baci / prod. Perugina / 1981.
3. Packaging, *Confezione* / mod. Baci del Piemonte / prod. Cuba.
4. Packaging, *Confezione* / mod. Baci di San Remo / prod. Balzola.
5. Chocolates, *Cioccolatini* / mod. Mon Cheri / prod. Ferrero.

SPECTATORS RING THE TEAMS.
TELELENSES BRING THE ACES
HOME.

*ARENA E SPETTATORI, CAMPO E
SQUADRE.
LA TELECAMERA PROIETTA
CAMPIONI IN CASA.*

Vitaliano Brancati
Paolo il Caldo

One April Sunday, the slopes of Monte Mario overlooking the Stadium of Marble were black with people. Throbbing like a medusa, the crowd spilled through the gates towards the streets which were already invaded by a dense and deafening cloud of motor scooters. Where they were coming from was hard to tell, perhaps from the depths of the earth, but the cloud stretched along the entire visible length of the Lungotevere, filtering through endless lines of cars, some of which groaned painfully as they tried to back around and into the traffic flowing in the other direction. The multitudes of pedestrians obscured the streets and sidewalks like dust raised by the moving cars, slowing down and blocking everything. Coming closer, the pitiful stuff making up these multitudes revealed itself as that substances referred to as flesh. Those who look upon it immediately associate it with a capacity for thinking and suffering, shutting their eyes with horror if they see it struck down. Thousands of faces shrank from the effect of distance and the comparison of each one with the mass of them all packed together. This mass even gave off an unpleasant sense of stupidity, joy, and wild anger, clearly demonstrated by the jackets hurled into the air, pants being pulled off, flasks of wine drained by those standing on the seats of their cars, the sweating, the shouting, the arms of women caressing pedestrians passing within reach of the open windows of cars, people jumping into fountains, others making good the bets they'd won or lost with sudden promises greeted by mixed applause and whistling.

"Roma! Lazio!" These two words, like clouds still dark after a long hailstorm, were charged with the electricity of thousands of people. On the slopes of

1 quando ti senti un po' così...

2

3

The most frequently attended sports events:

Soccer	32.2%
Tennis	15,1%
Athletics	12.9%
Boxing	12.7%
Skiing	12.1%
Bicycle racing	11.1%
Swimming	11.0%

During the season '81/82 the soccer pool (Totocalcio) has produced an income of 650 million dollars, equal to 12.5 dollars pro-capita.
4,310 official games are played every year.
Attendance for the 1980-81 season totalled 148,056,456.
Four newspapers entirely dedicated to sports events are published daily.
80.8% of expenditures on sports events are dedicated to soccer.

Sports maggiormente frequentati da spettatori:

Calcio	*32,2%*
Tennis	*15,1%*
Atletica leggera	*12,9%*
Pugilato	*12,7%*
Sci	*12,1%*
Ciclismo	*11,1%*
Nuoto	*11,0%*

*Nella stagione '81/82 le scommesse sul calcio (Totocalcio) hanno dato un incasso di 854 miliardi, pari a 15.023 lire per abitante.
Si svolgono 4310 partite ufficiali in un anno.
La frequenza alle partite di calcio, nell'anno 1980/81, ha totalizzato 148.056.456 spettatori.
Ogni giorno escono 4 giornali interamente dedicati allo sport.
L'80,8% della spesa per assistere a manifestazioni sportive è assorbita dal calcio.*

IO LA CONOSCEVO BENE

1965

ANTONIO PIETRANGELI

Stefania Sandrelli

Monte Mario, groups of spectators cold from the winds of dusk were seated around dying fires. In the middle of the deserted soccer field lay the black ball, now empty of all the furious force and skill it had contained when it seared the sky and ground with straight and curved lines.

Vitaliano Brancati, "Paolo il Caldo", Bompiani, Milano 1980. Translated by Robert Kleyn.

4

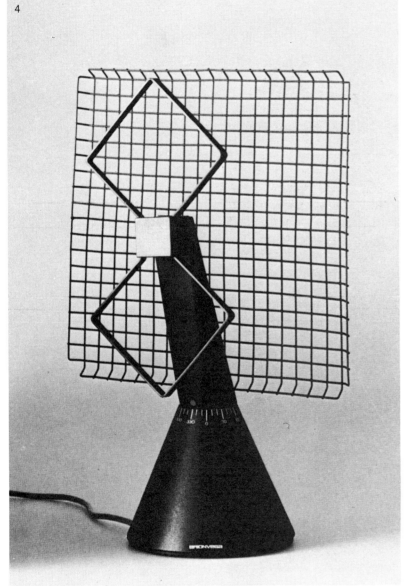

5

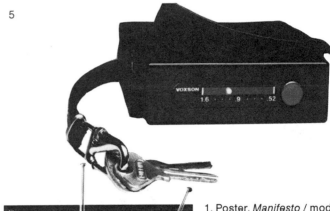

1. Poster, *Manifesto* / mod. Caffè Sport / des. A. Testa / prod. Carpano.
2. Television set, *Apparecchio televisivo* / mod. Algol 4 / des. R. Sapper, M. Zanuso / prod. Brionvega / 1966.
3. Shoes, *Scarpini* / mod. Top / des. Danieli / prod. Diadora / 1980.
4. TV Antenna, *Antenna televisiva* / mod. Robot / des. M. Zanuso / prod. Brionvega / 1981.
5. Portable car radio, *Autoradio estraibile* / mod. Tanga / des. R. Bonetto / prod. Voxson / 1980.
6. Radio receiver, *Radio ricevitore* / mod. RR 127 / des. R. Sapper, M. Zanuso / prod. Brionvega / 1966.

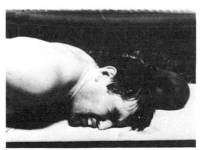

PIRANDELLO, NONO, VERDI, FELLINI. THE SET IS WHERE WE LIVE.

PIRANDELLO, NONO, VERDI, FELLINI. LUOGHI DI SCENA, LUOGHI DI VITA.

Alberto Arbasino
The Brotherhood of Italy

The moment he arrives at the theater, Rovescally is ushered to a box filled with aging girls who have been waiting for him, and they bow to him and he bows back and they kiss and bow. Enter Belotta in a lobster-color fake Chanel gown. Giulio tells Ferdinando that she probably forced the seamstress to use that color, explaining that those styles are usually found in beige flecked with lilac and pink, just like a very subtle tweed, and that only the lining should be gaudy. Andrea has just hurried off to the Teatro Nuovo to look for Klaus. Immediately Desideria is drawn into a group of flashy Roman socialites, together with some other tall young beauties all wearing the same delicately colored voile dresses. They greet Fulk excitedly, but before they manage to embrace him, he somehow stumbles over Canobbiana, crouched in front of the bar. She wears a cluster of monkeys on her head making her so unbelievable that everyone stares at her as if she had come out of a film about Atilla the Hun. "They don't think this is my hair, do they?" she asks Fulk in her deep voice, taking his arm so that he'll pull her up.

In less than ten minutes, I've had enough of the play and its embarassing blunders, poor imitations of Franca Valeri and Giulietta Masina, its local color right out of the 1944 version of Malaparte (black American soldiers and loose women), a surrealist skit with a painter and his dummy right out of a 1937 Vogue, vaudeville punch lines which aren't funny. It's shameful, and it's entitled, "Tell U.S. A Story". So I head off to Terni to play around in the bombed-out gardens wild with action and overflowing with spontaneity. What a city! What a life!

Returning calm and relaxed, I find everyone leaving the theater, their swollen wigs illuminated by the gilded lights of

---

It takes a lot of patience to convince people that a civilized man "lives" on art without even realizing it.
The tune he whistles while he shaves was written by a composer, and the people who prepare his morning newspapers and his evening TV comedy are writers; the lovely material of his wife's dress is unquestionably the creation of a designer, as is the refined elegance of the cutlery and plates that he proudly displays on his table. What would his office be like without the reproductions of paintings that give "tone to the place"? But this is only craftwork and that is simply commercial art, they might object. But without art neither one nor the other would exist. Mondrian has changed the face of our homes (although not always for the best); Matisse can be found on summerwear and Calder in toys, just as Stravinsky and Prokofiev peep out of the sound-tracks of movie box-office hits made for people whi would be horrified if anyone talked to them about classical or contemporary music.

Giancarlo Menotti

Ci vuole pazienza per dimostrare ai concittadini che l'uomo civile "vive" d'arte senza neppure accorgersene. La melodia che fischietta mentre si rade è pure stata scritta da un compositore, e sono scrittori quelli che gli preparano il giornale del mattino e la commedia serale alla TV; la bella stoffa del vestito che indossa sua moglie è indubbiamente stata ideata da un designer, e così le eleganti posate e i piatti che sfoggia sulla sua tavola. Che cosa sarebbe il suo ufficio senza la riproduzione di quadri che danno "tono al locale"? Questo è artigianato, quest'altro arte commerciale, si obietterà.
Ma senza l'arte né l'uno né l'altro esisterebbero. Mondrian ha cambiato il volto delle nostre case (anche se non sempre per il meglio), Matisse si ritrova sulle stoffe estive, Calder nei giocattoli, così come Stravinski e Prokofiev fan capolino nelle colonne sonore dei film di cassetta, per un pubblico che inorridisce se gli si parla di musica classica o contemporanea.

Giancarlo Menotti

2

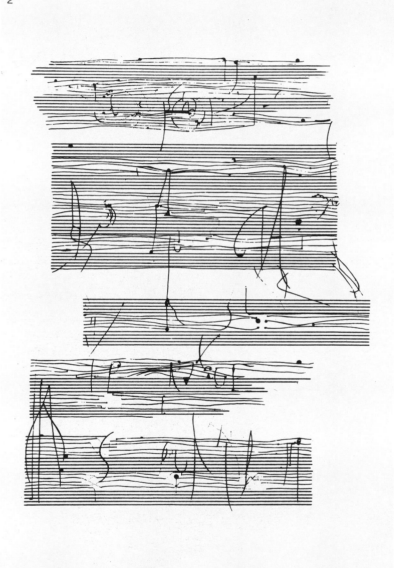

1

PROVA D'ORCHESTRA

1979

FEDERICO FELLINI

the piazza. Andrea is playing a game of some kind with a handsome young man at least sixty years old, not very tall, but with a smooth face and very lively. The introduction: "An abott, a lay abbot, of course, to be savored like a jujube". Tiny little feet, thin white hair, a bow-tie, he taps people lightly on the shoulder, always in motion. Elsa embraces him yelling, "Fuck-fuck-fuck-fuck, what would I do without this wonderful man!" Desideria, far away, surrounded by her friends, winks at me: "You see, they still take Cocteau seriously!" She nods at the doors of the Caius Melissus theater which are closing behind her.

"Skits and plays where a circus tent is the metaphor of the human condition!" declares the handsome abott. (Their game is to catalogue what they can't stand to see anymore, either on stage or screen, indoors or out.)
"Rehearsals of miracle plays," says Andrea, "fake Medieval performances where the people of some backward region play the roles of Joseph and Mary, the Ass and the Ox, Faith, Prudence, and Justice!"
"How about the police investigation that symbolizes all other forms of searching!"
"Particularly if it tends to uncover the abyss at the bottom of our hearts!"

"All those protagonists with names like He, Anyone or Everyone!"
"Even if they're called The Man, The Girl, The Girl next door, or The Traveller!"
"And naturally Pic, Mec, Zac, Din, Don, Dan, and other names for detergents!"
"The heart that bleeds while the carnival roars with excitement! Carnivals meaning all dances or parties, masked balls or sock hops!"
"Two lovers in an amusement park separated between one ride and the next! A 'Pierrot Lunaire' who dies of love for a modernday Colombina!"
"Every circus, every clown, every travelling salesman whether happy or

sad! Call us nasty, call us racist, but their emotional torments don't interest us any longer!"
"All mimes, Marcel Marceau included!"
"All parodies of classical ballet, beginning with 'Death of a swan'!"
"All mannequins, no matter what they're made from, and all cat masks!"
"All musicals, revues, or ballets where, in the second act the protagonist has nothing to do so leaves on a trip and finds himself in the middle of a samba in Brazil or a can-can in Pigalle!"
"All stories with a hero who always falls in love with the same woman who always appears in different guises!"
"Even those where a bunch of French

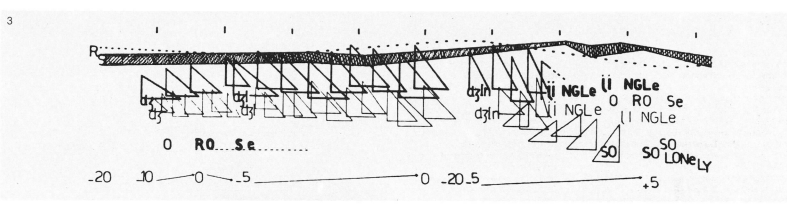

1. Loud speaker, *Altoparlante* / mod. Altoparlante 3W / des. M. Cuneo / prod. Ghieri / 1978.
2. Score, *Spartito musicale* / mod. Sensltlvo per Arco Solo / des. S. Bussotti / 1959.
3. Score, *Spartito musicale* / mod. Thema (Omaggio a Joyce) Voce e nastro magnetico / des. L. Berio / 1958.
4. Ear phones, *Cuffia stereo* / mod. BWA / des. Denys Santachiara / prod. BWA Recording sas / 1981.
5. Score, *Spartito musicale* / des. L. Nono / 1972.

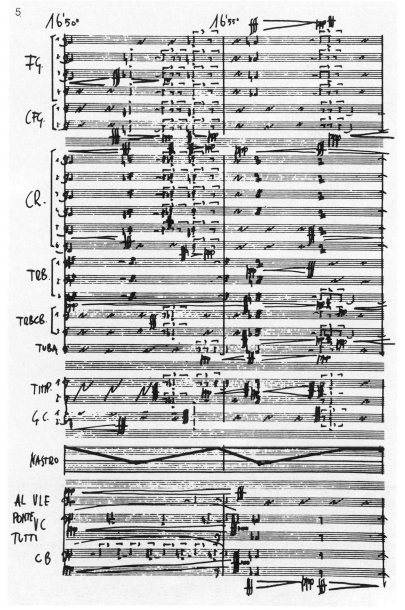

actors dress up like eighteenth century idiots and go to a chateau for no other reason than to exchange flippant remarks like, 'Women are like watches: when they're ripe they fall off the tree!'"

"No banalities... All political or existential parables which are set in Nowhere or in Beige!"

"All those allegories where the light of faith glimmers in the dark of night!"

"Don't forget about messing around with tape recorders and other such devices, particularly when they're played in reverse to produce that typically annoying screech!"

"The car accident during the last five minutes in order to cut through the knot of a complicated situation!"

"...That's the true deus ex car. Let's go eat," Elsa giggles, then yells for everybody to hear, "Take it easy, take it any way you can get it!" It's a beautiful warm night with a large moon. We set off for the restaurant on foot. The dinner is delicious except for the food, Raimondo is in good humor, and Sandro de Feo, our theater critic, gives us this wonderful number: "Whenever I go to the theater and find the set isn't ready and the actors and grips are running around in their street clothes getting everything in order... too bad, they didn't manage in time. They should have been ready, they really should

have, but they're not... But if I even suspect a work in progress... I can be a real beast!"

As we leave the Unicorn and Pentagram, everybody wants to come along. They insist and we go. The group grows along the way. Raimondo is in the rear and Andrea is coming along as well, with many people he knows from the demi-monde. It's already late, and in the quiet, deserted streets, the only sound is an occasional, "The Ambassador's wiiife is upset and she's always burping and telling her father, say what you liiike, he's not your son, that's whyyyy..." Everybody from the restaurant ends up following us, socialites and

nobodies both, one of those typical Roman events that begins with, "What the hell, let's all go!" and ends up with a noisy ascent through dark gardens behind an old stone wall. There's a bit of a breeze and the lanterns flicker. "Well, it's an old story that Roman matrons are in the habit of fooling with goats, you find it already in Juvenal. Of course the goat clamps her beneath him with his hooves and won't let her go. When at least he gets hungry, he finds her hair in his face, so grazing her is his natural reaction. So she ends up possessed and bald." I hear an old man's voice behind me, a monotonous litany in an English accent. Who knows

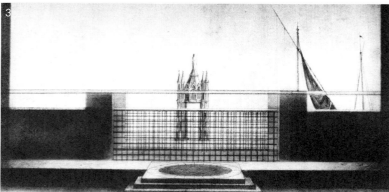

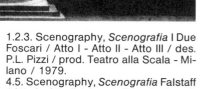

1.2.3. Scenography, *Scenografia* I Due Foscari / Atto I - Atto II - Atto III / des. P.L. Pizzi / prod. Teatro alla Scala - Milano / 1979.
4.5. Scenography, *Scenografia* Falstaff / Atto I - Atto II / des. A. Frigerio / prod. Teatro alla Scala - Milano / 1980.
6.7. Scenography, *Scenografia* Simon Boccanegra / Atto I - Atto III / des. A. Frigerio / prod. Teatro alla Scala - Milano / 1971.

who half these people are? Somewhere in the middle, two women are wearing enormous cloaks, one in purple satin, the other in black velvet, exactly like hooded conspirators at a masked ball. But they turn out to be nobodies with bare wide shoulders the color of cheese, and gaudy halter tops that slide down the moment they begin to dance. When they reach the landing, they're out of breath, looking like they're about to grab their brooms and fly out the window.

The house is dark and only the moon lights up the black salons we cross without finding the light. Out on the terrace, some candles shine on the long table. Shouting and leaping in the air, Boudeuse and Bordeuse hurl themselves at us. I don't know the real names of these two creatures of the night, but every time I step into some pleasure joint around Via Veneto late at night, they're always there screaming, "The overies are burning!" and "What a wonderful old dragon!" and "Excuse me, are you dancing with him or with her?" Whenever they hear certain words, their specialization is to jump up, yelling, "No one says that anymore! That's been out since 1939!" (Or 1946 or 1923.) Hanging there, they perform frenetic entrechats with their feet, or else arabesques, adding, "Like the scruff of a wolf's neck and Körmendi's novels!" (Or else like a plucked eyebrow, or having a house on Via Archimede, or the films of Rossellini, or pizza.) Finally they land, screaming, "But the poor soul doesn't suspect a thing!" A gloomy blond horse with thick sideburns executes a series of caracoles right behind them. He has an apartment on the Appia Nuova, that types him, but then he's Boudeuse's assistant, helping her with those plush velvet set designs. Which is why Andrea and everyone else knows him as "Boudeuse's help-mate."

They light the remaining candles, but there are only a few. From the yellow penumbra of the corners sprout forth tigers and wicker chairs, saints, the blessed, busts and flowers. While we're waiting for Raimondo, Giulio has the maid bring some coca-cola and white wine from the kitchen, along with some pastry left from last night's party. We're all about to collapse, it's just another evening of Alles Zusammen, everybody out of the chorus line. Gazzaniga arrives with Renato and some Milanese friends, and they stop in the doorway, cautious, barely smiling, looking around. "What's happening?" they ask slowly, not going out to the terrace, not leaving either.

One of the nobodies turns on the ste-

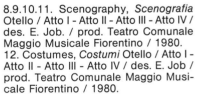

8.9.10.11. Scenography, *Scenografia* Otello / Atto I - Atto II - Atto III - Atto IV / des. E. Job. / prod. Teatro Comunale Maggio Musicale Fiorentino / 1980.
12. Costumes, *Costumi* Otello / Atto I - Atto II - Atto III - Atto IV / des. E. Job / prod. Teatro Comunale Maggio Musicale Fiorentino / 1980.

LA LUNA

1972

BERNARDO BERTOLUCCI

Jill Clayburgh
Matthew Barry
Veronica Lazar

reo and begins to move her rear end to a cha-cha, alone, calling the others. Vigorously unbuttoning her red jacket, Bellotta says, "I'd like to stay." "Then you'll get a ride back with the professor?" Gazzaniga asks. "Yes, he's picking me up. And be careful of those two fine gentlemen, if you wouldn't mind mentioning it to the chauffeur," replies Bellotta, explaining that she's referring to her bassett hounds. They might be thirsty.

Gazzabiga promises to take care of them and leaves with Renato and the others. The dancing nobody is the laughing stock of Rome, some one tells Andrea, because in the three years she lived with a wealthy TV director, all he ever did was call her up at home every evening to say, "Go ahead and eat at home, we'll go to a movie later." And when the affair ended to the music of a sound track and the two of them met to decide how to pay the rent, they each had the same idea ot the same moment exactly: "I'm too careless with money to take on that responsibility." Ferdinando steps out of the kitchen and says, "Derek hasn't moved an inch the whole day. He's still sleeping beneath all those flowers... Maybe he's deead?" "It doesn't matter, it doesn't matter, I'll take the milk train and I'll be fine," interrupts a tall old man with a white moustache. "I'm sorry, Prince..." says Ferdinando. Shivering, the Prince takes his hand as if to kiss it, while he holds a plaid cashmere rug with the other. "My dear friend, all that matters is that someone remembers to get me to the station by four-thirty," he says to Ferdinando, almost embracing him. "Everything will be fine, I'll be quite comfortable."

"Have you been to Paris recenty?" Bellotta asks Andrea, stepping in front of him with an empty glass in her hand. "Do you think there's any Armagnac?" "I don't know," he answers, "when were you there last?" "I just got back, just now. It's never been so beautiful, that city."

Three or four couples dance. Elsa clutches the help-mate designer, her hands all over him. I'm starting to get fed up.

"The Algerians haven't bombed it yet?" asks Andrea. "Oh, you hear explosions once in a while, but it's not a problem," she says, snapping her dentures at him a couple of times. "Couldn't you find me something to drink?"

I'm expecting a "ffancu..." from Andrea, but someone has brought out a roulette wheel with a green baize cloth, just like those you buy at tobacco shops, and ten or twelve people crowd into the gorgeous dining room pulling

---

Anyone working in a large opera house today operates in a space and with a machine conceived over 250 years ago. The director and stage designer staging an opera create variations on an old theme and try to force the theatrical machine. But with the passing of time, technical advances and changes in fashion, this machine has tended to become more and more "closed", and the richer it becomes in equipment, the smaller becomes the space allotted to imagination and creative freedom. These objective difficulties are added to those deriving from new theatrical experiences which present "man" in a different light and in sharp contrast to his stage image in the past. The result is that the stage cannot be considered only a place to decorate but also a place to "organize", the dominant components being the music and the orchestral pit, along with the acoustics and visibility of the house. Luckily the stage director and designer have plenty of room to work in; the stage set with its laws evokes inner spaces, poetic vistas, suggestions contained in things not fully perceived; and our minds let the imagination run free on our left as audience, while it "closes" on the imagination to the right. In "Don Carlos" (staged for La Scala's bicentennial year in 1977, with Ronconi directing, Abbado conducting, and scenes and costumes by Luciano Damiani) the movement of the processions and the marches of the Carnival, etc. could only be from right to left and no other way, while the revolt against the King (Part II, Scene 4) could only come from the opposite direction.

The traditional Italian and European operatic repertory indeed offers the stage director and designer highly interesting opportunities which go far beyond mere reconstruction.

Luciano Damiani

Chi lavora in un grande teatro oggi, opera in uno spazio e con una macchina concepita più di 250 anni fa. Il regista e lo scenografo, con le loro messe in scena, creano varianti al vecchio tema, tentano di forzare la macchina teatrale che con il passare del tempo, le conquiste tecniche e il mutare delle mode è diventata sempre più "chiusa" e più si è arricchita di mezzi, meno spazio è rimasto alla fantasia e alla libertà creativa. Queste difficoltà oggettive contribuiscono, insieme alle nuove esperienze teatrali che presentano l'"uomo" in misura diversa in contrapposizione all'immagine scenica del passato, a far sì che il palcoscenico non sia da considerare solo un luogo da "arredare" ma anche un luogo da "organizzare", con componente dominante la musica e la fossa dell'orchestra, l'acustica e la visibilità ne fanno parte.

Il regista e lo scenografo hanno spazio per operare, il quadro scenico con le sue leggi evoca spazi interni, fatti poetici nella loro totalità e il nostro cervello lascia all'immaginazione correre all'infinito alla nostra sinistra di spettatori, mentre "chiude" all'immaginazione a destra. Nel "Don Carlos" (Bicentenario del Teatro alla Scala, 1977, regia di Ronconi, direttore d'orchestra maestro Abbado, scene e costumi L.D.) il procedere dei cortei, delle processioni, delle sfilate del Carnevale, ecc. ecc. non poteva che avere luogo da destra a sinistra e solo così poteva svolgersi, mentre la ribellione al Re (parte seconda, scena quarta) non doveva che avvenire dalla parte opposta.

Al regista e allo scenografo l'opera lirica del repertorio tradizionale italiano ed europeo, che è il più diffuso nel mondo, offre ancora spunti di notevole interesse che vanno ben oltre la ricostruzione.

Luciano Damiani

1

3

5

Bellotta along like the extras in 'La Traviata'.

"Andrea, do you want to leave?"

"Just a moment. Have you had your cookies tonight?"

"Of course! But who are all these people?"

"Awful people I try hard to avoid on the Via Veneto. Now I can console myself, finding them all here, together."

"Oh, come on! With Boudeuse around?"

"Why not? It doesn't seem to stop Elsa."

"He obviously wants it both ways. With Boudeuse, he earns his keep. But once in a while he'll want to take another look at the golden temple."

In the far corner, overlooking the Piazza del Duomo, Boudeuse has Berceuse dressed up like a holy vision draped in red tablecloths. Some cases of liles are set around her, she has a halo around her head, a bed quilt does as the golden backdrop, and she has a circular Chinese fan in her hand. Berceuse grasps it like a Madonna on parade, softly singing her own Gregorian chant from a comic opera. "A miracle? A miracle!" screams Boudeuse celestially, and everyone responds, "Hosanna! Hosanna!" People in the street below stop to look up and a car which can't get through the crowd honks its horn.

A recently arrived group, all very fine, manages to transmit its highest compliments. "How exquisite, how râpe!" A moment later all sorts of things are crashing down to the street below – plates, pillows, flowers, all Raimondo's glasses, all the Marquise's vases, the candles still in the candelabras. Little falsetto screams, the hee-hawing of donkeys. Who knows who started it, but some of the wilder ones have to be stopped from throwing the chairs and statues down, with the chairs already on the railing.

"Isn't Raimondo here? asks Ferdinand. We haven't seen him hough, he's not around. Neither is Desideria.

"Come on, let's go," Andrea urges.

"Think he's still out somewhere?"

"He'll be sleeping out. Probably at Alberico's."

The dining room is full of smoke, and the light reminds me of a film série noire. Giulio stops us at the roulette table and, indicating Bellotta who has her back turned, asks, "Who the hell is that? She's like one of those old ladies in Montecarlo. The bitch has already taken one of my en plein, yelling that it was hers."

A short fat man with an asymmetric belly acts as croupier. He's not wearing a tie, but he does have a green visor. He rakes in the chips, calling out several

Scenography, *Scenografia* Don Carlos / des. L. Damiani / prod. Teatro alla Scala - Milano / 1977.
1. Atto II - Scena I.
2. Atto II - Scena II.
3.4. Atto II - Scena VI.
5. Atto III - Scena IV.
6. Atto IV - Scena II.
7. Costumes details, *Particolari costumi*.

times, "Whose is this split? No one claims it, everyone's moving around. The chip is worth five thousand lire. Bellotta, her back turned, doesn't see us. As the fat croupier rakes in that last ship, she exclaims loudly, but as if to herself, "I could't swear to it, because like a fool I wasn't paying attention..." And she looks around. "But it seems to me it was mine!" No one says anything. "Too bad! I suppose it's too late now!" she insists. The croupier looks at her. Precisely at the wrong moment, Klaus arrives and bows to her, even though Andrea shushes him furiously.

"Too bad!" she repeats loudly, turning toward the croupier. She leans back to ask Klaus if he'll be spending the winter in Milan. Somewhat disconcerted, he replies yes, whispering something about La Scala. "Ah, I'm so glad they transferred you there," she says condescendingly. "Does Elvezio know already? He'll be pleased, too. And where will you be teaching? At the university? or the business school?" Andrea gesticulates, don't answer, she's crazy. "Signora!" calls the croupier, "we're all friends here, if you like, you can split it with the bank."

"I'm not asking for charity!" Drawing herself up grandly, she pulls on her gloves, then her jacket. We slip away quickly, before she has time to say anything else to us and to avoid a very unpleasant argument between a very decided grey man in grey trying to leave with a nervous black woman in black. Very loudly and dramatically, she repeats, "I'm having a good time here. Just because you're my children's psychoanalyst doesn't give you any right to tell me what to do! So what do you want?" He's upset to the point of slapping her, and she's desperately looking around for someone to talk to so that she can say to him, "Can't you see I'm talking to someone?"

"Have you seen Raimondo?" we ask Giulio in the hall. He shakes his head saying, "I looked in his room, too, but he's not there." "They'll have gone somewhere together, probably to play charades. She won't have let him go alone." Now we're really leaving.

The moon, larger than before, sometimes disappears behind the towers. There's not a soul out at this time of night. We laugh at Elsa's car as it passes us going uphill, the help-mate beside her in the passenger seat.

Alberto Arbasino, "Fratelli d'Italia", Einaudi, torino 1976. Translated by Robert Kleyn.

A film is the result of the relationship that an author establishes with a reality; but the result also of the relationship that the created product establishes with the public. If there is anything that has made the Italian cinema recognizable, it is its identification with the life of its country and with its own time. There is hardly a moment in its daily life or its political events, in its will to know or its feelings of hope, its questions about small and big problems — that has not been represented by the Italian cinema in its continuing quest for the truth. Our concern about our place in the world and our anxious desire to known and to live are reflected in the magic space of the screen. A screen which has been infused with life by the events represented, but which has given its audience poetic truths in return, making each one feel as if he himself were the leading figure in those events and that quest. This, I would say, is what the Italian cinema has represented in the world since the war.

Francesco Rosi

Un film è il risultato del rapporto che un autore riesce a stabilire con una realtà e del rapporto che il prodotto creato riesce a stabilire con il pubblico. Se c'è qualcosa che ha reso riconoscibile il cinema italiano è stata la sua identificazione con la vita del Paese e con il proprio tempo. Non c'è stato momento di costume o politico, non volontà di conoscenza o sentimento di speranza, non interrogativo su piccoli come su grandi problemi che non siano stati rappresentati dal cinema italiano in una continua ricerca di verità. La nostra preoccupazione di come ha trovato riflesso nello spazio magico dello schermo, che ha ricevuto vita dai fatti rappresentati e ha restituito verità poetica allo spettatore, facendolo sentire protagonista a sua volta di quei fatti e di quella ricerca. Questo credo sia stato il cinema italiano nel mondo dagli anni dopo la guerra fino a oggi.

Francesco Rosi

1

ASSESSORATO ALLA CULTURA DEL COMUNE DI ROMA

DOPPIO GIOCO DELL'IMMAGINARIO

23 AGOSTO/13 SETTEMBRE 1978
BASILICA DI MASSENZIO

1. Poster, *Manifesto* / mod. Doppio Gioco dell'Immaginario / prod. Comune di Roma / 1978.
2. Advertising, *Pubblicità* / mod. Golia / des. M. Rizzi / prod. D. Caremoli / 1979.

THE HAND BEYOND THE PENCIL

ALESSANDRO MENDINI

In the general impasse now afflicting architecture, even the pencil has been called in question, the instrument and means that sums up the whole planning process.

But what lies beyond the pencil?

According to a friend of mine, beyond the pencil lie many more technological and sophisticated designing tools, including photography, the computer, and the motion-picture camera: "the hope of a metamorphosis of the drawing-board, the utopian dream of designing with different pencils".

However, in my opinion, if we are to find a way out of this impasse and free ourselves from this complex of ours about pencils and transfer grids, we shall have to revive, on the contrary (or simultaneously) some primordial means, what lies beyond the pencil is not the evanescent abstraction of film but instead the hand of man, a revival of the anthropological physicality of designing.

For it is only in this way or in the dialectic exchange between these extremes that a true *tabula rasa* can be created, the possible ground for examining *ex novo* the problems of design.

If the traditionally accepted meaning of design as something exclusively determined by the pencil is in a state of crisis, and if the pencil is only the abstract symbol of a project, the hands represent a much more concrete symbol, for they symbolize the very act of creating.

Let us think about these things a moment in so far as they regard specialists like ourselves, and without the foolish illusion and ambiguous seduction of "do-it-yourself". It becomes immediately clear that the hands of intellectuals have atrophied, and that in fact a philosopher could probably do without hands altogether. Science Fiction imagines man in the year 2000 with an enormous head and tiny hands: the more intellectual work becomes, the less skillful the hand is.

Using one's hand for writing is easy, using it to embroider is very difficult, and so on to the virtuoso uses that pianists, surgeons, and jugglers make of their hands.

The cleverest man with his hands is, of course, the magician, ironically the only one whose trade is useless.

Does this leave us with the paradox that there is something absurd about the highly skilled use of one's hands?

Indeed, it is easy to use one's hands not only in intellectual work but also in "unskilled" or alienating work like that of a porter or the worker who has only to push a button.

However, one of the highest levels of interest in the use of the hands can be found right in designing, when there is creative intent behind the execution of a "handmade" article.

There was a time when the architect was also a sculptor and a mason; it was only later that he became a designer, and still later a conceptual artist capable of designing without even using his hands (in designing film sets, for example).

The architect's and designer's trade must become a trade just like that of the potter, the baker, and the shoemaker, if designing is not to lose its humanity.

This is what it should become, even if we no longer know how to use our hands in just the right way, as they do. We would have to undergo a long process of reacquiring the old skills, a long physical exercise like relearning long forgotten movements, manual sensitivity, and rhythms of work.

For far too long now we have been acting metaphorically, at a remove from our work, and have lost our sense of the material quality and the craftsmanship of things.

The "project" as a mental operation should be counterbalanced by "fabrication", a manual operation.

LA MANO OLTRE LA MATITA

ALESSANDRO MENDINI

Nella impasse generale dell'architettura è imputata anche la matita, cioè quel mezzo, quello strumento che sintetizza di più l'iter del progetto.

Ma cosa c'è oltre la matita?

Secondo un mio amico oltre la matita ci sono dei mezzi di progettazione più tecnologici, più sofisticati, anche la fotografia, il computer, la macchina cinematografica: "la speranza di una metamorfosi del tavolo da disegno, l'utopia di un progetto con matite diverse".

Io penso invece che per uscire dalla impasse, per liberarsi dal complesso della matita e dei retini trasferibili, occorra al contrario (o contemporaneamente) riproporre semmai un mezzo primordiale: oltre la matita non c'è l'astrazione evanescente del film, c'è invece la mano dell'uomo, la ripresa della fisicità antropologica del progettare.

Perché solo in questo modo, o nella dialettica fra questi estremi, si crea una vera tabula rasa, il possibile terreno per parlare ex novo dei problemi del progetto.

Se è in crisi l'accezione tradizionale di un progetto legato solo alla matita, se la matita è solo il simbolo astratto del progetto, le mani rappresentano un simbolo ben più concreto, quello dell'atto di fabbricare.

E pensiamo a queste cose per quanto riguarda noi specialisti, fuori dallo stupido miraggio e dalla ambigua seduzione del "fai da te".

Constatiamo subito che gli intellettuali hanno le mani atrofizzate, che un filosofo le mani potrebbe addirittura non averle affatto. La gantascienza presenta l'uomo del duemila con una testa grandissima e con le mani piccolissime: più un lavoro è intellettuale meno abile è la mano.

Usare la mano per scrivere è facile, usarla per ricamare è difficile, fino al limite del virtuosismo, quello del pianista, del chirurgo, del giocoliere.

Il più abile a usare le mani è il prestigiatore, proprio colui che fa un mestiere inutile.

Allora siamo al paradosso che anche l'uso esasperato della mano rasenta i confini dell'assurdo?

Infatti risulta facile usare la mano oltre che nei lavori intellettuali, anche nei lavori "manovali" o alienati, quello del facchino o quello dell'operaio destinato a schiacciare un bottone.

Uno dei maggiori gradi di interesse nell'usare la mano è proprio invece nel progetto, quando si accoppia intimamente una intenzione ideativa con l'esecuzione di un "manufatto": una volta l'architetto era scultore e muratore, solo dopo è divenuto un disegnatore, e ancora dopo un concettuale che può progettare senza l'uso delle mani (film-architettura, appunto).

Quello dell'architetto e del designer deve diventare un mestiere come quello del vasaio, del panettiere, del calzolaio pena la disumanità del progetto.

Bisognerebbe che diventasse così, anche se non sappiamo più usare la mano in quel modo giusto, e occorrerebbe un lento processo di riappropriazione, un lungo esercizio fisico come per reimparare movimenti, sensibilità e ritmi perduti.

Troppo tempo abbiamo agito per traslati, abbiamo perso il senso materiale e esecutivo delle cose.

Al "progetto", operazione mentale, andrebbe opposta la "fabbricazione", operazione manuale.

1. Project, *Progetto* / "Il mobile infinito" / des. Alessandro Mendini, Studio Alchimia / 1981.
2. Interior design, *Arredamento* / des. Carlo Mollino / 1950.
3. Drawings realised by computer, *Disegni realizzati dall'elaboratore elettronico* / mod. Alfetta GT / Alfa Romeo.

LA CASA
È QUEL TEMPIO
INVIOLABILE
CHE ESCLUDE
LE AZIONI
CHE AVVENG=
ONO

NELLE ALTRE
CASE

1 cm = 15 cm

I L   M O B I L E   I N F I N I T O

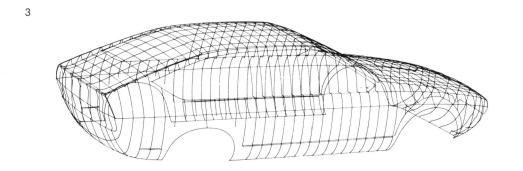

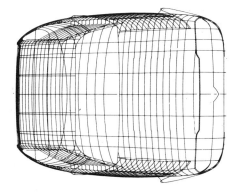

ITALIAN DESIGN IN THE YEARS OF "GREAT EXPECTATIONS"

GIOVANNI KLAUS KOENIG

The Origins and Strife Among the Various Tendencies
Italian design met with its first successes on the international scene during the fifties, mostly as a result of a few models of such outstanding originality that they brought about a complete change in product design in their respective fields. For the most part, these were: 1) the *Vespa* motorscooter by Piaggio, a vehicle which spelled out a never and more comfortable way of travelling on two wheels; 2) Pininfarina's Cisitalia sports car, which enabled drivers to win races in comfortably covered cars and no longer awkwardly seated in low-slung two-seater sports models; 3) Olivetti's typewriters and calculating machines, which brought a touch of cheerful lightness into the heavy hours of office work.
These instances, which were known everywhere, were only the vanguard of a much wider movement that could be considered nothing less than an explosion in the history of Italian taste and customs. On closer examination one realizes that the fire had been lit much earlier by the young architects of the thirties, who carefully watched American design in the years of the New Deal. But their prototypes either never went into production or were produced in very limited numbers.
The "great expectations" of Italian democracy, aroused by the proclamation of the Republic (1946), owing to the slowness so typical of design (it takes from three to five years to pass from the idea of an object to putting it into production), were not fulfilled until the fifties in a great number of designs. Many of them have now been forgotten, but it might be worth mentioning them to help us remember.
To begin with, to understand the great breadth of that movement, we should first distinguish among the various tendencies. As for the winner among these, industrial design, with its furnishings and its private means of transportation, there is little to add to what has already been said. The winner's story is always written immediately, and fairly well; but not so with the story of the defeated.
The first tendency, which was very strong in those years, was what we might call, to borrow a term from literary criticism, "national-populist". It sought not to revolutionize productive structures, but to provide new models for artisan work-shops, so as to revitalize this kind of activity without losing the inimitable manual qualities of artisan work. A tendency, this, which has enjoxed great success in the field of fashion and of the accessories of class. Two names are enough here — Gucci and Pucci, both of them Florentines. But the field of design products was blocked by its own productional structures, all of them tending towards a sort of forced-march industrialization. Furniture-makers went on calling themselves artisans, but they owned machine tools that would arouse the envy of a mechanical industry, and the manual aspect remained no more than an appearance.
The second tendency, half-defeated because it was also bound to the manual work of artisans, was the one which maintained that creative freedom was superior in importance to all other factors, and that it should be independent of manufacturing requirements and the laws of the market. The Bugatti cars of 1929-32 were conceived in the same way, and no one protested because they cost three times more than the other models and because one had to wait a year for delivery. But it was no mere chance that these companies had to close down.
Certain very beautiful objects of the fifties have remained unique, specially-made, "autograph designs" connected with past and unrepeatable occasions. Their pictures circulated only in the pages of reviews, like reproductions of the paintings of private collections, so their influence on the history of design was only indirect. An influence felt more in the minds of specialists in the field than through owners. In the same category we may include both interior design and "ephemeral" work (pavilions for fairs or exhibitions), because in these cases, too, what we have are unrepeatable, unique autograph designs whose circulation is limited in space and time, and whose memory is entrusted almost entirely to photographs (which is more or less what happened in the case of Mies Van der Rohe's Barcellona pavilion).

National-Populist Tendencies
Let us choose an example that symbolizes this tendency quite well: the pedal-operated toy car called "Disco volante" (Flying Saucer), designed by Raffaella Crespi for Bonacina in 1958. Instead of imitating

---

IL DESIGN ITALIANO NEGLI ANNI DELLE "GRANDI SPERANZE"

GIOVANNI KLAUS KOENIG

Genesi e lotta fra le tendenze
Il design italiano conobbe la sua prima affermazione in campo internazionale durante gli anni Cinquanta, soprattutto per merito di alcuni modelli così originali da rinnovare il campo stesso degli oggetti ai quali appartenevano. E principalmente: 1) il motoscooter Vespa della Piaggio, che significava un modo diverso e più comodo di viaggiare su due ruote; 2) la berlinetta sportiva Cisitalia di Pininfarina, che permetteva di vincere le corse su strada guidando comodamente al coperto e non più negli scomodi spyder; 3) le macchine da scrivere e da calcolo Olivetti, che rinnovavano con allegria il severo paesaggio d'ufficio.
Questi episodi, conosciuti ovunque, non erano che le punte di un movimento assai più vasto, che può considerarsi una vera esplosione nella storia del gusto e del costume italiano. A guardar bene, il fuoco era stato acceso assai prima, dai giovani architetti degli anni Trenta, attenti al design americano degli anni del New Deal; ma i loro prototipi o non erano mai entrati in produzione od erano stati prodotti in serie limitatissime.
Le "grandi speranze" nella democrazia italiana, accese con la proclamazione della Repubblica (1946), per la lentezza propria del design — fra pensare un oggetto e metterlo in produzione passano dai tre ai cinque anni — sbocciarono negli anni Cinquanta in molti oggetti di design. Molti di essi sono ormai dimenticati, e converrà farvi cenno pro memoria.
Anzitutto, per far comprendere la vastità di quel movimento, vanno distinte le diverse tendenze. Su quella vincente — l'industrial design per le forniture d'arredo ed i mezzi di trasporto privato — vi è poco da aggiungere a ciò che si sa già. La storia dei vincitori è sempre stata scritta subito, ed abbastanza bene: ma diversamente vanno le cose con gli sconfitti.
La prima tendenza, molto forte in quegli anni, è quella che potremmo chiamare, in analogia con la letteratura, "nazional-popolare". Essa cercava di non rivoluzionare le strutture produttive, ma di fornire nuovi modelli ai laboratori artigiani, onde rivitalizzare questo tipo di attività senza perdere l'inimitabile manualità dell'artigiano. Tendenza che ha avuto successo — e lo ha ancora — nel campo della moda e degli accessori di classe: basta fare due nomi — Gucci e Pucci, ambedue fiorentini —. Ma nel campo del furniture-design fu invece bloccata dalle strutture produttive stesse, tutte tese verso una industrializzazione a tappe forzate. I mobilieri continuavano a chiamarsi artigiani, ma possedevano macchine utensili da fare invidia ad una industria meccanica, e la manualità restava pura apparenza.
La seconda tendenza, sconfitta a metà in quanto anch'essa legata alla manualità artigiana, era quella che sosteneva la supremazia della libertà creativa su ogni altro fattore, e la sua indipendenza dalle esigenze produttive e dalle ferree leggi del mercato. Le Bugatti del 1929-32 erano automobili concepite nello stesso modo, e nessuno protestava perché costavano tre volte gli altri modelli, e bisognava aspettare un anno per averle. Ma non a caso queste Case hanno chiuso i battenti.
Certi oggetti molto belli degli anni Cinquanta sono restati dei pezzi unici, fuori serie, "design d'autore" legati ad occasioni irripetibili. Le loro immagini hanno circolato solo sulle pagine delle riviste, come i quadri delle collezioni private, e quindi la loro influenza sulla storia del design è stata solo indiretta. Non è passato attraverso i fruitori, ma solo nelle menti degli specialisti.
Nella stessa categoria può essere compreso sia l'interior design che l'effimero (padiglioni per fiere od esposizioni), in quanto anche in questi casi si tratta di pezzi unici irripetibili (di design d'autore) la cui circolazione è limitata nello spazio e nel tempo, e la cui memoria è affidata quasi interamente alle loro immagini fotografiche (come d'altronde è avvenuto per il padiglione di Barcellona di Mies Van der Rohe).

La tendenza nazional-popolare
Scegliamo un esempio emblematico di questa tendenza: l'automobilina-giocattolo a pedali "Disco volante", disegnata da Raffaella Crespi nel 1958 per Bonacina. Invece di imitare, in lamierino od in plastica, le automobili vere, la proposta della Crespi aveva molti pregi. La struttura della carrozzeria in canna d'India, tondeggiante

1. Toy, *Giocattolo* / mod. Disco volante / des. Raffaella Crespi / prod. Bonacina / 1958.
2. Newspaper rack-table, *Tavolino portariviste* / des. Carlo Mollino / 1950.
3. Rocking chair, *Poltrona a dondolo* / des. Roberto Mango / 1952.
4. Knock-down table, *Tavolo smontabile* / des. Franco Albini / prod. Poggi / 1951.
5.6. Dining-table, *Tavolo da pranzo* / des. Carlo Mollino / 1951.
7. Racing car, *Auto da competizione* / mod. Bisiluro / des. Carlo Mollino / 1955.

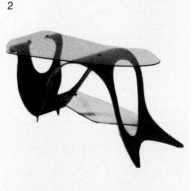

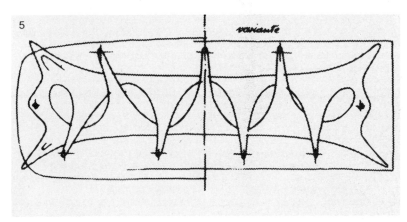

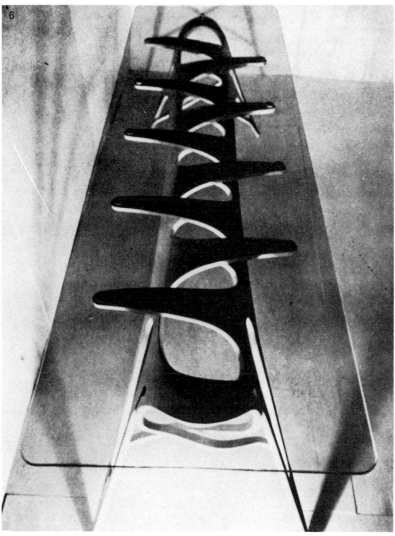

real cars made of chassis-sheet or plastic, Crespi's model offered a great many advantages. The chassis of this model was made of rattan cane and it was aerodynamically rounded off like the Alfa Romeo 3000 of the Mille Miglia races (which in turn recalled science-fiction vehicles). It was 1) more resistant to bumps than plastic and therefore safer; 2) it gave the child a chance to exercise his imagination and complete this "open-ended" design, which is just what children love to do; 3) at the same time it acquainted them with artisan technology, because the child can join the two canes by himself, while once the plastic model is broken it can only be thrown away.
(Parenthetically, it might be said that, unfortunately, Batman, Godzilla, and the TV comics have blocked this road. And it is we who are responsible for the intellectual deterioration of our children who, when they find out much later, turn all their impotent rage against us and the rest of the world.)
Another original object is the rocking-chair designed by Roberto Mango, in 1952. It consists of a truncated conical wicker seat, a light metal framework, and two non-parallel wooden rockers.
Bestriding this tendency and the more refined technological positions are the objects designed by Franco Albini. Among the most beautiful of them is his 1951 collapsible table, whise lightness is the fruit of Albini's passion for working materials almost to the breaking point, and then using sections of variable thicknesses according to the stress. His best-known object may be considered his 1956 bookshelves, with stanchions whose positioning is achieved by regulating the pressure against ceiling and floor. This started a long line of bookshelves of the same kind. As always in Albini, the doubling of the tapered stanchions follows criteria of uniform resistance and maximum lightness. The moveable shelves, alternating with the cabinet units, ensure the transverse stiffening of the system and brighten the severity of the overall design.

Carlo Mollino: Reckless genius
Carlo Mollino (Turin, 1905-1973) was described by Sandro Mendini as a mythical personage "who played around with architecture in his free time and dedicated himself to his hobbies full time". His collected papers, recently acquired by the Turin School of Architecture provided evidence of his many vocations. Famous as a photographer and historian of photography, skier and master of acrobatic skiing, daredevil flier, airplane designer, racing-car designer, and professor of architecture design, he was, last but not least, an architect.
There were too many things here, perhaps, for anything of his to remain beyond the construction he worked so hard at for so long: the new Teatro Regio of Turin. His love for Kitsch — the true Kitsch of Ludwig II of Bavaria, which is a virtue of great rarity — made him the perfect counter-figure for Albini and the Calvinistic functionality of the "Ulm style" fashionable in the sixties. His pupils Roberto Gabetti and Aimaro D'Isola invented neo art-nouveau, followed by Vittorio Gregotti and today Mollino is being rediscovered by young architects. But he is still too charged with "rugged individualism", with shouts of non-conformity, to be considered a precursor of the post-modern movement. Which, in fact, has adopted as its putative fathers (in the exhibition at the Corderie in Venice), much quieter personages like Ignazio Gardella and Philip Johnson.
Let's take a look at his dining table of 1951. The linear plane of crystal reveals the supporting structure: the span is expressed in two arches made of bent plywood beams also bending the other way to form two series of tongues alternating in direction and flexible enough to be adapted to the hyperstatic state of the system (nine tongue supports for the plane, and asymmetrical: five on one side and four on the other).
An organic form, then, like the skeleton of an animal or a frond, but unexceptionable as a construction, with a designing logic that follows no simplifying process and no Cartesian axis. What about the price? Forget about it. This work is outside the logic of the marketplace and mass-production.
This exploit had been preceded by his 1950 magazine-rack table in the same materials, a work in which artistic gesture took precedence over all other considerations, and with a total lack of rhythmical elements. Whereas in his thick maplewood table of 1955, sometimes

come l'Alfa Romeo 3000 delle Mille Miglia (che a sua volta ricordava gli oggetti di fantascienza) era: 1) più resistente agli urti della plastica ed anche più sicura; 2) lasciava adito alla fantasia del bambino di completare a modo suo quest'immagine "aperta", ed è proprio ciò che i ragazzi amano fare; 3) li introducevano contemporaneamente nelle tecnologie artigianali, perché la legatura di due canne si può rifare da soli, mentre una plastica rotta si butta via.
(Parentesi: purtroppo, i Batman, i Godzilla, i fumetti in TV hanno cancellato questa strada. E noi siamo responsabili del rincretinimento dei bambini, che quando poi se ne accorgono, crescendo, riversano le loro rabbie impotenti contro di noi ed il mondo intero.)
Altro oggetto originale è la poltrona a dondolo disegnata da Roberto Mango, nel 1952, composta da una seduta tronco-conica in vimini, da un leggero telaio metallico e da due pattini in legno non paralleli.
A cavallo fra questa tendenza e la tecnologia più raffinata vanno posti gli oggetti disegnati da Franco Albini. Fra i più belli vi è il tavolo smontabile del 1951 la cui leggerezza è frutto della passione di Albini di far lavorare i materiali ai limiti della resistenza, e quindi usando sezioni di spessori variabili a seconda degli sforzi. L'oggetto più noto è la libreria del 1956, con i montanti regolabili in pressione da terra a soffitto, che fu il prototipo di una numerosa stirpe di librerie consimili. Lo sdoppiamento dei montanti fusiformi segue, come sempre in Albini, criteri di uniforme resistenza e di massima leggerezza. I ripiani mobili, alternati ai contenitori, assicurano l'irrigidimento trasversale e vivacizzano la severità dell'insieme.

Carlo Mollino: genio e sregolatezza
Carlo Mollino (Torino, 1905-1973) è stato definito da Sandro Mendini come un personaggio mitico "che ha giocato con l'architettura a tempo perso ed ha invece preso i suoi hobbies a tempo pieno". Il suo archivio, recentemente acquisito dalla facoltà di architettura di Torino, ne ha mostrato le molteplici vocazioni. Famoso come fotografo e storico della fotografia, sciatore e maestro di sci acrobatico, pilota acrobatico e progettista di aerei, progettista di auto da corsa ma anche scenografo del cinema, arredatore e designer, professore di composizione architettonica ed infine architetto.
Troppe cose, forse, perché restasse qualcosa di lui oltre all'opera tanto a lungo sofferta: il nuovo Teatro Regio di Torino. Il suo amore per il Kitsch — quello vero, di Luigi II di Baviera, che è virtù rarissima — ne faceva l'esatto contraltare di Albini e della calvinistica razionalità dello "stile Ulm", di moda negli anni Sessanta. I suoi allievi, Roberto Gabetti e Aimaro D'Isola, inventarono il neo-liberty, seguiti da Vittorio Gregotti e Molino viene oggi riscoperto dai giovani. Ma è ancora troppo carico di "segni forti", di grida di non-conformismo, per essere considerato precursore del movimento post-moderno. Che infatti ha adottato, come padri putativi (nella mostra alle Corderie veneziane), personaggi più tranquilli con Ignazio Gardella e Philip Johnson.
Guardiamo il suo tavolo da pranzo del 1951. Il lineare piano di cristallo svela la struttura portante: in lunghezza si hanno come due archi, ma queste travi in compensato curvato si piegano anche nell'altro senso a formare due serie di lingue, alternate come verso ed elastiche quel tanto da potersi adattare all'iperstaticità del sistema (nove appoggi del piano, asimmetrici: cinque da un lato e quattro dall'altro).
Una forma organica, dunque, come lo scheletro di un animale o la foglia di una felce, ma costruttivamente ineccepibile, con la logica del disegno che non segue nessun processo semplificativo, nessun asse cartesiano. Il costo? Meglio dimenticarlo, ma non siamo nella logica del mercato, né nella produzione di serie.
Questo exploit era stato preceduto dal tavolo portariviste del 1950, negli stessi materiali, in cui il gesto aveva il sopravvento su tutto, con una totale assenza di elementi ritmici. Mentre nel tavolo di acero massiccio del 1955, usando stavolta un diverso tipo di materiale, Mollino approda a forme ritmiche e simmetriche (le quattro gambe ed i sostegni del tavolo), ma con la stessa logica. Questa volta più vicina alle ossa dei quadrupedi, sempre per ottenere la massima leggerezza.
Mollino si cimentò anche con le auto da record. È suo il "bisiluro" modello Le Mans del 1955, con il radiatore ad elementi superficiali (come gli idrovolanti da corsa della Coppa Schneider). Mollino rivoluziona la classica disposizione delle masse nelle auto sportive, ottenendo così un Cx ineguagliato.

1. Observation car, *Belvedere* / Elettrotreno ETR 300 / des. Giulio Minoletti / prod. Breda.
2. Exhibition Pavillion for Breda, *Padiglione Breda* / des. Luciano Baldessari / XXX Fiera Internazionale di Milano / 1951.
3. Foam rubber toy monkey with copper wire armouring, *Giocattolo in gommapiuma con armatura in filo di rame* / mod. Zizi / des. Bruno Munari / 1953.
4. Electro-mechanical clock, *Orologio elettro-meccanico* / mod. Emeras / des. Gino Valle, John Myer, Michele Provinciali / prod. Solari / 1956.
5. Plastic unit bathroom, *Unità bagno in plastica* / des. Alberto Rosselli / prod. Montecatini / 1957.

6. Portable television set with screw-on legs, *Televisore portatile con gambe avvitabili* / mod. RV 126 Movision 17 / des. Pierluigi Spadolini / prod. Radiomarelli / 1954.
7. Television set with revolving screen, *Televisore a cinescopio orientabile* / mod. 17/18 / des. Sergio Berizzi, Cesare Butté, Dario Montagni / prod. Phonola / 1956.
8. Sofa, *Divano ad ali mobili* / mod. D70 / des. Osvaldo Borsani / prod. Tecno / 1954.

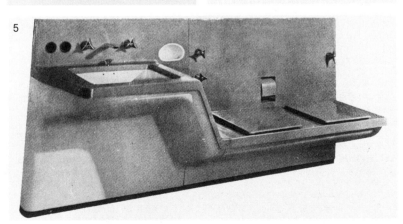

using a different kind of material, Mollino achieves rhytmical and symmetrical forms (the four legs and the supports of the table), but with the same logic. This time closer to the bones of quadrupeds, but always with the purpose of obtaining the greatest possible lightness. Mollino also took up record-making racing cars. His was the 1955 Le Mans "double-torpedo" model, with radiator of surface elements (like the hydroplane racers of the Schneider Cup Meets). Mollino revolutionized the classical layout of the masses in racing cars, thereby achieving an unequalled Cx (coefficient of penetration).

Other architects with fertile imaginations

Mollino was not alone; there were others like him. Of his generation was Luciano Baldessari, who worked on the Breda pavilion at the 1952 Milan Fair, leaving a trail of expressionism — a sort of Möbius strip — which authoritatively emphasized the amusing itinerary followed by visitors. Here too the flourish, as in Max Bill's contemporary sculptures, reigns supreme, with a logic all of its own inherent in the form itself and perfectly justified in an ephemeral structure, which is there to enjoy esthetically (but there were only some photographic panels to put on display).

In the fifties the Breda company (railroad construction) was the leading firm in the field of public railroad transporation. Giulio Minoletti, who worked for it, designed the interiors and the line of the ETR 300 electric train called "Settebello" (because of its seven coaches). With its observation car — at that time completely unknown on European railroads — it gave passengers the unforgettable thrill of travelling at 185 km/h. The ovoid front of the observation car and the shapes of the seats could have been Mollino's work rather than Minoletti's, the design was so similar.

Bruno Munari is another architect who always worked with the same freedom, since the time of his complicated "useless machines", Rube Goldberg-like mechanisms for cutting butter or killing mosquitoes. The Fascists published all his *divertissements* without realizing that they were perfect parodies of the hierarchical structures of the time and Munari cheerfully went on making fun of them.

His 1953 toy monkey ZIZI (which won a Compasso d'oro award) is still one of the most famous Italian objects for children: lined with tough foam rubber and constructed with copper rods, ZIZI could take any position, just like a true manikin.

Technological Design

Other objects of Bruno Munari's represent also the integration of creative imagination and industrial technology. His 1957 anodized aluminum ash-tray, designed for Danese, is composed of two simple elements obtained by the shearing of box-shaped sections of anodized aluminium — black outside, natural-colored inside, extractable for cleaning. This object has become "definitive" and has been reproduced in tens of thousands of units in all sizes. Now that its formal features are fairly commonplace, Munari's ash-tray has become a "banal" object, an unnoticed presence on the domestic scene as well as in the office.

Among the standard-bearers of the technological tendency were: Alberto Rosselli (1921-1976) the founder of the ADI and managing editor of *Stile industria*, the first Italian review of industrial design. As early as 1957 he had already designed a complete unit of bathroom facilities which consisted of a wall equipped with all the necessary fixtures. Osvaldo Borsani, designer and co-owner of Tecno, with his armchairs whose back can be lowered at various angles, and with his 1955 divan-beds, which quickly spread everywhere and marked the beginning of real industrial production of furniture. Gino Valle, with his alphanumeric watches for Solari, which gave rise to an information system now used by almost all the airports in the world and in many railroad stations. Lastly, Pier Luigi Spadolini, who with the 1954 Radiomarelli *Movision* television set designed the first widely-sold low-cost portable Italian TV receiver, a model with a metal body and screw-on legs. The *Movision* was the first decisive step towards dismounting that sort of pocket theater of japanned wood with gilt fillets that constituted the principal fetish in Italian homes of the fifties.

Quanto era rigoroso in questo modello, altrettanto libero fu nel disegnare il pullman pubblicitario per l'Agipgas (1952), le cui forme a coleottero, dalla coda abbattibile che si trasformava in scala posteriore d'accesso, costituivano un segnale pubblicitario fortissimo, altrettanto funzionale, per lo scopo previsto, del coefficiente di penetrazione dell'auto da record.

Altri architetti ricchi di fantasia

Mollino non era solo, ma in buona compagnia. Alla sua generazione appartiene Luciano Baldessari, che nel padiglione della Breda alla fiera di Milano del 1952 tracciò un segno espressionista — una specie di nastro di Moebius — che sottolineava con autorità il divertito percorso dei visitatori. Anche qui il gesto, come nelle sculture coeve di Max Bill, domina sovrano, con una sua logica del tutto interna alla forma stessa, e che è perfettamente giustificata in una struttura effimera, tutta da godere esteticamente (da mostrare, vi erano solo dei pannelli fotografici).

La Breda (costruzioni ferroviarie) era negli anni Cinquanta la Casa di punta nel campo dei trasporti pubblici su rotaia. Per essa lavorava anche Giulio Minoletti, che progettò gli interni e la linea dell'elettrotreno ETR 300 ("Settebello", perché composto da sette carrozze), sul cui belvedere — restato un unicum nei mezzi ferroviari europei — molti ricorderanno di aver provato il brivido dei 185 km/h. Il muso ovoidale del belvedere e le strutture dei sedili potrebbero essere di Mollino invece che di Minoletti, tanto vicino era il loro gusto.

Anche Bruno Munari ha sempre lavorato con la stessa libertà, fino dal tempo delle sue complicate "macchine inutili", come i marchingegni per tagliare il burro o per uccidere le zanzare. I fascisti pubblicarono i suoi divertissements senza accorgersi che erano perfette parodie delle strutture gerarchiche di allora e Munari continuò bellamente a prenderli in giro.

La sua scimmietta giocattolo ZIZI del 1953 (premiata col Compasso d'Oro) resta uno dei più famosi oggetti italiani per bambini: rivestita in gommapiuma resistente, la sua struttura in tondino di rame gli permette di assumere qualsiasi posizione, come fosse un manichino vero.

Il design tecnologico

Altri oggetti di Bruno Munari rappresentano anche una integrazione fra invenzione creativa e tecnologica industriale. I suoi portacenere di alluminio anodizzato del 1957, per Danese, composti da due elementi semplici, ottenuti per tranciatura di profili scatolari di alluminio anodizzato — l'esterno nero, l'interno color naturale, sfilabile per la vuotatura — sono diventati un oggetto "definitivo", riprodotto in diecine di migliaia di esemplari di tutte le dimensioni. Consumate le sue emergenze formali, il portacenere di Munari è oggi un oggetto "banale", un'inosservata presenza sia nei paesaggi domestici che in quelli di ufficio.

Vessilliferi della tendenza tecnologica furono Alberto Rosselli (1921-1976), fondatore dell'ADI e direttore di Stile Industria, la prima rivista italiana di industrial design, che già nel 1957 aveva progettato una intera unità di servizi da bagno che costituivano una parete interamente attrezzata; Osvaldo Borsani, design e proprietario della Tecno, con le sue poltrone ad inclinazione regolabile ed i divani letto (1955) che conobbero una immediata larga diffusione, e che segnarono l'inizio di una produzione veramente industriale del mobile; Gino Valle, con i suoi orologi alfanumerici per la Solari, che dettero origine ad un sistema di informazione oggi diffuso in quasi tutti gli aereoporti del mondo ed in moltissime stazioni ferroviarie. Ed infine, Pier Luigi Spadolini, che col Televisore Movision della Radiomarelli (1954) disegnò il primo televisore economico italiano di larga diffusione, portatile, a carrozzeria metallica con gambe avvitabili. Il Movision fu il primo passo decisivo verso la distruzione di quella specie di teatrino domestico, in legno laccato nero con filetti dorati, che era stato il feticcio principale delle abitazioni italiane all'inizio degli anni Cinquanta.

RISVEGLIO
GLI OGGETTI QUOTIDIANI

Italo Calvino
Le città invisibili

La città di Leonia rifà se stessa tutti i giorni: ogni mattina la popolazione si risveglia tra lenzuola fresche, si lava con saponette appena sgusciate dall'involucro, indossa vestaglie nuove fiammanti, estrae dal più perfezionato frigorifero barattoli di latta ancora intonsi, ascoltando le ultime filastrocche dall'ultimo modello d'apparecchio.

Sui marciapiedi, avviluppati in tersi sacchi di plastica, i resti della Leonia d'ieri aspettano il carro dello spazzaturaio. Non solo tubi di dentifricio schiacciati, lampadine fulminate, giornali, contenitori, materiali d'imballaggio, ma anche scaldabagni, enciclopedie, pianoforti, servizi di porcellana: più che dalle cose che ogni giorno vengono fabbricate vendute comprate, l'opulenza di Leonia si misura dalle cose che ogni giorno vengono buttate via per far posto alle nuove. Tanto che ci si chiede se la vera passione di Leonia sia davvero come dicono il godere delle cose nuove e diverse, o non piuttosto l'espellere, l'allontanare da sé, il mondarsi d'una ricorrente impurità. Certo è che gli spazzaturai sono accolti come angeli, e il loro compito di rimuovere i resti dell'esistenza di ieri è circondato d'un rispetto silenzioso, come un rito che ispira devozione, o forse solo perché una volta buttata via la roba nessuno vuole più averci da pensare.

Dove portino ogni giorno il loro carico gli spazzaturai nessuno se lo chiede: fuori della città, certo; ma ogni anno la città s'espande, e gli immondezzai devono arretrare più lontano; l'imponenza del getto aumenta e le cataste s'innalzano, si stratificano, si dispiegano su un perimetro più vasto. Aggiungi che più l'arte di Leonia eccelle nel fabbricare nuovi materiali, più la spazzatura migliora la sua sostanza, resiste al tempo, alle intemperie, a fermentazioni e combustioni. È una fortezza di rimasugli indistruttibili che circonda Leonia, la sovrasta da ogni lato come un acrocoro di montagne.

Il risultato è questo: che più Leonia espelle roba più ne accumula; le squame del suo passato si saldano in una corazza che non si può togliere; rinnovandosi ogni giorno la città conserva tutta se stessa nella sola forma definitiva: quella delle spazzature d'ieri che s'ammucchiavano sulle spazzature dell'altroieri e di tutti i suoi giorni e anni e lustri.

Il pattume di Leonia a poco a poco invaderebbe il mondo, se sullo sterminato immondezzaio non stessero premendo, al di là dell'estremo crinale, immondezzai d'altre città, che anch'esse respingono lontano da sé montagne di rifiuti. Forse il mondo intero, oltre i confini di Leonia, è ricoperto di crateri di spazzatura, ognuno con al centro una metropoli in eruzione ininterrotta. I confini tra le città estranee e nemiche sono bastioni infetti in cui i detriti dell'una e dell'altra si puntellano a vicenda, si so-

vrastano, si mescolano.

Più ne cresce l'altezza, più incombe il pericolo delle frane: basta che un barattolo, un vecchio pneumatico, un fiasco spagliato rotoli dalla parte di Leonia e una valanga di scarpe spaiate, calendari d'anni trascorsi, fiori secchi sommergerà la città nel proprio passato che invano tentava di respingere, mescolato con quello delle città limitrofe, finalmente monde: un cataclisma spianerà la sordida catena montuosa, cancellerà ogni traccia della metropoli sempre vestita di nuovo. Già dalle città vicine sono pronti coi rulli compressori per spianare il suolo, estendersi nel nuovo territorio, ingrandire se stesse, allontanare i nuovi immondezzai.

Italo Calvino. "Le città invisibili", Einaudi, Torino 1977.

Giorgio Bassani
L'Airone

Non subito, ma risalendo con una certa fatica dal pozzo senza fondo dell'incoscienza, Edgardo Limentani sporse il braccio destro in direzione del comodino. La piccola sveglia da viaggio che Nives, sua moglie, gli aveva regalato tre anni prima a Basilea in occasione del suo quarantaduesimo compleanno, continuava, nel buio, a emettere a brevi intervalli il suo acuto e insistente, anche se discreto. Bisognava farla tacere. Limentani ritirò il braccio, aprì gli occhi, e si volse, gravando col fianco sul gomito e allungando il braccio sinistro; e nel momento stesso che li raggiungeva con la punta delle dita la delicata, già un po' consunta pelle di daino della Jaeger, e premeva il pulsante d'arresto della suoneria, dalla posizione, sul quadrante, delle sfere fosforescenti, lesse l'ora. Erano le quattro: l'ora appunto a cui, la sera avanti, aveva stabilito di svegliarsi. Se voleva arrivare a Volano un'ora prima che cominciasse a far chiaro — si disse —, era necessario che non perdesse neanche un minuto. Fra una cosa e l'altra, alzarsi, andare al gabinetto, lavarsi, radersi, vestirsi, mettere un po' di caffè nello stomaco, eccetera, non ce l'avrebbe fatta a montare in macchina prima delle cinque.

Infine, non appena ebbe acceso la luce e, seduto sul letto, si fu lentamente guardato attorno, preso da un improvviso senso di avvilimento fu tentato di lasciar perdere, di non partire. Dipendeva forse dal freddo della stanza, o magari dal lume troppo debole che pioveva giù dal lampadario centrale: certo è che la camera da letto dove, a parte un breve periodo subito dopo sposato, e a parte, poi, naturalmente, l'anno e mezzo di Svizzera, aveva dormito fino da ragazzo, non gli era mai sembrata così estranea, così squallida. Lo scuro armadio che occupava, alto, largo e panciuto (sua madre l'aveva sempre chiamato l'armadio "bombé"), buona parte della parete di sinistra; il

pesante cassettone della parete di destra, sormontato da un piccolo specchio ovale, così opaco che non serviva a niente, nemmeno a farcisi la cravatta; la vetrinetta mogano e cristalli dei fucili, là in fondo, piccola accanto alla bigia sagoma verticale della mantovana; le sedie; la gruccia a rotelle su cui, fino dal pomeriggio del giorno avanti, sua madre aveva collocato in evidenza il costume di lana, completo di maglia e mutande lunghe (il resto dell'insieme da caccia, stivali compresi, l'aveva messo di là, nel bagno); i vari passepartout — quello del diploma di laurea, e quelli delle fotografie, in prevalenza di montagna —, attaccati ai muri un po' dappertutto: ogni mobile, ogni suppellettile, ogni oggetto che gli veniva sott'occhio, lo urtava, lo infastidiva. Era come se lo vedesse per la prima volta; oppure, più esattamente, come se soltanto adesso gli fosse dato cogliere un suo aspetto meschino, antipatico, assurdo.

Sbadigliò. Si passò una mano sulle guance e sul mento, ruvidi di barba, scostò le coperte, mise le gambe giù dal letto, prese da una sedia la vestaglia di lana color cammello, la indossò sopra il pigiama, infilò le pantofole; e dopo qualche istante era alla finestra, a guardare attraverso i vetri e le imposte socchiuse giù nel cortile.

Da vedere non c'era quasi niente. Il cortile era talmente immerso nelle tenebre che il pozzo, al centro, si distingueva appena. Ciò nonostante, dalla finestra della cucina dei Manzoli, i portinai, usciva una lista di luce bianchissima: tanto viva da arrivare a toccare in cima all'alto muro di fronte, prospiciente su via Montebello, i rami superiori del grande rosaio rampicante da cui, l'estate, la parete interna del muro veniva ricoperta quasi completamente. Raffiche di scirocco li agitavano, li scompigliavano. Secchi e leggeri, si muovevano a scatti: come se fossero percorsi ogni tanto da una scarica elettrica. Non pioveva: finché il vento durava, non sarebbe piovuto.

Si volse a guardare verso l'androne. La porta dell'appartamento terreno, occupato dalla famiglia Manzoli, si era appena aperta. Ne usciva dell'altra luce (assai meno viva di quella che filtrava dalla finestra della cucina): contro la quale venne subito a profilarsi una figura curva e infagottata.

— Romeo è già in piedi —, constatò. Seguì attento e immobile tutti i successivi movimenti del portinaio. Lo vide avanzare, accostarsi alla cancellata di ferro battuto che separava il portico dal cortile, socchiuderne un battente, uscire all'aperto, scrutare, in alto, il cielo buio, e infine, essendosi accorto evidentemente di lui, il padrone, togliersi il berretto.

Giorgio Bassani, "L'Airone". Mondadori, Milano 1976.

PER STRADA
LA CITTÀ RIVIVE

Savinio
L'automobile

Nel capitolo sulla meccanica del Trattato delle Opere Segrete della Natura e dell'Arte, Ruggero Bacone dice che presto si vedranno delle vetture senza cavalli e delle macchine che porteranno l'uomo in giro per l'aria. È chiaro che il dotto francescano di Oxford preannunciava così quella macchina che gli aggiornati e i brachifoni chiamano auto, e quell'apparecchio volante che si scrive aeroplano e si pronuncia aereoplano. Ricordiamo per inciso che Gabriele D'Annunzio, il quale amava dare nomi nobili alle cose che a suo sentire avevano nomi ignobili, propose di chiamare l'aeroplano "velivolo", ma non ebbe successo: sorte comune a tutti coloro che per ragioni o estetiche o di altro genere tentano deviare il corso naturale della lingua. Per l'occasione oscuri filologhi scoprirono che "velivolo" non era invenzione di D'Annunzio ma di Chateaubriand, e ricordarono "le pêcheur napolitain dans sa barque vélivole", citato nel volume VI, p. 164, delle Mémories d'Outre-tombe. Le parole di Ruggero Bacone si innalzano a profezia, se si pensa che questo cultore della Grande Opera, la quale come si sa era la ricerca della pietra filosofale, nacque nel 1214, morì nel 1294, e dunque visse sette secoli prima della nascita dell'automobile e dell'aeroplano. Non è chiaro tuttavia se queste ardite anticipazioni Bacone le trasse da una sua personale facoltà divinatoria, o se gliele suggerì quell'androide che, a imitazione di Alberto Magno, egli si era fabbricato da sé e gli aveva insegnato a parlare, e quello, in compenso, gli rivelava i segreti del futuro. Comunque fosse fu accusato di stregoneria e buttato in carcere, onde lo trasse Clemente IV, grande amico dei cabalisti e un po' cabalista egli stesso. Oltre all'automobile e all'aeroplano, Bacone predisse anche la campana per le esplorazioni sottomarine e il ponte sospeso. Queste previsioni di Bacone sono citate a prova della sua straordinaria genialità, ma resta a stabilire quale nesso preciso c'è tra genialità e "pensiero meccanistico". Per me, un infallibile segno di intelligenza (qui parlo d'intelligenza in senso assoluto) è l'orientamento "meccanistico" della mente. Avevo una certa stima di Ruggero Bacone finché lo credevo dedito soltanto all'alchimia e alla magia: l'ho perduta da quando so che egli si preoccupava anche del progresso meccanico del mondo. Sempre curioso mi riesce, curioso e sconfortante che tanto caso si faccia del progresso meccanico del mondo, e nessuno del suo progresso morale. È veramente così necessario il meccanismo alla salute, al benessere, alla felicità dell'uomo? Eravamo felici, felici e orgogliosi che l'automobile e l'aeroplano fossero penetrati così profondamente nella nostra vita da farci credere che non ne potevamo più fare a meno, e le restrizioni dovute allo stato di guerra sono bastate a

dimostrarci che si può vivere anche senza "la macchina" e senza "l'aereo". Gran differenza è tra come viaggiamo noi e come viaggiava Platone, ma non mi risulta che eguale differenza sia tra come ragiona un uomo d'oggi e come ragionava Platone. Dirò anzi... a questo i fisiocrati oppongono che il progresso mentale è una sacrilega illusione, una sfida a Dio. La quale risposta a me puzza della più sordida viltà morale.

Alberto Savinio, "Nuova enciclopedia", Adelphi, Milano 1978.

Luciano Mastronardi
Il meridionale di Vigevano

Sto camminando verso l'ufficio. È sabato. C'è mercato nella Piazzetta del mercato. Quello di Vigevano è un mercato silenzioso: non si sente nessun richiamo. Gli ambulanti se ne stanno seduti dietro i banchi, con gli scaldini in scossa; oppure in piedi, a scaldarsi vicino ai fuochi accesi fra un banco e l'altro.
Sulla porta delle Poste, ancora chiusa, dei vecchietti se ne stanno seduti coi libretti delle pensioni nelle mani. Dinanzi al palazzo delle Poste, c'è un bar, dove ogni mattina vado a prendermi il primo caffè. A quest'ora è pieno di impiegati che, mentre fanno colazione con cappuccini e brioches, affondano lo sguardo su pagine di giornali. Dietro il banco, il padrone sta trafficando alla macchina dell'espresso, mentre un garzoncino d'una dozzina d'anni, con l'aria spaurita e tesa di chi è al primo lavoro, lava tazzine e bicchieri e cucchiaini, e serve.
C'è tepore di protezione qui, anche se l'aria è lugubre. Ogni tanto sguardi furtivi vanno all'orologio, seguiti da sospiri compressi. Le otto e venti. Serpeggia una sorda irritazione.
"Ho detto due bustine!".
"Lo voglio macchiato latte!".
"E il bicchier d'acqua?".
"È stata lavata bene la tazzina?".
Questi appunti sono rivolti al ragazzino, che, con aria confusa, si fa in quattro a portare seconde bustine, servire bicchieri d'acqua, e riportare al padrone chicchere di caffè per allungarlo.
Qualcuno lo manda dal tabaccaio a prendere un pacchetto di nazionali, spicciati ragazzi'; qualche altro gli dà la giacca da smacchiare, c'è caduta una gocceta di caffelatte, ragazzi', vacci piano con lo smacchiatore, che si può bruciare lu panno.
Gli impiegati portano tutti camicie nuove dagli splendidi colletti, l'abito già fatto, stiratissimo, i calzini che arrivano poco sopra le caviglie, e che, nelle gambe accavallate, lasciano vedere una pelle bianca.
Parecchi si stanno fumando la prima.
Ci sono anche impiegate che parlano con la padrona del bar, seduta alla cassa, dei loro fastidi, che sono poi sempre gli stessi. Una ha una serva che è un mostro, non esagero, signora, un mostro. Tutte le mattine racconta l'ulti-ma mostruosità della serva:
"Ieri stava cercando di avvelenarmi!" sta dicendo, drammatica. "Me ne sono incorta in tempo; è stata la mano di Dio!".
Un'altra impiegata sta contando dei suoi rapporti con la suocera, con aria schifita:
"Il Signore dovrebbe farla morire, mia suocera, se è giusto come dicono!".
La padrona del bar ha un fare che le delude. Dice sempre e subito di sì, sì sì sì sì. Oggià oggià. Oppure, come ha fatto adesso, mentre l'impiegata le contava dell'avvelenamento della serva, sembra cadere dalle nuvole:
"Oh ma cosa mi dice mai! Oh pensi, pensi che gente c'è al mondo. Ma che cosa, neh!".
Il padrone del bar e la moglie hanno una strana somiglianza fra loro, che a prima vista si prenderebbero per fratello e sorella. Sono meridionali. Prima avevano una rivendita di giornali; poi hanno aperto una fabbrichetta di scarpe; ora hanno rilevato questo bar.
Adesso gli impiegati si alzano. Sono quasi le otto e mezza. Mentre la padrona dà i resti, e augura buon lavoro e buona giornata, il padrone e il garzoncino rimettono a posto le pagine dei giornali e puliscono i tavolini sporchi di briciole e di segni rotondi dei piattini.
L'ufficio dove lavoro è nel palazzo attiguo a quello delle Poste. Sul portone sta il portiere che ha tre modi di salutare diversi, conforme la posizione dell'impiegato che passa. Per i capi si leva il cappello; per gli impiegati comuni si porta la mano alla visiera; per gli avventizi si limita a un sufficiente cenno della mano.
Sua moglie invece è più liberale. Fa subito conoscenza con gli impiegati, e, dopo qualche momento, comincia a picchiare affettuosi schiaffetti sulle guance.
"Io non ho figli, ma sono sicura che, se ne avessi uno, mio figlio avrebbe tutta la sua bella faccia, tutta la sua bella intelligenza, e avrebbe fatto la sua strepitosa carriera!" ha detto a tutti gli impiegati della Tributaria, delle Imposte e delle Ipoteche, che saranno una cinquantina.
Per gli avventizi ha una frase anche per loro:
"Coraggio, gli ultimi saranno i primi. L'ha detto San Paolo!" dice, con l'aria vanitosa di chi fa una citazione.
Come mi vede, mi dice:
"Allora, dottore, ha pensato a quello che lo ho detto?... Uhm?... che si ricordi che, a Vigevano, di brave belle buone ragazze non è una mega!".
"Non lo metto in dubbio!".
"Ragazze proprio come una volta...".
Quando i portinai possono combinare un matrimonio, sono così contenti che sembrano loro gli sposi. E siccome quasi tutti gli impiegati statali di Vigevano vengono dal Meridionale, la portinaia, in base ai matrimoni combinati e ai figli che se ne sono nati, ha fatto una specie di teoria delle razze, che, a ogni nuovo matrimonio, viene ampliata, e magari modificata. I figli nati fra calabresi e vigevanesi sono più intelligenti che belli. I figli nati fra siciliani e vigevanesi sono piuttosto piccoli. Fra abruzzesi e vigevanesi vengono fuori figli, uhm!, così e così; invece fra vigevanesi e sardi vengono fuori dei fiò, che a dirgli belli è dirgli ancora poco. Fra toscani e vigevanesi vengono fuori dei prepotentoni...
"Quando ha deciso di mettere la testa a posto, che me lo dica!" mi dice, sulla soglia dell'ufficio.
Entrato nell'ufficio, mi sentii inopportuno. Seduto dietro a una scrivania, il capufficio guardava, severo come un giudice, Attilio, l'impiegato d'ordine, che gli stava dinanzi confuso. Come mi vide, Attilio diventò ancora più confuso. C'era un silenzio polveroso nella stanza. Il capufficio teneva delle carte in mano, con gli occhi fissi su Attilio, il quale muoveva gli occhi imbarazzati qua e là sugli scaffali.
Io finsi di niente, e mi sedetti al mio tavolo.
"Gliel'ho già detto parecchie volte: il timbro deve essere chiarissimo, diritto!" disse il capufficio.
"Non ho fatto apposta. Mi è scappata la mano!" borbottò Attilio.
"Il contribuente, quando vedrà questa carta, che concetto si farà di noi?" seguitò il capufficio, parlando fra i denti. E, dopo una pausa, posando i fogli sulla scrivania:
"Si rende conto?".
"Di cosa?" borbottò Attilio.
"Che questo ufficio non fa per lei. Lei deve andare alle Poste. Là può timbrare come vuole.
"Ma...".
"Mi dia ascolto, faccia domanda per fare il postelegrafonico. La faccia. Io glie-la appoggio. Il ministro delle Poste è stato padrino della mia figliola. In mia parola e...".
"Ne parlerò con mia moglie!" borbottò Attilio.
Il capufficio si avvicinò alla finestra. Dopo un momento chiamò Attilio. La finestra dà sulla Piazza del mercato.
"Eccola là sua moglie, vede?" diceva il capufficio, "là, al banchetto della polenta, adesso sta comprando. Se vuole andarsi a consigliare, le permetto di uscire!" seguito col suo accento cantilenante. Il capufficio ha una cadenza strana nel parlare; a volte dà l'impressione che canti.
Dopo qualche secondo di silenzio, il capufficio seguitò:
"Non è dignitoso che la moglie d'un impiegato del nostro ufficio vada per mercati a comprare polenta...".
"Glielo seguito ripetere!" disse Attilio.
"Per un postelegrafonico invece la cosa è diversa. Il nostro Regolamento parla chiaro: l'impiegato e i suoi familiari devono tenere una condotta...".
"Però non c'è niente di male, alla fine!" disse Attilio.
"Mi dia retta: vada a fare il postelegrafonico!" disse il capo, entrando nel suo studio.
Rimasti soli, Attilio si accascia davanti alla macchina da scrivere. Prese da un cassetto dei moduli H 3 118, e cominciò a ricopiare quella carta male timbrata. L'aria seguitava a essere carica del suo nervoso. Anche il ticchettare della macchina era nervoso.
Usciti poi i fogli, li mise sul tavolo, e con mano tremante, aria tesa, occhi attenti, cominciò a timbrare.
"Timbrati bene?".
"Molto bene!" dissi.
Mi seguitava a guardare con antipatia.
Sul mezzogiorno venne la figlia del capufficio, a prendere papà.
"Di' un po' ai miei subalterni: chi è il tuo padrino?" le domandò il capo.
"Il mio padrino è sua eccellenza il ministro onorevole..." disse la ragazza.
Il capo ci guardò con aria superiore, come dire: vedete chi conosco io!
Uscendo, mentre dava il braccio alla figlia, ripeté ad Attilio:
"Faccia domanda alle Poste; mangiapolenta!".
Quando padre e figlia se ne furono andati, Attilio origliò all'uscio, e come sentì i passi allontanarsi per il corridoio, prese due fogli protocollo e prese a timbrare, picchiando colpi da far vibrare scrivanie e tavoli.

Luciano Mastronardi, "Il meridionale di Vigevano", Einaudi, Torino 1964.

AL LAVORO
GLI OGGETTI
INSONNI

LA MANO ATTREZZO.
OGNI UFFICIO UN REAME.
TEMPI E METODI.

Paolo Volponi
Il memoriale

Mi presentai dunque, la mattina del 26 giugno 1946, alla portineria della fabbrica, dalle guardie che mi guidarono sino all'Ufficio Personale e Manodopera. Dietro la guardia traversai velocemente una parte del pianterreno senza poter guardare e capire dove passavo. Sentivo più forte, proveniente da ogni parte, il rumore delle lavorazioni. All'interno era più preciso, un rumore elettrico e di tante macchine in movimento. Ripeto però che il rumore scaturiva da ogni parte, anche dai muri e dai pavimenti della fabbrica. Camminando non incontrai alcun reparto di lavoro: solo per un attimo, nel vano di una porta che si chiudeva alle spalle di un giovane, vidi un tavolo illuminato, un tavolo di vetro, illuminato di prima mattina. A un certo punto traversai un andito immenso, un salone coperto da grandi vetri e nervature di ferro, dal quale partivano molti corridoi e altre sale che si spezzavano appena fuori della luce piegando verso l'interno. La guardia mi guidò verso il corridoio più pulito, l'unico che fosse intonacato di bianco. Dopo averlo imboccato bisognava salire tre scalini, affrontando una luce più alta e trovando sui due fianchi molte porte a distanza regolare. In fondo, il corridoio era chiuso da una specie di anticamera, dove la guardia mi lasciò indicandomi un gruppetto di persone in attesa. Nessuno parlava e l'unico rumore era sempre quello della fabbrica, un poco attutito. Qui si porgeva l'orecchio ad altri discorsi, a giudicare dalle facce di tutti quelli che aspettavano. Era una pausa, in quel corridoio bianco, illuminato, dal pavimento di linoleum, che ci veniva imposta.

Nei cinque giorni trascorsi dalla visita alla fabbrica, mi ero convinto che la chiamata al lavoro potesse essere una cosa buona e a mio vantaggio. Non avevo alcuna paura di essere rifiutato, perché in quei cinque giorni mi ero sentito già presente dentro la fabbrica. Avevo persino sognato di lavorare, di dover compiere un lavoro molto impegnativo costruendo un complesso meccanismo, simile alla macchina di un orologio. Mi capitava, nel sogno, che verso la fine del lavoro la mia costruzione si mettesse a suonare, contrariamente a quelle di tutti gli altri che in fila accanto a me facevano lo stesso lavoro. Il suono della mia macchina non cessava se non ne smontavo un pezzo, tale da comprometterne la completezza. Ma d'improvviso arrivava un capo, con l'aria del giovane operaio di Chivasso, il quale annunciava a tutti che secondo le ultime istruzioni le macchine avrebbero dovuto effettivamente suonare.

Aspettavo soprattutto di entrare nel corpo della fabbrica, di arrivare di fronte alle macchine, alla bocca del rumore; di mettere in atto il tentativo, ormai ben preparato, di una vita nuova, tanto che mi sembrava crollata ogni cosa

dietro di me, la preoccupazione stessa dei mali. Proprio per questo avrei dovuto immaginare le sventure che mi sarebbero accadute dopo la mia assunzione in fabbrica.
Lo stesso senso di vuoto e insieme l'attesa sicura della novità io li avevo provati molti anni prima, quando con mio padre e mia madre lasciai la Francia. Allora io non volevo partire, con la volontà accanita che può dominare un ragazzo di tredici anni. Non volevo tornare in Italia e mio padre cercava di convincermi con discorsi da adulto, che mi ripugnavano del tutto. Mio padre diceva di sentirsi stanco e anche malato e di non avere alcuna sicurezza in terra straniera. Diceva che l'Italia era cambiata e che con il fascismo era diventata un paese ricco, pieno di possibilità per un lavoratore e più ancora per l'avvenire di un ragazzo. Tutto questo servì soltanto a rendermi più angosciosi gli ultimi giorni di permanenza ad Avignone ed a svuotarmi d'ogni pensiero e ricordo dell'infanzia trascorsa sino a quel momento. In ultimo mi prese una grande frenesia di tornare in Italia; a Candia, che mio padre aveva descritto come un bellissimo paese. Alla stazione di Avignone, nel momento di partire, mi sentivo come nel corridoio di fronte all'Ufficio Manodopera: non mi restava nulla dei dodici anni trascorsi ed aspettavo soltanto il treno per l'Italia, l'arrivo a Candia, nella casa sul lago. Invece, da quel momento nella stazione, in cui il mio distacco e il mio viaggio si compivano come se immediatamente e con un passo solo avessi potuto valicare la distanza tra Avignone e Candia Canavese, cominciarono molti miei dolori: la morte di mio padre, l'iscrizione in ritardo di due anni all'Avviamento industriale, la solitudine per tutta la gioventù e poi la guerra e la prigionia.
Proprio per questo avrei dovuto capire che dalla mia esagerata aspettativa, dalla mia sicurezza d'entrare nella fabbrica, sarebbero cadute su di me disgrazie nuove e ben tristi.
Posso incolpare con sicurezza quei momenti smemorati di fronte all'Ufficio Personale.
Riguardando la mia vita posso vedere che il male ha sempre lottato contro di me dal giorno in cui sono partito da Avignone e che da allora si è servito dei fatti più attesi e più innocenti, delle mie stesse speranze, per colpirmi facilmente e con forza.
Se quell'Ufficio Manodopera si fosse presentato come uno strumento del male, io sarei fuggito o l'avrei vinto con la mia forza. Invece io fui ingannato per quanto ero indifeso. Entrai in quell'ufficio senza pensare affatto che la mia vita avrebbe potuto essere sconvolta; entrai senza alcuna eccitazione con la speranza di essere immediatamente avviato al lavoro.

Paolo Volponi. "Il memoriale", Einaudi, Torino 1981.

Primo Levi
Lilit e altri racconti

Spariti in pochi istanti il fischio e il brivido, si ritrovava lucido, con il nocciolo della poesia chiaro e distinto; non aveva che da scriverlo, ed ecco, gli altri versi non tardavano ad affollarglisi intorno, docili e vigorosi. In un quarto d'ora il lavoro era fatto: ma a Pasquale questa folgorazione, questo processo fulmineo in cui la concezione ed il parto si succedevano quasi come il lampo e il tuono, non era stato concesso che cinque o sei volte nella vita. Per sua fortuna, non era poeta di professione: svolgeva un lavoro tranquillo e noioso in un ufficio.
Avvertì i sintomi sopra descritti dopo due anni di silenzio, mentre sedeva alla sua scrivania e stava controllando una polizza di assicurazione. Li avvertì anzi con un'intensità inconsueta: il fischio era penetrante e il brivido era poco meno di un tremito convulso, che scomparve subito lasciandolo pieno di vertigine. Il verso-chiave era lì, davanti a lui, come scritto sul muro, o addirittura dentro il suo cranio. I colleghi alle scrivanie vicine non gli badavano: Pasquale si concentrò selvaggiamente sul foglio che aveva davanti, dal nocciolo la poesia si irradiò in tutti i sensi come un organismo che cresca, ed in breve gli stette davanti e sembrava che fremesse, appunto come una cosa viva.
Era la poesia più bella che Pasquale avesse mai scritto. Stava lì sotto i suoi occhi, senza una cancellatura, in una scrittura snella, alta ed elegante: sembrava quasi che il foglio di velina da copia su cui era scritta stentasse a reggerne il peso, come una colonna troppo esile sotto il carico di una statua gigante. Erano le sei; Pasquale la chiuse nel cassetto e se ne tornò a casa. Gli parve giusto concedersi un premio, e nel tragitto si comperò un gelato.
Il mattino dopo scappò in ufficio con precipitazione. Era impaziente di rileggere, perché sapeva bene quanto sia difficile giudicare un'opera appena scritta: il valore e il senso, o la mancanza di valore e di senso, diventano chiari solo il giorno dopo. Aprì il cassetto e non vide la velina: eppure, ne era sicuro, l'aveva lasciata sopra tutte le altre carte. Frugò fra queste, prima con furia, poi con metodo, ma si dovette persuadere che la poesia era sparita. Cercò negli altri cassetti, poi si accorse che il foglio era proprio lì davanti a lui, nel vassoio della corrispondenza in arrivo. Che scherzi fa la distrazione! Ma come non essere distratti, davanti all'opera fondamentale della propria vita?
Pasquale era sicuro che i suoi futuri biografi non lo avrebbero ricordato per altro: solo per quella "Annunciazione". La rilesse e ne fu entusiasta, quasi innamorato. Stava per portarla alla fotocopiatrice quando lo chiamò il direttore; ne ebbe per un'ora e mezzo, e quando ritornò alla sua scrivania la copiatrice era guasta. L'elettricista la riparò per le quattro, ma la carta sensibile

era esaurita. Per quel giorno non c'era niente da fare: ricordando l'incidente della sera prima, Pasquale ripose il foglio nel cassetto con grande attenzione. Chiuse, poi si pentì e riaprì, infine richiuse e se ne andò. Il giorno dopo il foglio non c'era.
La faccenda diventava seccante. Pasquale mise sottosopra tutti i suoi cassetti, richiamando alla luce carte dimenticate da decenni: mentre frugava, cercava invano di ritrovare nella memoria, se non tutta la composizione, almeno quel primo verso, quel nucleo che lo aveva illuminato, ma non ci riuscì: anzi, ebbe la precisa sensazione che non ci sarebbe riuscito mai. Lui era un altro, altro da quel momento: non era più lo stesso Pasquale, e non lo sarebbe ridiventato mai, allo stesso modo che un morto non rivive, e che non passa due volte sotto un ponte la stessa acqua di un fiume. Si sentì in bocca un sapore metallico, nauseante: il sapore della frustrazione, del mai più. Sedette sconsolato sulla poltroncina aziendale, e vide il foglio appiccicato al muro, alla sua sinistra, a pochi palmi dalla sua testa. Era chiaro: qualche collega gli aveva voluto fare uno scherzo di cattivo gusto; forse qualcuno che lo aveva spiato e aveva scoperto il suo segreto.
Afferrò il foglio per un lembo e lo staccò dal muro, quasi senza incontrare resistenza: l'autore dello scherzo doveva avere usato una colla di cattiva qualità, o averne usata poca. Notò che la carta, sul rovescio, era leggermente granulosa. Mise la velina nel sottomano, e per tutta la mattina manovrò in modo da non allontanarsi dalla scrivania, ma quando suonò la sirena di mezzogiorno, e tutti si alzarono per andare a mensa, Pasquale vide che il foglio sporgeva dal sottomano di un buon dito. Lo estrasse, lo piegò in quattro e lo infilò nel portafoglio: dopo tutto, non c'era motivo di non portarlo a casa. Lo avrebbe copiato a mano, oppure lo avrebbe portato in copisteria; sotto quell'aspetto non c'erano problemi.

Primo Levi, "Lilit e altri racconti", Einaudi, Torino 1981.

Ercole Patti
Diario Siciliano

UN PO' DI OLIO
Novembre 1969
In questi giorni la mattina c'è un bel sole dolce e mite. Nelle prime ore del pomeriggio il cielo si annuvola e viene giù una leggera pioggia che fa luccicare le foglie degli ulivi, le palette dei fichindia, le foglie del gelsomino che ricopre l'alto muro di pietre laviche, i due alberelli di limoni che stanno sotto gli ulivi. Al tramonto smette di piovere, più tardi spuntano le stelle sulle foglie bagnate che si asciugheranno nella notte sotto la luna.
Ho fatto raccogliere le olive dei pochi vecchi alberi che circondano la mia ca-

MERCATO FINITO.
MERCATO INFINITO.
LAVORI IN CORSO.
L'ORTOFRUTTICOLO.
LA SCORZA DI LIMONE NEL VERMOUTH.
CHI VA A PRENDERE IL BAMBINO?

sa per cavarne un poco di olio. Nell'aria autunnale fra l'erbetta fresca ancora bagnata dagli spruzzi di pioggia del giorno prima le olive cadono strappate dalle mani del contadino; sul telo di nailon disteso sotto l'albero risuonano con piccoli rumori sordi come una soffice gradinata. Alcune sono macchiate di scuro da un lato e questo anziché danneggiare l'olio che ne verrà fuori sembra invece, a quanto dice il contadino, che influirà favorevolmente sulla sua qualità. Comunque si tratterà di pochi litri di olio che saranno sufficienti per i miei soggiorni saltuari in questa casa davanti al mare.

Sul terreno in mezzo all'erbetta si alza qua e là qualche roccia anch'essa fiorita di pianticelle venute fuori dopo le recenti pioggie; in mezzo all'erba accanto alle pietre e sotto i tronchi degli ulivi nascono asparagi di campo che si alzano snelli dalle loro macchie spinose. Facendo un piccolo giro intorno in mezzo all'erba umida se ne può raccogliere un mazzetto giusto da farne un piattino di contorno.

Un ragazzo con un minuscolo paniere va recuperando le olive cadute nelle pieghe delle rocce o in fondo all'erbetta fresca, sul coperchio del pozzo, sul pergolato e in mezzo alle sperdute pianticelle di basilico e di erbette selvatiche che costeggiano i vecchi muri, sul ciglio dei muri stessi; e queste semplici e artigianali operazioni compiute nelle pause di sereno della stagione incerta danno un sapore piacevole alla piccola raccolta.

Riunite le olive in due grossi sacchi (quelle raccolte ieri sono calde come se fossero state accanto al forno, cominciano a fermentare) le portiamo all'alba al frantoio del paesetto vicino. La macchina percorre la stradetta tortuosa che passa in mezzo ai giardini di limoni ancora addormentati nell'aria pulita; le automobili che incontriamo hanno i fari accesi nella tenue luce del giorno che sta per nascere.

Nel frantoio tra lo sfolgorio di vivide lampade mattutine naviga l'odore forte delle olive macinate. Le due massicce ruote della macina girano su se stesse triturando polpe e noccioli. Dopo una prima spremitura quella poltiglia fragrante viene distribuita entro piatti e robusti dischi di rafia che, sistemati uno sull'altro con un massiccio blocco di legno sopra, vengono poi collocati sotto il potente torchio di acciaio; sotto quella dura premuta il primo olio viene fuori leggero da un tubo e va piano nella tina.

Tolta dai dischi di rafia la poltiglia odorosa viene messa ancora a palate nella macina; le grosse ruote vi rotolano ancora sopra, dopo di che va di nuovo insaccata entro i dischi di rafia e messa ancora sotto il torchio. Per tre volte il pastone di olive sfrante viene rimesso nella macina e per tre volte sotto il torchio; alla fine, ridotto in blocchi compatti come calcinaccio secco, si butta via ormai inservibile.

L'olio giallo e opaco scende silenziosa-

mente nella tina; poi dalla tina viene pompato su fino a un recipiente collocato in alto da dove scende giù lungo un tubo passando attraverso una piccola macchina splendente di nichelatura modernissima in mezzo a tutte le cose antiche che ci sono intorno; la macchina con un moto centrifugo lo divide dall'acqua: da una delle due bocchette esce l'olio giallino e opaco dall'altra l'acqua quasi dello stesso colore, soltanto un pochino più pallido.

Di tanto in tanto per facilitare l'operazione sarà versata ancora dell'acqua nell'olio grezzo e la macchina nichelata la dividerà con estrema precisione dall'olio sicché il liquido che esce dal tubo situato più in basso e va in un grande recipiente è olio puro e denso pronto per essere portato via, mentre quello che sbocca più fluido un poco più in alto, nonostante il bel colore emulsionato quasi verdolino, è soltanto acqua sporca che va a finire in uno scarico. Adesso che l'olio è raccolto nel grande recipiente, con una "quartara" di latta della capacità di otto litri e mezzo lo si misurerà a mano a mano che lo si tirerà su per metterlo nei barili e nei bottiglioni. L'odore dell'olio nuovo piglia alla gola con una forza inebriante. Ogni cosa nell'ampio camerone è imbevuta di questo potente e sano sentore che riempie le narici e sembra attraversare i vestiti e le suole delle scarpe.

In un angolo i sacchi dai bordi arrotolati pieni di olive verdi sono in attesa che venga il loro turno per essere buttati nella macina. Carichiamo nell'automobile la nostra damigiana di olio verde che ci servirà fino al prossimo raccolto. Dal cortiletto che costeggia lo stradale si vedono passare le macchinette dei sensali e dei piccoli imprenditori che cominciano la loro giornata. Davanti alla porta del frantoio c'è un grande gelso folto di foglie verde scuro, ogni tanto un passero vi si caccia dentro o ne esce.

Ercole Patti, "Diario siciliano", Bompiani. Milano 1975.

Corrado Alvaro
Itinerario Italiano

EMPOLI, IL POPOLO, I VETRI

Uno dei fatti più nuovi dell'Italia d'oggi, è lo sviluppo delle industrie in paesi vecchi, e per esempio in Toscana. Lungi dallo sfigurarvi, donano all'ambiente e al paese, e anziché sopraffare il vecchio colore d'una vecchia vita, lo fanno risaltare meglio. Prima di tutto c'è lo spettacolo di come l'italiano si trasforma a contatto con la vita organizzata e collettiva, che non è dei meno interessanti: egli porta sempre qualcosa dell'artigiano; e poi la nascita dell'industrialismo in Italia non è quella cosa nuova e strana che si è creduta per un pezzo. Al tempo del grande artigianato e delle vecchie corporazioni, le città ebbero centri nati da quell'assetto; poi divennero i musei di quel lavoro; noi l'Italia fummo abituati a considerarla così: si rimpiansero i più abili artefici e artigiani d'Europa, ma si torse il muso davanti ai fumaioli delle fabbriche. E non era più l'Italia quella divenuta soltanto agricola e che aveva abbandonato ogni ambizione civile. Nacquero perciò tanti monumenti senza scopo, che imitavano nell'apparenza le vecchie logge e i vecchi palazzi d'arte. Qualche cosa però non era andato perduto, e cioè la capacità del lavoro a crearsi i suoi monumenti e le sue testimonianze come l'avevano avuta un tempo i tintori o i lanieri, perché in conclusione, come altrove "tout finit par des chansons", in Italia tutto si concluderebbe in architettura e in arte. Basta tuttavia che la società si organizzi su un dato schema, che ritrovi in qualche modo la sua attitudine naturale, perché quella funzione torni in pieno. Non saranno più i palazzi dell'Arte d'un tempo; sarà una torre, una colonna estiva, un campo di gioco, e la vita si riannoda al vecchio filo, e questo lavoro senza volto, come era considerato il lavoro industriale, riprende il suo vecchio potere. Gl'impresari cambiano, la tendenza è la stessa.

A Empoli mi accadde di pensare a queste cose davanti al suo vecchio Duomo. I ragazzi giocavano in piazza, vi si attardavano donne coi bambini in braccio; una fontana ricorda la munificenza d'un signore che dotò la città d'acqua potabile, e sotto un calice di marmo grondante acqua, quattro donne di marmo sorridono nude. Non è più la nudità d'un tempo, è già la nudità moderna che ricorda la camera da letto. Il popolo intorno a questi nuclei formò i suoi, fatti di botteghe sotto i portici, di vecchi caffè, di mescite di vino, d'insegne che avevano portato qualche cosa di artisticamente popolare nello zinco verniciato. E poi le merci sulla strada, questo mercato quotidiano che ricorda da vicino la vita, la sua lotta, il contado, i mercati. C'è un modo di disporre e di mostrare le cose del vivere che ha della composizione. Si starebbe delle ore qua in mezzo, e si correrebbe non so quanto al richiamo di questo vino dal sapore di vecchie rose, di vecchi vasi.

La razza vuol pur dire. Per chi detesta la spocchia di certa vita moderna tutta nel parere quel che non si è, queste osterie a ogni passo che spengono l'arsura della strada polverosa, e i richiami delle trippe e della zampa, di tutto il mangiare semplice, è un meritato riposo. In mancanza d'altro, il popolo s'è fatto la sua decorazione per la vita quotidiana; ci sono i santi agli angoli, le insegne e le merci, e nulla è tanto eterogeneo che non entri in quest'atmosfera che è pur dura e di lotta. Perfino i prodotti a serie dei magazzini sembrano appesi a un albero di cuccagna, e riacquistano il vecchio prestigio dell'infanzia. E che dire di quest'insegna che porta scritto "Bazar fantastico"?

Empoli è in piano. I fuori porta si vedono dalle sue strade dritte tra balenii di biciclette che si confondono con quelli delle foglie degli olmi prese da un lungo tremito come se pullulassero, e la polvere, gli steccati gialli di qualche campo sportivo, i manifesti che laggiù sono più larghi e coloriti, come se tutto questo fosse l'annunzio d'una fiera e d'un Luna Park. Si dilungano laggiù i quartieri degli operai, perché Empoli ha almeno una quindicina di fabbriche di vetri. I carrettini dei fiaschi da impagliare sono fermi davanti alle porte. D'estate i vetrai son chiusi, ma sono arrivato in tempo, quando era ancora fresco, a vederne alcuni ancora aperti.

Ci s'imbatte a un certo punto nell'Arno, con lo stesso color verde che ha Firenze. Di sera sono aperte le finestre, le donne cuciono sui balconi, e il contadino nei campi contigui non ha finito mai di lavorare. Su un banco del fiume all'asciutto giocano i ragazzi. Il tramonto rosso e il perdersi del fiume nel piano ricordano il mare. Sulla spalletta del fiume c'era un uomo seduto a guardare. Mi domandò se fossi venuto a Empoli per lavorare e poi, saputo che venivo da Roma, "Oh, — mi disse — venite per l'appunto da Roma: come corre il Tevere? Io ci manco dal 1885, e ho sempre pensato se corre più il Tevere o l'Arno. Aspettavo qualcuno per domandarglielo". Ecco che cosa può pensare un uomo solitario sulla spalletta d'un fiume. Mi chiese anche notizie di Prato, giacché viaggiavo, ma non di più lontano. In quella venne avanti un ciabattino, a prender aria, col fare filosofico dei "ciaba" di tutti i paesi del mondo, e l'atteggiamento di chi tira i due capi dello spago nelle braccia un po' discoste. Il grande nuovo articolo che preparava una vetreria era uno spettacolo di partita di calcio. Su una tavola disegnata al modo dei campi di gioco, erano disposti i giocatori: la maglia di colore, la testa di vetro bianco; e il naso e lo stemma della loro squadra erano le cose più rilevanti. Questo un gran magazzino di tali manifatture: c'erano rose, fiori e frutti di tutti i colori, vasi e lampade. La fragilità del vetro è una cosa di cui bisogna ricordarsi ad ogni momento, abituati come siamo ad essere circondati di cose non fragili. A un certo punto vien quasi il panico di quella estrema

*DI LORO CHE NON CI SONO.
GOMITI STRETTI. GOMITI SUL
TAVOLO.
PROTEINE, VITAMINE...?
MANGIO LA PASTA.*

deperibilità. Ecco cose fatte per consumarsi; eppure esistono vetri di mille e duemila anni di vita dissepelliti dalla terra dove hanno dormito per secoli. S'immagina quanti esemplari, a migliaia, si sono rotti per uno che ha varcato il tempo. A un tratto questa di vetro mi sembra come un'umanità: corre il mondo, accompagna la vita, viaggia, si ferma in qualche angolo ignorato. Passano i tempi, crollano monumenti di pietra, di alcuni non rimane che un ricordo vago, si disperde perfino la traccia della pianta d'una città, e questo bicchiere, questo pupazzo, questo vaso, ricordo d'una civiltà, della vita, dura in qualche lembo di terra.

Fuori, a perdita d'occhio, ci sono i depositi delle damigiane e dei fiaschi nudi, separati da muriccioli tra magazzini confinanti. Paiono orti di grosse zucche; i fiaschi si levano a pareti sotto le tettoie, con tutti i toni del verde. È un mondo assai precario. Ancora una volta penso per esempio a una grandinata su questi vetri. Ma in un altro magazzino chiuso, le oliere all'infinito, le bottiglie, quegli oggetti che noi consideriamo come presenze e forme nelle case, qui acquistano quasi aspetti di tribù; a momenti quelle oliere che sono con due sacchetti legati sembrano una famiglia immensa di fratelli siamesi; altre oliere da trespolo, coi loro turaccioli, paiono delle bambine con la testina e il collaretto; e su questo tema, all'infinito, gli operai che limavano gli orli dei vetri con le macchine, sembrava avessero da fare con un mondo infantile o nano, che si fosse moltiplicato allo stesso modo quelle degli animali, per generazione, e le razze diverse erano i diversi colori d'ognuno sotto le stesse forme. E i vasi per fiori, gli ornamenti dei salotti, aprivano bocche mostruose o sembravano pezzi d'anatomia. C'erano violente simpatie e antipatie; ognuno di quegli oggetti ricordava un ambiente, i comodini da notte, le avide bevute notturne nel bicchiere trovato a tastoni, la bottiglia della camera d'albergo, il bicchiere dell'osteria, le rotture in casa e il nuovo rifornimento di vetri, e gli ospedali, i cestini da viaggio. E si scorgevano vecchie forme, antichissime, della nostra infanzia, o di paesi visitati, o veduti in qualche museo, forme che furono dei Fenici, ripetute all'infinito da tanti anni e secoli, dietro l'ispirazione d'un artigiano ignoto che trovò quella prima misura all'emissione del fiato nella canna. Oggi escono da ognuna di queste fabbriche trentamila pezzi di vetro comune al giorno, e trecento di vetro artistico. È un lavoro che ha il carattere del lavoro comune come una scuola; il forno del vetro è come un gran calamaio cui attingono tutti, e in circolo ognuno si dispone con la sua canna. È come se concertassero degli strumenti. Dev'esser la stessa l'emissione del fiato, tant'è vero che ogni esemplare è uniforme, e fra l'uno e l'altro non v'è che un'oscillazione media di venti grammi di peso. Il soffitto è altissimo, di travi e d'assi, come d'un'antica fabbrica o d'un'antica chiesa; il gruppo degli operai sta raccolto in mezzo, tra i potenti ventilatori e le finestre; su una tabella, col gesso, sono scritti gli evviva e gli abbassi delle passioni quotidiane degli operai. C'è la solitudine del lavoro individuale e insieme un colore di vecchia comunità intenta a un lavoro che ha perfino del gioco, che è tutto dire per un'operazione delle più faticose. Ma forse in questo contrasto sta tutto il fascino di questo spettacolo. Soli e insieme, ognuno col suo grumo incandescente che passa attraverso tutti i colori e le forme, nasce come un frutto duro e verde, si colora come una bolla, s'infiamma a mano a mano che prende più aria; il ritmo delle canne lunghe disegna fra uomo e uomo, fra solitudine e solitudine, una coincidenza di linee e un gioco di rette ripetendo il ritmo convergente delle assi del soffitto. Sembra un grande concerto che non arriva a esprimersi altro che in forme rotonde, pressappoco come quella cornetta del jazz che pare riesca a stento a gonfiare una palla di gomma ficcata nel padiglione. Appeso in basso a una lunga canna si gonfia come una nota profonda il bottiglione, mentre dall'altra parte le bottiglie striminzite e verdi da un quarto di litro fanno un altro suono di questa musica acuto; lo stesso soffiatore è compreso di quel volume che nasce al suo fiato, come una pianta che vedesse ingrandire enormemente un frutto. In questa orchestra di forme, di cui non si sente a tratti che lo sgrigliolio dello stacco del vetro, sta quasi da parte un lavoratore di fino, che ha il privilegio d'un piccolo inserviente, l'aiuto d'un compasso di legno per le misure e per aprire e regolare le corolle del vetro. Il quale passa nelle sue mani attraverso tutte le forme, dal globo alla coppa, al piatto con una riepilogo rapido di tutta una discendenza di volumi geometrici. Il ragazzo vi aggiunge il piedino, il ragazzo stacca il dippiù, il ragazzo vi salda un ornamento, il ragazzo gli sta attorno come in uno di quegli esercizi perfetti di acrobazia che vediamo sui palcoscenici. E intorno tutto un coro è intento a sentir oscillare, gravitare, marmorizzarsi sotto il suo fiato le grandi bolle verdi. A tratti, in cima a un bastone bruciacchiato, i ragazzi portano al forno della tempera i recipienti finiti in cui aleggia ancora l'ultima fiammella e fa sprizzare scintille dal bastone. Le bottiglie stanno nel forno a indurire e sembrano pani.

Corrado Alvaro, "Itinerario italiano", Bompiani, Milano 1941.

Moravia
Io e lui

Elisa prepara la tavola; ed io la seguo con gli occhi, affondato nella mia seggiola-semicupio impiallicciata e imbottita. Chiude prima di tutto il piano della tavola in una sottotovaglia di flanella. Poi stende la tovaglia e allora, chinandosi in avanti, alza la gamba scoprendo un polpaccio insospettato, carnoso e rotondo. Incredibile: "lui" commenta: "D'accordo, è brutta. Ma, così per gioco, e anche un poco per far dispetto a tua madre, vorrei vedere cosa succederebbe se, per esempio, tu le passassi un braccio intorno alla vita".
"Sta' zitto, cretino!"
Elisa apre il buffet, ne prende i piatti, i bicchieri, le posate e via via, con le mani guantate di filo bianco, prepara la tavola per due commensali. Ecco la vecchia caraffa ben nota, di "mezzo cristallo", con la pancia larga e il collo lungo, piena a metà di vino. Ecco la bottiglia dell'acqua minerale, anch'essa dimezzata, con un tappo di plastica. Ecco le forchette, i coltelli, i cucchiai, con il manico d'argento e le iniziali della famiglia, in stile floreale, regalo dei nonni che a loro volta li avevano ricevuti in dono alle loro nozze. Ecco la saliera e la pepiera in forma di pulcini di maiolica gialla con le teste bucherellate. Ecco l'oliera dello stesso stile della caraffa del vino. Elisa, senza rendersene conto, sta preparando il luogo e gli strumenti di un rito. Già, perché mia madre non è religiosa, ossia "praticante", se non per abitudine e per dovere sociale; in chiesa si limita ad andarci la mattina di domenica. Ma i riti della tavola familiare, della visita mondana, del teatro, del cinema, della villeggiatura e di tutte le cose, insomma, che "si debbono" fare, costituiscono per lei, riuniti e collegati, una specie di religione piccolo-borghese, priva affatto di qualsiasi trascendenza ma non per questo meno osservata e "praticata". Religione, sia detto tra parentesi, meravigliosamente adatta a favorire il particolare tipo di sublimazione che permette a mia madre di mantenermi in un costante e irreversibile stato di inferiorità.
Mia madre entra. In silenzio si siede, spiega il tovagliolo, rettifica la posizione dei bicchieri. Quindi alza gli occhi e mi guarda. In quel preciso momento sto sedendomi a mia volta; innocentemente, stringo tra due dita la sigaretta accesa. Gli occhi di mia madre si appuntano, eloquenti, sulla sigaretta. Non mi seggo, guardo intorno cercando un portacenere, e non lo trovo. Mia madre dice: "Elisa, dia un portacenere al signor Rico". Elisa esegue; io schiaccio la sigaretta nel portacenere, seggo e poi naturalmente, dico la sola cosa che non dovrei dire: "Ma Sabina, dov'è?"
"L'ho mandata via".
"E perché? Non andava bene?"
Elisa rientra, a questo punto, reggendo con le due mani una piccola zuppiera. Mia madre si serve; poi mi servo anch'io. Una matassina di spaghetti giallini, luccicanti di burro, sta in fondo alla zuppiera. Mia madre è delicata di stomaco: in casa sua si mangia "in bianco". Metto nella scodella un paio di forchettate, ci spargo sopra il formaggio, giallino anch'esso, prendendolo dall'antiquata formaggiera di vetro. Mia madre non mangia, aspetta che Elisa sia uscita. Poi risponde, alfine: "Sabina, andava benissimo. Ma tu non la lasciavi in pace. Passi guardarla; ma anche telefonarle, fissarle degli appuntamenti! E non fuori di casa, ma qui, in casa mia, come stamattina!"
"Ma quando mai. Se è Sabina che ti ha detto questo, ebbene Sabina ha mentito".
"Sabina non ha mentito e non me l'ha detto".
"E allora come fai ad esserne così sicura?"
"Ero presente quando tu hai telefonato. Sabina mi ha dato il ricevitore. Ho ascoltato e ti ho udito mentre dicevi che stamane saresti venuto apposta un'ora prima per stare con lei. Credevi di parlare a Sabina e invece parlavi a me. Allora l'ho licenziata, scusandomi con lei, e ho assunto Elisa".

Alberto Moravia, "Io e lui", Bompiani, Milano 1971.

Carmelo Samonà
Fratelli

Tutto comincia dal modo di spostarsi e di collocarsi nei luoghi dove abitiamo. Quando mio fratello si muove, gli spazi ne risultano ulteriormente ampliati e sordi, le stanze scandite da ritmi incerti: qualsiasi vano può sembrargli un deserto in cui rischia di perdersi o, viceversa, una prigione troppo stretta in cui annaspa come un volatile zoppo. Autore di impulsi a prima vista discordi, va soggetto a sbalzi di umore che lo colgono all'improvviso e altrettanto rapidamente lo abbandonano e si sciolgono in intervalli di strana quiete. Sono due tempi, e due comportamenti, distinti. Nel primo riesce a spiccare grandi salti dal basso in alto, gira a vortice su se stesso o percorre a lungo una stanza lambendone le pareti sempre in un senso, fino a descriverne il perimetro cento e più volte, mentre col dorso delle mani o con le punte dei polpastrelli compie attenti rituali su alcune parti del viso, specialmente sugli occhi. Nel secondo appare più concentrato ed astratto: ma, comunque, si muove, prediligendo per lo più un solo oggetto (quasi sempre insignificante per me) sul quale rinnova impercettibili prove di ispezione tattile, olfattiva e visiva. In apparenza non c'è regola in questo moto: mio fratello sembra la vittima occasionale di una presenza estranea di cui subisce pazientemente, e al tempo stesso interpreta col proprio corpo, i capricci. Guardandolo meglio, però, intravedo nei suoi gesti un misterioso anelito produttivo; ho il sospetto che le

PIAZZA
LE FONTANELLE
OSSESSIVE

SARACINESCE GIÙ.
TRAFFICO... BREVE INTERMEZZO.
L'INDAGINE DEL PICCIONE.
CHIAROSCURO.
LA CITTÀ IN TESTA LA MAPPA IN
TASCA.

infinite ripetizioni, i salti, gli avvitamenti del corpo, le rare parole traccino nell'aria un disegno animato di cui lui stesso, e non altri, è il regista: forse è lui che possiede il controllo della malattia, la piega ai suoi voleri e la costringe a rappresentare umilmente uno spettacolo ininterrotto.

Sembra esservi, in questo, una ferma, febbrile volontà di risarcimento. Il rifiuto delle cose che hanno concretezza ai miei occhi corrisponde all'elaborazione, da parte sua, di verità alternative. Dal suo corpo affiorano, suscitati da un attimo di rapimento o da una breve concentrazione, piccoli universi aleatori, nei quali si trasferisce anche per lunghi periodi, e dove a me è dato il privilegio di entrare, ogni tanto, e di abitare con lui. Li chiamiamo, di solito, i Grandi Viaggi (per distinguerli dagli spostamenti abituali fra un punto e un altro della casa, che sono i Piccoli Viaggi e hanno, a differenza dei Grandi, un utile immediato, un profitto). Anche se i percorsi — e le relative destinazioni — non cambiano molto, sono imprevedibili le varianti e infiniti i modi di realizzarle. Prevalgono le fantasie di dimore sotterranee o volanti. Non macchine aeree, però, o elaborate sepolture; ma capanne sospese nel vuoto, stanze allestite alla meglio fra cieli immaginari, cunicoli e buche che si suppongono scavati tenacemente, a forza di unghie, sotto di noi. Si direbbe che mio fratello non possegga, almeno finché dura il suo viaggio, la nozione dell'orizzontale e del piatto su cui ci muoviamo, ma solo quella di un sopra e di un sotto conquistati verticalmente, tracciando linee di precipizio e di elevazione in certi punti del pavimento, o nell'aria.

In questi nuovi spazi viviamo, a intervalli, immersi in una solitudine laboriosa. È come una casa dentro la casa, un tempo dentro il tempo. Non vi sono unità di misura comuni, né brevità né lunghezza, né minuti né ore; non abbiamo intese calcolate fra noi. Procediamo uniti, ma i nostri gesti si ispirano, naturalmente, a intenzioni diverse. Mio fratello si muove in un continuo sforzo di aderire alla terra per penetrarla, di agitare l'aria per raggiungere le nuove sedi in cui ha deciso di collocarsi. Io fingo di assecondarlo per studiarne da vicino il comportamento; osservo la successione dei suoi movimenti, lo pedino a distanza, talvolta lo fermo bruscamente e gli propongo soluzioni concrete con cui ritorni di nuovo con me, nel mio mondo orizzontale, stabile e piatto.

Carmelo Samonà, "Fratelli", Einaudi, Torino 1979.

Guido Piovene
Viaggio in Italia

Torino

"Prima prende il corso grosso, e poi chiama". Chi ha parlato così? Gianduia?

È un cittadino torinese qualsiasi, a cui ho chiesto la strada. Il "corso grosso": corso Roma. Poi "chiama": chiede un'altra volta.

Se dovessi gettare qualche aggettivo alla rinfusa che ci suggerisca il miscuglio con cui Torino si presenta, direi francese, gesuitica, padana, montanara. E poi anche, paradossalmente, graziosa, vezzosa, leziosa. Il motto "piemontese falso e cortese" è il più ingiusto dei motti, perché il piemontese è sincero. Forse deriva dal contrasto tra il suo carattere angoloso, spinoso, e un certo rococò di parole e di modi. Francese la regolarità delle vie, piazze, palazzi, portici, con predominio di un Settecento aggraziato, ragionevole e un po' pignolo. Il lato gesuitico porta seco qualcosa, non proprio di spagnolo, ma di spagnolesco. Penso alle chiese e cappelle della città, tra cui la più sfarzosa conserva la Sacra Sindone. Un barocco giusto e sicuro, dovizioso ma senza ebbrezza, senza capriccio, né teatralità, né follia; lo stile più formale per rendere onore a Dio, indizio d'una religione intesa come serio dovere pubblico, e nel tempo stesso discreta, convinta, piena di contegno. Ho provato a Torino, in queste chiese, la speciale narcosi che viene dalla regolarità luccicante. Un piccolo Escoriale, narcoticamente funebre con i suoi ori, marmi, statue, sono le tombe dei Savoia a Superga. Ne emana un fastoso cupio dissolvi, un nichilismo religioso, che nell'ultima fase di questa famiglia reale si è impicciolito, laicizzato, divenendo realismo, cinismo ed avarizia. Ma il panorama di Superga porta subito un correttivo. L'ultima volta che vi andai un tramonto arancione splendeva dietro la corona dei monti; le cupole della città ed i monti del fondo, ritagliandosi neri e piatti su quel colore favoloso, sembravano a eguale distanza; il Po dava bagliori, la neve spruzzava i pendii; si esprimevano nel paesaggio una modestia montanara, una rusticità fine, un misto di signorile e di agreste. Torino è forse la più ibrida delle città italiane, ed il suo carattere ibrido non viene dagli apporti esterni, ma sorge tutto dall'interno, dalla sua anima rigida ma contraddittoria. Va più in là di Milano nelle punte di modernità industriale e sociale; ma alcuni dei suoi musei, bene pubblico, sono avaramente tenuti come beni privati. Il Museo egizio specialmente, nel quale sembra che un proprietario egoista badi più ad ammucchiare i propri acquisti per se stesso che ad esporli al visitatore. L'ibrido di Torino si rispecchia nelle sue strade. I negozi di manichini, di strumenti ortopedici prendono uno strano spicco (si direbbe oggi, surrealista) in quell'insieme regolare, squadrato. Certi negozi di

barbiere, mai rinnovati, rivestiti di legno, assomigliano a farmacie, e come le farmacie ottocentesche sono anche asilo di conversazioni pettegole. Le pasticcerie stesse, per cui Torino va famosa da oltre due secoli, tendono alla farmacia (o al negozio di pompe funebri) con un'austerità leggiadra. Quante volte mi sono estasiato davanti alle grandi vetrine, i cristalli rinchiusi tra pesanti cornici di legno nero filettato d'oro con scritte d'oro, e in quella cornice di lutto dolci preziosi, sfavillanti come gioielli, canestri lavorati di pastafrolla riempiti di frutta candita, ghiottonerie da monaca, cappucci ripieni di panna e spolverati di cacao! Poi, mi voltavo; e vedevo fluire nelle vie una nebbia leggera, che bisogna chiamare, alla francese, un voile, ammorbidendo i volti e addolcendo le luci. Ma i torinesi sono anche lenti, pesanti, riflessivi, ragioniereschi, alieni dai gesti e dalle astrazioni, religiosi ma in modo strettamente privato, privo di teatralità, resistenti alle opinioni altrui, avari di consensi e, se provano ammirazione, portati a tenerla per sé piuttosto che a manifestarla in applausi; gli unici italiani forse che possiedano più opinioni che idee, in un Paese come il nostro, nel quale le idee sono folte ma le opinioni rade. Il loro piatto prediletto è il bollito, altrettanto ricco di carni, ma più magro dell'emiliano; piatto padano che i francesi disprezzano, il più rustico e insieme il più raffinato dei cibi, vero cibo da critici, giacché la sua stessa sincerità non gli consente di fingere la perfezione, lo colloca su cento gradi, che il palato fine distingue, di riuscita diversa. Dalla padanità siano respinti ancora ai francesismo, al rococò, alla cipria. Alcuni piemontesi, famosi per le opinioni inflessibili, l'intransigenza, la coerenza morale, con nomea di ispidi, di intrattabili, di irascibili, uomini magri, segaligni, hanno vezzo, moine, sorrisetti, ritrosie, stravaganze da monaca e da damina. Dappertutto l'accostamento del buon bollito casalingo con cappuccio di panna spolverata di cioccolata. Il carattere ibrido (mai falso), si riflette nell'aspetto della città, le dà una speciale attrattiva di scatola cinese che nessun'altra città italiana possiede.

Napoli

Un tuffo nella Napoli popolare, Spaccanapoli per esempio ed i vicoli che la circondano, è sempre l'unico mezzo a nostra disposizione per capire sul vivo che cosa fosse una metropoli del mondo classico. Nemmeno Roma ce lo illustra con la stessa evidenza; parlo, s'intende, della vita, non degli stili. Dovunque si volge lo sguardo, si scorgono sotto scorci strani o in cannocchiali sghembi scale, tabernacoli, chiese, obelischi barocchi. I tabernacoli risplendono anche nel fondo dei cortili delle case d'abitazione, tra i festoni della biancheria; è un popolo, come tutti sanno, che ha confidenza col sacro, ed uno degli ostacoli a restaurare le chiese monumentali sono le abitazioni, ingrommatesi tutto intorno, appiccicate

alle cappelle, talvolta perfino sul tetto. Qui si vendono polpi, ed insieme brodo di polpi, la più economica di tutte le bevande calde, perché costa dieci lire; qui è la friggitoria, ed il banco dei "passatempi", che sono cibi minuti da sgranocchiare. Le ragazze in un "basso" mettono insieme fiori finti; l'antiquariuccio spia sulla soglia della bottega. Chi ha qualche lira, mangia: la pizza, lo sfilatino con dentro la pasta, il formaggio, la frittata, i fagioli. I bambini, le "creature", brulicano. Anche nei ristoranti medi, pochi sono gli avventori senza i bambini intorno. Napoli è una città allattante e poppante, perpetuamente gravida. Un semidio napoletano è l'amore; nella coscienza popolare, l'amore si redime con la procreazione. La povertà napoletana ha i suoi vizi, ma da uno è quasi esente, l'incesto, piaga dei quartieri troppo promiscui di altre metropoli: troppo profondo è qui il sentimento della famiglia e del sangue. Quante persone vivano in questa Napoli brulicante, popolaresca, si può appena congetturare: forse sulle 300 mila. Le classi alte hanno emigrato nel tempo verso il porto e le alture, lasciando qui le spoglie delle loro dimore. Molto è stato scritto sui "bassi", alloggio abituale del popolino: camere a pianterreno, che sono insieme dormitorio, salotto, laboratorio artigiano e bottega, e nelle quali le famiglie vivono accatastate. La mancanza di spazio e di servizi igienici fa sì che il gettare i rifiuti per la strada, l'esporre i panni ad asciugare, sia una triste necessità; il dormir poco, il restar fuori il più possibile, di giorno come di notte, quella nervosa vita stradale perpetua che ha tanta parte nel pittoresco di Napoli, è spesso un modo per evadere da sgradevoli abitazioni. Ma il risanamento di Napoli è opera lenta, in gran parte indiretta, e non può ottenersi mediante provvedimenti draconiani. Gli sventramenti inconsulti non sono preoccupanti solo per chi difende la bellezza artistica di una città, dove il nobile e il sordido, il monumentale e il cadente, formano un unico tessuto.

Guido Piovene, "Viaggio in Italia", Mondadori, Milano 1957.

POMERIGGIO DEL LAVORO
PERSISTENZA DEGLI OGGETTI

LA MANO ATTREZZO.
OGNI UFFICIO UN REAME.
TEMPI E METODI.

Carlo Emilio Gadda
L'Adalgisa

Alcuni vestono larghi pantaloni di fustagno, quasi un rozzo velluto, stretti, di poi, alle caviglie: altri, calzoni corti con fasce o calzettoni di lana di facitura buona e materna: e guizzano via sulle loro biciclette, a testa china, come se pensassero: "peggio per chi mi avrà nello stomaco". Quelli che procedono a piedi, recano a spalla una povera giacchetta sudando ancora nella sera, minatori assetati, frantumatori delle antiche rocce. Le mani degli uni sono gialle, o color terra, e, dentro, callose. Le mani d'altro sono rosate come se un acido le spellasse dal palmo: è la calce, è la pietra. I tintori, per l'effetto del cloro, e gli allievi salumieri, per quello del sale, hanno mani gonfie, che sudano perennemente dal palmo. In qualche viso rasciutto, bronzato, tra i peli d'una barba, sulle grinze della non pensionabile pelle, è rimasto uno schizzo di calcina: un neo bianco. I fabbri, i meccanici, i conducenti vestono talora combinazioni di tela turchina, ma poi fatte nerastre per filiggine e limatura con larghe macchie oleose: e il loro volto è più fosco che quello de' maestri. Però è meno secco, e si capisce che al risciacquarlo potrà riapparire più pieno. Garzoni discesi dai ponti e dai bilancini con la faccia tutta sbiancata dalle sfarinature del gesso, come Pierrot nel pallore della luna, come infarinati mugnai. È raro incontrare dei muratori obesi o paffuti. Negli adolescenti, chi guardi, stupisce la lunghezza e la grossezza dell'avambraggio e del polso, in rispetto al torace ancor esile. Taluno indossa una maglia: è azzurra, o rossa, o grigia, o rigata: con buchi. Se il colletto della maglia comporta bottoni, uno quasi sempre è mancante. Le bretelle, rare, per lo più si rivelano un po' vecchie, e sudate: o raggrinzite, scrofolose: e sono affette da complicazioni riparatorie di spaghi e legacci, che hanno coi bottoni superstiti rapporti piuttosto complessi. Ma qualche altro, simile a benestante, o forse il favorito di Fortuna, ha bretelle di gomma assai larghe, nuove, tese come sparo di fionda: le quali sogliono aderire in ogni moto, in ogni istante, al caldo e vigoroso impegnarsi del torace sulle fatiche dell'opera.
Grosse scarpe!, i muratori e gli operai di campagna, con chiodi d'acciaio a rosellina, nel tacco e tutt'ingiro la suola: che stridono sul lastrico e sulle pietre, e qualcuno lo perdono lungo il cammino, da bucar gomme ai ciclisti: perché ognuno, nel suo cammino, deve ci lasci alcun testimonio dell'andare e dell'essere, e nemmanco si avvede. Buone scarpe, o talvolta men buone, o fruste: e se la suola è consunta, un po' di più, allora, sostituisce quel tanto di suola che manca. I meccanici hanno scarpini da ciclista, leggeri e svelti come babbucce, ma tenute da certe stringhe di cuoio. Altri sono privi di calcagni: si conosce che le loro calzature, già lucide, esaudiscono in sugli inizi le liete

necessità domenicali, nello spicco della sagra, o nel breve fasto del ballo: poi, come al dì festivo succedono i lavorativi, così nell'avvicinare e nell'aggredire il lavoro, i loro piedi grossi, dai muscoli rudi, hanno deformato l'originaria eleganza dell'involucro. Il tacco è scemato fino al nulla, e in corrispondenza del dito piccolo la punta s'è staccata dalla tomaia, come per un'ernia del carnoso piede.
Passano donne e ragazze: e talora per alcuna si volgono gli uomini o ragazzotti e mormorano tra loro quello che pensano o che gli sembra di dover desiderare: camminano e ridono: incespica, nel voltarsi, il più ardito. Talora qualcuno ha uno sguardo, che una fanciulla sommessamente raccoglie: e allora quello, pure andando, si porta nell'animo come una speranza e una dolcezza consolatrice, dopo le stanche ore.

Carlo Emilio Gadda, "L'Adalgisa", Einaudi, Torino 1974.

Ottiero Ottieri
Donnarumma all'assalto

Martedì

"Eh, qui dottore, non ci viene mai nessuno. Su negli uffici state meglio" ridacchiava l'operatore della verniciatura, e subito si è fatto premuroso per accompagnare il suo ospite, collega, superiore: era incerto.
Le piccole carrozzerie delle calcolatrici come automobiline scivolano sui rulli del rapydstan, compiendo un tragitto di montagne russe, di curve, di rettilinei: durante il percorso vengono verniciate, stuccate, asciugate, riverniciate, passando tra fortissime lampade accese che le essiccano, come globi gialli di un lunapark.
Siamo passati per i forni; abbiamo girato per quei lavori non meccanici, meno nobili: le vasche elettrolitiche, la cosiddetta agganciatura. L'operatore fa su di essi una piccola smorfia di disprezzo, benché ci tenga a spiegarli, fiero della complessità invisibile e chimica dei procedimenti.
Dietro gli uomini dell'agganciatura, abbiamo fatto una sosta. Agganciano, seduti, i piccoli pezzi, sfornati dall'officina, ai telai, prima che i telai siano immersi nelle vasche elettrolitiche per la cromatura, la nichelatura. L'operatore mi dà un'occhiata. Sa anche lui che questi operai si divertono poco, ma non se ne preoccupa tanto, come noi del Personale, abituati a considerare l'agganciatura un lavoro adatto per inchieste e studi psico-sociali. Agganciano di corsa, un pezzo dopo l'altro, una fila dopo l'altra, da sinistra a destra e dall'alto in basso come se riempissero una pagina scrivendo, e ogni lettera fosse un pezzo da infilare a un uncino. La riempiono con ostinazione e velocità.
Finito un telaio, lo staccano brulicante e tintinnante di pezzi, e ne cominciano un

altro. Adesso i telai si muovono a pedale verticalmente, cioè si alzano e si abbassano in modo che la riga da riempire sia sempre all'altezza delle braccia: prima era la schiena che seguiva la riga, rompendosi. Il telaio mobile è stata una conquista tecnica e sociale.
Si vedono gli operai, come bambini al pallottoliere, infilare i pezzi per un piccolo foro al gancio, d'un colpo, allungando un braccio; velocemente ritirarlo; un altro pezzo, agganciare; un altro pezzo, agganciare. Terminata una fila, a capo.
Tra essi c'è un anziano, un manovale assunto perché invalido. Ci ha sentiti dietro di sé, ma non si è voltato. Alzava piano le braccia pesanti e cercava i ganci, uno per uno, mentre gli altri ormai agganciano senza guardare. Arrancava con una meticolosità senile, la nuca grigia e la schiena magrissima, dura.
"Gli altri camminano" dice l'operatore. "Questo non ce la fa. Me lo dovreste togliere".
E chi se lo prende?
"Sarebbero lavori da donne. Se nelle assunzioni, per via della disoccupazione, non dovessimo dare sempre la precedenza agli uomini...".
Ha strizzato gli occhi, un po' freddo, malizioso: "Tanto le nostre donne quaggiù non ci vengono. Non siamo in alta Italia, dottore...". Silenzio.
Vicino, altri operai sbrindellati, i meno eleganti dello stabilimento, in zoccoli, ficcavano i telai nelle vasche fumanti e acide. Tutti hanno salutato, alzando il capo dall'immersione, sorridendo per essere notati. Ma l'operatore aveva fretta di portarmi via, e che non mi fermassi, di tutto il reparto, proprio con quelli vestiti di stracci.
Gli premeva di mostrarmi l'aggiustaggio ai banchi, suo orgoglio: tre operai in piedi che battono al banco con un martello sulle carrozzerie per spianarle; danno colpi di lima per ridurre la "luce" nell'incastro fra la carrozzeria e una specie di coperchio. Benché manovrino in grande serie, i ritocchi sono sempre diversi e affidati all'intuito, all'occhio, all'arte, come nel ferro battuto; finalmente, il risultato è variabile nella qualità, non solo nel tempo, e dipende dall'estro umano: niente rallegra di più gli operai.
Egli ha voluto presentarmi questa sua squadra di aggiustatori. Essi, a testa bassa, hanno tirato via perché non avevano tempo. Tutti gli operai che lavorano ai banchi sono orgogliosi e vanitosi.

Ottiero Ottieri, "Dommarumma all'assalto", Bompiani, Milano 1959.

Beppe Fenoglio
La paga del sabato

All'angolo della piazza che prima portava il nome del re incontrò l'invalido Baracca che veniva sulla sua carrozzella tirata dai due cani. Fece con lui la traversata della piazza.
"Non ti ho mai visto in giro a quest'ora della mattina", gli disse Baracca e Ettore si chinò a carezzare sulla testa il cane di pelo rosso e poi rialzandosi rispose: "È che stamattina vado a lavorare".
Baracca si stupì un po' e poi gli chiese dove.
"Alla fabbrica della cioccolata".
"Sono contento per te perché è una bella industria".
Lui non voleva che Baracca gli facesse un più lungo discorso sul suo lavoro e perciò gli domandò dove andava lui. Baracca andava a mettersi davanti alla stazione, lì faceva accosciare i due cani e aspettava l'arrivo del treno. Faceva delle buone mattinate al treno, perché i forestieri si commuovevano per i due cani. Finito alla stazione, Baracca faceva trottare i cani verso la Cassa di Risparmio, si postava all'ingresso sotto il portico e anche lì prendeva soldi perché la gente che usciva dall'aver maneggiato denaro in banca ne lasciava quasi sempre qualche briciola a Baracca.
— Baracca ha studiato un buon sistema —, pensava Ettore quando l'ebbe lasciato. — Mette a frutto le sue gambe rovinate e si mantiene bene, tanti vorrebbero potersi mantenere così. Però Baracca se lo merita perché un giorno ha saputo decidersi. Tutta la città sapeva che era stato un buon operaio e che gli era capitata la disgrazia, ma nessuno si aspettava che pigliasse la strada dell'elemosina, che un giorno si facesse vedere per la città su una carrozzella tirata da due cani e con in mano un mazzo di pianeti di tutti i colori. Difficile per Baracca e per la gente è stato quel giorno, poi tutt'e due ci han fatto l'abitudine e da allora vive meglio di prima. Anch'io devo combinare in maniera che la gente faccia l'abitudine a qualcosa di deciso da me. Devo decidermi, potessi farlo oggi, perché se no corro il rischio di farcela io l'abitudine a lavorare sotto gli altri —.
Adesso camminava per una strada secondaria e pensava solo più che i suoi passi lo portavano a lavorare. Camminava e gli venne in mente suo padre, un quarto d'ora prima, sulla porta della sua bottega. Era commosso a vederlo uscire di casa per andare a lavorare, aveva degli occhi come un cane da caccia. Suo padre gli porse la mano e lui gliela strinse, ma stringendogliela lo fissava come se non lo riconoscesse. E pensava: — Tu sei mio padre? E perché non sei milionario? Perché io non sono nato figlio di un milionario? — Quell'uomo lì davanti gli aveva fatto un torto a farlo nascere figlio di padre povero, lo stesso che se l'avesse procreato rachitico o con la testa più grossa di tutto il resto del corpo.

STRADE AL CREPUSCOLO
LA VETRINA INCANTATA

LO STRUSCIO.
IL SISTEMA DELLA MODA.
APPUNTAMENTO ALL'ANGOLO.
LA SEDUTA DAL BARBIERE.
ZONA PEDONALE.
CRESCENDO DI VOCI.

Poi pensò a quel tale che fra un quarto d'ora gli sarebbe stato accanto ad insegnargli come si compila una lettera di vettura.
— Cristo, — disse.
Andando aveva visto in un'officina un operaio scappucciare un tornio e non aveva la faccia triste, né stanca né torva. Poi passarono sul loro camion gli operai della Società Elettrica, avevano un qualcosa di militare per le loro uniformi azzurre e il dischetto d'ottone sul berretto e l'ordine con cui stavano seduti sulle sponde del camion. Anche loro non gli apparvero tristi, né stanchi né torvi, gli apparvero invece come estremamente superbi.
Ma lui scosse la testa tutt'e due le volte, finché arrivò davanti alla fabbrica della cioccolata.
C'era già più di cento operai e operaie, in qualunque direzione guardassero, sembravano tutti rivolti verso il grande portone metallico della fabbrica, come calamitati. Non si avvicinò, anzi si allontanò, andò verso un orinatoio e di là guadava i crocchi dei lavoranti e il portone ancora chiuso. Da dov'era poteva vedere la sirena alta su un terrazzino della fabbrica, e gli sembrava che l'aria intorno alla tromba tremasse nell'attesa del fischio.
Finalmente arrivarono gli impiegati, otto, dieci, undici in tutto, non si mischiarono agli operai sull'asfalto, stettero sul marciapiede. Lui si nascose dietro l'orinatoio e li osservava attraverso i trafori metallici. — Io dovrei fare il dodicesimo — si disse, ma cominciò a scuotere la testa, non finiva più di scuoterla e diceva: — No, no, non mi tireranno giù nel pozzo con loro. Io non sarò mai dei vostri, qualunque altra cosa debba fare, mai dei vostri. Siamo troppo diversi, le donne che amano me non possono amare voi e viceversa. Io avrò un destino diverso dal vostro, non dico più bello o più brutto, ma diverso. Voi fate con naturalezza dei sacrifici che per me sono enormi, insopportabili, e io so fare a sangue freddo delle cose che a solo pensarle a voi farebbero drizzare i capelli in testa. Impossibile che io sia dei vostri.

Beppe Fenoglio, "La paga del sabato", Einaudi, Torino 1972.

Nanni Balestrini
La violenza illustrata

Descrizione
Ancora una volta la guerriglia si è scatenata nei giornali di Milano.
La vita operosa di Milano è stata sconvolta ieri pomeriggio da una ventata improvvisa di violenza e di furore senza precedenti anche nelle ore più buie della storia più recente della città. Per tutto il pomeriggio e fino a tarda sera le vie del centro sono state teatro di scontri aspri accaniti feroci tra le forze di polizia e folti gruppi di dimostranti appartenenti a gruppi di estrema sinistra. Decine e decine di feriti e contusi dall'una e dall'altra parte. Barricate. Automobili rovesciate e incendiate. Agenti strappati dalle macchine e duramente percossi. Gragnuole di bombe molotov. Acri barriere di lacrimogeni. Barricate. File di tram con i vetri in frantumi.
Ancora una volta la guerriglia si è scatenata nelle strade di Milano. Per oltre tre ore le zone del centro si sono trasformate in campo di battaglia. Da una parte le forze dell'ordine intervenute con estrema violenza e dall'altra estremisti di sinistra che hanno devastato si presume secondo un disegno prestabilito quanto hanno trovato sulla loro strada. È stato un attacco esasperato durissimo. Per oltre tre ore i guerriglieri armati con sbarre di ferro sassi biglie di ferro e di vetro razzi hanno incendiato automobili costruito barricate messo di traverso autobus. Centinaia di bombe molotov sono state scagliate dai dimostranti che hanno messo in atto la tecnica della guerriglia urbana radunandosi improvvisamente in un posto e aggredendo la polizia e quindi disperdendosi nelle strade laterali per ritrovarsi più tardi.
I dimostranti hanno portato la guerriglia per le vie del centro storico di Milano. Violenti scontri si sono susseguiti per oltre quattro ore con la polizia. I feriti tra le forze dell'ordine sono stati 49. 22 carabinieri 5 ufficiali 3 sottufficiali e 19 poliziotti. Nei vari ospedali continuano ad affluire civili parecchi dei quali appartengono a dimostranti. Molti di costoro però hanno preferito rivolgersi a medici privati. Questura e carabinieri hanno arrestato 82 dimostranti. Si sta facendo un bilancio dei danni. È stato seriamente colpito l'edificio del Corriere della Sera. Sono state incendiate decine di automobili.
La piazza si è scatenata oggi a Milano. Una piazza limitata a gruppi di estremisti di sinistra sufficienti comunque a creare incidenti gravissimi di cui soltanto il bilancio può dare l'esatta misura. Un passante è moribondo. Sembra sia stato colpito alla testa da un sasso o da un candelotto lacrimogeno poi abbia sbattuto contro un palo di ferro della segnaletica infine sull'autolettiga è stato colto da infarto. È gravissimo all'ospedale. Poi decine di feriti molte auto incendiate bombe molotov scagliate dovunque negozi presi d'assalto e semidistrutti tram danneggiati.

Forse mai come ieri la guerriglia urbana a Milano aveva raggiunto simili punte di asprezza di ferocia di violenza organizzata. La città è rimasta sconvolta non solo per gli scontri i sassi i bastoni le cariche e i candelotti lacrimogeni ma anche per le bombe molotov gli incendi le barricate erette in decine di strade con automobili private e autobus di linea. Per le decine e decine di automezzi di jeep della polizia e di tram semidistrutti a bastonate a sassate e con le bombe incendiarie. Per i danni numerosi in una vasta zona della città dove i guerriglieri hanno continuato per ore e ore a tenere impegnate le forze dell'ordine della polizia e di tram semidistrutti a bastonate a sassate con incursioni rapide e improvvise.
Gravi episodi di provocazione sono avvenuti oggi pomeriggio nel centro di Milano. Nel corso di prolungati scontri la polizia ha attaccato violentemente gruppi di estremisti. Un anziano passante colpito da un candelotto in fronte è ricoverato in fin di vita al policlinico. Gruppi di provocatori appartenenti a organizzazioni extraparlamentari sedicenti di sinistra hanno compiuto atti teppistici in varie zone della città e al Corriere della Sera. Una delle guerriglie urbane più cruente che mai si siano svolte a Milano. È durata molte ore e si è estesa a macchia d'olio. I punti caldi sono stati decine. Impossibile seguire con un filo di logica il succedersi degli avvenimenti che però sembrano avere seguito un disegno preordinato di provocazione.
Pochi minuti dopo le 16 da via Cusani proveniente pare da corso Garibaldi è giunto il corteo della sinistra extraparlamentare. La polizia gli ha bloccato l'accesso a largo Cairoli chiudendo l'imbocco all'altezza di Foro Bonaparte. Vi è stata una breve consultazione tra funzionari della polizia e organizzatori del corteo dopo di che gli opposti schieramenti si sono fronteggiati per alcuni minuti senza che nulla accadesse. Tutto faceva credere che il corteo avesse rinunciato a proseguire limitandosi a presidiare la zona adiacente a largo Cairoli.
Alle 16 circa 5000 persone si sono ammassate nelle strade adiacenti a via Ponte Vetero uno dei vecchi centri di Milano. Quando si è trattato di raggiungere largo Cairoli c'è stato un incontro tra organizzatori della manifestazione e il questore il quale esigeva che i partecipanti abbandonassero i bastoni delle bandiere e qualsiasi altra cosa potesse trasformarsi in armi. Ma il comitato organizzatore non ha aderito. Non voleva perquisizioni. Nel frattempo mentre la testa del corteo era attestata in attesa delle decisioni in via Cusani la coda si è mossa per via Broletto. Gli organizzatori affermano che volevano raggiungere via Dante e quindi largo Cairoli facendo un giro più lungo. Quando i dimostranti sono giunti quasi all'altezza di piazza Cordusio sono stati respinti dalle forze dell'ordine che hanno lanciato numerosi candelotti lacrimogeni.

I primi incidenti sono avvenuti verso le 16 in piazza Cordusio. Secondo la versione ufficiale la polizia che presidiava la zona ha notato un gruppo di dimostranti con caschi e aste di bandiere che si stavano dirigendo verso largo Cairoli e ha chiesto che venissero abbandonati. Sempre secondo la versione ufficiale i dimostranti avrebbero risposto improvvisamente con un lancio di pietre. Le forze dell'ordine hanno allora attaccato rincorrendo gli estremisti che nel frattempo avevano ripiegato in via Broletto. Qualche minuto prima un altro folto gruppo di dimostranti aveva raggiunto largo Cairoli provenendo da via Cusani. Anche questi portavano caschi fazzoletti e bandiere con aste di legno. A questo punto sono giunti gli echi dei candelotti lacrimogeni che le forze dell'ordine avevano fatto esplodere in piazza Cordusio. Poco dopo i due gruppi di estremisti si congiungevano.
I gruppuscoli della sinistra extraparlamentare avevano cominciato ad affluire per raggiungere largo Cairoli. Via Dante però era stata bloccata dalla polizia. I dimostranti molti dei quali portavano caschi da motociclista e avevano in mano aste di bandiere dopo brevi scaramucce si sono dispersi per le vie laterali cercando di raggiungere largo Cairoli. I primi violenti scontri sono avvenuti all'angolo tra via Cusani con corso Garibaldi dove la polizia aveva steso un fitto cordone formato da uomini e camionette. Vi è stato un primo lancio di candelotti lacrimogeni e i dimostranti hanno risposto col lancio di pietre e bottiglie molotov.
Dai gruppetti di sinistra disposti all'angolo tra via Dante e via Giulini sono partiti i primi sassi contro il cordone di agenti che impediva loro di raggiungere largo Cairoli. Sembrava un episodio quasi trascurabile fine a stesso. Ci sono stati gli squilli di tromba poi una prima carica, ma è stata la scintilla che ha scatenato la violenza. Una prima bottiglia incendiaria è stata fatta esplodere in piazza Cordusio in fondo a via Dante dove giungeva la coda del corteo attestato in via Cusani. I disordini sono scoppiati anche qui dove già i guerriglieri avevano formato delle barricate trascinando in mezzo alla strada numerose automobili private. Da largo Cairoli sono partite a sirena spiegata le jeep della polizia una dozzina di vetture a tutta velocità.
I dimostranti si sono ritirati ma nella fuga hanno cominciato a disselciare la strada formando nel contempo barricate con le auto in sosta. Pochi minuti dopo il secondo focolaio è scoppiato in via Cusani nel largo costituito dal confluire di via Broletto via Ponte Vetero e via dell'Orso. Al lancio di sassi e di biglie di ferro da parte degli estremisti le forze dell'ordine hanno risposto con i candelotti. E da questo momento è cominciata la guerriglia. Barricate strade disselciate sassaiole. Tutto sotto il fumo nero dei candelotti sparati dalla forze dell'ordine per disperdere i dimostranti.

CASA
L'IO ILLUSTRATO

STILE RINASCIMENTALE.
TECNOLOGICO MILANESE.
RICORDI ROMANI.
ARREDO BAROCCO.
LA GIUNGLA IN TERRAZZA.
SULLA CREDENZA GUARDA IL
TELEVISORE.

I primi incidenti sono scoppiati lontano da via Cusani in piazza Cordusio dove la polizia ha caricato un gruppo di estremisti. È stato questo l'inizio dei disordini. Cariche violentissime si sono susseguite lungo via Broletto via Dante via San Tommaso e via Rovello. In breve gli scontri si sono estesi in tutta la zona con punte di particolare violenza proprio in via Cusani dove si trovava il grosso dei manifestanti. Sono stati sparati centinaia di lacrimogeni quasi tutti a altezza d'uomo alcuni dei quali hanno danneggiato i tram e gli autobus in sosta. Provocatori si davano alla distruzione di numerose auto in sosta. Si è sentito un urlo levarsi dalla piazza e i primi sassi si sono incrociati con i primi candelotti lacrimogeni le due parti sono entrate in contrasto con una furia paurosa in un mulinare di calci di moschetto e di manganelli con il sinistro accompagnamento degli scoppi dei candelotti lacrimogeni e di quelli soffocati delle bottiglie incendiarie. La battaglia si è frazionata rapidamente in accaniti corpo a corpo dopo che le file dei dimostranti erano state travolte dalla prima carica in un susseguirsi di mischie serrate feroci senza risparmio di colpi. L'aria era piena di tondelli di ferro di bulloni di cubetti di porfido che filtravano fra le volute grigie dei lacrimogeni e i falò delle prime macchine incendiate. Hanno preso fuoco raggiunte dalle bombe molotov una decina di macchine private molte delle quali sono state messe per traverso a formare barricate.

Dalle 16 le strade del centro sono state sconvolte da gravissimi disordini. Gruppi di dimostranti della sinistra extraparlamentare si sono scontrati con le forze dell'ordine. È stata una vera e propria guerriglia nelle strade invase dai fumi acri delle bombe lacrimogene e mentre la gente sorpresa sui tram o sui marciapiedi cercava di trovare un riparo qualsiasi. I guerriglieri hanno impegnato a lungo le forze dell'ordine che hanno risposto con durezza a volte usando i moschetti impugnati dalla parte della canna e usati come una clava. In più di un'occasione agenti e carabinieri sono stati costretti a ritirarsi davanti all'incalzare dei terroristi e alla loro tattica. Molti passanti hanno vissuto momenti di panico molti altri si sono rifugiati nei portoni e in parecchi stabili i custodi hanno chiuso i cancelli.

Iniziati nel dedalo di viuzze nei pressi di largo Cairoli di fronte al Castello Sforzesco i disordini si sono estesi rapidamente fino a raggiungere via Solferino dove ha sede il Corriere della Sera. Precedendo l'arrivo dei reparti di polizia un centinaio di estremisti hanno attaccato i pochi agenti presenti. Una decina di bombe molotov sono state scagliate contro le finestre del giornale in particolare quelle della cronaca al piano terreno. Fiamme e fumo sono penetrati all'interno. Mattoni e biglie metalliche hanno raggiunto anche il primo piano dove sono andati infranti i vetri delle finestre della redazione e della sala telescriventi. Poi all'arrivo delle forze dell'ordine le cariche e le incursioni sono proseguite nelle strade adiacenti. Impugnando i moschetti dalla parte della canna le forze dell'ordine hanno nuovamente attaccato riuscendo a respingere gli estremisti che si sono poi diretti verso essa piazza del Carmine e le strade vicine. Gli stessi tram bloccati facevano da riparo agli estremisti che hanno continuato a bersagliare le forze dell'ordine con pietre biglie di acciaio e a volte rilanciando anche i candelotti inesplosi. In questa fase la polizia ha fermato numerose persone soprattutto giovani e giovanissimi alcuni inseguiti anche dentro i portoni delle case. Ragazzi e ragazze con i volti tumefatti sono stati portati in questura. Non erano ancora le 17. Si pensava ormai che gli incidenti stessero per esaurirsi con episodi di estrema gravità.

Nanni Balestrini, "La violenza illustrata"
Einaudi, Torino 1976.

Giuseppe Tomasi di Lampedusa
Racconti

Casa Lampedusa

Anzitutto la nostra casa. La amavo con abbandono assoluto e la amo ancora adesso quando essa da 12 anni non è più che un ricordo. Fino a pochi mesi prima della sua distruzione dormivo nella stanza nella quale ero nato, a quattro metri di distanza da dove era stato posto il letto di mia madre durante il travaglio del parto. Ed in quella casa, in quella stessa stanza, forse, ero lieto di essere sicuro di morire. Tutte le altre case (poche del resto, a parte gli alberghi) sono state dei tetti che hanno servito a ripararmi dalla pioggia e dal sole, ma non delle case nel senso arcaico e venerabile della parola.

Sarà quindi molto doloroso per me rievocare la Scomparsa amata come essa fu fino al '29 nella sua integrità e nella sua bellezza, come essa continuò dopo tutto ad essere sino al 5 aprile 1943, giorno in cui le bombe trascinate da oltre Atlantico la cercarono e la distrussero.

La prima sensazione che mi viene in mente è quella della sua vastità. E questa sensazione non è dovuta all'ingrandimento che l'infanzia fa di ciò che la circonda, ma alla realtà effettiva. Quando ne vidi l'area coperta di ripugnanti rovine, la sua superficie era di 1.600 mq. Abitata soltanto da noi in un'ala, dai miei nonni paterni in un'altra, dai miei zii scapoli al secondo piano, essa era tutta a mia disposizione durante venti anni, con i suoi tre cortili, le sue quattro terrazze, il suo giardino, le sue scale immense, i suoi anditi, i suoi corridoi, le sue scuderie, i piccoli ammezzati per le persone di servizio e per l'amministrazione — un vero regno per un ragazzo solo, un regno vuoto o talvolta popolato da figure tutte affettuose.

In nessun punto della terra, ne sono sicuro, il cielo si è mai steso più violentemente azzurro di come facesse al di sopra della nostra terrazza rinchiusa, mai il sole ha gettato luci più miti di quelle che penetravano attraverso le imposte socchiuse nel "salone verde", mai macchie di umidità su muri esterni di cortile hanno presentato forme più eccitatrici di fantasia di quelle di casa mia.

Tutto mi piace in essa: l'asimmetria dei suoi muri, la quantità dei suoi saloni, gli stucchi dei suoi soffitti, il cattivo odore della cucina dei miei nonni, il profumo di violetta nella stanza di toletta di mia madre, l'afa delle sue scuderie, la buona sensazione dei cuoi puliti della selleria, il mistero di certi appartamenti non finiti all'ultimo piano, l'immenso locale delle rimesse nelle quali si conservavano le carrozze; tutto un mondo pieno di gentili misteri, di sorprese sempre rinnovate e sempre tenere. Ne ero il padrone assoluto e di corsa ne percorrevo continuamente i vasti spazi, salendo dal cortile su per la scala gran-de sino alla loggia situata sul tetto dalla quale si vedeva il mare e monte Pellegrino e tutta la città sino a Porta Nuova e Monreale. E poiché con deviazioni e giravolte sapevo evitare le stanze abitate, mi sentivo solo e dittatore, seguito spesso soltanto dall'amico Tom che correva eccitatissimo alle mie calcagna, con la lingua rossa penzoloni fuori dal caro muso nero.

La casa (e casa voglio chiamarla e non palazzo, nome che è stato deturpato, appioppato come è adesso ai falansteri di 15 piani) era rintanata in una delle più recondite strade della vecchia Palermo, in via di Lampedusa al numero 17, numero onusto di cattivi presagi, ma che allora serviva solo ad aggiungere un piacevole saporino sinistro alla gioia che essa sapeva dispensare. (Quando poi, trasformate le scuderie in magazzini, chiedemmo il numero fosse mutato ed esso diventò 23 si andava verso la fine: il numero 17 le portava fortuna.)

La strada era recondita, ma non strettissima, e ben lastricata; e non sudicia come si potrebbe credere, perché di faccia al nostro ingresso, e per tutta la lunghezza del fabbricato, si stendeva l'antico palazzo Pietrapersia che non aveva né negozi, né abitazioni, a pianterreno, e che mostrava soltanto un'austera, ma pulita, facciata, bianca e gialla come si deve, punteggiata da molte finestre custodite da enormi inferriate che le conferivano un aspetto dignitoso e triste di vecchio convento o di prigione di Stato. Gli scoppi delle bombe, poi, scaraventarono molte di quelle pesanti inferriate dentro le nostre stanze prospicienti, con quali lieti effetti sugli stucchi antichi ed i lampadari di Murano può essere immaginato.

Ma se la via Lampedusa per lo meno per tutta la distesa della nostra casa era decente, non così lo erano le vie di accesso: la via Bara all'Olivella che portava in piazza Massimo era brulicante di miseria e d'accattoni, e percorrerla era un affare triste. Divenne un po' meglio quando venne tagliata la via Roma, ma rimase sempre un buon tratto da fare fra sporcizia e orrori.

La facciata della casa non aveva nulla di architettonicamente pregevole: era bianca con le larghe inquadrature delle aperture color giallo zolfo, il più puro stile siciliano del 600 e 700, insomma. La casa si stendeva nella via Lampedusa per una sessantina di metri ed aveva nove grandi balconi di facciata. I portoni erano due, quasi agli angoli della casa, enormemente larghi come si facevano prima per permettere alle vetture di svoltarvi dentro anche da strade strette. Ed infatti vi svoltavano con facilità anche gli attacchi a quattro che mio padre guidava con maestria nei giorni di corsa al galoppo alla Favorita. Varcato il portone dal quale si entrava sempre, proprio di fronte alla scala vi era un porticato con colonne di bella pietra grigia di Billiemi che sostenevano il soprastante "tocchetto". Di faccia al portone vi era infatti il grande cortile acciottolato e diviso in spicchi da file di

MOTORI E FRASTUONO.
FRASTUONO E MOTORI.
CHI GUIDA?
L'ALLARME HA LA CHIAVE.
INIZIO SECONDO TEMPO.
GELATO GRAVITAZIONALE.
L'ULTIMO TRAM.

lastriche. Esso era terminato da tre grandi archi sostenuti anch'essi da colonne di Billiemi, che portavano la terrazza che univa, in quel punto, le due ali della casa.
La scala grande era molto bella, tutta in Billiemi grigio a due rampe di una quindicina di scalini ognuna, incassate tra due muri giallini. Dove cominciava la seconda rampa vi era un ampio pianerottolo oblungo con due porte in mogano, una di fronte a ciascuna rampa, con dei balconcini a petto d'oca dorati.
E subito dopo l'ingresso alla scala, però dalla parte esterna, sul cortile, pendeva il laccio rosso della campana che il portiere doveva suonare per avvertire la servitù che si erano ritirati i padroni o che erano venute delle visite. Il numero dei colpi di campana, che i portinai eseguivano magistralmente, ottenendo, non so come, dei colpi secchi e separati senza noiosi tintinni, era rigorosamente protocollizzato: quattro colpi per mia nonna la principessa e due per le sue visite, tre per mia madre la duchessa e uno per le visite di lei. Succedevano però dei malintesi, così che essendo talvolta rientrata nella stessa vettura mia madre, mia nonna e una amica che avevano preso con sé nella strada, venne eseguito un vero concerto di 4 più 3 più 2 colpi che non finiva più. I padroni maschi, mio nonno e mio padre, uscivano e si ritiravano senza che per loro si scampanasse.
Terminata la seconda fuga della scala si sboccava nell'ampio e luminoso "tocchetto", cioè in un porticato i cui vani tra le colonne erano stati riempiti, per ragioni di comodità, da grandi vetrate di vetro opaco a losanghe. In esso vi erano pochi mobili, ma grandi quadri di antenati, e un grande tavolo a sinistra sul quale si posavano le lettere in arrivo (e fu lì allora che lessi una cartolina proveniente da Parigi indirizzata allo zio, nella quale una qualche sgualdrinella francese aveva scritto: "Dis à ton ami qu'il est un mufle"). La sala accanto che seguiva era un immenso ambiente pavimentato a lastre di marmo bianco e grigio, con tre balconi su via Lampedusa. Con grande rammarico dei miei genitori essa era di decorazione interamente moderna, poiché nel 1848 vi era caduta una bomba che ne distrusse il bel soffitto dipinto e ne danneggiò irreparabilmente le pitture murali. Per lungo tempo pare anzi vi crescesse un bel fico. Essa venne rifatta quando mio nonno si sposò, cioè nel 1866 o '67, ed era tutta a stucco bianco, con un "lambris" di marmo grigio. Era in questa sala grande che stavano i camerieri, bighellonando sui loro sedili e pronti a precipitarsi nel "tocchetto" al suono della famosa campana.
Varcata una porta di stoffa verde si entrava nell'anticamera che aveva le soprapporte di ritratti di antenati sul suo balcone e sulle sue due porte, un parato di seta grigia, e altri quadri. E l'occhio penetrava nella prospettiva dei saloni che si stendevano l'uno dopo l'altro lungo la facciata. Qui cominciava per

me la magia delle luci, che in una città a sole intenso come Palermo sono succose e variate secondo il tempo anche in strade strette. Esse erano talvolta diluite dai tendaggi di seta davanti ai balconi, talaltra invece esaltate dal loro battere su qualche doratura di cornicione o da qualche damasco giallo di seggiolone che le rifletteva; talora, specialmente in estate, i saloni erano oscuri, ma dalle persiane chiuse filtrava la sensazione della potenza luminosa che era fuori; talaltra, a seconda dell'ora, un solo raggio penetrava diritto e ben delineato come quello del Sinai, popolato da miriadi di granellini di polvere, e che andava ad eccitare il colore dei tappeti che era uniformemente rosso rubino in tutte le stanze. Un vero sortilegio di illuminazioni e di colori che mi ha incantato l'anima per sempre. Talvolta in qualche vecchio palazzo, o in qualche chiesa, ritrovo questa qualità luminosa che mi struggerebbe l'anima se non fossi pronto a sfornare qualche wicked joke.
Dopo l'anticamera veniva la stanza detta "del lambris", perché rivestita sino a metà altezza appunto da un lambris di noce intagliato: dopo ancora la stanza detta "della cena" con le pareti coperte di stoffa arancione a fiori, stoffa che ancora in parte sopravvive come tappezzeria dell'attuale stanza di mia moglie.
E a sinistra la grande sala da ballo con i pavimenti a smalto, ed i soffitti sui quali deliziosi ghirigori oro e giallo incorniciavano scene mitologiche nelle quali, con rustica forza e grandi svolazzi di panneggi, si affollavano tutti gli dei dell'Olimpo.
E dopo il "budoir" di mia madre che era molto bello con il suo soffitto tutto a fiori e rami di stucchi colorati antichi, di un disegno soave e corposo come una musica mozartiana.

Giuseppe Tomasi di Lampedusa, "Racconti", Feltrinelli, Milano 1980.

Pier Paolo Pasolini
Alì dagli occhi azzurri

Squarci di notti romane
Nelle notti di marzo l'acqua del Tevere ancora non assorbe la luce delle migliaia di fanali che da Ponte Milvio si sgranano fino a San Paolo: acqua e luci divisi da un leggero strato di freddo. In qualche sera, precocemente tiepida, si intravede quello che sarà il prossimo accordo tra la corrente e i lungoteveri, nella purezza muta, dura, tragica della primavera. Il paesaggio buio — aria e acqua — punteggiato da luci in interminabili file ricurve, e arabescato dal buio più fitto degli alberi cittadini... e allora, svanito lo strato di freddo, circola tra fiume e fanali un'aria tenuissima, impalpabile, tutta trasformata in odore. E l'enorme carnaio trafitto dai mille profumi che lo compongono si adagia sui lungoteveri come un gas che avveleni inavvertitamente, d'incanto: e tutti, almeno per un istante, sia pure senza saperlo, vorrebbero morire a quel profumo di asfalti lontani (il Pincio, Corso Trieste, la Città Giardino, i quartieri meridionali...), di pattume, di erbe odorose e di pisciatoi. Allora le rotaie del tram, affondate tra le piccole pietre dure del selciato, acquistano un'espressività muta, dura, tragicamente nostalgica: vedete, lì, la città, una città, coi suoi quartieri nuovi e i suoi pomeriggi in cui il bianco del sole è di una noia mortale: e tutto pervaso da una normalità che deprime come una leggera febbre di tisico. Su quelle rotaie dei tram, su quei marciapiedi, su quelle spallette dei lungoteveri infebbrati, su quelle scale che conducono al livello del fiume, coi gradini unti di feci, su quei ponti che si stagliano contro un cielo romano — corrotto e seicentesco, d'un nitore che non è mai puro, grandioso ma non infinito — su quelle aiuole dove l'erba è divorata da uno smeraldo insano, su quegli intonachi invecchiati al sole, che nessuno si curerà mai di ripristinare, come se fossero votati a una desolante eternità, il profumo delle prime notti precocemente primaverili, come un animale ridestato dal caldo, sfoga liberamente i suoi brividi che scoperchiano i cervelli. Questo meraviglioso soffio, anonimo e infernale, ricostruisce con una fedeltà spietata gli "squarci di notti romane" dell'anno passato...
... ...
Da Ponte Sisto all'Isola Tiberina si stende un pezzo di Tevere paesano: a sinistra il Ghetto che si mette a cantare improvvisamente, a gola spiegata, in Piazza delle Tartarughe, al Teatro di Marcello, in Piazza Campitelli, a destra la foresta materna di Trastevere. Di qua gli orizzonti sono occupati dagli spazi asfaltati del mattatoio, dei Mercati Generali, e, in fondo, del San Paolo, domenicale e tirrenico, incallito nella leggera sporcizia: di là si va a finire in Monteverde, enorme deposito di un Arar eterno, tra muraglioni papali e ferrivecchi, fin che si arriva al Ponte Bianco, area di costruzione spalmata di croste e disgu-

stoso ciarpame fuori uso; è di là che giungono nei lungoteveri civili gli odori più stupendamente afrodisiaci: gli odori che tentano ad arrendersi al vizio fino magari al sacrificio della vita — il paese dei masochisti, delle zanoide, degli antenuli e degli impotenti. In mezzo alla normalità della finzione quotidiana, col traffico che, come un immenso nodo gordiano di cui sia stata mandata a memoria la formula risolutiva, si risolve di momento in momento — sindrome sontuosa, luccicante, borghese e timorata — si depone come una polverina disinfettante il profumo della notte calda dell'anno scorso; e se nel connettivo delle strade nuove e deliziosamente stupide — deliziosamente, se preferite dai giovinetti abitanti nei vicoli luridi — è rado, intermittente, dipanato, ci sono certi posti in cui si concentra, si coagula, si intrica, puzza e marcisce come un ganglio infiammato.
Per esempio, intorno all'orinatoio che sorge in fondo a Ponte Garibaldi: presso la fermata della Circolare Rossa. Fra i tronchi degli alberi piatti e inodori e la spalletta del fiume, sul breve tratto di marciapiede dove si ammassano gli anonimi in attesa del tram, che li porti verso i loro appartamentini da pompe funebri — verso Monteverde o le distese etrusche di San Paolo.
Pensate, magari, all'Isola Tiberina illuminata dai riflettori color inchiostro o carta di caramella menta. Arrosolata gelidamente, in mezzo al buio sconsacrato del fiume, divenuto spettacolo, scenografia, gloria del comune di Roma, attrazione iridescente e velina. Pensate magari all'ST che passa soffice e greve sul ponte. E alle migliaia di ignoti che dilagano verso il Ghetto, verso Campo dei Fiori.

Pier Paolo Pasolini, "Alì dagli occhi azzurri", Garzanti, Milano 1965.

IL SONNO
DAL SEGNO AL SOGNO

SI LEGGE A LETTO.
LA MUSICA DEI VICINI.
UN CANARINO IN TAZZA?
PASSANO LE MOTO.
NOTTURNO FELPATO.

Luigi Malerba
Diario di un sognatore

Settecamini, 30-31 dicembre 1978
(La decisione di annotare i miei sogni giorno per giorno nel corso del 1979 incomincia a turbare i miei sogni e a condizionare i miei sogni con ventiquattro ore di anticipo).
Un sogno unico e muto è presente per tutta la notte. È come un quadro fisso sul quale avvengono solo poche "correzioni". Il quadro non è altro che la prima pagina di un quotidiano di cui non riesco a leggere la testata, con i titoli di notizie che non leggo per protesta, ma che provocano un mio commento: "Ecco un sogno che avrei preferito fare domani notte quando incomincerò a annotare i sogni".

Roma, 25-26 gennaio
Mi alzo dal letto e vado alla finestra per aprirla, ma la maniglia si stacca e mi resta in mano. Mi accorgo che il legno della finestra è consumato all'interno e ha conservata intatta solo la scorza esteriore. Se premo un dito sul legno, affonda in una materia spugnosa, molle e umida, di colore scuro. Mi avvicino a un cassettone della camera e scopro che anche il legno del mobile è marcito all'interno. Provo ancora a premere il dito e di nuovo la superficie cede e il dito penetra nel legno marcio. Faccio un rapido controllo e mi accorgo che tutti i mobili sono colpiti dalla stessa malattia. Anche le porte. Vado in bagno preoccupato, mi guardo allo specchio. Sono pallidissimo. Premo un dito sulla mia guancia e mi accorgo con orrore che il dito affonda anche qui come nel legno.

Roma, 26-27 gennaio
Scopro che il mio metro di acciaio brunito serve per misurare il tempo. Posso misurare il giorno, il tempo diurno, ma non quello della notte perché il metro è nero. Mi dico: È finito il tempo degli orologi.

Settecamini, 27-28 gennaio
Ancora una volta i ladri sono venuti a rubare nella casa di Roma. Faccio una ispezione attenta e devo constatare che hanno rubato le stesse cose che hanno rubato l'altra volta. Accetto la contraddizione senza difficoltà, contrariato soprattutto da questa nuova visita dei ladri.

Roma, 29-30 gennaio
Sono seduto nella platea di un teatro. Ogni spettatore tiene in mano uno spago collegato con uno degli attori che stanno recitando. Anch'io ho in mano il mio spago collegato con una attrice giovane e ogni tanto do un leggero strappo per "correggere" la sua recitazione. Gli altri spettatori fanno altrettanto.

Roma, 30-31 gennaio
C'è un'area romana che da anni frequento in sogno, a lunghi intervalli di tempo, ma ritrovandola sempre uguale come se esistesse nella realtà. È un avvallamento lastricato di cubetti di pietra a ridosso di un ponte sul Tevere, contornato da case antiche e basse che si aprono su due strade e una delle due potrebbe essere via Giulia, ma non è, e l'altra una stradina stretta e più povera. Le case sono tutte di sagoma asimmetrica, facciate con il tetto in spiovente laterale, finestre alte e finestre basse, finestrini non allineati, portoni su un lato anziché al centro. Nel piano terra del fabbricato centrale fra le due strade ci sono due ristoranti-bar con tavolini all'aperto, molto discreti, frequentati da gente silenziosa. Qui non passano automobili, mi piace arrivare a piedi, sedermi a un tavolino e fumare una sigaretta o bere qualcosa. Qui posso sperare di trovare anche degli amici. Poco lontano da questo luogo c'è una stradina trasversale dove una donna vende quadri d'autore sul marciapiede (riconosco un De Chirico). A terra c'è un mobiletto abbandonato, non appartiene alla donna che vende i quadri, una specie di comodino con uno sportello di vetro smerigliato che apro per nascondervi un rotolo di banconote che portano stampato nell'ovale un disegno di De Chirico. Un milione, forse di più. Dopo avere nascosto le banconote mi affido a una guida con il berretto a visiera che mi sta aspettando all'angolo della stradina. Entriamo in una galleria sotterranea, scoperta di recente, che passa sotto al Tevere. L'ingresso della galleria mi sorprende per la quantità enorme di statue romane disposte nelle nicchie della parete in vari ordini di altezza. Esprimo la mia meraviglia e ammirazione, ma mi accorgo presto che le statue sono tutte di plastica. Mi vergogno di essere caduto in un errore così grossolano e procedo lungo la galleria che ora assume l'aspetto di un lungo corridoio con il soffitto a volta, molto alto, decorato di stucchi e affreschi. Saranno autentici o falsi anche questi? Ai lati continua l'esposizione delle statue romane, sempre finte, disposte dentro nicchie luccicanti di dorature. La galleria prosegue con leggere curve e anche qualche pendenza, come una strada. Nonostante la falsità delle statue la scoperta della galleria è in sé strabiliante se non fosse altro per le dimensioni grandiose. Esco finalmente alla luce insieme alla mia guida attraverso una porticina seminascosta che dà su un giardinetto. La guida mi mostra ora sul greto del fiume una superficie di mattoni levigata dallo scorrere dell'acque e in parte coperta di sabbia: è il "sopra" della galleria. Ritorno nella stradina dove ho nascosto i denari. Non c'è più il mobiletto. Sono costernato. Trovo una donna, non quella di prima, all'angolo di una strada vicino a un mucchio di masserizie e fra queste scorgo il mobiletto dove ho nascosto le banconote. Lo apro, ma è vuoto. Non dico niente, so bene che sarebbe inutile. Devo rassegnarmi alla perdita del denaro anche se la cosa mi procura una grave pena. Mi aggiro per le strade senza meta con la nebulosa sensazione che sto aspettando di svegliarmi.

Settecamini, 3-4 febbraio
Deserto del Sahara. Sono sorpreso che non sia caldo come si dice. Non sento caldo, ma sto sudando in abbondanza. Sudore freddo. Un aereo arriva nel cielo, fa un giro in tondo disegnando una O (o uno zero?) e poi se ne va. Sono solo, ma laggiù all'orizzonte, su uno schermo lontano, vedo le immagini del film Casablanca. Cammino verso lo schermo. Quando sarò arrivato entrerò nel film.

Roma, 10-11 febbraio
Vicino a piazzale Clodio, addossato a una parete di roccia, c'è un ascensore esterno con le pulegge in vista, le funi d'acciaio, le guide, gli ingranaggi bene oliati, per salire a Monte Mario. Nell'ascensore può entrare anche una automobile, è più un montacarichi che un ascensore. Una ragazza con accento americano mi dice che vuole fare un cambio, la sua Porsche quasi nuova in cambio della vecchia Alfa Romeo di A.M. Perché ne parla con me? Dovrei dirlo io a A.M. che è mio amico. Va bene. A Monte Mario si può salire quando di vuole, uno fa come gli pare. L'ascensore sale silenzioso. La ragazza mi trascina in un angolo buio e incomincia a spogliarsi. "Così in piedi?". "Preferisco in piedi", dice la ragazza. Decido che non salirò a Monte Mario ma andrò in America lasciando "in sospeso" il rapporto con la ragazza.

Roma, 11-12 febbraio
Un nuovo sistema per spedire le lettere. Apro la finestra, deposito la busta chiusa su una corrente d'aria e la lettera parte per la sua destinazione. È una bella invenzione, finalmente hanno inventato una cosa utile. Richiudo la finestra e mi metto a scrivere un'altra lettera.
(È un sogno senza dimensioni, senza spazio, di brevissima durata e poi di nuovo il buio del sonno).

Roma, 12-13 febbraio
Una strada di Roma nei pressi di San Salvatore in Lauro. Ai lati della strada, sui due marciapiedi, giganteschi vasi di opaline colmi di cipria colorate. La gente passa per la strada, qualcuno toglie il coperchio a uno dei vasi e, con un grande piumino, si cosparge di cipria. Secondo sogno. Mi trovo nel sottopassaggio del Tritone e salgo la scala per raggiungere un bar sulla via Crispi. Esco sulla strada e da qui salgo un'altra scala, poi scendo, salgo di nuovo scale sempre diverse, mi perdo in un labirinto di scale senza trovare il bar.

Settecamini, 13-14 febbraio
Devo andare a un appuntamento in un luogo di cui conosco solo il nome, che ho scritto su un pezzo di carta. Il mio mezzo di trasporto è un veicolo informe, di materia molle, gommosa, di aspetto molto primitivo. Si distinguono sì e no le ruote, impastate con il corpo del veicolo. Non so nemmeno se devo cavalcarlo o entrarvi dentro. Mi rivolgo a un uomo seminudo e gli mostro il pezzo di carta perché mi indichi la strada. L'uomo non parla, ma a sua volta mi consegna un foglietto con una somma di piccoli numeri, forse i chilometri che devo percorrere. Mi guardo attorno e vedo solo colline di terra nera e brulla. Mi viene il sospetto di trovarmi nella preistoria, ma la cosa non mi sconvolge. Finalmente monto in groppa al mio veicolo "molle" e parto a grande velocità sfiorando il terreno.
(La carta non può essere preistorica, ma mi accorgo della incongruenza solo al risveglio).

Settecamini, 18-19 febbraio
La "testa del serpente" si affaccia dietro l'angolo di un palazzo, spunta sopra il tetto di una casa, fra gli alberi di Villa Borghese. È una testa evanescente come una nuvola, verdastra, ha gli occhiali e gli stessi tratti del viso di un famoso uomo politico italiano. Si vede, si riconosce, eppure nessuno reagisce, nessuno parla. Sono preoccupato e scandalizzato. È lui il capo della mafia, è lui che ha organizzato le trame nere e poi il terrorismo, c'è sempre lui dietro a ogni scandalo, e adesso vuole diventare presidente di tutto. Mi affaccio a un ponte sul Tevere e questa volta vedo la testa del serpente che scende tirandosi dietro un corpo molle che occupa tutto il letto del fiume.
(Mi pare che avvenga in questo sogni il processo inverso della metaforizzazione: una metafora viene qui tradotta in una immagine "reale" all'interno di un sogno).

Luigi Malerba, "Diario di un sognatore", Einaudi, Torino 1981.

GIRONZOLANDO.
VERDE OLIVA.
VERDE BOTTIGLIA.
GIORNALI A VELE SPIEGATE.
UN TAVOLINO AL SOLE.

UN AUTO, UN PULLMAN, UN TRENO,
UNA BARCA,... LE CASE MOBILI.
CIPRESSI IN FILA E PINI A
OMBRELLO.
LA VEDUTA È UN MONUMENTO
ANTICO.

Goffredo Parise
Sillabario n. 1

Una domenica di gennaio del 1942 una signorina di una certa età dai capelli rossicci raccolti a chignon decise di andare al cinema. Era stata pochissime volte nella sua vita e sempre per accompagnare i bambini ai cartoni animati (era governante in una casa molto signorile), salvo una volta, al film Salvator Mundi che aveva visto insieme alla famiglia il giorno di Pasqua di un anno che non riusciva a ricordare. In casa il cinema non veniva considerato molto bene ma quella domenica la signorina aveva deciso di andarci da sola e di non dirlo a nessuno.

Era un giorno di pioggia, il denso fumo giallo che usciva dalla ciminiera di una fabbrica dove si tostava orzo avvolse lei e il suo ombrello, soli viaggiatori lungo un interminabile muro di mattoni (tirava anche vento).

La signorina raggiunse il centro della città, a passi di tacco nel suo loden si avvicinò all'entrata del cinema Edison, si fermò a guardare le fotografie del film La città d'oro, uno dei primi film tedeschi a colori di quegli anni, e vide che al botteghino c'era una gran ressa di soldati e in generale di uomini: la signorina sapeva che quel film era considerato audace, sapeva anche che quel cinematografo non era dei migliori ma non voleva fare nessun caso a tutto questo (era cresciuta in un collegio di suore povere ma parlava perfettamente il tedesco ed era stata anche interprete) anche se, in quel momento, il suo cuore batteva un poco più forte. Per non ficcarsi in mezzo a tutti quegli uomini si fece forza e chiese al venditore di caramelle (un ragazzo ruminante liquirizia, dalla bocca nera) di comperare il biglietto per lei. Lo ricompensò comprando cinque caramelle ed entrò nella sala. Subito capì che si trattava di un cinema "popolare", che non c'erano quasi donne tra gli spettatori salvo alcune bionde sparse e altre poche donne con i mariti. Trovò un posto, un brutto posto tra una combriccola di giovinastri, e fece per entrare nella fila ma fu fermata da un tipo in divisa nera che la sorpassò dicendo: "Occupato".

Poi si spense la luce, la signorina si trovò in piedi addossata al muro proprio sotto la fessura del proiettore da cui usciva un forte odore di acetone e già questo odore inaspettato le diede un senso di mistero. Sullo schermo apparvero alcune immagini di alpini diretti non si sa dove, sfilate a Roma, infine una diva che sorseggiava per propaganda un caffè chiamato "astragalo". La luce si riaccese e la signorina vagò sempre più a disagio alla ricerca di un posto (aveva un cappello tirolese con una spazzola di tasso infilata nel nastro) finché una mano grossa, gonfia e fortissima l'afferrò per un braccio. Si volse impaurita ma aggressiva e vide un uomo anziano vestito di un mezzo paltò con larghi baveri rossi di pelliccia, che le sorrise e le indicò un posto vici-

no al suo.
La signorina disse "grazie" passò toccando con le sue le gambe dell'uomo che le parvero durissime e sedette. Sentì subito, dopo pochi istanti, una gran vampata di calore al volto (la sala era piena di fumo), sbottonò il loden, sciolse il nodo della sciarpa e proprio in quel momento si fece buio e incominciò il film a colori. La signorina si "innamorò" subito del volto della protagonista, una giovane tedesca nel ruolo di una contadina bella e pura, ma in seguito si rese conto che si trattava di un film molto più audace di quanto avesse mai potuto immaginare: "sentiva" che prima o poi i protagonisti si sarebbero baciati, quando non fosse accaduto di peggio: per un momento pensò di andarsene (ma dove?) poi si abbandonò a una certa spossatezza interiore provocata dal calore del cinema e dalla durissima e inerte gamba dell'uomo al suo fianco, che avrebbe dovuto scavalcare, inoltre le batteva forte. Anche una donna dietro di lei le batté un colpetto sulla spalla con dita che sapevano di mandarino e disse: "Scusi, potrebbe spostarsi un po' a sinistra?". La signorina si spostò a sinistra ma dopo un po' ecco di nuovo le dita di mandarino e la voce della donna che chiedeva: "Forse sarebbe meglio che spostasse la testa un po' a destra". La signorina obbedì. "Così?" disse, e la donna rispose seccamente: "Così".

Passò ancora del tempo e di nuovo la donna disse: "Senta, io non ci vedo". Un uomo che stava con la donna borbottò al suo fianco, la signorina non sapeva cosa fare, le persone intorno dicevano "basta, silenzio" e qui si intromise l'uomo rotondo in mezza pelliccia; si sollevò un poco con fatica e sbatté la sua dura gamba contro la poltrona di legno sollevando un suono di strumento musicale. Ci fu un breve battibecco in un dialetto che la signorina non conosceva ma che la parola "educazione". Alla fine la donna disse a voce alta: "Come si fa a venire al cinema con un cappello così?". La signorina avvampò e con un gesto rapido e secco, come un uomo che la saluta, si levò il cappello dalla testa, lo chignon si sciolse e alcune ciocche ingarbugliate di capelli rossi e grigi si sparsero intorno alle orecchie. Poi abbassò il cappello tenendolo sul grembo con le due mani e riprese a guardare il film: si baciavano, la bionda e pura contadina tedesca stava affondata in un letto con un grande piumino, le labbra gonfie e trementi nel viso accaldato, la camicia da notte di canapa tesa dal respiro affannoso. La signorina beveva quelle immagini disperata e col cuore in gola.

"Vado, non vado, resto, che vergogna, non emozionarti, sii superiore, che vergogna..." farfugliava la sua mente e qualcosa dovette anche sfuggire dalle labbra perché l'uomo al suo fianco, che di tanto in tanto le gettava una occhiata, disse piano: "Come? Come dice?" e le sorrise con una larga bocca di mangiatore. La signorina non rispose e aguzzò

lo sguardo verso lo schermo ma udì un rumore che veniva dall'uomo: era come un battito, dei colpetti che sorgevano dalla gamba inerte di lui e che si trasmisero alla sua: come dei colpetti a una porta. Lanciò due o tre volte un rapidissimo sguardo a destra in basso e vide che l'uomo teneva una delle sue grosse mani appoggiata alla gamba e poi con una, o più dita, tamburellava. La signorina si "innamorò" subito del volto della protagonista, una giovane tedesca nel ruolo di una contadina bella e pura, ma in seguito si rese conto che si trattava di un film molto più audace di quanto avesse mai potuto immaginare: "sentiva" che prima o poi i protagonisti si sarebbero baciati, quando non fosse accaduto di peggio: per un momento pensò di andarsene (ma dove?) poi si abbandonò a una certa spossatezza interiore provocata dal calore del cinema e dalla durissima e inerte gamba dell'uomo al suo fianco, che avrebbe dovuto scavalcare, inoltre le batteva forte. Terrorizzata la signorina non capiva come una gamba potesse produrre un suono simile (l'uomo bussava ora senza tregua, con le nocche, proprio come si bussa forte a una porta): immobile fissò ancora lo sguardo sullo schermo, dove si svolgeva la scena della seduzione ed ebbe un gemito, un breve urlo, tanto forte le batteva il cuore.

Goffredo Parise, "Sillabario n. 1", Einaudi, Torino 1972.

Raffaele La Capria
Ferito a morte

Cap. IV

Gaetano attraversa la strada, si ferma a guardare dal parapetto il mare grigio nella calura, acqua di lisciva. Sotto il livello della strada il rettangolo rosso del campo da tennis, e quei giocatori in calzoncini bianchi, grassi e ridicoli sgambettano dietro la palla. Cura dimagrante, il grasso si scioglie, un po' di moto consigliato dal dottore, per la pancia. Ai lati del tennis i due quadrati delle terrazze del Circolo Nautico. Comodi sulle sedie a sdraio a chiacchierare, e quegli altri distesi a terra nudi immobili in fila come morti. Con che impegno prendono la tintarella! Massimo sarà al Circolo? Sempre seccante arrivare a casa sua quando lui non c'è. Che dire alla signora: preparare un argomento di conversazione. Oppure scendere giù, nelle sale del Circolo, e domandare di Massimo De Luca. Pare semplice, è vero? E invece quel senso di imbarazzo, di vergogna, appena metti piede lì. Perché imbarazzo, vergogna? Non li conosci? Mangiatori di sfogliatelle, adorano Scarfoglio, al massimo sfogliano Il Popolo dai Cinque Pasti, o Folli Vindici e Pirati, Le Arringhe Celebri. Facondi e fecondi, già arringati dal Truce, preferiscono ancora e sempre i gigioni e la genia dei geni. Il lussurioso immaginifico li fe' sognare d'Oltremare, crispini e libici inneggiarono alla guerra lirica, e poi fascisti a quella lampo. Nello scatolone di sabbia cacammo sangue due volte e nella neve più volte lo sputammo, sempre in onore dei probiviri ossessionati dalla Tranquillità della rendita. Moderatori di ideologie, galantuomini, degne persone e belle figure: riserva di saggezza. Da qui comincia la disgregazione. Dunque sai chi sono, e dunque non è proprio il caso... Eppure: C'è il signor Massimo De Luca? Ed occhi indiscreti ti squadrano dal suo mondo, intuito e fiuto bestiale per annusare in te, non cane né lupo, l'ambigua vittima dell'assurda scala di valori da essi imposti e qui vigenti, ambigua per l'atavica predisposizione a subirli rifiutandoli... Insomma tutto questo, e l'impossibilità di fregarsene sdraiandosi come loro nudo al sole. Vergogna ed imbarazzo, invece, il grumo vischioso dei sentimenti e oscuri risentimenti sociali, meschini ma giustificati, anche quando si scaricano su Massimo, tuo amico. Questi inviti a pranzo la domenica, per esempio, ne farei volentieri a meno. Le lezioni a Ninì, anche quelle, tanto per il profitto che ne ricava... giustificàti in uno che gli è amico, sì, ma che a casa sua, anche se fa caldo, esita a togliersi la giacca. Gli dirò che parto, che vado a Milano, non sembra ancora una cosa reale —lontano da tutta questa perdita di tempo.

S'incammina lentamente. La facciata del decrepito casermone borbonico nasconde il mare alla vista. Sulla strada solito viavai di bagnanti, torrente affluito dall'interno del continente napoleta-

no, s'ingrossa la domenica e straripa dal marciapiede. Ragazzini scalzi di tutte le misure, neri allegri e denutriti, e le loro occhiate, il bianco degli occhi come spicchi d'aglio. Ne vedi uno, ti volti un momento, e allo stesso posto ne trovi due, tre: partenogenesi partenopea. Sfiorati dal passaggio snervante delle motorette, dagli autobus coi grappoli umani sul predellino, dalle macchine, sotto il sole di luglio — un sole!... Oltrepassato il casermone rossofragola, scoppia dal basso un vocio confuso, e sotto la strada, di nuovo il mare nell'arco dolce della spiaggia, chiuso dalla selva delle palafitte, sovraffollato come Borgo San Lorenzo — un chilometro e mezzo quadrato, 125 mila abitanti, con una densità di 480 abitanti per ettaro, considera le strade, lo spessore dei muri e lo spazio inutilizzabile, ottieni, cessi compresi, una densità di 2,5 abitanti per stanza. E ci sono quattordici chiese, che diminuisce ulteriormente lo spazio...

Si affaccia dal parapetto: sale il vocio feroce, si sgolano impastati di sabbia fino al mento, epilettici nell'acqua bassa davanti alla luce purissima sconvolgente del mare. Quel fastidioso senso di promiscuità ogni volta, anche poco fa, nell'autobus. Una specie di vertigine che ti attira verso quel ribollire di corpi di facce segnate dall'usura del vicolo. Basterebbe un solo sguardo di simpatia, dato o ricevuto, una semplice occhiata di riconoscimento, un nulla, per sentirsi fagocitato dal magma umano come un albero dalla lava, distrutto, l'appartenenza a se stesso perduta, risucchiato dalla prevalente unità psicologica, soprafatto e partecipe sulla spiaggia di colpe storiche. — I preti e i frati concitavano quelle genti con gli stimoli potenti della religione. Senza amore di parte, ma per guadagni e rapine, si giuravano sostenitori del trono Aniello Totonno Ciccillo, orde ingorde della Santafede elettrizzate dalla promessa del sacco risalivano la penisola. La Foresta Vergine che avanza, col Cardinale in testa, muovendo lentamente per dar agio alle rovine della Repubblica di crescere e alla fama di narrarle. Adoratori di Facciagialluta e facciatosta sognano ancora farina feste e forche, un re lazzarone, i guasti i pasti e i fasti del quarantaquattro, campano ancora per scommessa, nascosti al Padreterno nel gomitolo del vicolo: ultimi detriti dello sfasciume... Col capogiro distoglie lo sguardo dalla piccola Cina formicolante sulla spiaggia sotto i suoi occhi. Oltre l'ultima fila di cabine protesa nel mare come una barriera all'invadenza di quei bagnanti, in uno specchio d'acqua più tranquillo, la mole cadente e fastosa del Palazzo Medina domina la baia.

Lì il vocio della spiaggia arriverà attutito dalla vastità incombente del giorno, uguale al ronzio dell'insetto tra i gerani, a quello dell'aeroplano passato altissimo nel cielo lasciando una sottile scia di fumo. Dalla terrazza la signora De Luca lancerà uno sguardo casalingo al panorama come per assicurarsi che tutto è a posto, il Vesuvio là, viola-polveroso sulla cima, più giù il caldo caduto come una cortina di tulle confondendo i colori in una tinta unica grigiazzurra con leggere sbavature d'un rosa pastello, un gruppo di case o un paese, lontano, sulla linea della costa. — D'estate la domenica è un giorno impossibile, dirà, gridando tante volte la domenica...

Lo zio di Massimo, disteso sulla sdraio: Domenica scorsa hanno divorato tre missionari! — in terrazza, ad aspettare l'ora di pranzo. La signora De Luca non raccoglierà la battuta, non la capirà, i suoi sguardi continueranno a vagare, pieni di disapprovazione, sul mare domenicale folto di vele di barche di richiami, tutto in disordine, penserà, e si fermeranno sopra un punto oltre le cabine, oltre la folla dei bagnanti sulla spiaggia, oltre il casermone borbonico, dove biancheggia la palazzina del Circolo Nautico. "Di', l'hai fatta la zuppa inglese?". La voce dalla sdraio le impedirà di formulare il pensiero che ha fermato i suoi sguardi su quel punto, e il pensiero, acquattato lì, in un angolino del cervello, senza decidersi a venir fuori, accentuerà quel futile nervosismo, quella tesa distrazione, che poi ritrovi tante volte anche in Massimo. "Di', c'è o non c'è?" insisterà la voce dalla sdraio, e non ricevendo risposta inizierà il monologo: Oggi viene mammà, e tu lo sai che ci tiene al dolce, la domenica. Poi avete un invitato, ho il posto a tavola, non parlo di me che pure un ospite può considerarmi, tanto lo vedo che con me non fate complimenti. Ma insomma con tutta questa gente, non mi pare bello senza dolce... Finalmente il pensiero si farà largo nel cervello della signora De Luca e si manifesterà: È capace di restarsene tutto il giorno al Circolo, ma io dico, che ci fa tutto il giorno, senza farsi vedere, senza ricordarsi che ha una famiglia, senza avvertire, in certe occasioni della vita bisogna essere puntuali, se no dove andiamo a finire?" Andrà al telefono guidata da questo pensiero, farà il numero ed aspetterà col ricevitore all'orecchio che il cameriere del Circolo le chiami Nini, Massimo, il marito, qualcuno. Dalla terrazza arriverà fino a lei, insieme al lontano vocio della spiaggia, una canzone di protesta: No tu non mangi broccoli / carciofi o baccalà / Ti nutri di gardenie / di giacinti e di lillà... Se è possibile che un uomo di cinquantatré anni, dico cinquantatré — penserà la signora De Luca riferendosi al fratello che canticchia là fuori, e lascerà anche questo pensiero incompleto come tutti gli altri. Piantata lì, col ricevitore in mano, e riattaccherà indispettita.

"Lei ha sempre in testa un pensiero e un soprappensiero", sta dicendo Massimo, come se fosse la prima volta. Assumere l'aria un po' divertita richiesta dalla circostanza, dall'atmosfera un po' speciale di commedia che si trova la domenica a tavola coi De Luca, sapendo in anticipo tutto quello che si farà e si dirà, senza capire perché Massimo vi collabora. Certe volte è irritante. Per esempio come fai a prenderlo da parte e annunciargli: Massimo, vado a Milano, ormai è deciso.

Sta dicendo: "Metti che il pensiero è: devo andare alle cinque dalla sarta. E il soprappensiero: Niní avrà comprato le scarpe? — Arriva Niní: Sei andato dalla sarta a comprare le scarpe? gli fa, e Niní: Ci andrò appena mi verrà un po' di appetito. Continuano cosí per un pezzo, e lei non s'accorge...".

Qui si deve ridere.

"Be' che c'è da ridere? Forse sarò stata un po' distratta".

"Per lei le persone sono divise in due categorie, le persone carine, che sarebbero poi i signori. E i cafoni, che sono tutti gli altri, quelli che incontri per la strada, nei filobus o al Circolo. Esistono anche due categorie intermedie, a dir la verità, quella delle brave persone e quella delle persone impossibili. Le sue amiche, per esempio, sono carine, gli amici e i clienti di papà sono cafoni, le sue sarte sono brave persone, se ritardano la consegna sono cafone. I comunisti sono cafoni e volgari, i monarchici sono signori, De Gasperi sembra un impiegato ma si vede che è un signore, e così di seguito...".

Lo zio: "Io come sono classificato?".

"Volgare e impossibile".

Qui altra risata.

"Lo sapevo, lo sapevo. E tu sei uno scostumato, ma fuori discussione, perché lei i suoi figli non li classifica".

"Gaetano è una brava persona, ma puzza di comunismo, la nonna è impossibile ma è una vera signora".

"E perché sarei impossibile?".

La signora De Luca: "Tu lo stai pure a sentire?".

La nonna: "Sai piuttosto a che stavo pensando oggi? Al marchese Solino Belmonte. A Roma, quando tua nonna era una delle prime bellezze della capitale, ricevuta da tutta la nobiltà...".

"E dall'Aristocrazia Nera", suggerisce lo zio.

"Ricevuta da Papi e Cardinali che tu poverino non te li sogni nemmeno che cos'erano quei ricevimenti! Già che siete di un'altr'epoca voi, e tu non so da chi hai preso, povero figlio mio!".

"Ho preso dal ramo plebeo della famiglia?".

"Certo non hai preso da me, e neppure dalle tue sorelle... che stavo dicendo?".

"Del marchese Solino Belmonte", fa Massimo.

"Ah, sì, questo marchese allora faceva la corte a tua nonna. Era l'epoca, signor mio...".

E si rivolge a me. L'epoca, dirà, in cui a Villa Borghese il re Umberto passando in carrozzella fece fare dietro-front al cavallo per lanciarle una regale occhiata... Se le parlassi dei tumulti di Milano del '98? Tentazione irresistibile. I soldati del Re Buono che sparano sulla folla, Turati e Anna Kuliscioff arrestati, e insomma tutta l'altra versione.

"...questo Solino Belmonte era straricco, casa magnifica, principesca, servitori in livrea, piatti d'oro, arazzi, non vi dico! E una sera, sentendomi cantare Vissi d'Arte, Vissi d'Amore, perdette la testa il pover'uomo. Allora la nonna era una vera bellezza non la vecchia che vedete adesso, e aveva una voce, una voce...".

Previsto. Infatti canta: "Viii - ssiii, d'Aaa - rte, Viii - ssiii, d'Aaa - more!" molto convinta, per un intero minuto, da un immaginario palcoscenico, sconnessa voce di soprano, e sul finale il braccio che allontana applausi, fantasmi del passato, re, marchesi... Assuntina incantata, col timballo di maccheroni, seguita da Mississippì a coda ritta.

"Caccia quel gatto!" dice la signora De Luca: "Io odio i gatti".

Lo zio, nel silenzio che segue le prime convulse forchettate: "Mangiare per me è l'ultima cosa", e aspetta la battuta di risposta.

"Si vede, si vede".

"La domenica faccio un'eccezione, se permettete".

"Ma se ogni volta che t'incontro mi domandi: che cosa avete mangiato oggi?".

"Ha parlato l'intellettuale della famiglia"!

"Massimuccio, lascialo stare. Lui è un po' grossier, capisce solo il pallone".

"Scusa, nonna, grossier non ti pare una parola troppo fine applicata a zio Umberto"?

"Hai ragione, pure il nome è sprecato, un bel nome di re".

"E il marchese Solino di Belmonte"?

"Pigliami pure in giro, caro mio. Se facessi un viaggetto a Roma, rimbambito com'è, una buona rinfrescata alla memoria gli darei, qualcosa me la lascerebbe...".

Ora, l'arazzo.

"Basterebbe uno solo degli arazzi che quel fetente tiene nel salone, per cambiare la nostra vita da così a così"!

"Ma quello è vivo o morto"?

"Vivo, vivo, certo che è vivo! Pure i moribondi sono vivi. Ce ne andremmo a Parigi, anche lei è invitato, sì, perché deve essere un bravo giovane lei, modesto, non è vero"?

Sul modesto Massimo mi strizza l'occhio, divertito. Vergogna ed imbarazzo.

"... e lì, caro mio, nonostante i miei settantadue anni, settanta-due, le farei vedere delle verve"!

Massimo ride incoraggiante, in maglietta azzurra, nero di sole come tutti loro. Sorriso di risposta dal pallido amico all'amico abbronzato.

"Pa - a - rìgi, o - o cà - ra, noirí - vedre - mo..."!

Niní! Come al solito in ritardo, sulle ultime parole della nonna, a passo di valzer entrando, "lavitauní - ti - trasco - rre - remo", con un immaginario calice di champagne traboccante.

"Vieni qua, siediti vicino a me, tu sì che sei nipote di tua nonna!"

Schioccano baci, affioranti lacrime di commozione.

"Vorrei vincere un terno al lotto, non molto, qualche milioncino. Allora...".

"Domenica scorsa ci accordammo so-

pra una cifra dai cento ai duecento milioni".

"È lo stesso. Con qualche milioncino la gente acquista fiducia e ti fa credito, 'ste cose le dovresti sapere".

"Non ci avevo mai pensato", fa la signora De Luca, colpita.

Niní sí, dirà, nel suo piccolo ci ha pensato. Per esempio a Positano, l'anno scorso il primo giorno che va al bar della Buca chiede un whisky, costa cinquecento e al cameriere lascia mille, il resto di mancia, cosí per tutta l'estate whisky a credito.

"E poi li pago io", dice il signor De Luca.

"Ci tratti sempre come se fossimo animali domestici che girano per casa".

"Hai detto bene cara, siete affezionati, siete irresponsabili...".

"Sempre esagerato!"

Nel silenzio il bravo-bravo-bravo dello zio, apparentemente senza una ragione, ma dentro c'è l'ammicco, perfino quando t'incontra e ti dice buongiorno ci mette dentro l'ammicco, il sottinteso avvio alla scenetta. Anche stavolta: "Bravo-bravo-bravo... e lei sarebbe il professore di Niní?"

Sorridere. Rispondere di sí. Sorriso: "Sí".

"Bravo-bravo-bravo".

L'intenzione è misteriosamente raccolta, tutti a ridere. Occhi ridenti dal mondo di Massimo puntati attraverso la tavola sulla mia forse-goffa giacca, sul mio forse-sciocco sorriso, sulla mia forse-buffa cravatta: vergogna ed imbarazzo.

"Ottimo elemento Niní, studioso, preparato, serio, puntuale: glielo dice lo zio".

"Niní è troppo intelligente per studiare!" dice la nonna.

"Bravo-bravo-bravo...".

"E poi ricordati che tu sei sempre stato un ciuccio, una sola cosa sai: il pallone".

"Per lo meno una cosa la sapevo fare. Il pallone ho imparato a calciarlo con Sallustro nella Villa Comunale".

"Tutti sporchi come operai, cosí tornavano".

Sul paragone, sguardo d'intesa di Massimo, ma evitato.

Evitato, e invece i miei occhi fissi negli occhi dello zio — accettando l'impossibilità della mente razionale di uscire dal labirinto meridionale, e perciò sei costretto ad inventare le Sabbie Mobili la Foresta Vergine ed altri miti che aiutano a capire senza vincere — attento a seguire parallelamente al corso di questi pensieri, la descrizione di una partita avvenuta tanti anni fa, attento come sulla Fenomenologia di Hegel, e dissociato, evitando lo sguardo di Massimo, occhi negli occhi dello zio, vergogna ed imbarazzo, a sentire di passaggi ricordati come mosse strategiche di una battaglia napoleonica, nomi elencati come quelli dei guerrieri dell'Iliade, Cavanna, Buscaglia, Vincenzi, Innocenti, Colombari, Visentin, Ferraris Secondo, Vojack, Mihalic, il due a zero dell'Italia Portogallo, il tre a zero dell'Italia Svizzera, si parla del '31 e del '32, gli anni

d'oro, quando i napoletani andavano nella nazionale, e Sallustro sotto l'area di rigore era un pericolo, a parare le sue cannonate un portiere si poteva rovinare... Parlerà come nuotando sott'acqua nella foga senza riprender fiato finendo a polmoni sgonfi con uno sforzo di volontà che impegna inutilmente gola e corde vocali, gutturalmente calando la sua voce farfuglierà nomi e date in un gracidio, le ultime parole colte stremate al traguardo dal mio occhio attento e volenteroso sulle sue labbra convulse, poi solo la sua faccia stralunata davanti a me, che finalmente inala, e Niní con ironica premura: Vuoi un bicchiere d'acqua zio?

Oppure Massimo approfitterà del momento per domandargli chi segnò quel gol della partita...

"Chi segnò con l'Ambrosiana nel '34?"

"Meazza al dodicesimo del secondo tempo".

"E il terzo gol della partita Napoli Roma nel '38?"

"Lo vedi che non sai niente? Non c'è stato un terzo gol. Finì uno a zero per il Napoli".

"Scusa, in che anno è scoppiata la seconda guerra mondiale?"

"Nel trentanove o nel quaranta, mi pare. Cretino?"

"E la guerra di Spagna?"

"Uuuh! È un esame o un pranzo?"

"Lo sai o non lo sai?"

"Non me lo ricordo".

Lo zio si presterà a recitare di buon grado la sua parte, vera del resto. Cambieranno magari le domande di Massimo: Hiroshima, la rivolta degli operai a Berlino, il processo dei medici, la guerra che continua in Indocina... ad ogni domanda Massimo mi inviterà a ridere alle spalle dello zio, i suoi sguardi respinti con imbarazzo e vergogna, mentre la signora De Luca: Perché dobbiamo pensare a queste cose tristi? — e lo zio passerà al contrattacco: Tu fa' lo spiritoso, ma voi con tutta la vostra storia ci perdete al confronto, noi eravamo ragazzi vivi, uscivamo dal fuoco, alla tua età tuo zio era un leone, appena si incontravano due o tre di noi in una strada, come per miracolo spuntava una palla, e finivamo che era scuro, eccetera.

Poi Niní, a seconda dell'estro: Siamo l'unica famiglia napoletana il cui primogenito può far precedere il titolo di sir al proprio nome.

"Ma perché dici tante stupidaggini?" gli dirà la madre.

"Il titolo fu concesso da Sua Maestà Britannica, un De Luca aveva aiutato l'ammiraglio Nelson ad impiccare Caracciolo".

"Non dire queste cose nemmeno per scherzo, lo sai che sono amica dei Caracciolo".

Dirà che un antenato De Luca travestito da donna entrò nella fureria del comando di Garibaldi fermo al Volturno, e fece sparire la cassaforte coi soldi per la truppa, e che questa è l'origine della ricchezza del nonno.

"Te la dico io quale è stata l'origine, la-

vorava".

"Sí lo so, babbo, alle sette del mattino eccetera, e tu pure facesti un affare, eccetera".

Oppure cercheranno di stabilire quale dei parenti ha causato la fine della fortuna del nonno, e allora interminabili discussioni su crisi, crak in borsa, il brillante, sperperi, inflazioni, il casinò di Montecarlo, fallimenti, suicidi, protesti e cambiali, insomma una specie di Medio Evo economico della famiglia — e la nonna concluderà dicendo che i soldi non fanno il vero signore.

"Quanto mi secca quando ti sento fare questi discorsi da comunista!" sta dicendo la signora De Luca: "Lo fai apposta per me, è vero Niní? Che c'entra la nobiltà della madre, vorrei sapere?"

"Io volevo solo dire questo: La madre di Guidino Cacciapuoti è una Santafede di Putignano".

"E che c'entra?"

"Niente, il figlio di questa nobile, si trova in galera per furto con scasso".

"Che c'entra la nobiltà, vorrei sapere. La colpa semmai è del Circolo, lo dico sempre io, ma tuo padre figurati, è il primo lui a dare l'esempio...".

"Già, io sono un delinquente: gioco a ramino con la signora Cotogna e il signor Fricelli a un soldo al punto".

"Come sei scocciante con questa signora Cotogna e 'sto signor Fricelli! Chi li conosce? Insomma se non fosse andato al Circolo a giocare e a far debiti, ora Guidino non si troverebbe in galera".

"Ha fatto la guerra, tiene quarant'anni quasi, potrà pure andare al Circolo".

"Sai quanto ha speso il bambino in una sola sera allo Shaker?" dice Niní: "Ottocentomila. Per portarci, pardon!, Carla Boursier che con Livio De Martino andava gratis dovunque".

"Gratis... s'è fatta sposare, altro che gratis. Ha fatto un bel matrimonio, non è stata scema".

"Ottocentomila lire!" strilla Assuntina entrata col vassoio del fritto misto.

Dorate alici croccanti. Allungo di Niní, colpetto di Assuntina, secco e rapido sulla mano furtiva, l'alice ricade nel vassoio.

"Niní, che brutto vizio tieni! Aspetta di essere servito".

"L'abbiamo fatta venire apposta dalla Scozia per lo stile del servizio a tavola", Niní mi spiega per inciso, in confidenza. La signora De Luca lo guarda perplessa, senza capire la battuta, poi si accorge di Mississippi:

"Assuntina, di nuovo è entrato. Caccialo".

"Babbo, ti ricordi l'anno scorso quando Pippotto Alvini morí d'infarto al Circolo?"

"Figurati se non me lo ricordo, me lo debbo ricordare per forza, ce lo ricorderemo tutti, per parecchio tempo, non dubitare".

"Sempre malaugurio, come suo padre", sbuffa la signora De Luca a capotavola.

"Giocarono per due notti e due giorni di seguito. In una di quelle due notti il ra-

gazzo Cacciapuoti con una chiave falsa entrò in casa Alvini all'ora giusta, perché la cameriera era andata al paese, e Flora chissà dove stava quella sera. Cosí fece fuori tre milioni di gioielli. Ora al processo pure quella storia è venuta a galla, ma Flora si è comportata bene, ha ritirato la denuncia".

Bianco vino ghiacciato appanna il bicchiere di Massimo, anche gli occhi già appannati, poi di là sul letto, nella controra, incapace di una lucida conversazione, tra i fumi di contagiose esasperate malinconie. Milano, gli dirò, è deciso, in settimana parto — lontano da tutta questa perdita di tempo.

"Il bambino purtroppo ha fatto la stessa operazione, una volta a casa di Cocò Cutolo, e poi a casa di Marino Perrella. Insomma per non mandarlo in galera il padre deve sborsare, pare, più di diciotto milioni liquidi, non so se mi spiego, e cosí le proprietà della Santafede di Putignano, liquidate. Al processo c'è stato il defilé delle sue amiche interrogate dal giudice, e nessuna ha ammesso di aver avuto rapporti intimi con Guidino, tranne Flora Alvini, viva la faccia!"

"Che peccato, un ragazzo tanto perbene, così carino!"

"Perbenissimo, con duecento chiavi false, le hanno trovate nella Giulietta che s'era fatta prestare da Cocò. Anche un piede di porco hanno trovato".

"Un piede di porco?"

"Mamma!... È una specie di leva per scassinare porte e serrature!"

"E perché dovrei saperlo? Lo dici con un tono...".

"Hanno trovato un'agenda con tutti i numeri telefonici e i nomi delle ragazze che si portava a letto. Sotto quello di Dorothy Rispoli ci stava scritto che accetta solo in macchina, sotto quello di Donatella Percuoco che accetta solo se mentre stai sul fatto le parli del più e del meno".

"Come sarebbe, del più e del meno?"

"Bella giornata oggi, che film hai visto ieri, andiamo a Capri domani, conosci Tizio e Sempronio, così, del più e del meno. Invece Adriana Citomarino è disposta tutti i giorni, tranne il sabato, perché è molto religiosa e la domenica va a messa, allora le sembra sconveniente, il giorno prima...".

"Gesù, Gesù, Gesù...".

"Assuntina, si può sapere perché tu ti scandalizzi?"

"Che debbo fare? Debbo dire che brave ragazze?"

"No, no, ma si sa benissimo che tu pure, con Gennarino...".

"E già! Mi hai presa per una di quelle guagliottelle che conosci tu?"

"Per favore, Assuntina, sta' a posto tuo, va' a prendere un po' di vino, che è finito. E a te, Niní, quante volte ti debbo ripetere di lasciarla in pace? Non si può fare più nemmeno una conversazione a tavola, lei deve sempre intromettersi, quando mai s'è visto?"

"Pensa che ingenuo, però! Entra di nascosto nella casa del commendator Marzullo che già non lo può sopportare per la ragione che sapete. Quella sera

ORDE DI CICLISTI.
I CANI PUNTANO.
CACCIARE LE SEPPIE, CERCARE I RICCI.
SI VEDE DAL GOLFO.

SCOPONE, BOCCE, PALLA A MANO.
CAMBIO MARCIA.
STRADA E PISTA, ASFALTO E NEVE.

invece di restare al Circolo, al tavolo di baccarà, Marzullo se ne ritorna a casa un po' più presto del solito. Guidino dalla finestra dell'appartamento lo vede, e nella furia si dimentica delle scarpe».
«Le scarpe?»
«Se l'era tolte per non farsi sentire».
«Ma se non c'era nessuno in casa?»
«Mamma!... Da quelli di sotto, no? E poi si fa sempre, per precauzione, è sempre meglio fare tutto in silenzio. Ora vuoi vedere com'è furbo? Tu sai la mania che lui tiene per le scarpe, le comprava da Marino a venticinquemila lire il paio, quelle inglesi, una meraviglia, di cuoio bulgaro, rossicce, con la fibbia di lato. Be', lui scappando se le dimentica. Come se a Napoli tutti portassero le scarpe che vengono da Regent Street. Non ci voleva Sherlock Holmes per arrestarlo. Ora, se tutto finisce bene al processo, dice che se ne vuole andare in Venezuela».
La voce di Massimo, spenta da noia e vino: «Il Venezuela è passato di moda!»

Raffaele La Capria
Ferito a morte

Cap. VI

Che acqua quel giorno! Metteva allegria. Roccia biancastra stellata di ricci neri, spaccata da lunghi crepacci, ombrose tane e grossi massi tra zone di sabbia smagliante, e lì tra sabbia e scoglio, in lento moto a mulinello, le colonie dei saraghi. A volte due o tre si staccavano dal girotondo e si rincorrevano, saraghi zebrati, col muso piccolo sporgente a punta e il corpo piatto, e quelli di razza, con la testa a bisonte e un solo anello nero nella strozzatura della coda. Presto! Occhiali, tubo, fucile — il fucile nuovo, alla prima prova, appena arrivato da Genova — e il salto in quell'acqua, il colpo gelido, il tubo gorgogliante, il corpo giù tra miriadi di bollicine impazzite, le mani più grandi del normale attraverso il vetro degli occhiali strette sul fucile luminoso, e lo spazio attonito cresceva, m'inghiottiva... poi la spinta verso l'alto, come due mani delicate alla vita che ti riportano a galla, la pressione diminuita, e quel nuoto planante nel silenzio assoluto. Tutto questo era ancora nuovo. E ad ogni sommozzata la fuga precipitosa dei saraghi che correvano a rintanarsi negli spacchi della roccia, quella luce ferma, pomeridiana, dove il contorno di uno spigolo di roccia si stagliava netto come filo arrotato di lama. Davanti al vetro degli occhiali ondeggiava lionato il ciuffo dei capelli, ogni tanto dovevo scostarli, come una tendina... Tre cefali, tre piccoli siluri plumbei sempre alla stessa distanza davanti a me, fuori tiro ma vicini. Nuotavo sopra un lastrone di roccia in pendio che finiva in una valletta sabbiosa e uno dei cefali si fermò a brucare sopra un masso a forma di cono. Distaccato dagli altri sentì la cosa che ero io arrivargli goffa addosso e sfrecciò via un attimo prima che il colpo partisse, disorientato con frenetici zig-zag cercando i compagni, e poi sicuro nella loro rotta. In quel momento, era grossa mannaggia, e mi trovai col fucile scarico, la spigola passò. Pareva un aeroplano da bombardamento, una fortezza volante quando d'improvviso la vedevi apparire nel cielo di Napoli. Ricaricato in furia il fucile, sistemato lo spago, mi voltai ed era troppo lontana, scomparsa. La valletta sabbiosa incassata come il letto di un fiume tra due sponde ripide di roccia finiva in imbuto in un crepaccio, e gusci di ostrica biancheggiavano sulla sabbia, come ossa di animali davanti alla tana. Piccoli saraghi di vetro si mossero. Lenti come ventagli, indugiarono ancora prima di entrare nel buio dello spacco. Nuotai verso il fondo, la pancia strisciante sulla sabbia, seguendo il canalone fino all'apertura: larga abbastanza. Ci infilai il braccio armato di fulice e tutta la testa, mentre con la mano libera mi trattenevo a uno sperone dello scoglio. Li vidi subito, due saraghi, grandi, luminosi dentro la tana, fermi e tranquilli nel buio. Il più grosso profilato, sotto tiro. Al

posto del sarago il bagliore di un piatto d'argento, l'asta scossa da un tremito, la sabbia del fondo smossa. Colpito. Risalii, l'asta se ne venne via senza intoppi: colpito di striscio, peccato. Ricaricai, poi ci fu un rimescolio sul fondo, tra i massi della scogliera poco distante si alzò una nebbiolina d'acqua gassata che li avvolse per un momento, e da quella nebbia luminosa emerse un'ombra grigia, solitaria, che veniva come un ordigno metallico verso di me. La spigola. Pareva ancora più grossa, non mi era sembrata così grossa prima, mammamia! L'acqua rimasta nell'ansa del tubo grattava, respiravo appena e nuotavo piano con delicatezza per portarmi sulla sua traiettoria senza spaventarla. Indifferente e calma, ma forse non ce l'avrei fatta a tagliarle la strada, veniva troppo veloce. Allora cambiai tattica, espulsi l'acqua rimasta nel tubo e nuotai forte. Come previsto il rumore la spaventò, dirottandola verso la scogliera. Difficilmente fanno dietro-front. Unico pericolo, che superasse il punto di passaggio obbligato tra il mio fucile e gli scogli, prima che arrivassi alla distanza di tiro. Adesso la vedevo bene, in tutti i particolari: la grinta della bocca bordata di bianco carnoso con gli angoli piegati in giù, l'occhio fisso, il rilievo delle squame, la zigrinatura orofumo lungo il corpo già vibrante di allarme. E dietro vedevo, immensa, la mole dei macigni della scogliera. L'attimo decisivo — a picco puntandola dritto sulla parte più grossa dove il corpo s'allarga — e sentii che l'asta entrava in quel corpo. Trafitta si rovesciò di fianco, splendida tutta d'argento, con la pinna irta sul dorso, la bocca aperta nello spasimo, il corpo a mezzaluna e come paralizzato. Il peso dell'asta la trascinava così, a fondo, sopra un liscio scoglio bianco, e il sangue saliva dalla ferita come un filo di fumo rosato nell'acqua. Poi l'asta cominciò a tintinnare sullo scoglio, lo spago uno strappo, teso nelle mie mani, la spigola con l'asta infilata nel corpo tentò, si dibatté, frenetica. Ma l'aletta dell'arpione s'era bene aperta, non aveva più scampo. Risalii a galla, respirai due o tre volte a pieni polmoni, le orecchie mi ronzavano, e arrivò quel richiamo, la voce infantile di Ninì: Maaa...ssimo! Maaa...ssimo! Il fucile stretto tra le gambe, ritirai lo spago, afferrai l'asta, con l'altra mano la viscida argentea carne tremante che tentava ancora di sfuggire alla mia presa, pollice ed indice a tenaglia nella rossa apertura delle branchie, e così, viva, la tenni. In quel momento di nuovo la voce di Ninì... Come ora: "Maaa...ssimo! Maaa...ssimo!"

Raffaele La Capria, "Ferito a morte", Bompiani, Milano 1975.

Tommaso Landolfi
Mano rubata

"Mi sembra", disse, "che sia venuta l'ora del poker".
"Che poker?" chiese qualcuno straccamente.
"Propongo", riprese lui, "che si giochi una specie d'eliminatoria, mano per mano, di modo che alla fine rimanga un solo vincitore".
"E poi?"
"Il vincitore resterà vestito, o almeno avrà il diritto di farlo, e tutti gli altri dovranno spogliarsi, denudarsi completamente: che ne dite?"
"Uhm, per proposta è un po' vecchiotta, nevvero?" — rispose un marchese scultore e figlio di ex-ministro; mentre le donne gridavano in cantino per semplice onor di firma.
"Lo so, ma potrebbe lo stesso esser divertente".
"Sì?"
"Si può sempre provare".
"E proviamo", concluse l'altro con indifferenza. Ma nessuno si muoveva o si mostrava particolarmente sollecito di passare ai fatti; il che servì soltanto a rinfocolare Marcello.
"E allora?" insistette egli, "proprio non vi va?" Poi, facendosi accanto a Gisa e guardandola ormai nel bianco degli occhi, soggiunse: "Lei cosa ne dice?"
La fanciulla, si capisce, aveva inteso alla prima che la proposta di Marcello la concerneva personalmente, sebbene non potesse indovinare la furiosa esclusività dei suoi desideri; ma era fin lì rimasta senza batter ciglio. Ora, interrogata direttamente, si turbò forse, se non che il suo abituale pallore le fece scudo; ad ogni modo rese al giovane una lunga occhiata e non rispose subito. A Marcello d'altra parte (che le stava davanti quasi come nudo) durante questa corta pausa apparve d'un tratto nella sua vera luce la pericolosa avventura in cui s'era tanto storditamente lanciato. Difatto il gioco proposto comportava l'eventualità per lui appunto di doversi denudare innanzi a lei vestita; prospettiva che lo fece fremere e inorridire.
"Non vedo perché si rivolga proprio a me", rispose ella da ultimo, seguitando a fissarlo.
"A Lei come a un altro".
"Ebbene, non sarò io a guastarvi la festa", replicò con una certa aria di sfida.
"Vedete? lei accetta. Qua un mazzo di carte: chi comincia?" si mise a gridare Marcello con voce falsa. In realtà si augurava ormai che sopravvenisse qualche impedimento e che tutto andasse a monte.
La padrona di casa invece, seppure svogliatamente, fornì il mazzo di carte; si passò a precisare le modalità del gioco, a discutere il sistema d'eliminazione eccetera. E intanto l'imbarazzo o meglio l'angoscia di Marcello aumentava: da una parte, è vero, raggiava l'agognata nudità della fanciulla quale premio d'un trionfo negli imminenti ludi, ma dall'altra egli si rappresentava tanto al vivo se stesso sconfitto e nudo e tre-

mante di vergogna davanti a lei e a tutti, che non era dubbio di dove pendesse la bilancia. Nondimeno che fare? ritrarsi, dopo essersi dato dattorno in quel modo, e con ciò confessare pubblicamente la propria timidezza, la propria viltà, confessarla oh Dio alla fanciulla, la quale oltre tutto aveva saputo prendere fermamente il suo partito? La sola cosa che non bisognava fare: e che allora? La sua fantasia, la sua volontà, erano come prese da balbettamento, ma annaspavano pure, e annaspando lo guidarono a una via d'uscita (sebbene anch'essa perigliosa): occorreva lasciare ai perdenti un'alternativa. I perdenti dovevano poter scegliere tra il denudarsi e alcunché d'altro; così, se tra loro fosse venuto a trovarsi lui stesso... Stava per proporre la felice variante, allorché il solito marchese disse bisciolando:
"Guardate però che il giochino come ci disponiamo a farlo non appare, nevvero, per nulla promettente. È faccenda, come dire, troppo letterale: uno vince, gli altri si spogliano, un bel momento poi si rivestiranno, e tanti saluti. Che diamine, val davvero la pena di durare tanta fatica per ottenere un risultato così banale? No: io proporrei invece, che so, di offrire ai perdenti un'alternativa. Che dovrebbe essere dosata appuntino eccetera, e ci fornirebbe almeno indicazioni sul grado d'orgoglio di ciascuno".
"Come sarebbe?" chiese una voce femminile.
"Lascia stare, carina", rispose uno dei pittori: "un po' difficile per te. Ma beh, quanto all'idea del nobile collega, son d'accordo. Stabiliamo dunque questa alternativa".
"Ma che", disse un altro, "il vincitore la immaginerà a suo piacere".
"No, no!" intervenne Marcello vivacemente. "Che dite: si deve stabilire subito, ché ciascuno sappia fin d'ora a cosa va incontro".
Il giovane invero, che in un primo momento era stato lieto di quell'aiuto insperato e quasi divinatorio, vedeva ora, col consueto ritardo, quanto malfida fosse difatto la situazione. L'alternativa, cioè, non poteva essere inaccettabile (ché allora avrebbe danneggiato lui stesso), ma neppure accettabile (ché perdendo, Gisa di certo vi si sarebbe appigliata). E insomma, di nuovo egli era infra due e non sapeva che pensare.
"E va bene", gli rispondeva nel frattempo uno, "dichiariamola sicché, codesta alternativa. Così? quale deve essere?" Discussero varie proposte all'acqua di rose, senza mettersi d'accordo. Finalmente un altro disse:
"Oh diavolo: sta' a sentire, di' tu, Marcello, che hai inventato tutto; di' quello che ti pare e noi accetteremo la tua proposta senza più discutere".
"Volete che sia io a stabilire l'alternativa?"
"Sì", risposero in parecchi.
Era il momento di decidere; decidere in una tra viltà e baldanza, tra rinuncia e

volontà, certezza di conquista, tra meschinità da limaccia e furente passione. Vinse stavolta la passione. V'era bensì un'ulteriore difficoltà, e Marcello se ne rese conto: proporre qualcosa di veramente inaccettabile, di estremo o lesivo, non avrebbe significato far cadere forse la proposta nel vuoto? Nessuno addirittura l'avrebbe presa sul serio. Ma il giovane era ormai lanciato e (come spesso ai timidi avviene) doveva fatalmente trapassare il segno.
S'era fatto silenzio. In questo silenzio Marcello disse dunque:
"Ebbene, l'alternativa sia... la morte".
"Come?"
"Che, che?"
"La morte!"
"Nientemeno!"
"Sì", riprese egli, "la morte o diciamo il suicidio: chi non volesse spogliarsi sarà libero in cambio di suicidarsi, subito e in nostra presenza".
"Interessante!" disse il principe del sangue con un mugolio da falso intenditore di quadri.
"Per nulla", ribatté il marchese scultore. "L'alternativa non mi sembra bene scelta né in alcun modo feconda; anzi la direi, nevvero, propriamente inutile, anzi ancora non è affatto un'alternativa: chi mai potrà prenderla in considerazione, scegliere di uccidersi piuttosto che spogliarsi?"
"Non si sa mai!" rispose Marcello esasperato e vagamente ansioso.
"Ma è uno scherzo".
"E sia. A buon conto, mi avevate fatto arbitro e promesso di non discutere, se non erro. Sicché accettate o non accettate? È la sola cosa che dovete dirmi".
"Accettiamo sicuro", disse dopo un momento la padrona di casa.
"Sì sì accettiamo, se è per questo", confermarono alcuni.
"E lei che dice, le sta bene il patto?" chiese Marcello a Gisa.
"Ma guarda", rise lei senza alcuna apparente commozione, "ma guarda che ha preso ogni volta a interrogarmi in particolare; non sapevo che la mia opinione fosse tanto importante. Ma sì, mi sta tutto bene: con quale diritto se ne dubita?"
"Allora siamo d'accordo su ogni cosa, e cominciamo", soggiunse gravemente Marcello.
Quella pronta e generale accettazione era facilmente spiegabile: ciascuno per suo conto aveva pensato che in ultima analisi dall'alternativa si poteva sempre prescindere. Se Marcello voleva scherzare, lo facesse a sua posta; se lo scherzo era poco divertente, pazienza; e finalmente si trattava senza più di spogliarsi in caso di perdita, il che a loro, nulla costava.
Eppure in mezzo a loro erano, ignorati, due ai quali invece molto costava il mostrarsi ignudi, qualunque e quantunque impellenti fossero di ciò i motivi. Tra questi due doveva accendersi, invisibile e disperata, la mischia.
L'eliminatoria non risultò punto agevole; le mani di poker si susseguivano con lentezza, lasciando volta a volta

inoperosa la maggior parte della compagnia. Si faceva tardi; l'alcool rinvispiva occasionalmente alcuni, ma infruscava un tantino le menti dei più. Marcello, non per caso, si trovò accanto a Gisa e, lui stesso stupito al suono della propria voce, le disse d'un tratto:
"Noi due insieme solleveremmo il mondo".
"Lo so", fu la sorprendente e semplice risposta.
Ma tutti erano più o meno annoiati. Da ultimo toccò a Marcello prender le carte; per vero dire egli e da parte sua la fanciulla avevano già precedentemente perduto una mano ciascuno, senonché, in base alle cavillose regole stabilite da un letterato specialista di questi giochini, avevano facoltà d'appello o di rientrata. C'era un pittore che reggeva al comando da tre o quattro mani: contro di lui fu chiamato in ultima istanza a misurarsi Marcello, con altri due.
Occorreva vincere fino alla fine; ed occorreva intanto, è ovvio, vincere questa mano. L'angoscia del giovane, un istante sopita, gli si risollevò dentro convulsamente.
Le carte erano distribuite coperte, e ciascun giocatore le voltava da sé; poi si procedeva all'eventuale scarto; infine si leggevano i risultati ottenuti e si proclamava il vincitore della mano. Durante la distribuzione, egli tese la sua violenza alla sorte; quindi, invece di seguire l'esempio degli altri, che andavano peritosamente rialzando gli angoli delle proprie carte e sbirciandole col capo quasi coricato sul tavolo, scoprì d'un tratto le sue. E rimase abbagliato: cinque cuori, benché non tutti contigui, gli si allineavano davanti. Colore. Nondimeno la sua gioia fu subito amareggiata dalla vista degli altrui giochi, tra i quali erano presenti ben due tris, che minacciavano altrettanti poker (il quarto gioco non poteva riuscire che a un full). Marcello sudava freddo; ma quelli dei tris cambiarono le carte, e rimasero tali.
Aveva vinto. Ma nelle prossime mani? Le prove da superare erano ancora parecchie... Tuttavia un colore servito era pure una cosa; un segno; forse la sorte aveva inteso dichiararsi. Calma, calma: presto per cantar vittoria; lasciarsi prendere da un senso di sicurezza, d'euforia, poteva essere pericoloso (e perché mai pericoloso? forse che le carte cambiano a seconda dei nostri sentimenti o che possono magari mutar faccia a dispetto? Certo che cambiano: a seconda dei sentimenti e anche delle persone)... Entrarono i nuovi giocatori. E Marcello rivinse: facilmente, "a bischero sciolto" come dice la gente del "traffico", della nobile arte. Rivinse; poi rivinse ancora colla squadra seguente; e ancora e ancora. E non poté più difendersi dal senso di sicurezza, d'euforia eccetera: aveva la fortuna in pugno.
E così venne l'ultima mano, la decisiva tra tutte; sarebbe bastato perderla perché tutti i precedenti sforzi (quali egli li considerava, e non benignità della sor-

te) tornassero in nulla. In questa ultima mano doveva giocare, tra gli altri, contro la sua diretta antagonista; lo aveva quasi dimenticato; se ne avvide all'improvviso, se la vide innanzi, e tutta la sua spocchia sparve come nebbia. Qui, qui era il vero cimento, qui doveva provarsi la solidità della sua fortuna. Furono di nuovo distribuite le carte. Di nuovo troppo commosso per indugiare, egli le voltò d'un tratto: due dieci, i magri ganci di due sette, una quinta carta manifestamente inutile (una dama di cuori, però!) Come, possibile? possibile che la sorte lo tradisse in questo supremo momento? Guardò le carte degli altri: due degli avversari erano superiori a lui in partenza, sebbene non vi fossero giochi chiusi, il che del resto non significava un bel niente. Cerchiamo soltanto di non perdere la testa. Dunque: due doppie coppie superiori alla mia; ma il pericolo non è probabilmente da quella parte, chiudere un full è molto più difficile di quanto non si creda; il pericolo è piuttosto, e per l'appunto, in quella sua scala aperta dai due lati; è così facile invece che entri, una scala aperta dai due lati. Vedi là, è una scala spogliata, misera, freddolosa, o meglio è solo un progetto; ma queste meschine scalucce, se chiuse, battono per perfino un fulgente tris d'assi (e ciò francamente è ingiusto)... Provò l'impulso di scartare tre carte, tenendosi la coppia di dieci; così, se anche avesse fatto solo tris, e se nessuno degli altri avesse fatto full... Se, se: è follia. Nondimeno qualunque full eventualmente chiuso dagli altri sarebbe stato superiore a quello eventualmente chiuso da lui stesso... Oh, che follia davvero ragionare in questi termini, cedere allo smarrimento.
Lo scarto era cominciato. Le due doppie restarono tali; la sua scala al contrario, come previsto, risultò chiusa. Chiusa per sotto, con un miserabile sette; ma quel sette passato di là rendeva ancor più improbabile il suo proprio full... A questo punto il gioco era divenuto una singolar tenzone: si trattava di battere quella scala o di non batterla; si trattava, ora veramente, o di denudarsi davanti a lei vestita o di restar vestiti davanti a lei nuda.
Anche Marcello (che s'era poi deciso a scartare sennatamente) ebbe la sua carta; e non aveva il coraggio di voltarla, la viltà era più forte dell'ansia; chiese il permesso di stillarla. Raccolse dunque le quattro carte già scoperte, i due dieci e i due sette, in mucchietto serrato e le ribaltò; vi pose sopra, sempre coperta, la carta sconosciuta, la carta del destino; quindi rovesciò l'intero mazzetto e lo afferrò saldamente. Per quell'ultima e risolutiva mano tutti s'erano avvicinati al tavolo. Lei lì non aveva neppur levato gli occhi; impassibile, pareva unicamente occupata nell'osservare gli annaspamenti del giovane:
"Fa' pure con comodo, non c'è fretta", disse qualcuno con una certa ironia. Marcello spiegò in fretta, a ventaglio, le

prime quattro carte; e, con una quasi impercettibile trepidazione del polso, provocandone coll'indice lo scorrimento, si accinse a scoprire il segno della quinta. Tuttavia la manovra procedeva con una lentezza per lui medesimo esasperante; anziché fare i movimenti necessari, egli, si sarebbe detto, li evitava con ogni cura, pari a chi mimi una marcia senza avanzare. Oppure la carta era di quelle "profonde"; certo l'angolino guatato restava bianco, né il segno s'annunciava in alcun modo, con uno di quei puntini o accenni di linee o spigoli o rotondità che il giocatore sa riconoscere.

"Beh, coraggio: son le quattro", disse un altro.

Tommaso Landolfi, "Tre racconti", Vallecchi, Firenze.

Giorgio Manganelli
La volta degli angeli

La facciata di Santa Maria Novella mi affascina non per la grazia, la sottigliezza, l'estro delle sue decorazioni; ma piuttosto per il fatto che la grazia è troppo affollata, la sottigliezza smentita dal palese piacere, il voluttuoso godere del movimento delle linee, e l'estro insidiato da una innocente imprudenza. La facciata di Santa Maria Novella non affascina perché in qualche modo perfetta, ma perché è palesemente, squisitamente sbagliata, si consente un eccesso che a Firenze è del tutto assente, eccetto in qualche "luogo" barocco, dove opera una rottura decisamente colta. Ma questa facciata non è colta; è furba. Guardate quale ilare irrequietezza comunichino quelle volte in basso, interrotte dal subito moto verticale delle due porte, e dal grande frastuono del potere centrale; non è possibile non godere, da complici, di quella ulteriore alleanza di rettangoli e semiarchi, della ordinata e burlesca fila di quadrati sopra la prima trabeazione, e delle grandi e fittamente lavorate volute che s'arricciolano al di sopra, puntando verso un timpano vagamente prelatizio.

Su questa saletta buona di una casa benestante e felicemente plebea, vennero eseguiti ulteriori giochi; giacché puro gioco fu l'aggiunta nella parte inferiore di due cinquecenteschi strumenti astronomici, una sfera armillare — indicava plasticamente i moti dei pianeti — e un gnomone — l'asta che manovra l'ombra sulle meridiane; un gioco saputo, che sembra indicare la parentela cosmica di questa casuale delizia, questo disegno squisito e apparentemente distratto. Ma certo la suprema astuzia, il grande gioco di questa facciata lo si deve all'intervento di Leon Battista Alberti, che riuscì a inserire la sua magra ma docile matematica nel contesto di questo stupefacente gioco, in una superficie in cui non c'è spazio che non si muova e danzi. Due semicolonne, due pilastri, un arco, una lunetta; nei quattro capitelli tutta la pazienza e la dottrina di una citazione fatta per pura grazia, nulla di intimidatorio; ma quel luogo nel luogo, il portale dell'Alberti, è la suprema rivelazione che tutto ciò che leggiamo come gioco e sovrabbondanza di letizia immaginale, e la rapida e leggera sapienza, l'insondabile saggezza felice dell'angelico popolo dell'aria, e dei loro complici terrestri giacché ciò che si chiama "arte" è anche complicità. Se giustapponete l'immagine di questa facciata alla facciata di San Miniato al Monte — la chiesa fuggita oltre la periferia di Firenze per sottrarsi alle sevizie del Battistero — saprete subito dove si collochi, nella grande "rissa geometrica" di Firenze, la facciata felice di Santa Maria Novella. Non lontano da Santa Maria Novella si innalza un sistema di luoghi che è tra i più intensi e singolari di Firenze: San Lorenzo. San Lorenzo — una delle chiese cui venne impedito di trovar pace in una facciata — è un luogo che in sé raccoglie luoghi violentemente conflittuali, è un campo di battaglia mentale. Se l'interno è una delizia di aria e pietra, come faceva il Brunelleschi, i punti, decisivi sono altri: la Sagrestia Vecchia, del Brunelleschi, la Cappella dei Principi, la Sagrestia Nuova di Michelangiolo. San Lorenzo è una sorta di principesco e cortigiano cimitero dei Medici, dal quattrocentesco Cosimo, "padre della patria", il banchiere più ricco d'Europa, al morbido e falotico Gian Gastone, Granduca e "postremus", ultimo, della dinastia in cui s'era tramutata la facoltosa e ambiziosa famiglia, e che aveva lasciato il duro e bellicoso Palazzo Medici per il fascinoso e sottile adescamento di Palazzo Pitti. Tuttavia San Lorenzo non è un mausoleo.

La Sagrestia Vecchia è quel che possiamo attenderci dal Brunelleschi, l'uomo che pensò Santo Spirito e la Cappella dei Pazzi; è un uomo matematico, ma la sua matematica abita l'aria, i numeri sono angeli e, miracolosamente, respirano. Le pareti non hanno peso, la cupola irresistibilmente chiama verso l'alto. Un lieve senso di freddo e di castità, una impossibile miscela di astrazione e di grazia regge e tiene assieme questo "luogo" minuto ed esatto, che ha la terribilità della discrezione assoluta.

All'esterno di San Lorenzo, si innalza l'edificio che accoglie la cripta dei Medici — quelle delicatamente tragiche tombe dei principini morti nella cuna —, la Cappella dei Principi, la Sagrestia Nuova. La Cappella è, dicono, la massima struttura in pietre dure che si dia al mondo; e qui stanno giganteschi sarcofagi, statue, stemmi, motti, il grandioso ma inconcluso mausoleo dei Medici. Questo mito del grande mausoleo aveva turbato a lungo le fantasie dei granduchi; e Francesco I, uomo stravagante e sottile, aveva dato mano a raccogliere le pietre; e Ferdinando I, fratello e successore del precedente, aveva posto mano all'opera, sui disegni di un altro Medici, Don Giovanni. Dunque, questa Cappella è una sorta di idea che i Medici proponevano di sé, in quanto popolo di sovrani morti. Qui dentro vi è qualcosa che nel disegno mentale di Firenze è raro: il lusso. I Medici, che si sapevano dei risaliti, borghesi faticosamente cooptati nella nobiltà diastica europea, avevano una idea ornata, fastosa, esibizionistica della propria eternità. Questo fasto non celebra le glorie di una famiglia tra le più singolari d'Europa, piuttosto ne adorna la scomparsa, queste pietre splendenti sono pietre cortigiane che pronunciano una sovraccarica orazione d'addio, un'orazione non finita, giacché anche le pietre cortigiane, ad un certo momento vennero accolte nella cerimonia della morte. Questa Cappella non adorna i Medici morti, ma la morte, la fine, la polvere taciturna che furono i Medici di Firenze. Accanto alla Cappella, passando per un breve corridoio adorno di due misteriose statue mostruose, enigmatiche ma del tutto pertinenti, si apre la Sagrestia Nuova di Michelangelo. È del tutto evidente che questa Sagrestia è da sempre in guerra con l'altra, per quel che è possibile far guerra ad un disegno, elusivo e fuggiasco, del Brunelleschi. I bianchi e i neri dei muri tolgono ogni illusione; questi muri non aspirano alla condizione dell'aria. Le poderose statue, pietra di carne, del Giorno e della Notte, del Crepuscolo e dell'Aurora, e le due immagini principesche, stanno a presidio di una immobile catastrofe, una uccisione minata nella pietra. Se guardate la cupola, vedete subito dove sta il segreto punto matematico della sfida. La cupola a cassettoni è esattamente l'opposto della cupola del Brunelleschi; non abbraccia e adesca l'aria, la rifiuta, forse la cattura e trasforma in sasso, in questo luogo in cui tutte le metamorfosi sono in direzione della sconfitta. Michelangelo costruisce, colloca, definisce, e la sua potenza sta in questa coabitazione di tirannia e di sconfitta; questo teologo della pietra è un inventore di tombe, di allegorie della disfatta, una sconfitta immobile, dalla quale è ormai assente il fragore della battaglia. Nella rissa geometrica il mito del Battistero non poteva andare oltre questa argomentata catastrofe, cui, a distanza di pochi metri, si contrappone la mite, aerea diserzione dell'altra geometria, quella della Sagrestia Vecchia. Firenze è una città letteralmente sacra, tutta racchiusa nella cerchia del mito cristiano; e non dubito che di questa città impossibile si potrebbe dare una lettura strettamente teologica; e forse Firenze stessa lo sapeva, se in un codice quattrocentesco della Città di Dio di Sant'Agostino, una miniatura dà i connotati di questa città: ed è Firenze. Questa sacralità, questo aroma di eterno, di conclusivo stinge anche sugli edifici che diciamo civili. E vorrei chiudere questo catalogo di luoghi arbitrariamente prediletti, con poche righe su un luogo che amo: Palazzo Rucellai, dell'Alberti. L'Alberti parte da un'idea globale dell'edificio che potrebbe concludere in un trionfo della matematica minatoria; ma egli sfugge, con la sua incredibile delicatezza di gesti, costruendo una facciata infinitamente e minutamente mossa, stabile ed irrequieta, inventando una pietra che sembra sensibile al vento, che reca in sé una continua vocazione metamorfica, un veloce gioco di citazioni nei tre ordini architettonici, ma una citazione collocata in un contesto anomalo, come già era accaduto nella facciata di Santa Maria Novella. Lo stemma della famiglia Rucellai, qui collocato nella seconda trabeazione, appariva anche sulla facciata della chiesa: un alacre, araldico disegno di vele.

Giorgio Manganelli, "La volta degli angeli"

Giorgio Manganelli
"Scoprire" in piazza

L'anno scorso ho scoperto la Finlandia; ho cominciato quest'anno scoprendo Firenze. Dopo tutto, è una questione di ordine alfabetico. Tutto ciò ben s'addice alla mia nevrosi, che unisce ambizioni enciclopediche e manie rigorosamente metodiche. Prima della Giamaica dovrebbe venire la Francia. Non voglio negare che pare più naturale usare il verbo "scoprire" per la Finlandia, periferica dimora di betulle e di aurore boreali, che non per Firenze. Firenze non è, come Helsinki, al termine del più lungo volo non-stop del continente europeo; è a tre ore scarse da Roma, dove vivo, e poco più da Milano. Ogni anno passo più d'una volta per la stazione di Firenze. Tuttavia ho dovuto attendere un'età provetta e qualcosa di simile ad una tardiva passione per incontrare Firenze. Quando, nel settembre dello scorso anno, mi recai a Firenze per rendere onore a Pinocchio, erano anni che non vi mettevo piede. Certamente, non fosse stato per amore di Pinocchio, questo infantile psicopompo, io avrei risposto di no. Ma per amore di Pinocchio ho sfidato le mie ansie, la mia codardia, e il pezzo di legno da catasta mi ha dato in cambio Firenze; ma come sempre, Pinocchio non sa fare i conti; la sua matematica è fiabesca.

Mi si può chiedere, comunque io mi chiedo perché abbia per tanti anni tenuto a bada Firenze; perché sia stato necessario Pinocchio per farmi sospettare che una delle più singolari esperienze della mia vita stava a una manciata di minuti in treno da casa mia. Oh, io lo so, lo so benissimo. So perché conosco Lucca, Pistoia, Modena e Ascoli Piceno meglio di Firenze. Prima di parlare di Firenze, tenterò di spiegare questa apparente anomalia .

Per anni, ho creduto ciecamente alla interpretazione ufficiale di Firenze. Firenze è una città bella, bellissima, meravigliosa; è un capolavoro, una cooperativa di capolavori, un museo abitato, l'ottava meraviglia, una città esclamativa, una città da urlare, da svenire, un riassunto di storia dell'arte. Firenze è una città eminentemente estetica. È strano come capiti di prendere alla lettera le sciocchezze della più trita propaganda turistica. Come abbia faticato a capire che una città come Firenze "non poteva" essere giudicabile come "bella" e nemmeno come un "capolavoro": perché queste erano le due parole proibitive, in queste si riassumeva il divieto di scoprire Firenze.

Esaminiamo i due termini. In primo luogo, io non credo che esistano città che si possano definire "belle". Qualunque cosa sia, una città non si lascia giudicare con un termine a mala pena tollerabile per un sonetto o un quartetto. Se una città è "bella", ci deve essere del marcio. Io non ci vado. Una città è un reticolo di luoghi, percorsi, soste, angoli, include edifici ed assenze di edifici; include tutte le possibili città che sorgono davanti ai nostri occhi, a seconda dell'itinerario che percorriamo. Ho visto Calcutta; Calcutta non è "bella", nel senso che una definizione estetica diventa fatua davanti ad uno dei luoghi chiave per l'interpretazione del pianeta. Calcutta è un luogo totale nel quale l'essenza mitica della città si cela e si svela; la città si propone come luogo simbolico, magico, come pagina da interpretare, come tessuto di significati, di allusioni, di fantasie; una città è un luogo occulto, nella quale un muro logorato dalla muffa, un edificio decrepito, una sterminata piazza non pavimentata, trafitta da pozzanghere e ciuffi di dura erba, propongono una storia segreta, una favola in cui l'orrore e lo splendore ostinatamente coabitano. Percorrete i quartieri più fitti di una città orientale. Non ditemi che sono "tipici". Quegli agglomerati di luoghi evidentemente precari sono proposizioni, immagini significanti, sono soprattutto ipotesi sul mondo, microcosmi. Nessuno oserebbe definirli "belli"; non intendo dire che sono "brutti", che è lo stesso discorso; direi che guardarli come luoghi di sosta estetica, parcheggi della nostra anima di gusto colto e raffinato, significa non guardare nulla. E qui si tocca con mano qualcosa che accade spesso da sospettare: vale a dire, che la così detta estetica sia una astuzia laica per non venire a contatto con la materia mitica e violenta, il luogo dionisiaco, che abita un oggetto. Quest'ultima proposizione è deliberatamente ambigua: la parola "oggetto" può essere tanto complemento che soggetto, come le parole "luogo dionisiaco". Torniamo a Firenze. Se l'aggettivo "bella" per Firenze è pertinente, può voler dire che Firenze è una città totalmente identificabile con la propria vocazione estetica, un luogo che si consuma nella propria "bellezza", oppure può voler dire che l'interpretazione estetica è stata imposta su di un luogo estremamente significante, affinché quel luogo stesse fermo, non inquietasse, non fosse materia d'altro che di colto svagamento, fosse, come s'è detto, un luogo esclamativo; insomma, Firenze "bella" è una città esorcizzata; non fa male, è solo una fonte inesauribile di letizia intellettuale, non conosce demoni, non significa nulla, non allude, non è una allegoria del mondo. O Firenze è a questo modo, o qualcuno ha cercato di dissanguare Firenze, di persuadere il mondo che Firenze è come Calcutta.

Se Firenze è un luogo eminentemente o esclusivamente estetico, ne deriva un'altra conseguenza: che noi siamo invitati a contemplarla come un maniacale concentrato di storia dell'arte. Con sollievo noto di aver scritto "maniacale". La follia che guidò Francesco I granduca di Toscana a fondare la galleria degli Uffici può diventare criterio interpretativo di una intera città. La città è una galleria di edifici illustri, ciascuno dei quali reca addosso la propria etichetta, con data e autore. Una città ha una storia, in questo caso una storia dell'arte. Ma è vero? Io ne dubito. Abito a Roma, una città che esibisce oggetti lungo un arco di duemila anni. Tuttavia, quando percorro questa rimarchevole città, io posso solo culturalmente adoperare questa sterminata dimensione temporale. Per me, Roma è simultaneamente il Colosseo, San Pietro, Piazza Navona, Piazza Bocca della Verità, la Torre delle Milizie, l'arco di Tito, la Santa Teresa del Bernini e Stazione Termini. Ne risulta un tessuto impossibile, se pretendiamo che una città sia un luogo pacifico; ma sta a noi vivere questo discorso urbano per quel che acconsente di essere, per le letture che sollecita, per le ipotesi di mondo che accoglie nella sua mappa. Una città è sempre e tutta contemporanea; è fatta di elementi incompatibili, se colti uno per uno, ma che hanno molte cose a dirsi, se noi ci facciamo messaggeri dall'uno all'altro; e, naturalmente, mentre trasportiamo i messaggi, segretamente li leggiamo.

Se io nego alla città che contemplo il carattere di formazione storica, o meglio il rifiuto di leggerla secondo gli strati storici, ne viene che io non vedo più gli edifici in reciproca dialettica; o meglio, si tratta di una dialettica immobile, senza svolgimento, che non si conclude più, né mai si concluderà; e questo non è l'ultimo fascino di una città. E credo che appunto a Firenze, che sembra volere imporre una lettura di storia dell'arte, questo diniego della storia sia essenziale. Tutto è contemporaneo, tutto è intemporale, e i conflitti non si risolveranno più. Ed ecco che la città reclamizzata come luogo perfettamente dilettoso, dimora della assoluta bellezza, diventa il luogo in cui i conflitti perdurano immobili, irrisolti e irrisolvibili, in cui diverse ipotesi di mondo si lacerano e si compongono: una città tragica, una città significante, una città come Calcutta.

"Capolavoro": ecco una parola che per anni mi ha tenuto lontano da Firenze, giacché detesto, come mi pare ragionevole, il concetto di capolavoro, e a Firenze pare che tutto sia o finisca per diventare capolavoro. La parola "capolavoro" ha qualcosa di odioso, di prevaricante. Se un'opera mi viene presentata come un capolavoro, si presuppone che io non muoverò obiezioni; cadrò in uno stato stuporoso, dirò "oh!", "ah!", congiungerò le mani in atto di supplica, come una "pietà di me"; posso anche trattenere il respiro e ruotare le pupille. Il capolavoro non si discute; merita solo il "culto della personalità". È tirannico; limita la libertà di stampa e di parola. Pensate alla Gioconda leonardesca, ed alla quantità di sciocchezze che si sono scritte, anche in ottima prosa, su quel "capolavoro". O il Partenone: oh, un giorno mi piacerebbe parlare del Partenone. Se Firenze è una città capolavoro, non mi interessa. L'istinto mi porta a cercare i luoghi minori, gli oggetti controversi, i mondi periferici, le forme distratte o schive. Non voglio l'immagine esatta, ma l'immagine che partecipa dell'errore.

È strano che solo il viaggio a Firenze mi abbia rivelato dove stava l'inesattezza del ragionamento, una inesattezza sgomentevole. Debbo essere un poco antropomorfico, ma non credo infondatamente. Un'opera, un oggetto, un'ora di luce diventano "capolavori" per nascondersi. Se un luogo è centrale, trasformandosi in capolavoro viene occultato, spostato, diventa periferico e acquista i privilegi dell'errore; intendo dire, che il capolavoro diventa ignoto, è qualcosa di cui non si parla, diventa destinatario di discorsi elusivi ed erratici. Non c'è travestimento più perfetto del "capolavoro".

Dunque, se una città non può essere "bella", se non deve essere un capitolo di "storia dell'arte", se può essere "capolavoro" solo per nascondersi, per rendere più intricato l'itinerario di scoperta, in che modo si potrà parlare di Firenze, o più propriamente, di qualsiasi altra città? Che cosa è una città? Vorrei rispondere con una citazione da un libro delizioso uscito in questi giorni in italiano: "L'idea di città", di Joseph Rykwert (Einaudi): della città egli dice: "più che a ogni altra cosa essa somiglia a un sogno". A questo modo, mi proverò di parlare di Firenze.

Giorgio Manganelli, "Scoprire" in piazza.

ONDE DI AMORE.
FIORI, BACI, E CIOCCOLATINI.
L'INVOLUCRO DELLA MIA PASSIONE.

ARENA E SPETTATORI, CAMPO E
SQUADRE.
LA TELECAMERA PROIETTA
CAMPIONI IN CASA.

PIRANDELLO, NONO, VERDI, FELLINI.
LUOGHI DI SCENA, LUOGHI DI VITA.

Alberto Savinio
Amore

Chi può vantare una "completa" esperienza dell'amore? Solo un mostro di molteplicità, un uomo-polipo fornito di tanti tentacoli, quanti sono gliinnumerabili desiderii che danno al nostro vivere un'apparenza di senso, un'illusione di necessità, e che tutti assieme costituiscono il grande inganno della vita. E di quale amore si parla? L'esame generale della questione ci porterebbe un'altra volta in altomare, e soltanto l'esame particolare di ciascun genere d'amore potrebbe fornirci forse qualche lume: amore dell'uomo a Dio e reciprocamente, amore dei figli per i genitori e reciprocamente, amore fraterno, amore della gloria, della ricchezza, delle arti, amore sessuale, amore platonico, amore per le bestie, per la natura grezza o per quella manufatta, amore per se stessi, ecc. ecc. Ma anche l'esame "specializzato" di ciascun genere d'amore ci lascerebbe probabilmente con un pugno di mosche. È una ragione ineluttabile quella che vieta tra noi e l'amore ogni possibilità d'incontro; ed è che nel punto stesso in cui l'amore sta per nascere, l'amore muore. (Che brutta unione fanno queste due parole: due caramelle ammollite dal caldo e appiccicate assieme). Muore soltanto l'amore dei sensi, come purtroppo sappiamo? No, ma qualunque amore, anche quello della ricchezza, che muore nell'atto stesso in cui l'uomo acquista la ricchezza. Durano solo gli amori inappagabili, gli amori che non hanno possibilità di arrivare all'amore, ossia al possesso della cosa desiderata. Come l'amore della vecchia zitella per il suo pechinese; perché salvo in casi di sadismo sovracuto, la vecchia zitella pur nei più accecanti accessi passionali e isterici, non supera nelle affettuose manipolazioni del suo pechinese il limite oltre il quale essa stritolerebbe tra le sue mani amorose la bestiola per farla sua, al che l'avvia l'accesso passionale e isterico: l'amore. Altra cagione che vieta l'attuazione dell'amore, ossia il risultato in senso amorico del desiderio, è che nel momento in cui entriamo in possesso della cosa amata, l'amore per la cosa amata perde il suo carattere transitivo, si confonde con l'amorproprio e da questo è assorbito. Stupisce la donna che nel momento in cui l'uomo dovrebbe essere più amoroso che mai, ridiventa egoista e incomunicante. Anche negli amori più grandi, negli amori sublimi, nell'amore di Petrarca per Laura, l'amante ama se stesso, e in questo caso anzi l'intransitività dell'amore è provata dal suo impoetarsi, dal suo cristallizzarsi nello stato "intransitivo" per eccellenza. L'amore dunque? L'amore propriamente non esiste. È una ipotesi, una grande, una smisurata ipotesi. Per un errore di contesto quanto d'espressione, la cui origine si perde nella notte del linguaggio, si confonde l'amore con la "preparazione dell'amore", ossia col desiderio.

L'amore indica piuttosto l'effetto della naturale inclinazione e della passione suscitata dalle attrattive della forma esterna, che il resultato della scelta e della riflessione, quello che i Romani espressero colla voce diligere composta da legere che significa scegliere. Ed è bene che sia così. Desiderio è l'illimitato, l'infinito. Amore è la morte. (Nuovo significato da dare al binomio amore-morte). E ora dovrei passare a parlare del desiderio, ossia di ciò che in effetto è l'amore. Ma qui davvero mi manca l'esperienza o piuttosto mi va mancando. I desideri ci tengono fermi alla vita, come gli ormeggi tengono ferma la nave al porto. Ma a poco a poco i desideri muoiono, gli ormeggi si rompono senza che noi ce ne accorgiamo, e domani la nostra nave salperà tranquilla e libera di desideri. Si avvererà allora la "grande ipotesi"?

Alberto Savinio, "Nuova Enciclopedia", Adelphi, Milano 1978.

Vitaliano Brancati
Paolo il caldo

Una domenica di aprile, tutte le pendici di Monte Mario intorno allo Stadio di marmo, erano nere di folla, nella quale si andava propagando, come il palpito che increspa le meduse, il moto per uscire dai recinti e tornare sulla strada, già per suo conto invasa dalla nuvola dei motorini, fitta fitta e stordente, in continua partenza non si sapeva bene da dove, forse dal fondo del suolo, e prolungantesi per tutto l'arco visibile del Lungotevere attraverso file interminabili di automobili da cui, gemendo dolorosamente, alcuna cercava di uscire a marcia indietro per incanalarsi nel fiume del ritorno. Sui marciapiedi e in mezzo alla strada, la moltitudine dei pedoni, come la polvere stessa suscitata da quel moto di macchine, faceva velo, annebbiava tutto, rallentava e impediva, finché avvicinandosi, rivelava la pietosa sostanza di cui era fatta, quell'elemento che si chiama carne, al quale subito chi guarda associa la sua capacità di pensare e di soffrire, e chiude gli occhi con raccapriccio se lo vede colpito, senonché qui, nella forma stessa che componeva pigiando le centinaia di migliaia di facce rimpicciolite dalla distanza e dal confronto di ciascuna con la somma di tutte, non privo di uno sgradevole senso di stupidità e di gioia e rabbia ferine, delle quali erano prove lampanti le giacche buttate all'aria, i pantaloni sfilati di sotto alle scarpe, i fiaschi bevuti a garganella stando ritti sui sedili delle vetture, il sudore, gli urli, le carezze delle donne sporgenti il braccio dalle vetture a sconosciuti pedoni che le capitassero a tiro, i salti dentro le fontane pubbliche, risoluzioni repentine accolte da fischi mescolati ad applausi, con le quali si adempivano scommesse perdute o vinte.

"La Roma! La Lazio!" In queste due parole, come nella nuvola che, dopo avere grandinato lungamente, rimane nera, si concentrava ancora l'elettricità d'infinite persone, mentre sulle pendici di Monte Mario si andavano spegnendo i fuochi appiccati alle erbe da gruppi di spettatori che, sedendovi intorno, si erano sentiti troppo esposti al vento del crepuscolo, e in mezzo al campo deserto giaceva il nero pallone, vuoto ormai di tutta l'ira e la forza e la perizia con cui aveva trascritto in cielo e in terra rette e curve velocissime.

Vitaliano Brancati, "Paolo il caldo", Bompiani, Milano 1980.

Alberto Arbasino
Fratelli d'Italia

Al teatro, Rovescalli viene subito sistemata in un palco con parecchie altre bambine della sua età che l'aspettano, e si fanno infatti una quantità d'inchini e di baci. Entra la Bellotta in un finto Chanel color aragosta, e l'avrà preteso lei così, evidentemente, dalla sartina che gliel'ha copiato, perché Giulio spiega a Ferdinando che normalmente quei tailleurs lì vengono in beige variegato di lilla e rosa come un tweed smortissimo: squillante dev'essere se mai la fodera. Andrea è corso al Teatro Nuovo per Klaus; e Desideria viene subito riassorbita da un fastoso gruppo di mondani di Roma, con un paio d'altre belle alte e vestite uguali a lei di veli di colori tenuissimi. Fulk lo festeggiano straordinariamente; ma prima che lo abbraccino una per una fa in tempo a scivolare sulla Canobbiana accovacciata sotto il bar con una cloche di scimmia in testa talmente incredibile che la stanno molto fissando: pare uscita dal film su Attila: "Non crederanno mica che siano i miei capelli, questi?", domanda lei cavernosamente a Fulk, facendosi dare il braccio per tirarsi su.
Ma dello spettacolo mi bastano neanche dieci minuti: impacciate che bassamente imitano la Masina e la Valeri, malapartismi da 1944 coi negri e le segnorine, lo sketch surrealista col pittore e il manichino, tipo "Vogue" 1937; battute un po' da avanspettacolo, però non divertenti. Da vergognarsi; e si intitola "Tell U.S. a Story". Così filo giù a Terni a farmi un po' di sciocchezze nei giardini bombardati, che tripudiano di movimento e traboccano di spontaneità. Che città! Che vita!
Tornando molto più tranquillo e disteso, sono lì tutti fuori sulla piazza che escono, e una luce dorata illumina le parrucche gonfie. Andrea sta facendo un giuoco apparentemente divertente con un bel signorino d'una sessantina d'anni, non grande ma liscio in faccia e vivace. "Un abate laico da assaporare come una giuggiola", lo presenta: piedini piccoli, pochi capelli bianchi, cravatta a farfallino, colletti sulle spalle, mobilissimo, e la Elsa se lo abbraccia urlando: "cazzo-cazzo-cazzo, non so come farei senza questo simpatico!" mentre i mondani continuano a fluire intorno. "Prendono ancora Cocteau sul serio! Visto?" ammicca in lontananza Desideria in mezzo ai suoi, e indica dietro a sé le porte del Caio Melisso che stanno chiudendosi.
"Sketches e commedie dove un tendone da circo rappresenta una metafora della condizione umana!" dichiara il bel signorino. (Il loro giuoco è una specie di catalogo delle cose che non si possono più assolutamente vedere su scene e su schermi, sia all'aperto che al chiuso).
"Prova di sacra rappresentazione finto-Jacopone", dice Andrea, "dove tutti gli abitanti di una certa area sottosviluppata interpretano parti di Giuseppe e Ma-

ria, Asino e Bue, Fede Prudenza e Giustizia!

Anche la finta inchiesta poliziesca che simboleggia tutt'altre indagini!

"...E specialmente se tende a scoprire abissi nel fondo dei cuori!

"Tutti i protagonisti simbolici con nomi come Egli, Tizio, Ognuno o Ciascheduno!

"Anche se si chiamassero l'uomo, la Ragazza, La Prima Vicina, la Seconda Vicina, il Viandante!

"E naturalmente anche Pic, Mec, Zac, Din, Don, Dan, e altri nomi di detersivi!

"Il cuore che sanguina mentre il carnevale impazza! Nel carnevale si comprende ogni ballo o festa o veglione o quattro salti!

"I due amanti che si prendono nel lunapark fra una giostra e l'altra! Il Pierrot lunare che muore per amore di una moderna Colombina!

"Tutti i circhi, tutti i clowns, tutti i forains, allegri o tristi! Saremo infami, saremo razzisti, ma i loro tormenti sentimentali non ci interessano più!

"Tutti i mimi compreso Marcel Marceau!

"Tutte le parodie del balletto classico a cominciare da quella della 'Morte del cigno'!

"Tutti i manichini in qualunque materiale, e tutte le maschere in forma di testa di gatto!

"Tutti i musicals o riviste o balletti dove nel secondo tempo non avendo più niente da fare il protagonista parte per un giro del mondo trovandosi in mezzo a una samba brasiliana e a un cancan a Pigalle!

"Tutte le storie con un protagonista che s'innamora tante volte della stessa donna che gli riappare in diversi travestimenti!

"Anche quelle dove dei francesi d'oggi si travestono da coglioni del Settecento in uno château al solo scopo di scambiarsi marivaudages sul tipo di 'La donna è come l'orologio: quando è matura casca dall'albero'!

"Non sbraghiamo... Tutte le parabole politiche o esistenziali che si svolgono nel Nulla o nel Beige!

"Tutte le allegorie dove sotto le porcellerie s'intravede la Fede!

"Non si dimentichi il baloccarsi con magnetofoni o altri apparecchi riproduttori meccanici del suono, tanto peggio poi se girati all'indietro per produrre il caratteristico fastidiosissimo stridore!

"L'incidente di macchina usato negli ultimi cinque minuti per sciogliere di colpo un intrigo troppo complicato!

"...Cioè la vera macchina ex-deo, andiamo a mangiare", ridacchia la Elsa gridando un po' a tutti: "Manica larga! Bocca buona!" La notte è bella, tiepida, con una lunona. Ci avviamo a piedi verso il ristorante; e poi il pranzo è tutto molto piacevole, tranne il cibo, con Raimondo d'ottimo umore e un certo delizioso numero di Sandro de Feo: "Se arrivando a uno spettacolo vedo che la scena non è pronta, e attori e macchinisti si aggirano vestiti da strada mettendo a posto delle cose... Pazienza, non

hanno fatto in tempo... avrebbero dovuto, sarebbero stati tenuti, e non ci saranno riusciti... Ma se faccio tanto di sospettare un work in progress... posso diventare una belva!".

Questi qui dopo l'Unicorno e il Pentagramma vogliono venire almeno una volta sull'altana anche loro, e insistono; così si va. Poi per la strada il gruppo s'allarga. In fondo anche Raimondo come Andrea e come tutti loro ne conosce molto, di demi-monde. È già piuttosto tardi, nelle strade silenziose e deserte si sente solo qualche "l'ambasciatrice ha delle angosce e fa dei rutti, e continua a ripetere a papà: tu dici sempre cosìì perché non è tuo fiiiglio...", ma quelli che erano al ristorante finiscono per venirci dietro tutti, mondani e ordinari, una di quelle cose romane tipiche tipo "ma cche cce ffrega, si va tutti insieme!"; e poi si finisce per salire vociando fra gli orti bui dietro i muri di pietra. C'è un po' di vento, e fa oscillare le lanterne. "Perché la matrona romana, sempre si è usato che facesse delle cretinate con il caprone, già in Giovenale si trova la storia, e il caprone naturalmente con i suoi zoccoloni ha una presa energica, non la lascia andare, soltanto alla fine gli viene la fame, e trovandosi lì davanti i capelli di lei è troppo naturale, li bruca come se fossero erbetta, così lei alla fine si trova posseduta e calva", sento una voce di vecchio di dietro, monotona come una litania: con accento inglese. Si va insieme a gente che per una buona metà nessuno conosce, con in mezzo due opera-cloaks immensi, uno di raso viola e uno nero di velluto, che veramente sembrano congiurati in domino, col loro cappuccio. E poi si vede che sono delle ordinarie anche quelle, con delle schienone nude un po' formaggiose e dei reggipettacci che scappan fuori da tutte le ascelle appena provano a ballare; quando arrivano su in anticamera veramente pare che stiano per riprendere la loro scopa e volar via dalla finestra.

La casa è buia e non trovando le luci soltanto la luna entra a illuminare i saloni neri che attraversiamo. Sull'altana un paio di candele sono accese sul grande tavolo. Si precipitano avanti a tutti urlando con salti altissimi Berceuse e Boudeuse, due creature della notte che non so come si chiamino in realtà, ma le vedo ogni volta che metto dentro la testa in qualche luogo di delizie intorno a Via Veneto sul tardi, e stanno sempre strillando "l'ovaia in fiamme!" e "bravissima la vecchia" e "ma scusi, lei con chi sta ballando? con lui o con lei?". Appena sentono una parola, fa la loro specialità che spiccano questi balzi altissimi, gridando per aria "non s'usa più! non s'usa più dal '39!" (o dal '46, o dal '23). Facendo, sempre per aria, dei frenetici entrechats coi piedi, o delle arabesques, aggiungono "...come il bavero di volpe e i romanzi di Körmendi!" (oppure come il sopracciglio depilato, o la casa a via Archimede, o i film di Rossellini, o la pizza), e finalmente scendendo

strillano "ma l'infelice non lo sa!". Subito dietro viene caracollando un cavallone biondastro e fosco, a basettoni, vestito come il Rouge e il Noir: perfino con redingote e collettoni svolanti, mi pare, al buio. Appia Nuova, non si sbaglia, come genere; ma aiutante di Boudeuse, di suo mestiere scenografo capitonné; e per questo Andrea e tutti lo conoscono come "l'aitante di Boudeuse".

Tutte le candele le accendono; ma non ne sono rimaste mica tante, in giro, e dagli angoli affiorano dentro una penombra gialla i vimini e le tigri, e le sante, le beate, i busti, i fiori. In attesa di Raimondo, Giulio fa tirar fuori dalla cucina della coca-cola e del vino bianco; e ci sono anche dei piatti di dolci avanzati da ieri. Franano tutti giù, trenta o quaranta persone, è proprio una serata tipo Alles Zusammen, questi faranno certamente i cori. La Gazzaniga con Renato e le altre milanesi arrivano cautamente fino sull'orlo del ponte, con un sorriso appena, e guardano attorno. "Cosa si fa?" si domandano adagio, senza scendere nell'altana e senza andarsene.

Una ordinaria ha messo una cha-cha sul grammofono e comincia a muovere il didietro da sola chiamando gli altri. "Io rimarrei", dice la Bellotta, slacciandosi vigorosamente la sua giaccaccia rossa. "Allora torna su col professore?" le chiede la Gazzaniga. "Sì, verrà a prendermi. Mi raccomando quelle due dignitose figurette, se vuole avere la compiacenza di ricordarlo al suo chauffeur", risponde la Bellotta, spiegando che si riferisce ai bassotti, potrebbero avere sete.

La Gazzaniga promette e se ne va con le altre, e con Renato. L'ordinaria che balla viene attualmente dileggiata, dicono a Andrea, perché in tre anni che ha fatto la sciocchina con un regista della televisione pieno di soldi è stata solo capace di sentirsi telefonare da lui ogni sera "mangia pure a casa tua, che andiamo al cinema dopo", e quando è poi passata con un musico di colonne sonore e i due signori si sono incontrati per decidere chi le paga l'affitto, hanno avuto nello stesso momento la stessa battuta, "sono troppo vigliacco nelle cose di soldi per prendermi questa responsabilità!" Ferdinando si avvicina uscendo dalla cucina e dice: "Derek non s'è mosso da oggi. Dorme ancora con tutti i suoi fiori addosso... Sarà mica morto?". "Non importa, non importa, per me prendo il treno del latte e va benissimo", interrompe un gran vecchio alto coi baffi bianchi. "Mi spiace, principe..." gli fa Ferdinando; ma il vecchio gli afferra tremando una mano come per baciargliela, e con l'altra solleva un plaid di cashmere "Caro amico, basta solo che qualcuno si ricordi di portarmi giù alla stazione per le quattro e mezza", gli dice quasi abbracciandolo, molto commosso. "Andrà benissimo e viaggerò comodissimo".

"È da tanto che non è più stato a Parigi?" domanda la Bellotta intrufolandosi

sotto Andrea col bicchiere vuoto in mano. "Un po' d'armagnac non sarà possibile averne?".

"Ah, non so", le fa lui. "E lei quando c'è stata?".

"Adesso, torno proprio adesso, mai stata così bella, la città".

Le coppie che ballano tre o quattro. Una è la Elsa che ha già afferrato l'aitante e gli sta prendendo in mano tutto. Ma comincio a essere stufo.

"Non l'hanno plasticata?" chiede Andrea alla Bellotta.

"Oh, si sentono i rumori di un po' di bombe, ma non dànno fastidio", fa lei, battendo un paio di volte la dentiera. "Non mi cerca qualche cosa da bere?". M'aspetto il "vaff..." di Andrea, ma hanno portato su perfino una roulette col suo tappetino, di quelle che si comprano dal tabaccaio, e s'infilano in dieci o dodici nella sala da pranzo meravigliosa a giocare, trascinando via la Bellotta come le comparse della "Traviata".

"Andrea, andiamo?".

"Aspetta un momento. Tu l'hai già avuto il tuo benefizio, stasera?".

"Certo! Ma chi sono, tutti questi?".

"Gente spaventosa, che faccio di tutto per evitare a Via Veneto; e adesso ho la consolazione di trovarli qui tutti insieme".

Alberto Arbasino, "Fratelli d'Italia", Einaudi, Torino 1976.

FIRMS PARTICIPATING IN THE EXHIBITION
AZIENDE PARTECIPANTI ALLA MOSTRA

ABET LAMINATI
Viale dell'Industria, 21
12042 Bra (Cuneo) - Tel. 0172/423611

ACEA - Azienda Comunale Elettricità ed Acque
Piazzale Ostiense, 2
00154 Roma - Tel. 06/5799

ALESSI S.p.A.
Via Priv. Alessi, 6
28023 Crusinallo (NO) - Tel. 0323/641601

ALFA ROMEO
Via Gattamelata, 45
20149 Milano - Tel. 02/93391

ALFATEC S.p.A.
Via Giuseppe di Vittorio, 28
20068 Peschiera Borromeo (MI) - Tel. 02/540555

ALFEO S.r.l.
Via Brughiera
20010 Pregnana Milanese (MI) - Tel. 02/9391301

AMF MARES SUB S.p.A.
Via Cerisola Borghetto, 37
16035 Rapallo (GE) - Tel. 0185/60871

ANI
Via Arzignano, 72
36072 Chiampo (VI) - Tel. 0444/672555

ARTELUCE S.p.A.
Via Moretto, 58
25100 Brescia - Tel. 030/280281

ARTEMIDE S.p.A.
Via Brughiera
20010 Pregnana Milanese (MI) - Tel. 02/9391301

AURORA DUE S.p.A.
Strada Abbadia di Stura, 200
10156 Torino - Tel. 011/241069

AUTOVOX S.p.A.
Via Salaria, 991
00138 Roma - Tel. 06/8401841

BASILE
Via Jenner, 51
20159 Milano - Tel. 02/6071841

BCS PROGETTI
Via Milano, 24
22050 Lomagna (CO) - Tel. 039/58400

BERETTA S.p.A.
Via Pietro Beretta, 18
25063 Gardone Valtrompia (BS) - Tel. 030/837261

BIEFFEPLAST S.p.A.
Via Marconi
35030 Caselle di Selvazzano (PD) - Tel. 049/630111

BULGARI
Via Gregoriana, 56
00100 Roma - Tel. 06/6791640

ALFONSO BIALETTI & C. S.p.A.
Via IV Novembre, 106
28023 Crusinallo (NO) - Tel. 0323/642131

BIANCHI S.r.l.
Via Salomone, 41
20138 Milano - Tel. 02/5064451

BLOOM S.p.A.
Via Crocefisso, 21
20122 Milano - Tel. 02/8323644

BOERI SPORT
Via San Rocco, 5
20135 Milano - Tel. 02/573320

BALZANO
Via Sansovino, 243/63
10151 Torino - Tel. 011/252858

BORSALINO GIUSEPPE & FRATELLO
Corso Centocannoni, 23
15100 Alessandria - Tel. 0131/54241

BRIONVEGA S.p.A.
Via Pordenone, 8
20132 Milano - Tel. 02/2157241

BRUNATI S.p.A.
Via Strada Statale, 342
22040 Alzate Brianza - Tel. 0362/72743

BUMBLEBEE S.a.s.
Via San Galdino, 6
20154 Milano - Tel. 02/384202

BUSNELLI Gruppo Industriale S.p.A.
Via Kennedy
22020 Misinto (Milano) - Tel. 02/9640221

BWA RECORDING S.a.s.
Via D. Machelli, 7
42100 Reggio Emilia - Tel. 0522/21359

CABER ITALIA S.p.A.
Via San Gaetano, 125
31044 Montebelluna (TV) - Tel. 0423/29441

CALZATURIFICIO F.LLI DANIELI
Via Mazzini, 20
31031 Caerano San Marco (TV) - Tel. 0423/85621

CAMPAGNOLO S.p.A.
Viale della Chimica
36100 Vicenza - Tel. 0444/56933

CARPIGIANI BRUTO S.p.A.
Via Emilia, 45
40011 Anzola Emilia (BO) - Tel. 051/733021

CASA D'ARTE CERRATELLI
Via della Pergola, 44
50121 Firenze - Tel. 055/214601

CASA NOVA S.rl.
S.S. 77 Km. 74,5
62029 Tolentino (Macerata) - Tel. 0733/99075

CASSINA S.p.A.
Via Luigi Busnelli, 1
20036 Meda (MI) - Tel. 0362/70581

CASTELLI S.p.A.
Via Torreggiani, 1
40128 Bologna - Tel. 051/369921

CEA Costruzioni Elettromeccaniche ANETTONI
Via E. Filiberto, 27
22053 Lecco (CO) - Tel. 0341/422194

CHAUSSURES COLETTE
Via Monsignor Pogliani, 5
20015 Parabiago (MI) - Tel. 0331/553070

CINELLI S.p.A.
Via E. Folli, 45
20134 Milano - Tel. 02/2159874

COMELIT Compagnia Elettronica Italiana S.p.A.
Via D. B. Arrigoni, 3
24020 San Lorenzo di Rovetta (BG) - Tel. 0346/72180

CONSORZIO INDUSTRIE BALMA
Via di Vittorio, 10
10090 Cascina Vica Rivoli (TO) - Tel. 011/9592492

ENRICO COVERI
Via Visconti di Modrone, 26
20122 Milano - Tel. 02/702098

BRUNO DANESE S.n.c.
Piazza San Fedele, 2
20121 Milano - Tel. 02/866019 - 866296

DAYTON S.p.A.
Via Asolana, 76
31010 Oné di Fonte (TV) - Tel. 0423/58394

DOLOMITE S.p.A.
Via Feltrina Centro, 10
31044 Montebelluna (TV) - Tel. 0423/20941

DRIADE S.p.A.
Padana Inferiore
29012 Fossadello di Caorso (PC) - Tel. 0523/821648

ELAM S.p.A.
Via Molino, 27
20036 Meda (Milano) - Tel. 0362/73781

EUROLINEA INTERNATIONAL S.p.A.
Via Perini, 54
38100 Trento - Tel. 0461/984920

FABRA S.r.l.
Via Sansovino, 243/60
10151 Torino - Tel. 011/7395333

FANTINI F.lli
Via M. Buonarroti, 4
28010 Pella (NO) - Tel. 0322/969127

FASHION BOX S.r.l.
Via Schiavonesca Marosticana, 14
31011 Asolo (TV) - Tel. 0423/55447

FERRAGAMO SALVATORE S.p.A.
Via dei Tornabuoni, 2
50123 Firenze - Tel. 055/210756

FERRARI
Via Abetone Inferiore, 2
41053 Maranello (Modena) - Tel. 059/941161

FERRÉ GIANFRANCO S.r.l.
Via San Damiano, 2
20122 Milano - Tel. 02/708888 - 709394

F.I.L.A. Fabbrica Italiana Lapis e Affini S.p.A.
Via Sempione, 2/C
20016 Pero (MI) - Tel. 02/3532241

FILA S.p.A.
Viale Cesare Battisti, 26
13051 Biella (VC)

FIORUCCI S.p.A.
Via G. Di Vittorio, 10
20094 Corsico (MI) - Tel. 02/4482

FLOS S.p.A.
Via Moretto, 58
25100 Brescia - Tel. 030/280281

GABBIANO
Via De Gasperi, 6
25066 Lumezzane P. (BS) - Tel. 030/872616

GAGGIA S.p.A.
20086 Robecco sul Naviglio (MI)
Tel. 02/9470371

GHELFI
Via del Triumvirato, 28
40132 Bologna - Tel. 051/311905

GIOVANNETTI
Via Pierucciani, 2
51032 Bottegone (Pistoia) - Tel. 0573/544755

HERON PARIGI S.d.f.
Località "Soterna"
50032 Borgo San Lorenzo (FI) - Tel. 055/849073

ICARO OLIVIERI S.p.A.
Via Feltrina Sud, 87/A
34044 Montebelluna (Treviso) - Tel. 0423/29544/5

I GUZZINI ILLUMINAZIONE S.p.A.
S.S. 77 Km. 102
62019 Recanati (Macerata) - Tel. 071/980582

ILSA EXPRESS
Corso Pastrengo, 46
10093 Collegno (TO) - Tel. 011/784223

I.P.E. nuova BIALETTI S.p.A.
Via dei Mille, 3/A
28023 Crusinallo (Novara) - Tel. 0323/61611 - 612

I PELLETTIERI D'ITALIA S.p.A.
Loc. Levanella
52025 Montevarchi (Arezzo) - Tel. 055/9841-2-3

IRMEL S.p.A.
Via L. Comoli, 54/58
28026 Omegna (NO) - Tel. 0323/61234

IS.VE.I.E. S.r.l.
Via Mantova, 34
10153 Torino - Tel. 011/851846

ITALDESIGN SIRP S.p.A.
Via A. Grandi, 11
10024 Moncalieri (TO) - Tel. 011/6470333

ITALJET S.p.A.
Via Palazzetti, 5
40068 San Lazzaro di Savena (BO) - Tel. 051/455034

JADI LUISA
Via Cenni, 6
43100 Parma - Tel. 0521/494519

KAMIKAZE S.r.l.
Via delle Industrie, 1
20082 Noviglio (MI) - Tel. 02/9054065

KARTELL S.p.A.
Via delle Industrie, 1
20082 Noviglio (MI) - Tel. 02/905465

KING BOOT S.r.l.
Via Fiume, 15
40068 San Lazzaro di Savena (BO) - Tel. 051/410694

KRIZIA S.p.A.
Via Agnello, 12
20121 Milano - Tel. 02/872304

LAGOSTINA S.p.A.
Via IV Novembre, 45
28026 Omegna (NO) - Tel. 0323-642101

LA PAVONI S.p.A.
Via Archimede, 26
20129 Milano - Tel. 02/7496057

LOMBARDA GRANITI S.r.l.
Viale Montegrappa, 9
20124 Milano - Tel. 02/6597231

LORENZ S.p.A.
Via Marina, 3
20121 Milano - Tel. 02/5456166

LOTTO S.p.A.
Via San Gaetano, 131
31044 Montebelluna (TV) - Tel. 0423/29846

LUCI S.p.A.
Via Pellizza da Volpedo, 50
20092 Cinisello Balsamo (MI) - Tel. 02/6188233

MARCATRÉ S.p.A.
Via Sant'Andrea, 3
20020 Misinto (MI) - Tel. 02/9649451

MARTINELLI LUCE S.p.A.
Via T. Bandettini, 145
55100 Lucca - Tel. 0535/55008

D. MEAZZA & M. MASCIADRI S.n.c.
Via Crocette, 21
28022 Casale Corte Cerro (Novara) - Tel. 0323/60115

METODO E MISURE S.p.A.
Via del Lavoro, 2
36063 Marostica (VI) - Tel. 0424/75016

M.G.C. Manifatture Giovanili Contemporanee S.p.A.
Zona Industriale Sud, Via Cile, 6
35100 Padova - Tel. 049/761566

MISSONI S.p.A.
Via Luigi Rossi
21040 Sumirago (VA) - Tel. 0331/909170

MOLTENI & C. S.p.A.
Via Rossini, 50
20034 Giussano (MI) - Tel. 0362/81334

MPA Meccanica Plastica Agordina S.p.A.
Via Pragrande
32021 Agordo (BL) - Tel. 0437/62403

NAVA GRAFICHE
Via Martin Lutero, 5
20126 Milano - Tel. 02/2570251

NAZARENO GABRIELLI S.p.A.
S.S. 77 Km. 75,900
62029 Tolentino (MC) - Tel. 0733/971956

NORDICA S.p.A.
Via Montebelluna, 15/A
31040 Trevignano - Tel. 0423/818041

NUOVA FAEMA S.p.A.
Via Ventura, 15
20134 Milano - Tel. 02/2123

OCEANO S.d.f.
Via Borgonuovo, 20
20121 Milano

OFFICINE CIMBALI GIUSEPPE S.p.A.
Via Manzoni, 17
20082 Binasco (MI) - Tel. 02/9055501

OFFICINE MECCANICHE VALLIO S.p.A.
Via per Monastier, 4
31156 Vallio di Roncade (TV) - Tel. 0422/84321

OLIVARI B. S.r.l.
Via G. Matteotti, 140
28021 Borgomanero (NO) - Tel. 0322/844001

OLIVETTI S.p.A.
Via Meravigli, 12
20123 Milano - Tel. 02/88361

OLIVETTI SYNTHESIS S.p.A.
Largo Richini, 6
20122 Milano - Tel. 02/8864

O-LUCE ITALIA S.p.A.
Via Cavour, 42
20098 San Giuliano Milanese (MI) - Tel. 02/9840495

PERRY ELECTRIC S.r.l.
Viale Tunisia, 42
20124 Milano - Tel. 02/654881

PIAGGIO & C. S.p.A.
Via A. Cecchi, 6
16129 Genova - Tel. 010/5991

INDUSTRIE PIRELLI S.p.A.
Piazza Duca D'Aosta, 3
20100 Milano - Tel. 02/85351

PLASTIC SCREEN
Via Reguzzoni, 7
20125 Milano - Tel. 02/6437552

POLTRONA FRAU S.p.A.
S.S. 77 Km. 74,5
62029 Tolentino (Macerata) - Tel. 0733/971766

ROSSI & ARCANDI S.n.c.
Via Brenta, 4
36010 Monticello Conte Otto (VI) - Tel. 0444/595111

ROSSI DI ALBIZZATE S.p.A.
Via Mazzini, 1
21041 Albizzate (VA) - Tel. 0331/993200

RUFFONI
Via Magenta - P.O. Box 11
28026 Omegna (NO) - Tel. 0323/61990

SACIT S.p.A.
Via Carlo Torre, 27
20143 Milano - Tel. 02/8323741

SAIET S.p.A.
Via Serenari, 1
40013 Castel Maggiore (BO) - Tel. 051/700005

SAMES S.p.A.
C.so Siracusa, 195/A
10137 Torino - Tel. 011/3094844

SAN MARCO INTERNATIONAL S.r.l.
Via Montello, 73
31031 Caerano San Marco (TV) - Tel. 0423/85521

SANTINI E DOMINICI S.r.l.
Via Licia, 39
00183 Roma - Tel. 06/6784114

F.lli SAPORITI S.n.c.
Via Gallarate, 23
21010 Besnate (VA) - Tel. 0331/274198

SCI POZZI-GINORI
Via Ugo Bassi, 8/A
20159 Milano - Tel. 02/69602

SEIMM S.p.A.
22054 Mandello sul Lario (CO)
Tel. 0341/731112

SICME ILLUMINAZIONE S.r.l.
Via Triumplina, 25/U
25100 Brescia - Tel. 030/302368

SIMAC
Via Garibaldi, 20
20060 Gessate (MI) - Tel. 02/9502661

SKIPPER S.p.A.
Via S. Spirito, 14
20121 Milano - Tel. 02/705691

SOLARI & C. UDINE S.p.A.
Via Gino Pieri, 29
33100 Udine - Tel. 0432/43241

STUDIO ALCHIMIA S.r.l.
Foro Bonaparte, 55
2021 Milano - Tel. 02/808532

SUPERGA S.p.A.
Via Verolengo, 38
10149 Torino - Tel. 011/290701

TEATRO ALLA SCALA
Via Filodrammatici, 2
20121 Milano - Tel. 02/8879

TECNICA S.p.A.
31040 Nervesa della Battaglia (TV)
Tel. 0422/897421

TECNO S.p.A.
Via Bigli, 22
20121 Milano - Tel. 02/79341

TREZETA S.r.l.
Via E. Fermi
31011 Casella D'Asolo (TV) - Tel. 0423/52138

UNIFOR EMME 3 S.p.A.
Via Isonzo, 1
22078 Turate (CO) - Tel. 031/9689681

VALENTINO
Via Gregoriana, 24
00187 Roma - Tel. 06/672011

VENINI INTERNATIONAL S.r.l.
Fondamenta Vetrai, 50
30121 Murano (VE) - Tel. 041/445047

VIRO INNOCENTI S.p.A.
Via Garibaldi, 4
40069 Zola Predosa (BO) - Tel. 051/755211

VORTICE ELETTROSOCIALI S.p.A.
Via G. Verdi, 13
20067 Zoate di Tribbiano (MI) - Tel. 02/9064465

VOXSON S.p.A.
Via di Tor Cervara, 286
00155 Roma - Tel. 06/225831

ZANOTTA S.p.A.
Via Vittorio Veneto, 57
20054 Nova Milanese (MI) - Tel. 0362/40453

ERMENEGILDO ZEGNA & FIGLI S.a.s.
13159 Trivero (Vercelli)
Tel. 0323/642174

ZEN RUBINETTERIA S.r.l.
Via Repubblica
28026 Omegna (NO) - Tel. 0323/642174

ZUCCHETTI RUBINETTERIA S.p.A.
Via Mulini di Resiga, 27
28024 Gozzano (Novara) - Tel. 0322/94771

This catalogue was made possible through the contribution of
BULGARI INTERNATIONAL JEWELERS

Questo catalogo è stato realizzato con il contributo di
BULGARI